CONNECTIONS

A Guide to On-Line Writing

Daniel Anderson
University of North Carolina at Chapel Hill

Bret Benjamin
University of Texas at Austin

Bill Paredes-Holt
University of Texas at Austin

Allyn and Bacon
Boston London Toronto Sydney Tokyo Singapore

Vice president: Eben W. Ludlow
Series editorial assistant: Linda M. D'Angelo
Marketing manager: Lisa Kimball
Composition and prepress buyer: Linda Cox
Manufacturing buyer: Suzanne Lareau
Cover administrator: Linda Knowles
Editorial-production administrator: Mary Beth Finch
Editorial-production service: York Production Services

A Viacom Company
Needham Heights, Massachusetts 02194

Internet: www.abacon.com
America Online: keyword:College Online

Anderson, Daniel.
Connections : a guide to on-line writing / by Daniel Anderson, Bret Benjamin, Bill Paredes-Holt.
p. cm.
Includes index.
ISBN 0-205-26847-1
1. English language—Rhetoric—Data processing. 2. Report writing—Data processing. 3. Online data processing. I. Benjamin, Bret. II. Paredes-Holt, Bill. III. Title.
PE1408.A586 1997
808'.042'0285—dc21 97-25069
CIP

Printed in the United States of America.
10 9 8 7 6 5 4 3 2 1 02 01 00 99 98 97

CONTENTS

PREFACE

Overview

Although English departments and computer networks may seem like strange bedfellows, they are rapidly becoming inseparable partners. Each semester, more and more English and composition courses across the country incorporate computer technologies into their curriculum. This may mean that students exchange e-mail or do research on the Web; it may mean that courses are taught in computer-assisted classrooms (an increasingly common occurrence in liberal arts departments); or it may mean that courses focus on the many cultural expressions and ramifications of digital information. Because of this recent emphasis on computer-mediated communication, departments throughout the liberal arts, and particularly in the disciplines of English and composition studies, are beginning to rethink the ways in which both teaching and learning take place.

It is in this context of evolving forms of communication and education that we have written *Connections: A Guide to On-Line Writing*. Our goal is to produce a textbook that is specifically designed for students and instructors in writing classes who are interested in working with the Internet. We see *Connections* as a way of mediating between traditional print-based writing and newer forms of on-line communication. In the bulk of this text, we focus on writing activities that take place on the Internet, but we also believe that these activities can complement more traditional writing projects. Similarly, we believe that an understanding of the basic principles of rhetoric will help guide writers as they begin working with on-line media. The text, then, combines a strong rhetorical focus with a detailed exploration of Internet communication in order to help students become better writers in both print-based and electronic formats.

Connections could easily be incorporated into courses across several disciplines and within a variety of classroom situations. Because the text integrates a strong rhetorical foundation with practical advice for composing with on-line media, *Connections* will be particularly useful for computer-assisted writing classes at the undergraduate level (and, perhaps, in an advanced high school curriculum). In lower-division writing courses, *Connections* could be used in conjunction with a standard composition handbook such as *The Allyn & Bacon Handbook*. In slightly higher-level writing courses (particularly those focusing on topics related to computers and technology), *Connections* could function as the central writing textbook for the semester, perhaps in conjunction with a reader such as Victor Vitanza's *CyberReader.* Additionally, because of the growing interest in the Internet throughout the humanities, this is a textbook that might be adopted as an Internet guide by instructors teaching classes in philosophy, anthropology, communications, and other disciplines.

Approaches

Our main approach is to treat the Internet as a complex, rich, and useful tool for teaching rhetoric and composition. Because the Net is made up of communities that are continuously engaged in written conversations, it provides an excellent site for gathering information, critically examining written texts, and allowing students to compose for a large and interested audience. For this reason, our book focuses heavily on the ways in which language use and meaning can be seen as constantly evolving forces that are constructed through collaborative debate, discussion, and argumentation. Viewed in this way, the Internet is not only a vast storehouse of information or a communications tool, but also a living, breathing conversation.

Connections, then, treats the Internet as a fluid collection of media and communities. The communications technologies that comprise the Internet include media as diverse as e-mail, MU*s, newsgroups, and the World Wide Web, each bringing communities of users together by providing on-line spaces for collaboration and communication. Writers will be consistently challenged to make informed choices about what kinds of compositions will be appropriate and effective in a variety of contexts. *Connections,* therefore, is designed to explore the rhetorical complications of on-line writing and to provide strategies that will enable students to actively participate in on-line conversations and to make successful rhetorical decisions.

Connections offers students a number of advantages over current Internet writing guides. Primarily, we have attempted to move beyond the tendency of other books to focus solely on resource-based instruction. We do provide guidance for harvesting the enormous research potential of the Internet, but rather than recommending lists of sites (many of which will soon become obsolete) or providing step-by-step instructions for getting on-line, we concentrate on strategies and assignments that are designed to help students research and compose with these new media. By featuring strategies and activities in addition to resources, we hope that *Connections* will have a longevity and broad-based appeal that other guides have yet to capture.

Finally, we have worked to make *Connections* a modular textbook by dividing it into manageable chapters that might be assigned in conjunction with a particular class task or assignment. This format should allow instructors to pick and choose which sections of the book are the most useful for their particular class.

Organization

Connections is organized into four parts. **Part 1** introduces our model of rhetoric. We focus on a definition of rhetoric that is broad enough to include many types of communication but that emphasizes argumentation and analysis. The following three parts look at various forms of writing and research on the Net in terms of the rhetorical foundations laid in **Part 1,** concentrating on three broad categories of communication: research, collaboration, and compositional design.

Although **Part 1** is concerned primarily with rhetoric, **Chapter 1** provides an introduction to our model of composition and offers definitions and information about the Internet, looking briefly at each of the Internet media that we discuss throughout the book. Once the Internet terminology has been defined, we devote the remainder of **Part 1** to principles of rhetoric and communication. We stress the rhetorical situation and look at its elements, including the speaker, the message, and the audience. We also discuss the principles of effective argumentation and consider the contexts in which messages are exchanged, the purposes that inform messages, and the media that are used for different forms of communication. We conclude the first part by looking at the importance of critical reading. In **Part 1,** each chapter ends by asking students to draw connections between the Internet and the rhetorical concepts we have put forth.

Our second part focuses on using the Net as a research tool. We begin **Part 2** by looking at the value of research, suggesting that research can be an integral part of the writing process. Next, we investigate the nature of Internet resources and some of the challenges that they pose. We move on to talk in more detail about using the World Wide Web as a research tool, then spend some time looking at ways to tap into the conversational resources that are available on e-mail discussion lists and newsgroups. We close **Part 2** with a sample research session that brings together many of the strategies outlined in this section of the book.

Part 3 looks at opportunities for collaboration and conversation provided by the Internet. We start by outlining some of the ways in which knowledge is communally constructed, stressing the importance of collaborative activities for students. **Part 3** then looks at the collaborative nature of real-time environments on the Internet, including MU*s and IRCs. We also explore student collaboration on a local level with e-mail discussion lists, newsgroups and Web forums, and then we examine ways that students can interact with others on a global scale. We conclude by looking at collaboration on the World Wide Web and by arguing that the Web itself is a collaborative medium.

Our final part focuses more closely on some of the possibilities for creating extended on-line compositions. **Part 4** opens with a general discussion of the writing process and how design is shaped in electronic environments. We next focus on design as it comes into play in the virtual environments of the Internet. We talk about composing in MU* spaces and the complications of narrative and collaboration that arise. **Part 4** closes with four chapters devoted to composition on the World Wide Web. We begin with HTML basics, providing information about the process of composing Web pages. We next discuss the importance of page layout and then the many rhetorical and argumentative challenges of hypertextual Web composition. Finally, we explore some of the emerging trends in Web composition as a way of anticipating future possibilities for Web builders.

Features

Connections has a number of useful features that will enhance the on-line writing experiences of both students and instructors.

The *Connections* Web site: (**http://www.abacon.com/connections**)

The textbook is accompanied by an interactive Web site. This site offers more extensive Internet assignments, information about the latest versions of Internet client software, updates concerning new technological developments, links to related sites about on-line writing, information about copyright and other on-line issues, an on-line version of the Instructor's Manual, and much more. Additionally, we complement many of the exercises in the text with on-line message forums.

Flexibility of the Text

Because we cover both rhetorical principles and Internet activities while dividing the text into distinct, thematically arranged chapters, *Connections* supports a broad range of teaching goals. This flexibility will allow instructors to pick and choose the sections of the book that are most appropriate for their courses, whether they use *Connections* as the central text in a writing course or as a supplement to other materials.

Exercises and Class Discussions

Instructors will appreciate the fact that most chapters in *Connections* contain one or more classroom exercises, discussion topics, and writing assignments. These exercises are designed to get students thinking about how to use various Internet technologies and how to present themselves effectively in both traditional and on-line rhetorical situations.

Extensive Coverage of the World Wide Web

Not only do we explore the Web as a tool for research and collaboration, *Connections* provides four chapters that are specifically devoted to Web composition: **Chapters 17, 18, 19,** and **20** as well as **Appendix 5**. In these chapters, we address not only technical building skills but also rhetorical and design strategies that students will need to create effective Web sites. It is our hope that *Connections* can serve both as a resource and as a rhetorical guide for students who are beginning to compose on the World Wide Web.

Student Work

The text also contains a significant amount of student work. We include student e-mail and newsgroup postings, MU* projects, peer reviews, Web pages, and a variety of other on-line compositions. These student texts serve as examples that demonstrate ways to analyze and produce on-line writing.

Internet Nuts and Bolts

In **Chapter 1,** we have included a brief description of the various Internet media that will be discussed in the book. This section provides an easy-to-understand overview of E-mail, Newsgroups, MU*s, IRCs, Gopher, Telnet, File Transfer Protocol, and the World Wide Web, as well as a brief introduction to the principles of netiquette.

Key Terms

At the beginning of most chapters, we have briefly defined any important terminology that appears in the chapter. These definitions cover terms ranging from rhetorical concepts to Internet programming languages and are intended to help students quickly familiarize themselves with the basic vocabulary of the chapter.

Tips and Tactics

Many chapters conclude by outlining and reiterating important points and strategies. These sections offer students a kind of checklist where they can quickly get hints about ways of improving their own Internet research and writing skills.

Extensive Back Matter

The Appendixes contain a wide range of information that complements the material presented in the main body of the text. For instance, to help students with issues of citation and documentation we have reprinted Andy Harnack and Gene Kleppinger's "MLA-Style Guidelines for Citing Internet Sources," and have included an in-depth discussion of copyright information. Additional resources include a section on MOO building commands, a handy compilation of HTML commands, and a special section about Web building with frames and layers. Finally, we offer an extensive glossary of the terms used in the book.

Acknowledgments

We would like to take this opportunity to briefly thank the many people who have helped make this book possible.

First we would like to thank the wonderful publishing crew who have helped us with the development of *Connections:* Mary Beth Finch and Lori Ann Smith for their expert guidance with the production of the book, Doug Day and Malcolm Ward for their advice and encouragement, and all the others at Allyn & Bacon who have made books like this possible, including Joe Opiela and Lisa Kimball. And most importantly, we would like to thank our editor, Eben Ludlow, whose support and optimism about this project have been undaunted since we initially approached him with the idea for *Connections*. His advice about how to proceed with this textbook has been invaluable.

We would be remiss if we didn't thank our many colleagues and friends who have contributed to make the Computer Writing and Research Lab at the University of Texas such a rich space for teaching and learning. There are too many people to name individually, but we owe a great debt to the time, energy, and enthusiasm of the instructors who staff the CWRL. In large part, this book is a product of their constant efforts to productively integrate new forms of electronic communication into their classroom practice. In particular, we should thank the director, John

Slatin, whose commitment and dedication to the lab are in large part responsible for creating such a dynamic environment. We should also give special thanks to those instructors whose class sites and student projects appear in *Connections:* Tonya Browning, Nick Evans, Barbara Harlow, Mary Harvan, Katie Henninger, Albert Rouzie, Gina Siesing, and Natasha Sinutko.

We must also acknowledge the important roles that our students have played in the creation of this textbook. Not only have they provided many of the examples that we use throughout *Connections,* they have also been true partners in helping us develop the pedagogical principles that underlie this book. Along with offering a tremendous amount of advice, technical and otherwise, they have continually challenged us with the simple question, "why?" We thank them not only for investing so much energy in their learning, but also for helping us to revise our teaching practices to better accommodate the goals that we have for our classes.

Also deserving recognition are those colleagues who volunteered to crash test a manuscript version of *Connections* in their classrooms, in particular, Eric Jansson, D'Arcy Randall, Albert Rouzie, and Lynn Rudloff. Their faith in our drafty prose is commendable. Thanks also to Kazel Morgan and Ailise Lamoreux for their helpful comments about revising Part 1.

We are also indebted to our reviewers:

Tonya Browning
University of Texas at Austin

Marcia Peoples Halio
University of Delaware

Ed Klonoski
University of Hartford

Beth E. Kolko
University of Wyoming

Gregory VanHoosier-Carey
Georgia Institute of Technology

They challenged us to explain and justify our ideas about teaching, and their insightful comments have made *Connections* a much better textbook.

Thanks also to Andy Harnack and Gene Kleppinger for allowing us to reproduce a section of their on-line citation guide, *Online! A Reference Guide to Using Internet Sources* published by St. Martin's Press. Thanks to Xochitl Paredes-Holt for the use of her graphics.

Most importantly, we would like to thank the people who are closest to us. Writing any book demands a tremendous commitment, but writing a book about the Internet requires that all the work be done in just a few short months, simply because of the rapid changes that are taking place on-line. This has meant many long days and nights at the office, and it has often kept us away from the people we love. Their support and sacrifices have truly made this book possible. Daniel would like to thank Peter for showing me the amazing powers of the imagination, Palmer, whose unencumbered joy continues to renew my spirit, and Cindy, who lifts me more than words can say. Bret would like to thank Bob, Nancy, Ailise, Woodrow, and Clyde for their love and patience and for hounding me just enough to keep me on my toes. Bill is always indebted to Xoch for her patience, persistence, and tolerance.

WRITING ON-LINE

PART 1

CHAPTER 1

INTRODUCTION

Connections

rrrrrrrrrrrrrrring

rrrrrrrrrrrrrrring

JASON: Hello.

JILL: Hey, Jason, this is Jill.

JASON: Hi, Bill, I'm glad you called.

JILL: No, this is *Jill.* So I take it Bill hasn't called yet?

JASON: Oh, Phil! I totally agree! I can't believe those idiots in Congress haven't passed that bill yet either. Surely they have something to think about besides their own wallets?

JILL: I think we must have a bad connection. Hang up and I'll call you back . . . and by the way, don't call me Shirley. □

As we all know, the word "connection" refers to something that links or bonds things together. But what makes this telephone connection between Jill and Jason particularly bad? After all, they are linked—they are talking to each other. Yet the connection is clearly flawed.

We would like to suggest that there are two critical elements in any human connection: the mental or emotional attachment between the two conversants and the physical or technological medium through which they communicate. In order to establish a good connection, both elements must be in place. Jill and Jason's bad connection suggests not only a malfunction in the telephone wiring, but also a breakdown of interpersonal communication. Both of them are attempting to carry on a reasonable conversation, but for any number of reasons, they are unable to get their messages across, resulting in an exchange that's more like a bad comedy routine than a telephone call.

We decided to call this book *Connections,* then, to highlight the process of establishing meaningful connections between people through a communications medium. We were particularly concerned with the kinds of connections that were being established between writers on the Internet. As we began to formulate a plan for *Connections,* however, we soon realized that to help students make sense of the many forms of on-line composition, we would need to talk about the process of communication in general. In part, we wanted students to better understand Internet communication by first considering the principles and techniques of more traditional forms of writing. We wanted to acquaint students with strategies that have proven effective in print-based writing so that they would be able to apply those strategies to on-line composition. Our goal was twofold: to help writers consider their purposes as they present themselves as speakers to different audiences, and to help them apply these skills to on-line research, collaboration, and composition.

For a writing class, the Internet can serve as a valuable extension of the library. Besides offering many of the same materials that students might find in the stacks of a library, the Net provides unprecedented archives of government documents, up-to-the-minute information about important news and events, in-depth analysis of national and international issues, and vast storehouses of images, film clips, and audio files. These resources can be retrieved, studied, and analyzed by others who are interested in similar ideas. Doing this type of Internet research allows writers to see the many facets of an issue by making connections between their work and the work of others.

But in addition to providing researchers with a wealth of documents and information, the Internet facilitates numerous forms of interpersonal exchange. These kinds of connections offer a more dynamic, interactive way for writers and readers to collaboratively explore ideas through a process of dialog. Internet users can send e-mail from country to country, carry on debates in newsgroups or Web forums, and engage in real-time discussions on MU*s and IRCs. These exchanges blur some of the boundaries between written and verbal communication, requiring us to rethink the very definition of "writing" to make it more inclusive of the conversational composition that is taking place on-line.

In addition to these more spontaneous, informal compositions, the Internet lets authors establish connections between their ideas and their audiences by producing more extended projects. For instance, Internet authors can build projects in a MU*, using textual descriptions to create virtual environments. Additionally, authors might use the Web's hypertextual capabilities to situate their compositions within a matrix of background information, perhaps incorporating multimedia elements to help convey ideas. Traditional writing strategies certainly apply in these on-line writing situations, but electronic environments also require that authors consider new factors as they decide how best to inform or persuade an audience.

Connections, then, represents something of a bridge between traditional print-based writing and these newer forms of electronic composition. Throughout the book, we look at a number of Internet media—e-mail, newsgroups, MU*s, IRCs, and the World Wide Web—as a way of exploring the principles of written communication. *Connections* is not the type of Internet guide that offers only a collection of on-line punctuation, citation, and fact-finding resources that might help you write an essay. Nor is it a technical manual or builder's reference that expects you to compose all of your work in electronic environments. Rather, *Connections* is a writing textbook that uses on-line writing not only to teach you the principles of effective communication, but also to help you develop and express their your ideas.

Compositional Foundations

Throughout this book, we take two fundamental approaches to writing. We believe that writing is an ongoing process of discovery and that writing always takes place in the context of a larger community.

The Writing Process

Have you ever sat down to write an essay and ended up eight hours later with a completely different paper than the one you had in mind when you started? Well, if you have, you're not alone. In fact, most authors experience this process to some degree almost every time they write. Although this phenomenon may sometimes seem like indecision or a lack of focus, we believe that it points to one of the greatest benefits of composition—namely, that the slow, deliberate pace of writing allows authors to fully explore even the most complex topics. When we write, we are forced to scrutinize every idea that we put onto paper, carefully considering what we are saying, why we are saying it, and who might be listening.

It is this element of writing, the process of discovery and development, that *Connections* is most interested in. While we wouldn't want to suggest that exploration is the only goal of writing—usually, the final draft of an essay, article, or editorial will have implications that extend beyond self-fulfillment and self-education—we do believe that a tremendous amount of value can be gained from the writing process itself. Of course, this process is not limited solely to those moments when an author "puts pen to paper." Writers go through any number of stages during which their ideas are refined, focused, complicated, and revised.

For example, suppose you had to write a research paper, a project that most of us face at one time or another. After getting the assignment, you would start by coming up with a topic. You might brainstorm with your instructor or a classmate to assemble a list of possible options, pinpointing your areas of interest. Next you'd likely head to the library to find some information about your topic. After reading through some source materials, you would probably need to narrow the focus of your topic, choosing a particular angle or issue to explore in more detail. At this point, you might put summaries and citations from your research on note cards or produce an outline of your ideas. Next you might write up a draft, sitting down at the keyboard to organize and articulate your thoughts. You could show the draft to your instructor or to a peer and receive some preliminary feedback. Taking this feedback into consideration, you might head back to the library to do some further research or begin revising your paper, straightening out the main ideas before eventually proofreading and polishing the text.

As you can see, the writing process requires that authors remain flexible as they move through the various stages. There is no set order that authors must take, and there is no limit to the number of times that any one step might be repeated. For some authors, the process of narrowing a topic is the most difficult, so they might spend extra time brainstorming and researching. Authors who have problems organizing information into effective arguments might focus on outlining, drafting, and incorporating feedback into revisions. What's important to keep in mind is that your education takes place at every stage of the writing process and that the final draft of a project is only one piece of a much more involved and complicated set of documents and conceptual plans.

This is the approach that we take in *Connections,* emphasizing the ways in which all forms or stages of writing not only help to fulfill the larger goals of a project, but also contribute to an author's education and development. In doing so, we attempt to construct a broad definition of writing, suggesting that there can be value in many forms of communication.

Writing in a Community

We would be wrong, though, to imagine that the only goal of writing is to further an author's personal development and understanding. Remember that, for communication to take place, a connection must be established between two or more people. So, while we think that writing is valuable as a process of self-exploration, we also want to suggest that writing is a public act that always takes place within the context of a community.

Your first interaction with this communal context comes when you consider the audience for your compositions. To tailor your presentation so that it appeals to your readers, you must understand their beliefs and develop a sense of which issues are most important within that community. You'll also need to adhere to the group's conventions, find common ground where you can present your ideas to this audience, and accommodate any major objections that they are likely to raise.

Another way that writers interact with a community is through research. When you comment on an issue in your writing, you will almost certainly be entering into what might be considered a preexisting "conversation." By this, we mean that your remarks will be judged, to some extent, on how well they analyze, critique, and advance the debate that has already taken place among a larger community of writers and readers. That is why we devote **Part 2** of this book to the process of research. To write successfully, you'll have to position yourself within this conversation by demonstrating where your ideas complement the work done by other writers and where they move in new directions.

Finally, writers are always products of their environments. We write as members of a social community that is defined by a certain set of assumptions. In fact, each of us belongs to many of these communities: We live in the twentieth century, we might be Americans, we might be African Americans, we might be women, we might be Bostonians, we might be academics, we might be married, we might be unemployed, and so on. Each of these communities influences the way we act, the way we think, and the way we write.

As we move through the rest of this book, then, we'll continue to think about writing as a process that takes place within a community. We'll also continue to explore the connections between traditional ways of understanding communication and the new forms of writing made possible by digital media. We believe that this approach highlights the strengths of on-line writing. After all, the Internet can be considered to be both a single giant text and an evolving conversation. When we participate in the various forums on the Net—perhaps sending an e-mail message, posting to a newsgroup, conversing on a MU*, or building a Web page—we are not only interacting with others, but also producing written compositions. Of course, a newsgroup post usually isn't the equivalent of a formal written essay. However, it might be an important step in the process of writing a longer paper, perhaps a way of organizing research or brainstorming for ideas. And it is certainly an example of writing within a community, meaning that authors who hope to receive a response from the newsgroup audience will need to make any number of rhetorical choices to compose an effective post.

Because the Internet offers so many situations in which authors can communicate with an audience, it provides an exceptionally rich environment for students of rhetoric and composition. *Connections* is designed to help you analyze and participate in these complex on-line writing situations with the goal of improving your overall communication skills and helping you become a more effective writer.

The Layout of the Book

Connections is divided into four parts, each highlighting a different component of the writing process. **Part 1** is an introduction to the principles of rhetoric. Although each major chapter has a concluding section that examines issues of on-line communication, the emphasis in **Part 1** is on traditional rhetorical concepts and strategies.

Part 2 begins our primary focus on Internet writing situations by examining effective strategies for on-line research. We start by introducing some core principles of research, then examine some specific strategies for finding materials on the World Wide Web and for utilizing the conversational resources of the Net. We conclude with a sample demonstration of Internet research.

Part 3 is concerned with various aspects of collaborative writing. We open by discussing ways in which knowledge is communally constructed. Next, we offer suggestions for participating in real-time discussions, collaborating with other members of your class, and interacting with the larger Internet community.

Part 4 is devoted to principles of design in electronic compositions. We begin with an overview of design, then move on to discuss building in the text-based environments of MU*s. The remaining four chapters are devoted solely to Web design, moving from the basic principles of Hypertext Markup Language (HTML) to issues of page layout to the rhetorical considerations of Web design. The book concludes by looking at advances that are taking place on the Web as a way of speculating about where some of the future possibilities for communication may lie.

The remainder of **Chapter 1** will be an introduction to the various Internet media that we discuss throughout the book. If you're already knowledgeable about the Net, some of this may be familiar information. If, on the other hand, you can't imagine what the acronym "MU*" could possibly refer to, this section should get you up to speed on the basic Internet media and give you a crash course in some key terminology. We also offer a brief discussion of a few basic "rules of conduct" (netiquette) to help prepare you to participate in on-line communities. As you read through the book, you can always refer back to the following section if you are confused about any of the media we discuss.

Internet Nuts and Bolts: Servers, Clients, and Internet Media

When we hear the phrase "the Internet," we might first imagine a single communication medium like the telephone. But the Internet is actually a collection of different communication media. Things like e-mail, newsgroups, and the World Wide Web are all part of the Internet, but each has a distinctive language or "protocol" that allows it to share information. For example, most e-mail relies on the Simple Mail Transfer Protocol (SMTP). Any server or client that understands the shared set of commands and specifications of the SMTP protocol can transmit e-mail.

Servers and Clients

From a technical standpoint, the Internet can be thought of as a collection of computers, wires, and programs. Assuming that the computers and wires are in place, what really makes the Net function are the various programs that allow information to be shared. Those programs on the Internet that are designed to store and distribute files are called servers. For instance, a mainframe computer at your school will likely have a program (a news server) that subscribes to and organizes the messages in various newsgroups. Programs that contact servers and manage information for individual users are called clients. For instance, you might use a newsreading client (newsreader) to browse through the postings in a particular newsgroup or to compose and send your own messages.

Keep in mind that neither servers nor clients are particular machines, but the programs that allow the Internet to function by providing a way to transfer information. So for instance, when you log onto the mainframe at your school, you can activate a mail-reading client that resides on that machine. That client might contact the mail server that also resides on the same mainframe computer. In general, clients that reside on remote machines are more difficult to use. Whenever possible, you should try to use clients that run from your own personal computer. These local clients usually offer a graphical interface and more capacity for saving and managing information.

Client Options

Remote Clients Some basic clients are probably available directly from the mainframe where you have an Internet account. With these clients, you log onto your account and enter a command line to run programs located on that remote machine. These programs are generally unsophisticated and somewhat difficult to operate, but if your Internet access is limited or your machine can't handle large programs, these remote clients will be satisfactory.

Local Clients Local clients are programs that run on your personal computer, making them probably the easiest way to access any kind of Internet media. In general, they have more intuitive, readable interfaces than remote clients do, provide more powerful organizing and editing features, and make it easier for you to manage information. Although Web browsers are local clients that are designed to read files on the World Wide Web, you can also use many of them to access other Internet media, such as newsgroups and e-mail. While these Web-based clients are much more user-friendly than remote client software, they still have some limitations. As Web browser technology improves, though, these clients will likely become increasingly sophisticated.

Internet Media

Since there are actually a number of different media with specific protocols that make up the Internet, you'll want to know something about their different functions. In this section, we define the various media and provide some basic information about how they work. Occasionally, we offer suggestions about which clients to use, but because each institution will have a unique setup, you will probably need to check with your instructor or an experienced user about how best to access Internet media from your school. You can find additional information about client software at the *Connections* Web site.

E-Mail In many ways, e-mail is the most basic form of Internet communication. E-mail transfers messages and files from one account to another via their respective mail servers. Let's say someone named Bob Doe wants to send a message to someone named Bubba at the White House. Looking at their respective e-mail addresses in Figure 1.1 helps us visualize the process.

Bob Doe's e-mail address is "bob@mail.utexas.edu". When Bob sends this message, it will go from his account, "bob", to his mail server, "mail.utexas.edu". The mail server will transfer the message to the

■ **FIGURE 1.1** An E-Mail Client Interface

"whitehouse.gov" mail server, which will distribute it to the account "bubba". The @ character (usually pronounced "at") is part of every Internet e-mail address and separates the individual account from the mail server.

You will probably have two major options for handling your e-mail. You can log onto your account on a mainframe computer and activate a mail client such as Pine or Elm. You might also use a local client, either a Web browser that incorporates e-mail or a specific mail-reading program such as Eudora.

Newsgroups A newsgroup is a forum in which users exchange messages and other files with anyone else who frequents the group. Most colleges have access to Usenet, an extensive collection of publicly distributed newsgroups. These groups are topic-centered, meaning that each newsgroup is designed to address a very particular subject area. Topics can be relatively broad, as in **talk.abortion,** or as minutely detailed as that of a group such as **bionet.genome.arabidopsis.** Groups are arranged alphabetically by name under several umbrella categories. For example, under the prefix **talk** are groups that are designed for discussion of issues such as abortion, politics, philosophy, religion, and many others. Other prefixes include **alt** (alternative), **comp** (computers), **info, misc, news, rec** (recreational), and **soc** (social).

Your school probably provides access to Usenet through a local news server, a machine that collects and distributes files for each of the newsgroups that your school subscribes to. This means that not all groups will be available from your local news server and that some groups will be available only to your local community—for example, class newsgroups for courses at your particular college or university. Most colleges, however, offer thousands of groups, and most of the messages that you post will be accessible to newsgroup users all over the world.

To read and post to a newsgroup, you will need a newsreading program or client. You can often use a Web browser for accessing newsgroups, but their interfaces are more limited than those of local newsreading clients such as Nuntius or Newswatcher (Mac) or Free Agent (PC).

Internet Relay Chat (IRC) Internet Relay Chat (IRC) has been compared to CB radio because it allows users to "chat" on a number of different channels. These channels are accessed through an IRC server and are organized by topic. To use IRCs, you will need to know the Internet address and port number of an IRC server.

Once you are on a channel, you can have real-time interactions (exchanges that take place simultaneously) with the other users there. Usually, this is done by simply typing a message and sending it to the group. IRCs also allow users to perform actions. When you enter the "action" command followed by some text, the IRC server will append the text to your name so that the other users see you performing what you've written. For example, if a user named Gates entered the command as follows:

```
/me pulls out a poisoned pen and dashes off a check
for 150 million dollars
```

the other users would see the message

```
Gates pulls out a poisoned pen and dashes off a
check for 150 million dollars.
```

By combining messages with actions, IRC users interact and have real-time conversations.

MU*s (MUDs, MOOs, MUCKs, and MUSHs) MU* is the acronym we use to refer to the variety of text-based virtual environments that are found on the Internet. The names for these environments are often derived from the acronym MUD, which stands for Multi-User Dimension (MOO, for instance, stands for MUD Object-Oriented). Perhaps one of the best ways to describe a MU* is with a sample, as in Figure 1.2.

MU*s are constructed with textual descriptions that have been designed to create a virtual environment for users to explore. Many of the objects in MU*s are also programmed to interact with readers. For example, when a user enters the command "get letter" in the environment shown in Figure 1.2, the MU* responds by providing a description of the letter. The user can then choose to hold onto the letter or drop it.

MU*s also provide an excellent space for people to meet and engage in real-time interaction. By exchanging messages and actions, users can converse with other guests in the MU*. For instance, a typical MU session might look like this:

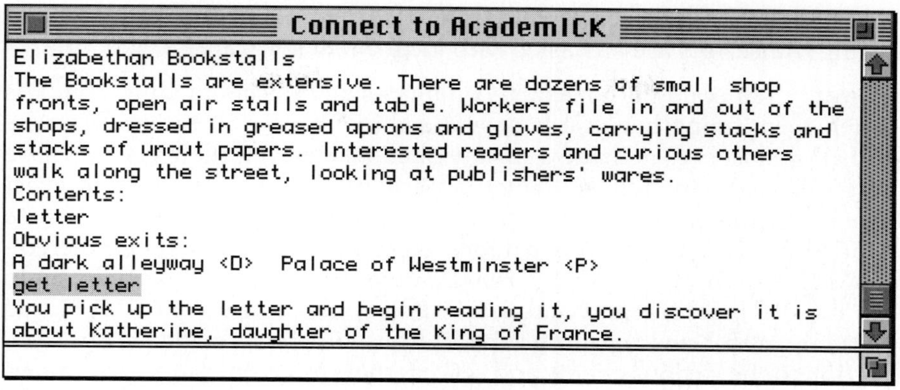

■ **FIGURE 1.2** A Section of the MU* AcademIck

You are in a small conference room with four chairs and no obvious exits.

You see
Alejandro
Sara
Marcus

Alejandro says "What did you think about the film? I think I'm going to write about the way the film deals with women in the legal system."

Sara says "Hi everybody. As the only woman here, I'm going to go out on a limb and say Alejandro is right. With this film we should write about women and the law.

Marcus coughs and hesitantly adds, "I guess that's OK, but I hated this movie. Can we write about how bad it was? I really thought it could have had a point if it had just talked about human rights laws and shown how violated the woman was. Instead, it just seemed to try and blame the woman for her predicament.

Conversation on a MU* is actually a combination of speaking and "emoting," the name for showing actions in MU* space. By using the "say" and "emote" commands, users can engage in complex interactions that are valuable for brainstorming and often take on a sense of narrative.

To connect to a MU*, you need to know the Internet address and the port number of the MU* server. Though the most basic of Internet connections will let you use MU*s effectively, interaction, navigation, and saving transcripts are all easier with local client software.

Telnet Telnet might not exactly qualify as an Internet medium, but it is worth mentioning because it provides direct access to Internet servers and allows users to activate a variety of clients, even if their systems have only minimal capabilities. Telnet is perhaps the most basic of Internet connections. It allows one machine on the Internet to connect directly to another. You might compare a Telnet connection to attaching an incredibly long wire from your keyboard to a remote computer. You can log onto the remote machine and activate FTP, Gopher, e-mail, IRC, MU*, and text-only Web-browsing programs. Because Telnet provides a raw connection to the various clients and servers that reside on remote machines, its command line interface can be clunky and it offers less functionality than do clients that you might use on your personal computer.

File Transfer Protocol (FTP) File Transfer Protocol (FTP) allows clients and servers to upload and download files. Since newsgroups, Gopher, and the Web also have the capability to transfer files, you may not need to use FTP. If you have a personal Internet account and want to publish a Web site, however, you'll probably use an FTP client to upload your HTML files.

Gopher Before the explosion of the Web, people browsed the Net with Gopher. At the time, Gopher was a vast improvement over Telnet sessions and FTP sites. Gopher made it feasible for companies, universities, organizations, and even individuals to begin publishing materials on the Internet.

Since the advent of the Web, however, Gopherspace has taken on a new role. Web browsers can read Gopher files, meaning that Gopher clients now seem rather limited. Perhaps more important, since the Web has made it possible to publish materials in a more dynamic, complicated fashion, most current Internet publishing takes place on the Web rather than in Gopherspace. Still, there are large archives of information available on Gopher servers, and for institutions that don't have full access to the Web, Gopher remains an important technology for researching on the Internet.

Gopher uses a set of protocols that operate on the metaphor of tunneling through a maze of "gopher holes" to find information. Gopher servers organize information hierarchically. When you log onto a Gopher host, you'll have a menu of top-level choices. By selecting any of the options, you "burrow" down to that next level, where there will be another menu of choices. As you move up and down through the tunnels, you'll find text documents, multimedia files, software archives, and even interactive sessions in which, for instance, you might be logging onto a library catalog or government database. Although a Gopher client cannot display the sounds and images that are found on the Net, it can often open helper applications to present the various media.

The World Wide Web The Web seems to be expanding so quickly that some see it as a fundamental change in the way we think about information. Things are undoubtedly shifting, but we like to think of the Web as more evolutionary than revolutionary. One of the things that makes the Web so powerful is the way it incorporates the earlier protocols of Gopher, FTP, Telnet, even e-mail. The protocol of the Web, Hypertext Transfer Protocol (HTTP), allows clients to access almost every kind of Internet file. Additionally, HTTP allows hypertextual links to be created between files, meaning that Web authors can compose projects that weave resources and ideas into complicated "webs" of information. They can also more seamlessly incorporate multimedia elements into their Web pages (see Figure 1.3).

To compose these pages, the Web provides writers with an authoring language that is understood by both servers and browsers: Hypertext

■ **FIGURE 1.3** A Course Web Site

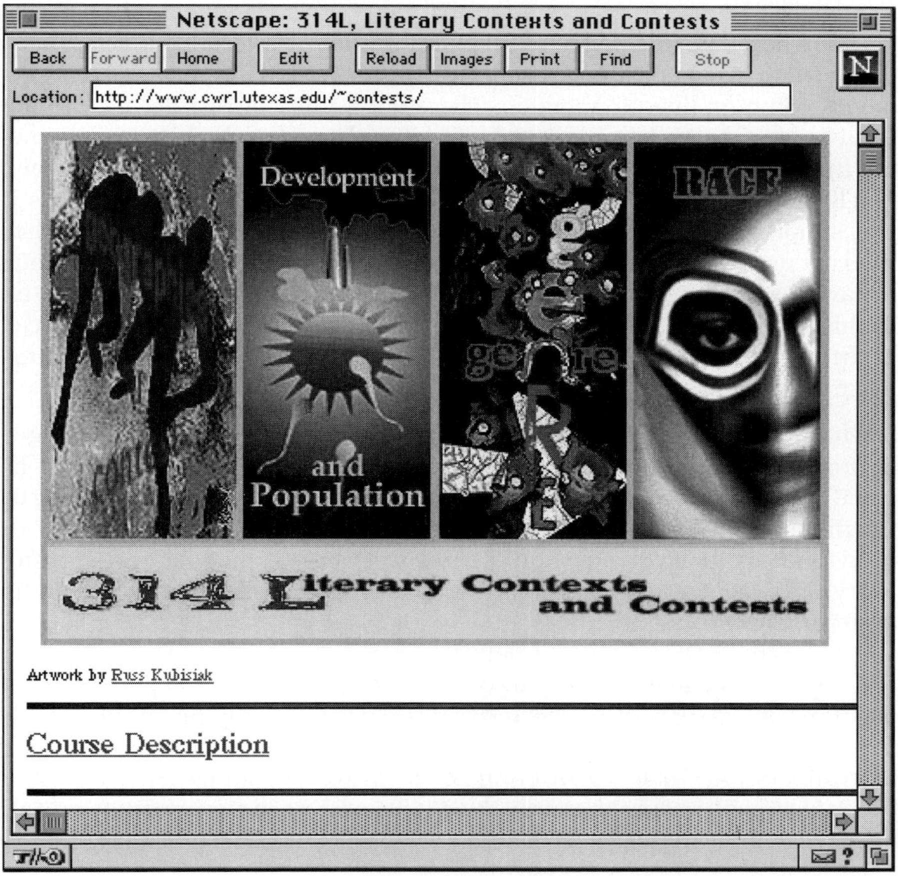

Markup Language (HTML). HTML allows writers to insert commands in their documents that can format text, make links, or display images. It sounds tricky, but writing for the Web is really not that difficult. In **Part 4,** we'll show how it's done.

To access the Web, you need a Web browser. Although the Web was intended to be a standardized environment, some browsers have added capacities that don't match the conventional Web protocol. Netscape, for instance, has consistently implemented features that don't follow the HTTP standards. Nevertheless, many of these features are quite handy, and a large majority of the people browsing the Web currently use the Netscape Navigator browser. We'll often use Netscape terminology in this book, but we try to focus on functions that work with all browsers. To get more information about Web browsers, see **Chapter 7** or the *Connections* Web site.

Netiquette

If you've heard people talk about the importance of Internet etiquette (netiquette) and worried about having to master a slew of new conventions before going on-line, don't panic. There are a number of rules for on-line behavior, but, believe us, none of them are as obscure and arbitrary as knowing that you should spoon your soup toward the outside edge of the bowl. You'll be able to handle yourself comfortably in most on-line situations if you simply follow the golden rule: Put yourself at the keyboard of other Internet users. If you simply consider how your audience will react to your behavior, you should be able to get a feel for the major tenets of netiquette. In this section we offer a few general guidelines, but check out the resources at **http://www.abacon.com/compsite/conversation/netiquette.html** for more information.

E-Mail First, control the tendency to automatically forward messages to other Net users. Because electronic communication is so easily duplicated and shared, users can redistribute messages with a single click of the mouse. Of course, if a message pertains directly to the interests of an individual or group, you should send it along. Obliviously forwarding every tidbit that you stumble across, however, will only clutter the paths of others on the Net.

Also, be sure to provide relevant subject headings for your messages and never send a message without a heading. Because many Internet users receive dozens of e-mail messages a day, they rely on subject headings to sort and prioritize their mail. If you have information about a virus that affects only Macintosh computers, using a heading such as "Mac Virus Alert" will ensure that only the people who need the information will have to read the message. In general, try to select a subject heading that is succinct and encapsulates the message. If you come up with a clever or playful heading, be sure that it still conveys the gist of the message.

A final point of e-mail decorum concerns responses. Because replies usually duplicate the original message in the body of the response, it's possible for messages to contain large amounts of text. Rather than forcing your reader to wait while the message transfers or scroll through a lengthy duplication of previous messages, it is best to edit or "snip" the original message. If a lengthy message concludes by asking "blahdie blahdie blahdie . . . who was that long-winded guy in Hamlet?," you can snip the "blahdie blahdie" and respond

```
>who was that long-winded guy in Hamlet?

Polonius. And speaking of windbags . . .
```

There will be times when you'll want to provide a full record of previous conversations by leaving an original message intact. In general, though, you should respect the time, bandwidth, and carpal tunnels of other users and include only the most relevant parts of earlier messages in your replies.

Newsgroups Because newsgroup postings and e-mail messages are so similar, many, if not all, of the recommendations we make for e-mail will also apply to newsgroup etiquette. Be sure to include appropriate subject headings and important passages from messages you're responding to. In addition, there are several conventions that apply more specifically to writing that takes place on newsgroups.

In deference to the popular potted meat product, Internet users have coined the term "spamming" to describe unsolicited messages. Spamming specifically refers to messages (often advertisements) that are posted indiscriminately to a large number of groups or lists. For instance, if you posted the same research query to 117 newsgroups, you would be spamming. In general, receiving unsolicited messages frustrates and angers Internet users. Before posting any message to a newsgroup, check that the forum is appropriate to your purpose and that your message is relevant to the group.

To avoid rubbing anyone the wrong way in your newsgroup replies, check the heading information of each message as you look through it with your newsreader. If the message was originally "cross-posted" to more than one group, the names of several newsgroups will appear in the heading. By removing the names of the newsgroups that aren't appropriate for your reply, you can avoid unnecessarily duplicating your message.

One way to ensure that your message generates constructive responses is to shepherd your posting through the group. Don't post a message and then take off for two weeks of bonefishing in the Bahamas.

Check that your submission has been posted to the correct group, then check back regularly to see what kinds of feedback it receives. If a heated response crops up, you can quickly apply some "flame retardant" by trying to amend or add to your original post. If a thread of discussion develops in response to your initial message, be sure to take an active role in the evolving conversation. Follow the progression of your message so that you can further champion your position, accommodate differing perspectives, and clarify any misunderstandings.

MU*s/IRCs As you think about decorum in MU*s and IRCs, keep in mind that these environments are usually informal and that interactions in these spaces are playful and spontaneous. Still, despite the rambunctious participation of real-time users, there are several basic rules and conventions that fall under the category of MU*/IRC netiquette.

The first guideline concerns offensive speech and behavior. Because MU*s and IRCs require the use of characters or nicknames, participants occasionally submit rude or hateful postings while hiding under the cloak of anonymity. Although users expect a fair amount of well-intentioned kidding in MU*s and IRCs, they often draw the line when messages become mean-spirited or threatening.

Similarly, you'll need to be responsible about using emotes and actions in MU*s and IRCs. As you interact in real-time spaces, don't make unwanted advances or pester other users. You can easily go around licking or kicking every character you see, but you do so at the risk of alienating other users and possibly being kicked out of the space. In particular, don't project actions or emotions onto other characters or put words into their mouths.

Finally, as you work in MU*s and IRCs, be responsible when trying on different personas and be respectful of the personas of others. You'll need to balance the positive benefits of experimenting with different characters with the negative consequences that can result from deceitful online identities. There is little harm in pretending to be an academic or a body-builder for a few hours, but avoid misleading people who think you are genuine and be careful not to carry the ruse too far.

CHAPTER 2

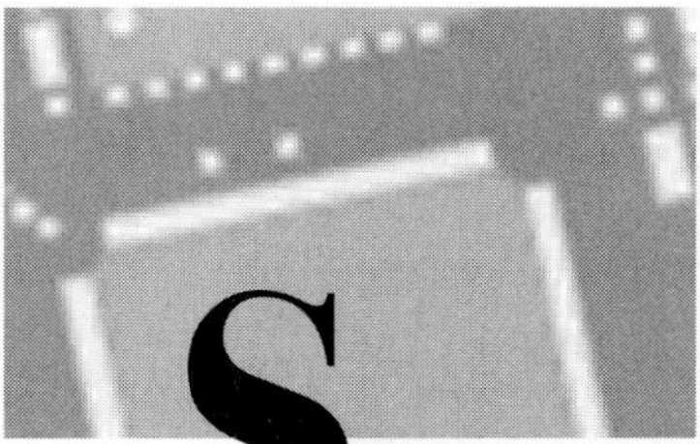

SITUATING COMMUNICATION

Rhetorical Foundations

It's hard to pin down the meaning of the term "rhetoric." If you've heard the phrases "marketing rhetoric" and "campaign rhetoric," you may have gotten the feeling that rhetoric is just a tool used by pitch-people and politicians to sell popcorn or put a spin on the latest poll figures. But rhetoric involves a much broader set of concerns. When authors construct Web pages or when students read Shakespeare, they use rhetoric both to create their own works and to better interpret the messages of others. Rhetoric, then, should be seen as facilitating both the practice and the study of all forms of communication.

Rhetoric is not necessarily good or bad—rather, it can be put to different purposes. Nike, for instance, has a rhetorical purpose in mind when using Michael Jordan as a spokesperson to sell shoes. Similarly, Martin Luther King, Jr., used rhetoric in his "I Have a Dream" speech for the purpose of attacking racial injustice. In each case, the point is to communicate as effectively as possible. You'll need to make your own judgments about the motivations and tactics of the messages you encounter, and studying rhetoric can help you better understand the complicated dynamics of communication. You can use rhetoric both to create arguments and to analyze the many messages that bombard you every day. □

KEY TERMS

Audience: The recipient(s) of a message in any communication situation. The audience can range from a solitary reader of a work to an auditorium of people at a speech or a concert to thousands of readers on the World Wide Web.

Authority: The credibility and expertise with which an author speaks. Authority is influenced by an author's status, knowledge, and experience. In messages, authority is conveyed by well-wrought arguments, fair-mindedness, well-documented support, an appropriate tone, and other compositional elements.

Context: The elements surrounding and informing any act of communication. The setting, the time, related events, and any other messages about a topic all influence the way any message is constructed and interpreted.

Credibility: The amount of trust that is placed in an author's competence, motives, and fair-mindedness. Also used to refer to the reliability of resources.

Message: (1) Used to denote "what is being communicated." The message is in some ways the "content" of communication divorced from its context. (2) Also refers to the "text" that is transmitted in any act of communication.

Rhetoric: The study and practice of communication. Rhetoric can be used both to analyze the messages of others and to compose messages of your own.

Rhetorical Situation: The relationship between the speaker, the audience, and the message at the moment of communication. It can also refer to additional elements of communication, such as the purpose of a message and its context.

Rhetorical Triangle: The relationship among three components of any communication act: the message, the speaker, and the audience.

The three are interconnected, but isolating each element for examination and evaluating their influence on each other helps us to better understand the complexities of communication.

Speaker: The communicator in a rhetorical situation. Also refers to the ways in which an author, writer, lecturer, or any other communicator is perceived through a message. A speaker can be a single author, a spokesperson, or even an entity such as the American Medical Association.

Communication and the Contingency of Meaning

Understanding rhetoric helps us see that the meanings of words and the processes of communication are contingent on the context in which messages are exchanged. When people accept the definition of a term or concept, it may not be because of some inherent truth about the word or idea. Rather, people arrive at the meaning of ideas based on a complex set of factors, including personal experiences and a context of communal understanding. This context is not always readily apparent, but it influences the way we relate to each other and our world. To illustrate, let's take a look at a somewhat conflicted moment in our relatively recent history.

The year 1992 marked the five hundredth anniversary of Christopher Columbus's "discovery of America." Across the country, there were celebrations. Hollywood produced several films to commemorate the event, cities hosted large festivals, and schools put on pageants and plays to recreate the voyage of the Niña, the Pinta, and the Santa María. For many, the year marked a triumphant moment in American history.

But not all of America was celebrating. Some Americans were questioning the premise that Columbus actually "discovered" a "new world." Obviously, this "world" and its inhabitants were not new in 1492. Indigenous civilizations had existed throughout the Americas for centuries. From their perspective, Columbus's exploration was not a discovery but the beginning of occupation and colonization by *conquistadores,* conquerors.

Our point here is to demonstrate that the way we use and interpret language depends on a number of factors, including our individual biases and cultural assumptions. Think about the complexities of a phrase such as "the discovery of America." How might the phrase mean different things for different people? When Americans refer to Columbus's arrival as a "discovery," the term suggests that the history and culture of America begin when Europe encounters and claims sovereignty over the "new world." For Native Americans, on the other hand, 1492 might mark the end, rather than the beginning, of cultural autonomy and national sovereignty.

Because Columbus believed that he was authorized to claim the "new world" for God and the King of Spain, he also felt the authority to name what he found. The names that he selected—in other words, the language he used to represent the people and regions that he encountered—had a major impact on the very development of America as a nation. Since Columbus was hoping to find a new trade route to India and the Far East, he called the people he encountered "Indians." Not only did this term have no historical or cultural connection to the indigenous people of the Americas, it carried with it a number of negative associations. Europeans associated the term "Indian" with the Far East and eastern religion, cultural identities that represented a great threat to Christian values. For Europeans in the late fifteenth century, the term "Indians" suggested exotic and pagan savages whose sole value was as cheap suppliers of silks and spices. It was only by mistake that Native Americans were associated with India at all, but this association brought with it a number of repercussions. Had Native Americans been referred to as "indigenous nations" for the last five hundred years, it might have been harder to justify the treatment they suffered at the hands of settlers. The term "indigenous" suggests a prior right to the land, while the term "nations" carries with it connotations of civilization and development. By labeling the indigenous people of America "Indians," Columbus influenced the way that European settlers treated the inhabitants of America for centuries.

You may have heard of the controversies surrounding the team names of the Washington Redskins or the Atlanta Braves and wondered what all the fuss was about. Some people argue that the reference to "Redskins" or "Braves" is not meant to insult anyone's culture or history. Because language and images shape our perceptions of the world, however, some people find these terms offensive. When Native Americans are represented as nothing more than a team mascot or noted solely for their ability to "Tomahawk Chop" an enemy, the rich and diverse histories of these peoples are overlooked and negative stereotypes are perpetuated. The way the indigenous peoples of North America have been, and continue to be, defined through derogatory representations in language determines, to some extent, the way that we understand and relate to these cultures.

Just as the word "Indian" cannot be divorced from its complex history, each word that we use has a number of important nuances and connotations. Remember that communication doesn't take place in a vacuum. The meaning of each word is contingent on its history, the cultural values associated with it, and the context in which it is used. As a writer, you have a responsibility to consider the implications of your language and to anticipate the ways in which an audience might interpret your words.

Exercise 2.1

Discussing the Implications of Language

We've talked about some of the implications of using the word "Indian," but this isn't the only word that is loaded with historical and cultural assumptions.

Working in small groups with your classmates, choose a recorder to write down your results as you discuss the different implications of the following terms:

- Congressman
- hacker
- mob
- computer virus
- nationalism
- Mother Earth
- patriotism
- Communications Decency Act
- mankind
- hysteria
- family values

What kind of cultural and historical influences might affect our understanding of the terms? Would these terms have different meanings for different groups? Do they privilege one group over another? What synonyms for these terms might be used to emphasize different perspectives? How would using these words influence the way that readers view your own compositions?

The Rhetorical Situation

One way to appreciate the contingency of meaning is to look at the rhetorical situations in which messages are uttered. Take, for example, the sentence "We need to appreciate the value of our land." By itself, the sentence seems pretty harmless. But what if the CEO of Shell Oil were saying this at an executive meeting of international oil and drilling companies? What if it were said by a representative of the Environmental Defense Fund in front of the U.S. Congress during a debate about leasing the rights to mine, drill, and log on public lands? What about its meaning if it were posted to a radical militia's Web site? The context in which something is said has as much impact on its meaning as the statement itself.

As you can see, the notion of "value" shifts depending on the rhetorical situation in which the message is uttered. If a mining company were speaking, "the value of our land" might refer to the worth of extractable mineral resources; for a government energy agency, it might mean how long mineral resources will power the nearest city; and for environmentalists, it might mean biodiversity and the quality of the air, land, and water.

As Figure 2.1 illustrates, any rhetorical situation brings together a number of elements. Every rhetorical situation will have a speaker, a message, and an audience. Additionally, communication always takes place within a larger context. Speakers, audiences, and messages exist in a specific time, place, and cultural moment. In fact, each individual, whether speaker or audience, has his or her own specific contexts that influence the ways in which messages are produced and interpreted. For communication to occur, then, there must be some sort of overlap between the contexts of the speaker and the audience. In other words, before a message can be conveyed successfully from a speaker to an audience, there must be some common ground on which to base their communication, whether it be a shared language, a commitment to a particular topic, or a set of cultural references and assumptions.

As we can see from the "value of our land" example above, we sort through complex communication every day (though we might not always think of it like that) and make judgments accordingly. As readers and writers it is our job to understand the influences of these rhetorical situations as we interpret and create messages.

■ **FIGURE 2.1** The Rhetorical Situation

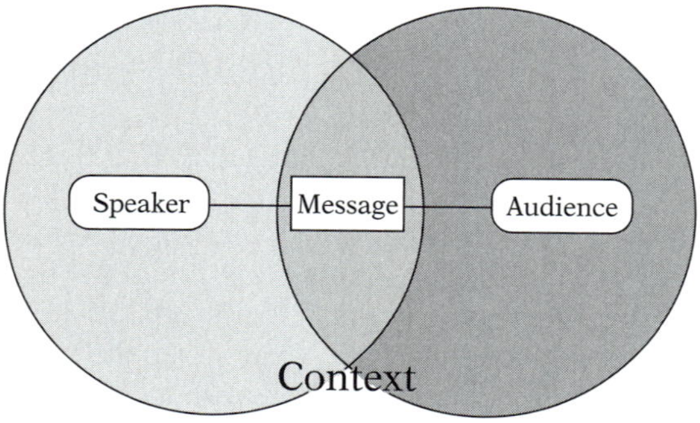

The Rhetorical Triangle

To better understand the rhetorical situation, we can use a device known as the rhetorical triangle (shown in Figure 2.2) to isolate some of the basic elements of communication. The rhetorical triangle derives its name from three poles of communication: the message, the speaker, and the audience.

The Message The message is the "content" of any act of expression. Think of the message as the idea or ideas that you are trying to get across and the positions that you are trying to argue. In an academic context, the message consists of the evidence, the supporting reasons, and the assumptions that underlie what you want to communicate.

The Speaker When we say "speaker," we don't just mean someone who verbally addresses an audience. Speakers can range from the author of an essay, to a public speaker, to a corporate entity. What is important is that she or he is the person who produces and/or delivers the message. The identity of the speaker determines in large part how a message is received. For example, a corporation that is a well-known industrial polluter will have a hard time convincing anybody about its noble plans for environmental protection. A speaker's identity carries meaning. That's why celebrities and sports figures are hired to endorse products. Their charisma and appeal are supposed to carry over to the manufacturer or product.

Writers and readers also gauge the influence of speakers by considering the speaker's authority. Authority is the amount of credibility and knowledge a writer brings to his or her messages. Words carry much more weight when presented by an expert on the subject. If four out of five doctors recommend Tylenol, we tend to believe that it's the best pain reliever on the market. Readers also assign credibility to publications and other

■ **FIGURE 2.2** The Rhetorical Triangle

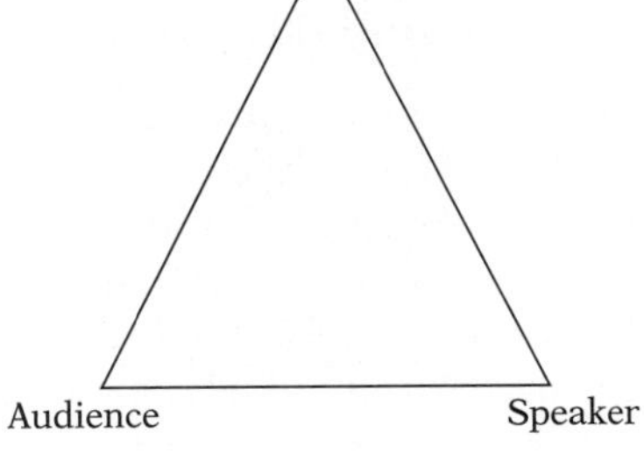

sources. We grant a much greater authority to health information that is presented in the *New England Journal of Medicine,* for example, than in the pages of *Cosmo.* (See **Chapter 5** for more information about examining sources.)

But you don't have to be an expert to write with authority (just look at us). You can also create credibility by presenting yourself as a knowledgeable and reasonable person. In addition to writing carefully and responsibly, you should respect your audience. Don't insult their intelligence with simplistic arguments or condescending language. Also, be fair to other positions. If you denigrate and insult people who disagree with you, you lose credibility with your audience.

The Audience Successful writers always anticipate how a particular audience will respond to their work. This awareness of audience helps to shape the message, determining whether it's confrontational, informative, congratulatory, or something more personal. Think, for example, about writing letters home after your first week at college. Would the letters to your best friend, to your parents, and to your favorite high school teacher be the same? Each letter would probably include some of the same events, but your audience would determine the tone of your letter, the events you chose to report, and the level of detail you included. You'd probably tell everybody about the first day of classes, but you might not tell your parents or your teacher that you slept through your eight o'clock lab because you had been out late sampling the local music scene.

Taking your audience into consideration means finding values that you have in common with the audience and appealing to their beliefs and assumptions. In the letter to your teacher, you would probably concentrate on your shared academic interests, perhaps discussing the textbook in your sociology class. You might appeal to your friend's fondness for good blues, marveling at the gravely voice of the singer at the local club. You would probably try to tap into your parents' belief in the value of hard work, telling them you were exhausted from the harried pace of the first week. In each case, you would be appealing to your audience's assumptions about what constitutes things like "good" and "bad."

Working with the Rhetorical Triangle

Though we've isolated the elements of the rhetorical triangle for analysis, we don't want to suggest that these are pure, distinct categories. In fact, the three parts of the triangle are inextricably linked. All communication depends on the presence of each of the elements, and any subtle shift in the speaker, message, or audience will produce a change in the others. Changes in the way you present yourself as a speaker must be represented in your message. Your message will also change shape as you begin to consider your audience. What's important is that you realize how these related elements can guide your writing and that you become conscious of the various elements as you work. Establish credibility as a speaker, compose with a sense of your audience in mind, and consider the rhetorical situation as you craft your messages.

Exercise 2.2

Appealing to an Audience

Working in small groups, use this exercise to help you think about the three points of the rhetorical triangle. As you work through the questions below, remember that the elements of the triangle influence each other in complex ways and can be hard to isolate. Consider this scenario:

As an environmental activist, you've been sent by the State Board of Tourism to address the Rockville city council and community leaders with a speech entitled "Why We Should Limit Mining to Protect the Environment." Rockville is a historic mining town in the Rocky Mountains that is facing increased pressure because operations are destroying the habitat of the Basalt River, which is famous for its population of native cutthroat trout. The city council is made up of two retired miners, a second-generation business leader, the school superintendent, and the town doctor.

The goal for this assignment is to come up with four reasons for limiting or banning mining that will appeal to various members of the city council. As you work, have a recorder write down your responses to these prompts.

- First, think about the makeup of the council. How would you characterize this audience? What values is each person likely to hold?
- Next, ask yourselves how you can appeal to their beliefs. For instance, are the town leaders committed to mining or to something more fundamental such as economic interests? Would an ex-miner have different priorities from those of a teacher or a doctor? Try to come up with four general strategies, one that will appeal to each council member's sense of value.
- Consider how best to present yourself as a speaker. What aspects of your position would you highlight for this particular audience? How might you dress? Would you speak informally? Would you present a lot of data or would you stick to more anecdotal evidence and generalized arguments? Why?

- Next, develop reasons for banning or limiting mining operations. Jot down what you come up with and select the four that are most likely to appeal to your audience. Work for a minute to rethink and fully articulate each reason. Ask yourselves why they may or may not prove convincing and adjust them for better success if you can. When finished, present the four reasons you have chosen to the class.

Exercise 2.3

Considering Audience, Speaker, and Message

The goal of this assignment is to practice looking at messages and drawing conclusions about their speakers and intended audiences. For each of the following messages, write a sentence or two describing the speaker of the message and the audience at which the message is aimed.

- Inquiring minds want to know.
- Operation Desert Storm was marked by the use of "smart bombs" and Patriot missiles.
- Commentary on the Internet often makes grand claims about the democratization of information and discourse via network connections. This view, of course, fails to take into account the level of wealth (personal, institutional, or national) required for individuals to gain access to computer hardware.
- Waste not want not.
- This architecture can be greatly simplified and its flexibility can be increased if we view the browser as a generic extension manager who acts merely as a dispatcher. Not only MIME extensions, but also the communication toolbox and the HTML viewer are subsumed as extensions.
- A duck walks into a drugstore and says, "Gimme some Chapstick . . . and, ah . . . put it on my bill."

The Rhetorical Triangle and the Internet

We've been talking about how important it is to understand rhetorical situations, particularly the relationships between speaker, audience, and message. As you begin reading and writing on the Internet, you'll find that a number of subtle shifts take place in on-line rhetorical situations. One difference is the way you consider your audience as you write. Although many instructors encourage you to imagine an audience for your assignments, most class papers are seen only by a single reader, the teacher. Writing on the Internet, however, fundamentally alters the dynamics of this rhetorical situation. For instance, if you were to post a message to a Usenet newsgroup, you would likely be addressing an audience of several thousand users from around the world, all of whom are interested in your topic. Additionally, these readers can and will respond to the messages you produce. By receiving this immediate feedback, you'll be better able to gauge the makeup of your audience and the effectiveness of your writing.

To demonstrate some aspects of on-line rhetorical situations, we offer here a brief discussion of a wayward student newsgroup message and the response it generated. As part of a larger assignment, students in a computer-assisted composition class were told to follow the discussion on a newsgroup. After conducting some outside research and considering the different participants in the newsgroup, students were asked to post a message that detailed their own position on an international issue.

One student who posted to the newsgroup **soc.culture.bosna-herzguna** in the summer of 1994, during debates about the U.S. role in the Bosnia conflict, tried to show that intervention on behalf of the Muslim minority was a moral issue.

```
What is going on here.  Why is everyone so against
not helping Bosnia. So are we going to let the
Muslims be killed of by those gready ass Serbs and
Croatians.  I'm not saying go in and destroy
every gun.  just make it fair. The Serbs are stedly
getting weapons and supplies from Serbia who is
helping the Muslims.  Then we can help them with the
peace process.  Give them what they want.  If
they want to be divided on ethnic lines lets help
them do that so we can get out as quick as possible.
Because no matter what, we will always be involed
while the conflict still occurs.  Please someone
leftwith a good heart agree with me I know yall are
out there.

Ali
```

This posting demonstrates why on-line writers must carefully consider their role as a speaker, the shape of their message, and the makeup of their audience. Although most newsgroup readers welcome some informality and generally don't check for spelling, this author's carelessness negatively affects her credibility. The message appears rather hastily written, includes a number of mechanical errors, and takes a fairly simplistic, albeit well-intentioned, approach toward the problem.

The sample also illustrates why authors must carefully present themselves as speakers. Note that the student who posted this message was named Alicia, but she posted under her nickname, "Ali." Mistakenly believing the student to be Muslim because of her nickname, one member of the newsgroup posted a pointed message responding to what he thought was a heavy Muslim bias.

> Actually Croats you bloody idiot. Before the war in Bosnia begun, Muslims received huge quantities of arms from CROATIA and CROATIANS (who according to you want to kill muslims). Those quantities of arms continued after the conflict between Croats and Muslims ended. I did not see you stinking muslim countries providing arms.
>
> Also don't dare forget you peace-of-no-good-trash that during the war in Croatia (1991/2), there were several thousands of MUSLIM volunteers in Serb ranks going to Croatia and killing Croats in Croatia for the benefit of Serbs. Bosnian president at that time opposed any recognition of Croatia as an independent state. If you want to talk about crimes, chew on that.
>
> Got that?

Even though this group member had been very constructive in replying to other student posts, his response to Ali's message was extremely negative. Although this respondent seems excessively intolerant and his message could easily be categorized as a flame, the student might have been able to avoid the personal attack had she thought more carefully about the initial posting. In part, the harsh response is driven by misconceptions about the religious status of "Ali." At the time, Croatia and Bosnian Muslims had a rather uneasy alliance against their common enemy, Serbia, a fact that Ali almost wholly ignored. In the past, however, relations between Bosnian Muslims and Croats had erupted into ethnic conflicts. By not recognizing the potential repercussions of her nickname, Ali's presentation of herself as a speaker inspired strong negative feelings that influenced the reception of her message.

Additionally, the original posting doesn't do the best job of tapping into the audience's shared values and beliefs. The respondent begins by correcting Ali's use of "Croatians." Because the respondent expected group members to be aware of the implications of religious identities and political events related to the conflict, he took Ali's misuse of the term as willful denigration of Croats and Croatia. Although most group members won't worry too much about the occasional slip-up, the response shows the need to understand and adhere to the terminology and conventions of a debate as closely as possible.

The importance of this example is that it highlights the need to take all of your writing seriously (but particularly writing that addresses a responsive Internet audience). It also shows that despite the many new rhetorical situations that we encounter on the Net, a careful application of proven rhetorical strategies is still the best path to successful on-line communication. Ali's posting had numerous problems in the accuracy and detail of the message; it didn't reflect a careful presentation of the speaker; and it didn't fully consider its audience and their assumptions. As a result, the post generated misunderstanding in an atmosphere where misunderstandings are filled with tension.

CHAPTER 3

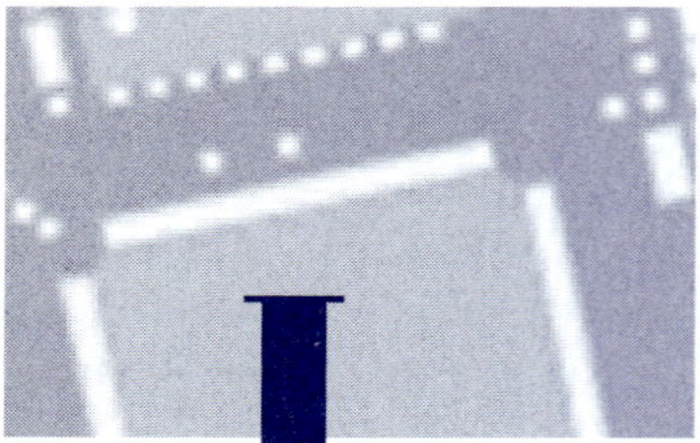

I DON'T WANT TO ARGUE ABOUT THIS ANYMORE

Defining Argument

Our culture often associates the word "argument" with the idea of a verbal fight. When we try to define argument, the images that leap to mind are nose-to-nose screaming matches between boyfriends and girlfriends, parents and children, or ballplayers and umpires. However, in the context of a writing class, the term "argument" has a somewhat different meaning. When teachers tell you to "construct an argument," they probably don't want you to recount the latest round in the "toilet seat: up or down" battle.

Of course, we all intuitively understand that if, in a formal assignment, writers try to shriek, break glasses, or kick dirt (or whatever the textual equivalents might be), they're not likely to convince anyone of anything. By taking on an overly defensive or adversarial tone, authors generally create more opposition than support. But the differences between arguments at home or on a baseball field and arguments in a writing classroom go beyond a simple matter of tone or word choice.

Arguments in the world of academics will be judged more by the persuasiveness of their logic than by their decibel level. Rather than provoking altercations, these arguments seek to move a conversation forward in an effort to educate an audience. □

KEY TERMS

Arguable Position: A position that addresses a topic or issue in which some type of conflict, disagreement, or disparity exists between two or more viable positions. Those positions must share a certain amount of common ground.

Argument: A claim that is explained by logical reasoning and often supported by evidence and that is intended both to persuade an audience and to move the audience toward a clearer sense of understanding.

Claim: A statement that stakes out a position or asserts a point.

Evidence: The data and materials that are used to support a claim.

Fact: Something that is verifiable within a specific group of people at a specific time.

Opinion: A claim that is based on personal preference.

Persuasion: Communication that moves an audience to action or convinces them to think in a certain way.

Argument versus Persuasion

If you've ever heard a political slogan or seen an ad on TV, then you are already familiar with persuasive communication. An act of persuasion can be thought of as something that moves an audience to action or convinces the audience members to think in a certain way. As such, persuasion is a rather broad category. The striking image of a single man who refused to get out of the way of a Chinese Army tank during the 1990 government crackdown at Tiananmen Square may have persuaded millions of people to oppose human rights violations in China. However, the government crackdown that suppressed the demonstration may have persuaded countless Chinese citizens to steer clear of protests in the future. On a less serious note, an e-mail message entitled "Important News" might persuade you to open it, or a dog that is wagging its tail might persuade you to reach down and pet it. Each of these communication acts provokes some kind of movement or change (whether physical or mental) from an audience. But are they arguments?

Not really. Although the goal of any argument is to make an audience think or act in a particular way, we believe that for something to be considered an argument, it must persuade an audience by using logical reasoning. The Marine colonel who simply orders his troops to run five miles might be persuasive, but because he hasn't provided any logical reasons for why they should be running (besides, "I said so!"), he hasn't constructed an argument. A baseball manager, on the other hand, is both persuasive and argumentative when he tells his team to run five miles after explaining that running is essential to a player's overall fitness and that it has a direct impact on both the offensive and defensive elements of the game. While persuasion can rely on any number of factors to move an audience (a colonel's authority, a powerful image, a catchy jingle), arguments attempt to persuade an audience by staking out a claim (a position that one is taking or a point that one is trying to make) and backing up that claim with logical reasoning.

Even when you do provide reasons for your claims, however, some people still won't be convinced. You may need to strengthen your arguments by supplying evidence to support your logic. You'll need to tailor your evidence to fit your argument. For instance, many scientific readers will expect an argument to be supported with some kind of statistical data. An argument in a history class might call for primary research materials, documents and artifacts that were produced during the period being investigated. A more issue-oriented research paper might require that you find articles or books that present the various sides of a debate. An argument in a newsgroup posting might need to cite previous messages. Evidence might also come in the form of examples, personal experience, and analogies. In general, evidence can be thought of as the data and materials that answer the question "Why should I believe this statement?" So far, then, our definition of argument might read something like "a claim that is intended to persuade an audience and that is explained with logical reasoning and often supported by evidence."

We can push this definition still further by adding one final element: Arguments should always move the conversation on a given issue toward education and understanding. By this we mean that writers should develop knowledge about a topic through research and anticipate and respond to opposition arguments with the idea of clarifying the issues, educating the audience, and advancing the discussion. Our definition of argument, then, assumes a kind of good faith effort not to obscure, confuse, or avoid the issues, but rather to add productively to an existing debate.

Our final definition of argument, then, might read something like this: "a claim that is explained with logical reasoning and often supported by evidence and that is intended both to persuade an audience and to move the audience toward a clearer sense of understanding."

Choosing Your Battles: Selecting an Arguable Position

Facts versus Opinions

Not all arguments can "forward the conversation." For instance, what is the problem with a study that, after a careful analysis of medical reports, argues that smoking is bad for your health? Or an article by a literary scholar arguing that James Joyce is the greatest modern author because his novels demonstrate the widest range of vocabulary and use the largest words? In the first instance, the argument is something of a "no-brainer." Because of the overwhelming evidence that has been collected by doctors in support of this position, the argument borders on the statement of a fact. Not many people (excluding executives from the tobacco industry) would disagree with the claim. In the second argument, the criteria for greatness (breadth of vocabulary and word size) are a matter of personal preference. If you believe that lots of long words determine literary greatness, then the argument is persuasive. But since we all probably have different criteria for what makes a book "great," this position is hard to argue.

Both of these examples might fit into a broad definition of "argument." Each supports a claim with reasons and evidence in an attempt to persuade its audience. But since the study about smoking is too close to being a fact and the article about Joyce is too close to being an opinion, neither of these positions can forward the conversation enough to make a good argument.

Figure 3.1 shows one way of looking at facts and opinions. Some people think of facts and opinions as polar opposites. People often try to define facts as "scientific," "permanent," and "true" whereas they think of opinions as "subjective," "temporary," and "unreliable." In our language,

■ **FIGURE 3.1** The Fact/Opinion Continuum

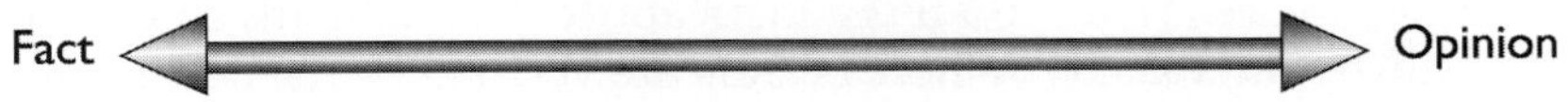

the word "fact" generally has a more positive connotation than "opinion." We often hear people say, "Just stick to the facts" or "Well, that's just your opinion" as a way of controlling a conversation or discrediting another speaker.

However, it turns out that automatically privileging facts over opinions overlooks some of their complexities. For instance, can we ever know for certain that something is "true"? Before Copernicus's astronomical work, Europeans were certain that the earth was the center of the universe. It was a "scientific fact." Before explorers were able to sail around the world, many people considered it a "fact" that the earth was flat. For some indigenous peoples in the South Pacific, it is a "fact" that sharks are the reincarnated spirits of their relatives, just as it is a "fact" for Christians that Jesus Christ is the son of God. If we think carefully about it, we will see that "facts" are not permanent truths, but rather culturally and temporally relative ways of understanding.

But we also cannot definitively say that there is no such thing as a fact. After all, we depend on facts and truths in order to function in our everyday lives. For instance, we all feel confident that gravitational forces are a constant fact of our existence. How could we live our lives if we truly believed that stepping off a building would not result in some rather painful injuries? There are certain common conceptions of the world on which we base our assumptions and activities. Clearly, then, we need to alter our notion of "fact" to balance our understanding that knowledge is culturally relative with our need for some degree of certainty.

We would suggest that a "fact" is something that is verifiable within a specified group at a specified time. If everyone in fifteenth-century Europe believed that the earth was the center of the universe, then that piece of scientific knowledge was a fact for that particular group of people—regardless of what modern astronomers now believe. In the same way, shark gods are a fact for a particular group of indigenous peoples on the Pacific Rim—regardless of what Christians, Jews, Buddhists, Muslims, or members of any other religion might believe. They are facts because the members of each group believe that they are true and depend on them as a structuring influence on their lives. What's important to note for our purposes is that once a group has firmly acknowledged something as a fact, there is little left to argue about.

Opinions have another way of inhibiting argument. For instance, is there any way to refute the statement "I like Alice Walker's novel *The Color Purple*"? Of course not. The speaker is not claiming that everyone should like *The Color Purple* or that Walker's novel is historically accurate. The statement simply claims a personal affinity for the book. This opinion may not be any less "true" than the facts above, but its truth can be confirmed only by the speaker. Whereas facts are verified by the consensus of a group, an opinion is held by an individual.

Our main point is that neither facts nor opinions make good arguable positions. Of course, people like Copernicus occasionally come along and disprove what has been considered scientific fact, and individuals often change their opinion, but if something is universally verified or wholly a matter of individual preference, there is little or no room to argue. Figure 3.2 redraws the relationship between fact and opinion. In this figure, we see a kind of continuum in which fact and opinion are much more closely related than we initially suggested. Both exist outside of the area of arguable positions.

Finding Common Ground

An arguable position must meet two important criteria. First, a viable argument must have two or more conflicting positions. As we have seen, both facts and opinions allow for only one viable position. Although the claim "smoking is bad for your health" has little opposition, the claim "we should ban smoking in public places" will provoke a number of possible arguments. The second criterion to look for in a viable argument depends on the first. Not only must there be two or more defensible positions, but these positions also must share a certain amount of common ground.

It is impossible to educate and persuade an audience if the speaker and the audience don't share at least a basic set of assumptions. This is often the problem in debates about abortion. People who are pro-life generally believe that a fetus is a human life from the moment of conception and that no human life, under any circumstances, should be willfully

■ **FIGURE 3.2** Revised Fact/Opinion Continuum

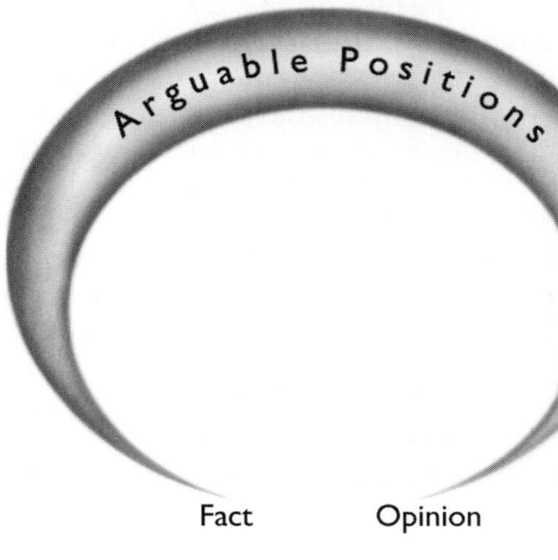

taken. By contrast, pro-choice supporters generally contend that although a fetus may be considered "alive," it is not yet a human being and therefore the mother's rights should be privileged over the fetus's rights. Although this issue sparks much heated debate, it generally produces very little true argument. The two sides begin with contradictory assumptions about the definition of human life, and because each side defends its basic assumptions so strenuously, there is little movement in the discussion.

Conversely, the debates about the welfare system in the United States generally share some common assumptions that make it more feasible to stake out an arguable position. Many of the participants in these debates agree that the current welfare policies are imperfect. They argue for policy changes that will ensure assistance for people who are in need but that will also reduce the number of people who are abusing the system. Of course, participants disagree about what kind of assistance should be given, who that assistance should be given to, and how best to limit abuse. Although arguments about welfare reform also occasionally degenerate into finger pointing and name calling, if participants make the effort to consider the shared assumptions that link the various camps, they are more likely to move the conversation forward.

Shared assumptions are not always plainly stated. When composing an argument, we need to actively search out the common ground between the various sides of a debate. In fact, the most important skills for any type of argumentative writing may be the ability to decide where meaningful conversation can occur and to concentrate our efforts on those areas.

So far in this chapter, we've fleshed out a working definition of argument. To summarize, an argument is a claim that is supported by logical reasoning and evidence and that is intended both to persuade an audience and to move the audience toward a clearer sense of understanding. Additionally, for a position to be arguable, it must address a topic or issue in which some type of conflict, disagreement, or disparity exists between two or more viable positions. Finally, those multiple positions must share some kind of common ground for the argument to productively advance the conversation.

EXERCISE 3.1

Determining Arguable Positions

Working in small groups, decide which of the following claims are arguable positions. If a position is arguable, explain why. If it is not arguable, explain why not, and rewrite the claim so that it becomes arguable. Choose a recorder to take notes and, when finished, discuss each claim with the rest of the class.

- Gay couples should be allowed to marry and receive benefits.
- Talking to kids about sex will make them want it more.
- Puerto Rico is part of the United States.
- All children should learn to play an instrument.
- We should erect a wall on the Mexican/American border to keep out illegal immigrants.
- Seattle is a nicer city to live in than Austin.
- E-mail hampers interpersonal communication.
- Hollywood has a responsibility to make movies that are less violent.
- Bulimia is a serious eating disorder.
- Aerosol sprays are bad for the environment.
- Gambling is a disease.
- The Internet should not be regulated as a broadcast medium.

Argument on the Internet

Throughout the rest of this book, one of our ongoing projects will be to examine how traditional understandings of argument are being altered as new forms of writing emerge on the Net. We will consider the compositional technologies of the Internet as tools that provide new opportunities and challenges for constructing on-line arguments. We will also explore how the very definition of argument is changing to better accommodate the demands and possibilities of electronic information media.

One of the ways in which argument is being transformed on the Internet is through the dialog and debate that take place in on-line conversational spaces. Exchanging messages in MU*s, newsgroups, e-mail lists, or Web forums generally doesn't lead to the type of extended arguments that instructors expect in formal writing assignments. These electronic forums can, however, provide an opportunity for members of a class to develop arguments through a process of exchange, debate, revision, and synthesis. Claims sent to collaborative forums are tested and refined as other members of the class respond with support or critique, offering alternative perspectives that complicate the initial message. The sample post shown in Figure 3.3 is taken from a Web forum that generated a lively exchange about course readings.

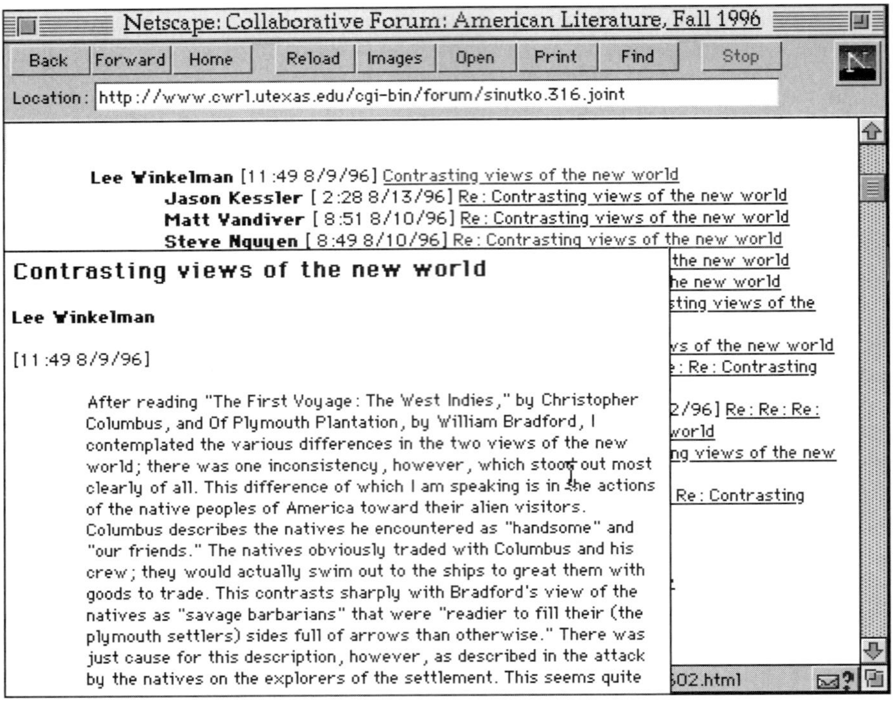

■ **FIGURE 3.3** An Initial Posting in a Thread

Figure 3.3 shows a thread from a message forum and the initial message or prompt that sparked the conversation. The opening post claims that the description of Native Americans given by the settlers at Plymouth Plantation in New England differs from the descriptions given by Columbus. The post concludes by suggesting that the settlers at Plymouth had "just cause" to describe Native Americans as "savage barbarians."

In the response shown in Figure 3.4, Steve Nguyen notes the significance of Lee's opening post but goes on to challenge the initial message. Steve suggests that the different descriptions of Native Americans can be explained by the particular motives and activities of both the traders who were traveling with Columbus and the colonists who were settling at Plymouth.

Taken together, Lee's initial posting and Steve's response create a point/counterpoint dialog that was further refined by the other messages in the thread. As a form of argument, these postings are best understood in the context of the larger discussion thread. In many ways, the perspectives represented by the various messages in the discussion form a kind of col-

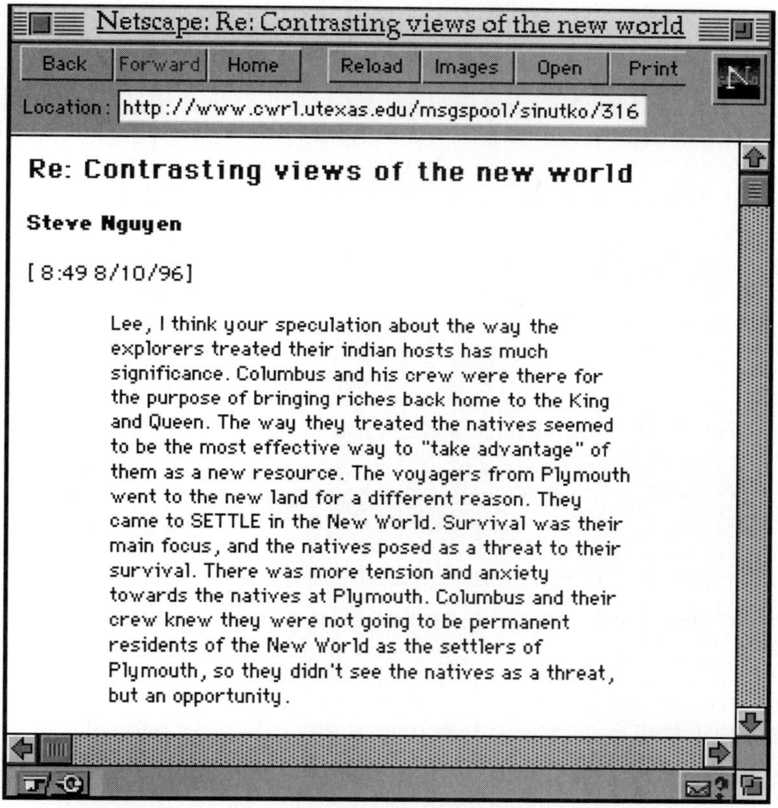

■ **FIGURE 3.4** A Response in a Thread

lective argument, which differs considerably from what we might find in a persuasive essay. We believe, however, that this type of exchange demonstrates the process of education and clarification that is fundamental to any argument. Additionally, these posts can be thought of as a stage in the process of writing a more formal essay. They provide an opportunity for authors to formulate their ideas and to consider what opposition arguments they will need to address if they are to convince an audience.

Another way in which argumentation is transformed on the Net is through the multimedia and hypertextual capabilities of the World Wide Web. Since the Web can integrate graphics, video, sound, and animation into a document, writers are afforded new opportunities of expression. Imagine the difference it could make for a film analysis project if an author could play a clip from a movie (and allow readers to replay it as many times as they wanted) rather than having to describe a critical scene and depend on the audience to remember its intricacies.

The sample shown in Figure 3.5 demonstrates how an argument can be enhanced by drawing on the hypertextual and multimedia capacities of the World Wide Web. This student project looked at the play *A Raisin in the Sun* by Lorraine Hansberry as well as the 1961 film adaptation of the play. It argued that traditional authority in the play represses the younger generation's identity. The student is able to bolster her analysis by including a clip from the film version. In the clip, the mother chastises and slaps the daughter, offering visual and aural support for the claim.

■ **FIGURE 3.5** A Multimedia Web Project

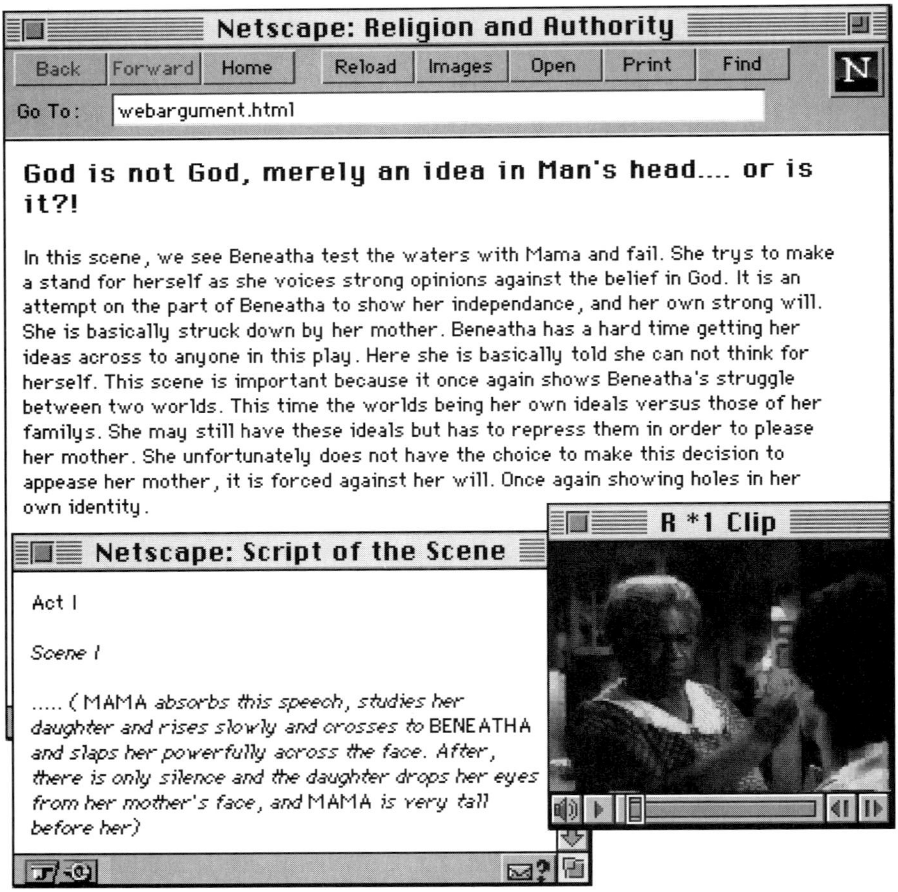

Additionally, the project capitalizes on the hypertextual nature of the Web by providing a link to the original script of the play. The stage directions,

> MAMA absorbs this speech, studies her daughter and rises slowly and crosses to BENEATHA and slaps her powerfully across the face. After, there is only silence and the daughter drops her eyes from her mother's face, and MAMA is very tall before her.

not only allow the reader to explore Hansberry's original text, they also further the argument by providing a sense of the power relationships that are treated in the play.

Using multimedia and hypertext provides new avenues for developing and supporting an argument. Be aware, however, that these avenues lead not only to new argumentative possibilities but also to new problems. For instance, not all arguments support multimedia as well as this film analysis project does. If you are arguing in favor of free speech on the Internet, a clip that depicts a student burning the U.S. flag won't automatically support your position. You'll need to provide context for the clip and show how it works to further your claims. Multimedia can distract from an argument just as easily as it can enhance it. (For more information about composing effectively with multimedia, see **Chapter 19.**)

In some senses, though, it is unfair and unproductive for Web authors to simply replicate standards of argumentation which were designed for print media. The evolving conventions for Web design demand that we organize information in completely new ways. They stress interactivity and multimedia presentation, rather than clear transitions and linear progression. Documents on the Web fit into the broad category of hypertext, a mode of writing that is based on the principle of linking together nodes, or pieces of information, rather than carefully tracing a linear path from point A to point B as you might see in a traditional essay. Because writing on the Web can be linked to documents all over the world, authors are able to construct arguments that are situated in a web of contextual materials.

Figure 3.6 demonstrates how Web authors are able to integrate multiple documents into a single project. This project links to documents that exist elsewhere on the Internet (for instance, the Human Rights Watch Web site), as well as to subsections of the student's own site (for instance, his discussion of U.S. foreign trade policy). The links also lead to several different types of materials. For example, the link to "economists counter these claims" leads to a document that provides oppositional arguments. In addition, the link to a "class discussion" leads to a Web forum that both

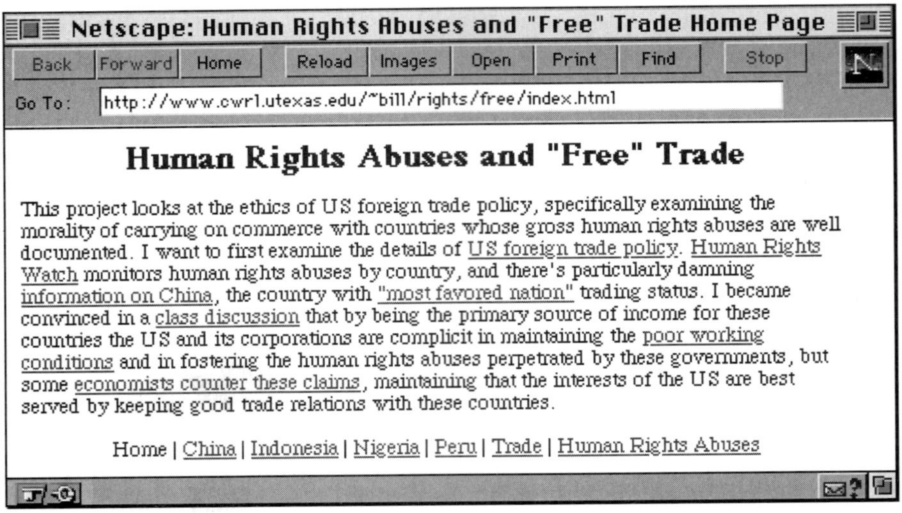

■ **FIGURE 3.6** A Web Project That Integrates Multiple Links

references an earlier conversation and offers readers a chance to contribute their own ideas to an ongoing debate.

Obviously, these new forms of hypertext and on-line composition provide writers with new challenges and opportunities. Well-written hypertextual arguments should still support a claim with logical evidence and attempt to move the conversation forward, but as we will explore throughout this book, electronic conversation, multimedia, and hypertext all are complicating the way we think about argumentation.

CHAPTER 4

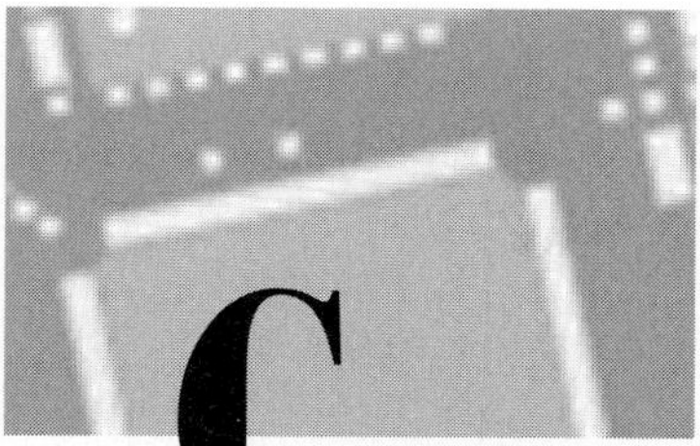

CONSIDERING PURPOSE

Tools for Analyzing and Constructing Messages

Every message—spoken, written, gestured, even photographed or painted—is an attempt to communicate with a purpose. Purpose can be seen as the aims or reasons that compel a speaker to present a message to a specific audience in a particular way. It determines the choices that authors make, shapes the way they organize information, and guides their writing process. As a reader, you can focus on authors' purposes to better analyze their messages. Similarly, by carefully considering your own writing goals, you can make more informed decisions about how best to communicate your ideas. □

Using Purpose to Analyze Messages

Many times, readers are so busy thinking about *what* a message is saying that they forget to think about *why* someone is saying it. But picking out the goal behind a complicated message can help us to better assess its meaning and role within a larger rhetorical situation.

KEY TERMS

Context: The elements surrounding and informing any act of communication. The setting, the event, the time, and any other messages about a topic all influence the way any message is constructed and interpreted.

Informative Writing: Writing that presents information without trying to persuade.

Medium: The mode of communication for a message. The term can be used generally, for instance, to distinguish electronic communication from messages in a print medium. It can also be used specifically to distinguish subcategories of communication such as magazines and newspapers or e-mail and the World Wide Web.

Persuasive Writing: Writing that tries to move an audience to action or toward an adjustment of the audience members' beliefs.

Purpose: The motives that compel a speaker to present a message to a specific audience in a particular way. Purpose also refers to the particular goals that an author has in mind at any stage of the writing process.

Style: The choices of arrangement and diction that an author makes. An academic style generally uses a specialized language and constructs complicated sentences to make logically reasoned claims. An informal style, on the other hand, often uses colloquial language and less rigid conventions.

Tone: Similar to style, tone is the attitude conveyed in a message. Depending on the mood that the author wants to set, the tone can be frivolous, joking, serious, conciliatory, confrontational, and so on.

Context

Thinking about purpose can contribute to our understanding of messages by allowing us to more closely examine the context in which they are exchanged. Take, for example, the American World War II propaganda poster shown in Figure 4.1.

It's clear that the context of World War II both influences the author's purpose and shapes the message of this poster. By projecting a strong female image, the poster encourages women who had previously

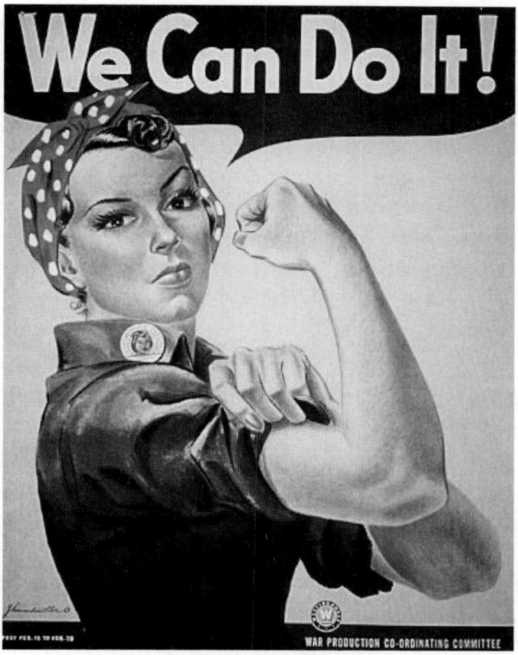

■ **FIGURE 4.1** A World War II Propaganda Poster

been absent from the labor force to contribute to the war effort. It is the unique context of 1940s wartime labor shortages that made such a message viable in the United States. Remember that before the war, manufacturing jobs were occupied almost solely by men. After the war, female workers were asked to leave the labor force and return to their roles as mothers and housewives. The author's purpose of recruiting women into the workforce, therefore, must be analyzed in light of the specific historical context in which the message was produced.

But there are always differences and similarities between our own social contexts and those of others. For instance, despite the advances of women in the workforce, this poster still has cultural relevance today. Women are still excluded from certain jobs, are forced to struggle for equal pay, and continually have to convince people that "We Can Do It." At the same time, our context causes us to interpret the poster differently today than we would have in 1943. Prior to the 1940s, women had been limited to work in the home or to a few jobs that were considered suitably "feminine," so the poster meant a radical transformation of cultural attitudes. Today it represents the continuation of a women's rights movement that has been progressing steadily in the fifty years since the war.

When we read the message today, we look at it as an historical artifact. We can no longer read it solely in terms of its original purpose of recruiting women to assist in the war effort. An artist today might still be able to use the image, but it would be put to a different purpose that was informed by our contemporary context. For instance, an artist who wanted to highlight the fact that very few women hold positions of power in today's corporate world might incorporate the poster into a collage that juxtaposes it with an image of seven well-dressed men sitting around a mahogany table at a corporate board meeting.

Media

Evaluating an author's purpose also helps us to understand the media in which messages are exchanged. The medium (in this case, poster art) should correspond to the purpose and will certainly influence the shape of the message. Because the message asking women to join the workforce is communicated in the form of a poster, it necessarily presents information in certain ways—for instance, by using bold, eye-catching images rather than extensive text that must be analyzed. The choice of poster art tells us that the author's purpose is to quickly impress a large audience on an emotional level rather than lead them toward a detailed analysis.

The aim behind the poster is to further the war effort, more specifically to change America's attitudes about women in the workforce. Because posters are colorful, highly visible, easy to understand, and simple to distribute, they proved to be an appropriate choice of media for this message. Obviously, writing a long book about the subject would have been much less effective as a means of achieving these goals.

As you can probably tell, there is a significant overlap between purpose, context, and medium. Thinking about purpose as we investigate communication sheds light on the context. Additionally, authors' choices of media tell us something about their purposes. As you interpret messages, then, pay careful attention to the purposes that drive the other elements of the communication situation.

Advocating for Yourself and Your Issues

No matter what walk of life you eventually choose, you are almost certain to come across situations in which you will be forced to advocate for yourself and/or an issue you believe in. Whether you are requesting a promotion, setting up a nonprofit organization's Web page, breaking up with your partner, or arguing about a city ordinance, you'll need to employ sound rhetorical strategies. As you meet these challenges, the more powerful your writing skills are, the more successful you are likely to be.

We'd be naive to think that this book will equip you with the tools you'll need to argue persuasively for yourself in every situation. However, we do think that the kinds of writing discussed in this book can have a concrete impact on real-world situations. Additionally, we believe that the writing you do will be less frustrating, more meaningful, and ultimately more convincing if it is driven by interests that are important to you.

As a way of bringing these real-world motivations into the writing classroom, some instructors ask students to compose letters to their congressional representatives or editorials for their local newspaper. This sense of purpose helps writers tailor their message to suit both the audience and the medium. For instance, the letter to Congress might be short and direct to serve the purpose of registering a complaint. Conversely, the purpose of an editorial is to influence a large audience, so the piece would probably need to be longer and argue logically but with a stylistic flair.

Composing these letters and editorials gives writers a sense of purpose that helps them craft messages that are more likely to move a real audience. Ideally, however, students will write to editors not because they are fulfilling an assignment, but because they have real-life concerns. If you were almost run over on your way to school each day by buses illegally using a bike lane to avoid traffic, then writing a letter to the editor about enforcing bike lane laws would have a purpose that extends beyond the assignment for a class. You would probably argue more forcefully because, in some sense, your life would be at risk each day that you commute.

As you move through your college career, you will likely write both to fulfill assignments and to address your own concerns. In fact, we'd like to think that these two purposes can be present in your writing at the same time. As you compose, think of ways to make your assignments meaningful to you. Whether your purpose is to address an everyday problem or simply to polish your prose, writing with a sense of personal investment will generally produce better results.

Learning the Process: Multiple Steps, Multiple Purposes

When you are working on a project (ideally, one in which you have some personal investment), your purpose will change as you move through the different stages of the writing process. For instance, if your purpose is to brainstorm about a debate or controversy, your writing will look much different than if your purpose is to convince a reader that a particular policy should be changed. The way you approach the task at hand will be determined by your purpose at that stage.

To better understand specific purposes, you should first consider the shifting nature of purpose. When you take on a writing project, the overriding purpose is to produce a finished version of the piece. But along the way there are numerous steps that you must follow. Perhaps you start by conducting research, narrowing the focus of your project, and summarizing and documenting the information that you find. You probably spend some time brainstorming, throwing out ideas, and exploring points of contention. You begin a draft of the assignment, fleshing out the ideas you've already brainstormed and developing the project's content. Later, perhaps, you show the draft to your peers and incorporate feedback into a revision. Each of these steps has its own specific purpose that works in conjunction with the larger purpose of the project.

Additionally, your sense of purpose can suddenly shift during any one of these stages. Perhaps while you are brainstorming about the causes of teen pregnancy, you realize that the lack of sex education is a major contributing factor in high teen birth rates. Your initial purpose might be to sketch out ideas and explore the topic, but once you hit on an idea, your purpose may be to run with it, to flesh it out as much as possible, and begin developing a thesis.

Form Follows Function: Shaping Your Argument to Match Your Purpose

Informative and Persuasive Writing

Although this book is mostly concerned with writing that takes the form of persuasive argumentation, at times you'll need to adjust the kinds of writing you do to meet your purposes. In addition to writing persuasively, you may often need to clearly present your audience with information.

Informative Writing Informative writing seeks to present information as clearly as possible. For instance, you may be trying to provide historical background for an issue, explain a complicated task, or relay observations. In informative writing, the currency, accuracy, and clarity of your information are of primary importance. In some settings—for instance, a sociology project examining student interactions in the dining hall—you'll want to be as objective as possible. Perhaps including statistics and detailed records of observations. In other situations—for instance, a project that gives detailed instructions about posting a home page to the Web—you may want to use graphics and illustrations to help your readers visualize the steps you are explaining. In every case, you'll want to hold your readers' interest. Use specific details and be as economical as possible to avoid numbing your reader with a boring flood of information.

Persuasive Writing Although persuasive writing can be anything that moves someone else to action, in this book we are most interested in persuasive writing that develops arguments. Arguments may take numerous forms. You might evaluate a text, define a term or concept, compare two or more items, establish a cause-and-effect relationship, or propose a solution to a problem. Each of these types of argumentation will demand a different approach to the topic and will probably take a different form, but the overall goal will be to persuade your readers.

Usually, arguments have a thesis statement somewhere early in the paper that announces the author's position. If the argument is complex, the author should map out its organization carefully in the beginning so that readers aren't confused. Additionally, persuasive arguments often address possible opposition to the points that they put forward.

Although we've separated informative and persuasive writing here for the sake of analysis, our aim is not so much to cover every possibility or to provide simple formulas that will generate an argument for you, but to help you begin thinking about your messages as dynamic and original creations that you shape in response to your writing goals. Often compositions include *both* informative and persuasive writing. For instance, if you were trying to inform an audience about the spread of AIDS, you might first have to persuade the audience that the public is still ignorant about the nature of this disease. Similarly, if you were trying to argue that insurance companies should provide better benefits for AIDS patients, you would need to inform your audience about the prohibitive costs of AIDS care. Let your purpose determine when and how you shift between informative and persuasive writing.

Style and Tone

Your purpose will also influence the style and tone of your messages. Style generally refers to the choices of arrangement and diction that an author makes in a composition. For instance, if you are writing to fulfill an assignment, you will probably choose an academic style—one that uses complete sentences written in standard English and includes citations and documentation. If you are writing to entertain, you will probably choose a more informal style, throwing in colloquial language, jokes, and the occasional mention of Cheez Whiz if it will better illustrate a point.

Tone is similar to style but refers to the overall attitude or mood conveyed in a message. If you are requesting help from the audience, you will most likely use a polite tone that shows your willingness to listen. If you are challenging someone else's point, you will need to select the appropriate tone in which to respond. For instance, if you believe that someone has deliberately misinterpreted your message or is not arguing in good faith, you might take an accusatory tone. Usually, though, you will get better results if your tone is even-handed and sympathetic. You might outline a few of the opposition's points that you see as legitimate and then raise questions about the ones you disagree with.

Consider your purpose and readership when you think about style and tone. If your message is aimed at a professor, it will take on a different tone than if it is aimed at your fiancée. If you were making a flyer for this weekend's tractor pull, you wouldn't want to write in a overblown, academic style. Adjust your style and tone to match your purpose and audience.

EXERCISE 4.1

Composing with a Purpose

Working in small groups, perform the following exercise to better understand how purpose influences the choices we make as we compose a given message. Choose a recorder to transcribe the group's work, and when finished, present the results to the rest of the class.

The goal for this exercise is to produce two "dear Jane or John" letters. In the first letter, imagine that your purpose is to let the other person down easy. You're no longer interested but have no hard feelings. In the second letter, your goal is to "let 'em have it." You're fed up and ready to burn all bridges. As you think about what to say in your letters, consider how your purpose is influencing your style and tone as well as any other rhetorical choices that you make.

EXERCISE 4.2

Argument and Information

Working in small groups, choose a recorder to transcribe the group's work, and when finished, present the results to the rest of the class.

The goal of this exercise is to come up with a list of the materials and arguments you would include if you were producing an infomercial trying to sell a new home HIV testing kit. You will need to both present information about the test and convince the public of the test kit's merits. Discuss how you might make such an infomercial. Come up with a list of the information you would present to your audience. Next, list at least three arguments that you would make to convince people to buy the product. Finally, flesh out one of those arguments, providing reasons that further your claims and evidence to back them up.

Purpose and the Internet

We've talked about the ways in which evaluating purpose empowers people, either by showing them the motivations behind what they read or by helping them influence their own audience. It's ironic, however, that while teachers of writing want students to see that their work can have an impact on the world at large, most of these students' compositions rarely make it beyond the instructor's desk.

On the Internet—even if there is no way to measure the ultimate impact of your words—you can be certain that your writing will find an active audience. Additionally, since many of the media on the Net are organized by topic, the audiences that you find are likely to have an interest in your subject. You may not be able to change everyone's opinion about welfare reform, but you can at least make your voice known to people who are actively thinking and talking about the issue.

This live audience will make it even more necessary for you to consider exactly what you are trying to accomplish and to make the right rhetorical choices to achieve that goal. Your first choice concerns what kinds of writing are most effective for both the Internet medium you wish to use and the particular aims of your project. Just as you wouldn't write a term paper on a postcard, you wouldn't create a four-paragraph essay in a real-time conversation. Each Internet environment lends itself to different kinds of writing; therefore, you'll need to choose the electronic forum that best suits your purposes.

For instance, the fast-paced interactions that take place during synchronous (real-time) conversations like those in MU*s or on IRC channels are geared toward exploring the merits of different perspectives on an issue. You can write freely in these environments with the aim of discovering as much about the topic as possible and generating new ideas.

The following sample demonstrates some of the properties of real-time electronic conversations. This excerpt was taken from a class discussion about the topic of Internet censorship and the Communications Decency Act (CDA).

```
Max Wright:  If we start to dictate what can and
can't be spoken on a global scale, where do we stop?
```

Where will that line move tomorrow? How far will it invade your daily life?

Sebastiano D. Montoya: Daniel: I don't believe the gov't should regulate the morals of an entire nation, since the government is not an accurate representation of the nation, which leads to a skewed vision of what morals are. If this were to happen on a large scale, we would probably be living in a Demolition Man society. (no salt, no cussing, no meat, no sex)
I don't know about that.

Tara Blankenship: Every day murderers get away with their crime and so do rapists. Are we allowing a society that allows anything to go? Look long term. What's considered obscene now won't be considered obscene in the future. It will only get less regulated. Now is the time to take action. A line needs to be drawn.

Jake Monford: What is CDA? I am not familiar with it.

Eilene D'Marco: I believe in free speech, but who doesn't tone down their language when a child is in the room? and what do you think of people who don't?

Charles Lau: Jake: Communications Decency Act

Note that several different threads of discussion appear in the sample. For instance, the second and third messages reveal two differing perspectives on censorship. Sebastiano D. Montoya claims that the government doesn't accurately represent the people of the nation and that regulations could lead to government repression. Tara Blankenship offers a different point of view. She responds to Max Wright's earlier concern about the difficulties of distinguishing between different types of censorship with the claim that the "line needs to be drawn" to preserve a moral foundation for the future.

In all of these messages, the authors concentrate on exploring ideas as freely as possible. It's not that there shouldn't be conflict and argument in these discussions or that sound reasoning and evidence shouldn't be provided. The point is that the kinds of debate you'll find in these forums tend to encourage the exchange of ideas rather than the development of complete arguments.

While writing in real-time situations will differ from communication on a newsgroup or e-mail list, no Internet medium is limited to a single type of writing. Each environment can be used for a wide range of purposes, depending on what kind of project an author is working on. For instance, in an argumentative project, you might use the World Wide Web to construct a site that persuades readers to think or act a certain way. For a more informative assignment, you might use Web pages to freely disseminate information.

The project shown in Figure 4.2 argues against the reliability and constitutionality of workplace drug testing. For this author, it was important that readers move through his claims and arguments in sequence. For instance, the author wanted to acknowledge some of the claims made by employers about the necessity of drug testing before refuting them with arguments about employees' rights to privacy and the unreliability of the tests. This project, then, begins with the opposition and moves sequentially through the refutation. Figure 4.2 shows that the project has been designed in a linear fashion. Instead of using a menu that represents the contents of the entire site and letting readers select where to go, the

FIGURE 4.2 A Linear Web Argument

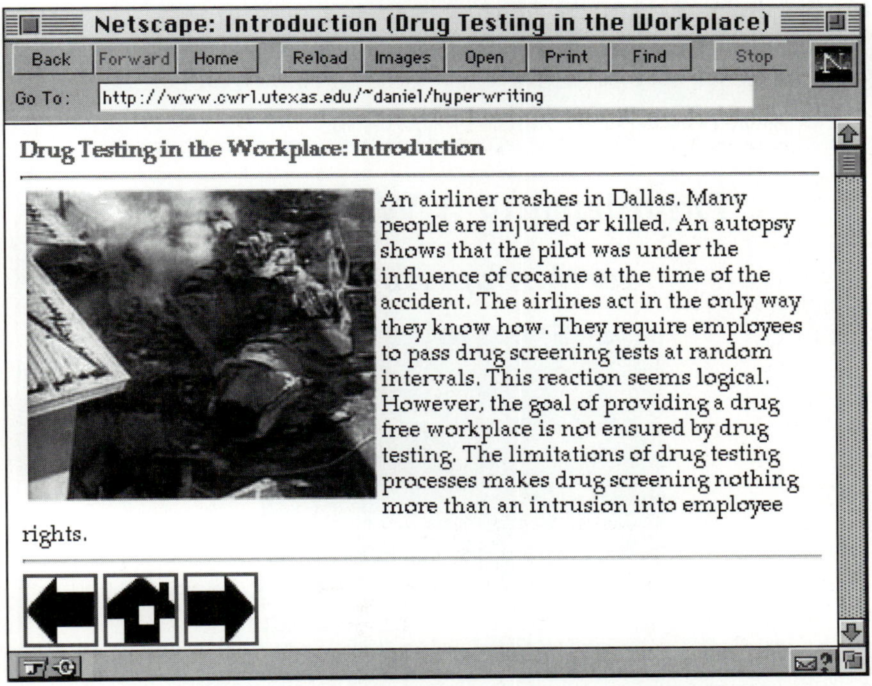

project uses forward and back buttons to lead the reader through the information in the order that the author desires.

To contrast, let's look at a Web page that has a different purpose. Figure 4.3 shows a project that was developed as part of an informative writing assignment. In this project, students were asked to teach something that they had learned about writing or technology during the semester. As you can see, this author takes a different approach to presenting information. Rather than limiting the reader to forward and backward movements, the author provides a menu that links to all of the elements of the site. A reader who already knows about writing with HTML need not pass through that section. This model places more control in the hands of the reader and meshes more closely with the goals of the project.

Our final point is not that one project is more successful than another or that your informative and argumentative projects must follow set formulas. These authors chose to present information in the manner they felt would be most appropriate for their purposes. Because on-line writing provides so many new and unfamiliar rhetorical situations, it is essential that you think carefully about your goals and how best to implement them.

FIGURE 4.3 A Nodal Web Argument

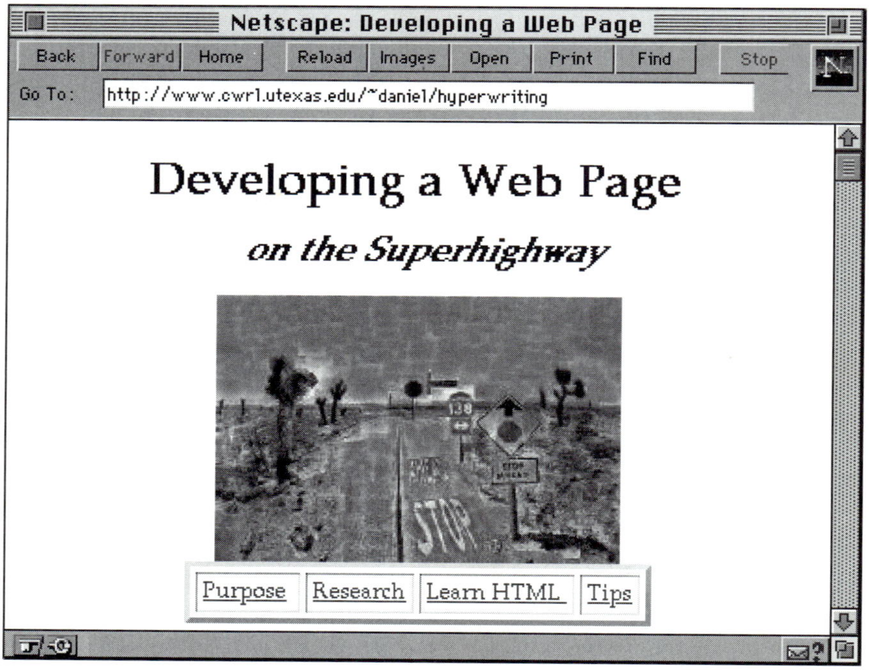

CHAPTER 5

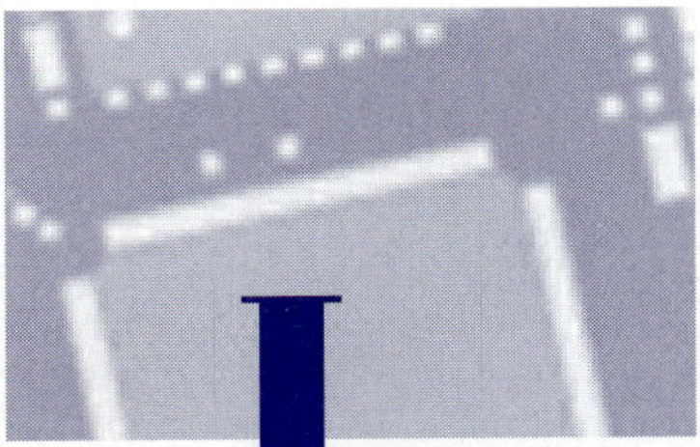

I KNOW I READ IT SOMEWHERE

The Importance of Critical Reading

Every day, we face a host of complex interpretive situations. Advertisements, newscasts, seminar meetings, and even messages your dad leaves on the answering machine all need to be carefully analyzed. We perform some of these acts intuitively. For instance, knowing that Dad and Aunt Helga haven't spoken since that ugly Jell-O incident at the family reunion in 1983, you will take Dad's latest ranting about "that side of the family" with a grain of salt. Because you are familiar with the context of the message, interpreting its nuances seems to come naturally.

Understanding messages in less familiar contexts, however, requires a bit more effort. Remember that any act of communication is situated within a larger rhetorical context. As readers, we need to evaluate messages in terms of their overall purpose, their speakers, their audiences, and their relationships to other texts. Additionally, before we can fully assess the position of a message within this larger context or incorporate a message into our own writing, we should understand some of its internal organization—

its thesis, logic, claims, evidence, and assumptions. Sophisticated "consumers" of information have critical reading skills that allow them to conduct in-depth analyses of a broad range of messages. □

KEY TERMS

Assumptions: The premises on which any claim is based. As the term "assumption" suggests, these premises are usually unstated.

Claim: A statement that stakes out a position or asserts a point.

Credibility: The amount of trust that is placed in an author's competence, motives, and fair-mindedness. Also used to refer to the reliability of resources.

Critical Reading: An approach to analyzing messages that looks at both their successes and their failures. Critical reading considers texts in terms of their purposes, contexts, and media and evaluates them by examining their component parts.

Evidence: The data and materials that are used to support a claim.

Fair Summary: A summary that articulates the basic message of a text without critique or commentary. In general, a fair summary represents an author's argument as closely as possible.

Genre: Primarily a literary term used to describe the differences between works such as plays, poems, and novels. Additionally, it can be used more specifically to distinguish subcategories such as romance or detective novels.

Purpose: The motives that compel a speaker to present a message to a specific audience in a particular way. Purpose also refers to the particular goals that an author has in mind at any stage of the writing process.

Skeptical Reading: An approach to analyzing messages that focuses on the weaknesses of a text. A skeptical reading tries to find fault with a message in as many ways as possible.

Sources: The materials that authors use as they research. Academic projects generally require that authors document their sources.

Sympathetic Reading: An approach to analyzing messages that focuses on the strengths of a text. A sympathetic reading tries to flesh out the major claims and trace the development of an argument.

Thesis: The main point that an author is trying to get across.

Messages and Their Components

The term "critical reading" can be somewhat misleading. When instructors ask you to read a text critically, they want you to do more than just point out its flaws. Critical reading requires that you look at both the successes and failures of messages. It demands a much broader approach—one that considers both the message as a whole and its individual parts.

To demonstrate how to read critically for the components of messages, let's take a careful look at a sample article.

Ban Boxing

Robert E. McAfee

As a practicing physician, I am convinced that boxing should be banned.

First, boxing is a very visible example that violence is accepted behavior in our society—outside the ring as well as inside. This sends the wrong message to America's youth, and at a time when so many kinds of violence are on the rise, it is a message we should stop.

Second, boxing is the only sport where the sole object is to injure the opponent. Think about what a knockout really is: It is a cerebral concussion that knocks the victim senseless! Boxing, then, is morally offensive, because its intent is to inflict brain injuries on another person. And it is medically indefensible, because these injuries so often lead to irreversible medical consequences, such as a subdural hematoma, non-fatal acute intracranial hemorrhages, "punch drunk syndrome," progressive neurological disorder, and serious eye conditions.

Third, medical science can't take someone who has suffered repeated blows to the head and restore that person to normal function. Many physicians, with new methods of brain scanning, have seen an otherwise young and healthy individual sustain serious and permanently disabling injury due to boxing, sometimes in just one fight. This causes many physicians to conclude that our society should ban boxing. And sadly—slowly but surely—as many of our nationally known veteran boxers can no longer hide the long-term effects of brain injury, the public is beginning to understand what only doctors and family members previously knew.

What about the argument that injuries occur in other sports? Quite simply, in those sports, injuring the opponent is not the accepted method of scoring or winning. And in those sports, there is an attempt to wear protective equipment that will minimize injury. But scientific evidence shows there is no really effective way to prevent boxing injuries that may have a lifetime effect—even from one fight.

And finally, to those who say boxing "gives poor kids an opportunity to get out of the ghetto," I have a better suggestion. Let's take each young person with that precious, undamaged brain and combine some education with that same commitment to excellence he has for boxing. I guarantee that youngster better success over a lifetime—and perhaps a longer and healthier life, too.

Boxing is morally and medically offensive. So as a physician, I believe boxing should be banned.

This article, written by Dr. Robert McAfee, was originally printed as an editorial in *USA Today.* Although we find the argument convincing, approaching it from a critical perspective helps us better understand its strengths and weaknesses. As we move through the rest of this chapter, we'll use McAfee's article as a point of reference and a way of providing examples for the various critical reading strategies we discuss.

Purpose

As we saw in the previous chapter, thinking about the purpose of a message helps us better understand its construction as well as its situation in a larger rhetorical context. Question the purpose of a message as you read. Is it meant to provide you with information? Is it asking you to buy something? Is it trying to convince you of something? If you can determine the larger purpose of a message, you can use that awareness as a starting point for further analysis.

For example, in "Ban Boxing," McAfee's basic purpose is to reach as broad an audience as possible and convince that audience that a popular sport should be banned because of its detrimental medical consequences. McAfee would have written a different letter if his purpose had been to convince the International Boxing Federation to require protective headgear in all matches. He would have written yet another kind of letter had he been asking the readers of *USA Today* to write to their congressional representatives urging them to sponsor legislation banning the sport. It seems that the purpose of this piece is to enlighten an audience in the hope of beginning a larger movement to end boxing, rather than to influence a specific policy decision.

Genre

"Genre" is primarily a literary term that is used to describe the differences between works such as plays, poems, and novels. It can be used more specifically to distinguish subcategories such as romance or detective novels. What's important for our purposes is that genres carry with them certain expectations about the form, length, tone, and style of a composition. We expect to find different kinds of writing in a newspaper column, for instance, than we do in the owner's manual for a VCR.

Genre, then, will help to determine what you should look for in any given message. For instance, "Ban Boxing" takes the form of a brief editorial. The piece does not provide detailed background information about the history of boxing or document the medical sources it draws on. Like most editorials, however, it makes a number of forceful claims in a concise, coherent manner. Knowing the genre helps us to determine the appropriateness of the message's content.

Thesis and Claims

Sometimes arguments can be distilled into a precise thesis statement. A thesis won't always be clearly announced in a message, but you can think of it as the main point that an author is trying to get across. An argument will generally consist of a thesis supported by additional claims. Claims are statements that stake out a position with logical reasoning and evidence (see the section entitled "Evidence" below). The thesis itself is a kind of claim, but we're using the term "claim" here to specifically describe the series of assertions or positions that are put forward to support the thesis. Picking out the thesis and the supporting claims reveals the logical structure of the argument and provides an opportunity for assessing which points are adequately supported by reasoning and evidence.

In "Ban Boxing," the thesis seems particularly simple. Ban boxing. McAfee supports this thesis with four additional claims, three of which he plainly numbers. First, he states that boxing sends a bad message. Second, he argues that the object of boxing is to injure someone. Third, he suggests that boxing causes brain damage. The article makes a final claim toward the end when it argues that education is the best way to help urban children.

Evidence

Evidence is the data and materials that provide the necessary support to convince an audience about the validity of a claim. Using evidence shows that you are knowledgeable about the topic and enhances the overall believability of your argument. Evidence can take the form of statistics, surveys, interviews, personal experience, or anything else that will help bolster a claim.

In "Ban Boxing," a certain amount of the evidence seems to come from McAfee's personal experience. His experience as a physician allows him to discuss the effects of boxing without relying on any specific studies or data. Additionally, throughout the piece, there are veiled references to scientific evidence. The way that the third claim refers to "new methods of brain scanning" suggests that there is scientific support for the claim without specifying where the evidence comes from. This would be troubling in a longer, academic essay, but because of the genre and the author's credibility, we are more willing to forgive this lack of specificity and failure to document sources. McAfee's final point about education may not be as convincing because it doesn't supply even the personal experience that supports his medical claims.

Credibility

As you evaluate sources, you should also assess the author's credibility. Is the author an expert on the subject? Is she or he well informed about the issue and familiar with its controversies? Does she or he seem to present the material well? Does the author demonstrate a fair-minded approach to the issue? Does the author bring up opposing points of view merely to dismiss them or equitably represent the multiple perspectives on the issue? In general, you should evaluate whether the author seems to be trustworthy and competent.

In "Ban Boxing," McAfee announces his authority immediately by speaking "as a practicing physician." This claim supports his credibility by establishing that he has sufficient expertise to make medical evaluations and by implying that he has practical experience with boxing-related injuries.

When McAfee begins to speak about education, he is attempting to address the opposing argument that boxing provides opportunities for disadvantaged youths. His guarantee that education will lead to success, however, may require additional support because his credibility as a physician doesn't carry the same weight in discussions of education and social reform. To make this claim with authority, McAfee would need to provide additional evidence, perhaps citing statistics about the amount of civic funding spent on boxing programs that could be funneled into education or about the limited number of boxers who actually make it "out of the ghetto."

Sources

Sources are the materials that authors use as they research a project. Academic writing requires that authors document the evidence they use so that future researchers can track down information. Working with sources also demonstrates that authors have some knowledge of the discussion circulating around an issue. You should always examine the evidence and sources that are used in a text to determine their reliability. If an author claims that smoking increases lung capacity but cites the *Timbuktu Picayune* as the source, you might want to double-check the reliability of the claim. Also, be sure to examine the breadth of sources being used in a project. To accurately represent an event, issue, or theory, authors usually need to demonstrate a knowledge of several points of view and consult a wide range of sources.

Assumptions

Assumptions are the premises on which any claim is based. As the term "assumption" suggests, these premises are usually unstated. Though unpacking these hidden assumptions can be frustrating, it is one of the most essential critical reading skills. For example, the claim that animal testing is inhumane and therefore should be stopped relies on the unstated assumption that all inhumane treatment should be stopped. This claim also assumes that ethical standards that are normally reserved for humans apply equally to animals. The argument necessarily implies that inhumane treatment of rats, whether meant to find a brighter eye shadow or to discover a cure for cancer, is unequivocally wrong and should be stopped. Because arguments usually hinge on such unstated assumptions, bringing them to light often reveals the fundamental principles on which an argument is built.

In "Ban Boxing," the claims are clearly stated but still rely on unstated assumptions for support. For example, the first claim is that we should ban boxing because it sends a bad message. On the surface, this claim seems legitimate, but it relies on the unstated assumption that we should ban all messages that we don't approve of. This assumption is harder to defend. After all, doesn't the First Amendment to the Constitution protect our right to freedom of expression? The many conflicts that circulate around flag burning and erotic art should tell us that censoring any kind of message is much more complicated than it might initially appear. Who gets to decide what messages are good or bad? What criteria will be used? By interrogating the unstated assumption that "bad messages should be banned," we begin to sense the wider ramifications of McAfee's claim.

The claim that boxing should be banned because it causes brain damage operates on a similar assumption. Like hang gliding, drag racing, and rock climbing, boxing is a dangerous sport. But that doesn't necessarily mean we should take away people's right to do it. Can the government or anyone else legislate what consenting adults do with their bodies? Who decides what behavior is acceptable? The assumption that society should ban things that cause bodily harm (the justification behind laws mandating motorcycle helmets or seatbelts) helps us to understand the claim in a more critical light. It also provides us with what is perhaps our strongest argument against the piece. It might be valuable to provide more education to young fighters about the potentially damaging consequences of their sport. However, mandating that they cannot box simply because it's bad for them seems overly restrictive, especially when they might earn tremendous amounts of money in the ring.

Sympathetic and Skeptical Approaches

Another useful strategy for critical reading is to take different approaches to a text so that you can bring to light various aspects of the message. The most simple of these shifts can be accomplished by reading alternately as a sympathetic or skeptical reader.

The Sympathetic Reader

A sympathetic reader tries to learn as much as possible about the strengths of a text. As you read, assume that the author's evidence is reliable and has sources to back it up. Although McAfee's claims about education and urban children generate a number of questions, sympathetic readers will forgo exploring any of these avenues until they have heard the author out. Sympathetic reading simply follows the main claim of the piece and traces its development.

To practice sympathetic reading, you might write a "fair summary." A fair summary should encompass the basic message of a text, pointing to the genre and purpose of a piece while explaining the thesis, the claims, and possibly some of the evidence. In general, a fair summary represents the author's argument as accurately as possible without pointing out its weaknesses and lapses in logic. Here is a sample summary of McAfee's article:

> In the *USA Today* editorial "Ban Boxing," Robert McAfee, a licensed physician, argues that boxing should be banned because it is immoral and because it causes irreparable physical damage. First, he

claims that boxing is immoral because it promotes violence. For McAfee, boxing is unacceptable because "the sole object is to injure the opponent." He argues that a knockout "is a cerebral concussion that knocks the victim senseless" and that there is no protective equipment that can prevent this kind of injury. Because the injuries from boxing are often permanently disabling, McAfee finds them medically indefensible. Finally, he suggests that if we invest money and energy in education rather than boxing, young people will have a better chance of success over a lifetime.

Note how the summary presents a sympathetic reading of the author's message rather than highlighting problems with the article. It follows the original article's movement, outlining McAfee's claims and supporting reasons. Without providing every detail, the summary offers enough information so that someone who has never read the piece could understand the basic elements of McAfee's editorial.

Reading sympathetically, however, still requires that you think critically. A sympathetic reading should go beyond summary by also pointing out the rhetorical elements and strategies that authors use. Note how each passage presents evidence, explains background information, establishes the credibility of the speaker, or reaches out to the audience. This sort of critical reading not only focuses on what authors are saying, but also takes special notice of how they say it.

The Skeptical Reader

Playing the role of a skeptical reader is probably closer to what we are accustomed to when we think about analyzing an essay. A skeptical reader tries to find fault with a message in as many ways as possible, interrogating every element of the message. Does the author present enough evidence to back up every point? Is the support one-sided? What about the author's use of sources—are they reliable? Does the author lack credibility? Look especially for instances in which the author seems biased or unfair to the opposition.

Like the sympathetic reader, the skeptical reader also thinks about the text in terms of its rhetorical devices. Are there moments in the text where the author appeals only to your emotions rather than to your sense of reason? Does the author try to confuse the issue by using technical jargon? Does the author try to deflect attention from complicated or controversial points in an argument by offering easy answers? Think about

McAfee's shift to being concerned about education. Does it help to advance his logical argument, or does it serve some other purpose?

The shift from medicine to education can be seen as a rhetorical device. McAfee is trying to anticipate and respond to an opposing argument: that boxing provides a way out of poverty for urban youth. McAfee responds to this claim by suggesting that education is more effective. However, for years, people have emphasized education as a way of helping inner-city youth. Since the results of many of these efforts have been mixed at best, McAfee's proposal is both unoriginal and oversimplified. A skeptical reader will stop and try to find out what's behind this rhetorical move and begin exploring the validity of the opposing point of view.

Combining Critical Reading Strategies

Although we've separated the sympathetic and skeptical reading strategies here, in most circumstances, readers shift easily between the different modes. Most reading requires a flexible approach—one that implements different strategies depending on the demands of the situation. As you read through any work, you should temper your sympathy with a healthy dose of skepticism and vice versa.

As part of your critical reading process, stop and examine the validity of whichever approach you have been taking. As a sympathetic reader, have you forgiven too much? Did you already agree with the author before reading the piece? Are the arguments less convincing than you first supposed? Does the argument support its claims with enough evidence and adequately address opposing points of view?

As a hostile reader, have you been too harsh? Are the inconsistencies that you identify in your skeptical reading really problems with the essay, or were you nit-picking in order to have something to say? Do the problems go to the heart of the argument, or are they minor points to which the author could probably respond if given the chance?

Remember, too, that the strategies of sympathetic and skeptical reading often take place simultaneously. What is most important in the end is that you strike an appropriate balance between acceptance and critique. Even the best essays have weak points, and poorly written pieces often have something valuable to say. By shifting between approaches, you will be able to bring out the strengths and weaknesses of whatever you read.

Reading Critically to Write Better

As we have seen throughout the past four chapters, rhetorical principles can be applied to both the analysis and the composition of messages. Although critical *reading,* as its name suggests, is inherently geared toward the analytical side of this equation, it is also crucial for at least two major writing activities: incorporating source materials and revision.

Working with Sources

As a rule of thumb, never assume that your audience has read the sources that you are citing. For this reason, the tools of summary and sympathetic reading are extremely important whenever you incorporate outside materials. Even, or perhaps especially, when you are working with sources that you disagree with, you owe it to your readers to present those opposition arguments as evenhandedly as possible. If you choose to refute those arguments later by first providing a fair summary, you will inform your audience about alternative perspectives and establish yourself as a much more knowledgeable, credible speaker. Even your opposition will have to give you credit for dealing with their arguments head-on rather than ignoring them or taking cheap shots at remarks that have been pulled out of context.

When it is time to refute other arguments, the strategies of skeptical reading will be the most useful. First concentrate on the major problems that you have located in the source. Rather than itemizing each minor flaw, try to focus on the places that seem the most problematic: an author's questionable assumptions or purposes, gaps in reasoning, problems with evidence, or perhaps a lack of important source materials. By focusing on the most essential elements of a text, you will be able to clearly and persuasively articulate your opposition to the piece.

Finally, it is important to note that your research cannot make an argument for you. It is your responsibility to articulate exactly how you are using the research to further your argument. Have you situated the quotations within the context of your paper? Have you discussed and drawn conclusions about the citations that you're including? You will also need to incorporate sources into your own writing gracefully. Does the quotation fit grammatically with the surrounding sentences? Does it interrupt the flow of the writing?

Revising Your Own Work

When it comes to editing and revising your own writing, sympathetic and skeptical reading take on new roles. You still want to be a sympathetic reader to the extent that you are able to determine which parts of your argument will be the most believable to an audience. However, you will generally spend more time interrogating your own writing as a skeptical reader to make it stronger.

A skeptical reading is useful at both the global and local levels. You will probably want to begin by examining your argument as a whole. Can you clearly articulate your purpose? Will your audience share your assumptions? Does your thesis state precisely what you want your argument to say? Are there any holes in the logic of your argument? Is each of your claims supported by sufficient evidence? Does your piece have a clear organization? Have any content-level issues been left out or poorly stated? By using your critical reading skills to analyze your argument at this global level, you can identify areas that need fundamental revision.

After you have worked out any major kinks in your essay, you can narrow the focus of your critical reading. Once you're confident that the basic argument is sound and that most of your text will remain in the final piece, you can begin working at the sentence level. Do your tone and style remain consistent throughout? Do each sentence and each word say precisely what you are trying to articulate? Are there any places where you stumble over grammar, syntax, or diction? At this stage, it can be helpful to read the piece aloud, listening for any awkward phrases or confusing sentences. At the final stage of local revision, the purpose of your critical reading should shift toward polishing and tightening the essay. Check for spelling errors and ensure that your format and documentation styles are correct. Examine the details, making sure to cross the *T*s and dot the *I*s.

Critical Reading and the Internet

When we gather information on the Internet, the range of items that we must evaluate expands considerably. In most ways, this is a positive development; the more perspectives we contend with as we're exploring an issue, the better. For instance, if we read traditional news sources such as the *L.A. Times* or *Newsweek*, we see only a handful of outlooks. However, we can generally rely on the accuracy and credibility of print sources. After all, most print publishers try to edit for clarity, check for accuracy, and screen out frivolous information.

On the Net, however, it is often difficult to tell whether the resources have been edited as rigorously, and some sources obviously haven't been edited at all. This means that you will need to evaluate a wide range of materials, many of which will not be worthy of your time. Unfortunately, offensive speech, junk marketing, and idle bickering make up a fair share of Net information. By reading sympathetically, you can occasionally find valuable information in these pieces. In general, however, Internet sources require even more careful skeptical reading than their print-based counterparts do.

You can apply all of the strategies of critical reading discussed in this chapter to the on-line materials that you find; however, you may need to alter your focus somewhat for each of the different Internet media. To illustrate, let's look briefly at a message about legalizing gay and lesbian marriages that appeared in the Usenet newsgroup **alt.politics.homosexuality** immediately after a Hawaiian judge ruled in favor of same-sex marriages.

This newsgroup is particularly interesting because its users are anything but homogeneous. In this forty-eight-message thread of discussion, postings ranged from homophobic threats of violent attacks against gays and lesbians to extended analyses of constitutional history. This was by no means a one-sided discussion—in fact, it was hotly contested, with authors frequently attacking previous posts. Some of these objections were well-reasoned arguments; others were emotional, "gut-level" reactions.

We've chosen to critically read a post that refutes an earlier message. Although it is one of the more civil posts in the thread, it still contains a small degree of what might be considered sniping. In general, though, it turns what is a snide comment about the ruling judge in the Hawaiian court case into a meaningful discussion of both same-sex marriage and legal philosophy.

```
>There was compelling interest and most people
>agree. One judge, drunk with his power, sits up
>there and simply says, I know better then 70% of
>the population.


Shawn,
  Perhaps you should check out the judge's written
opinion. The state's witnesses (under cross-
examination) admitted that gay parents are just as
effective caregivers as straight parents. The judge
ended up quoting them in his opinion.

  I'll agree that popular sentiment is against the
idea of same sex marriages (more along the lines of
"equal legal and economic benefits are fine but
don't let them gays have the word 'marriage'").
However, the courts' role in our political system is
to protect the minority from the tyranny of the
majority. The judge didn't come up with this equal
treatment idea out of thin air ... it was a logical
result of the Hawaiian state constitution guarantee
of equal treatment before the law (a guarantee
imposed on the state by popular vote BTW).

Later,
Steve
```

Steve is responding primarily to Shawn's assertion that the judge, "drunk with his power," overstepped his authority by making a ruling that went against strong popular opinion. In a section of the original post (not quoted in Steve's response), Shawn had argued that gay marriages shouldn't be legal because they are damaging to children. Steve's post responds by directing Shawn back to the judge's opinion, telling him to review the evidence that is cited there. Although this is something of a backhanded comment, Steve effectively uses the judge's opinion as a source, citing the fact that the state's own witnesses (i.e., those people arguing against same-sex marriages) agreed that gay and lesbian parents are "just as effective caregivers as straight parents." This suggests two things: first, that there is significant evidence to refute the notion that same-sex marriages would be damaging to children and, second, that the judge has carefully considered the arguments about child welfare and has made his decision on the basis of the evidence presented in court rather than as a way of satisfying his lust for power.

In his second paragraph, Steve further develops his defense of the judge by considering the purpose of the judiciary as a whole. He writes that "the courts' role in our political system is to protect the minority from the tyranny of the majority," suggesting that federal judges are appointed rather than elected precisely so that they will *not* fall under the direct control of majority opinion. He argues that the judge merely upheld the principles of "equal treatment" set out in Hawaii's state constitution.

A closer look at Steve's second paragraph also reveals a subtle argument about a gray area in public opinion polls. He concedes that a majority of people oppose same-sex marriages but complicates the definition of what it means to "oppose." Steve points out that most people aren't against giving gay and lesbian couples "equal and legal economic benefits," but rather, they are unwilling to grant the formal status of "marriage" to the union of same-sex couples. As critical readers, we can examine the assumptions that might underlie this narrow distinction. If people's objections are not based on economics or legal definitions, they must be grounded in a moral or social definition of marriage that is reserved specifically for heterosexual relationships.

As you can see, Steve's posting raises a number of interesting points that might be important for a paper discussing the issue of same-sex marriages. But it also has some points that must be approached skeptically. Although it alludes to the judge's opinion and to testimony given in favor of gay parents, the post doesn't cite that material or provide any direct quotations to help develop Steve's point. His claim that public opinion favors economic and legal benefits for gay and lesbian marriages would be stronger if it provided some supporting evidence. Similarly, although Steve makes some valuable arguments, they are advanced in several broad claims in the course of two brief paragraphs and never fully articulated.

This is not to say that the post would make a poor resource—on the contrary, we think Steve's arguments are an insightful response to Shawn's earlier post and that they make a valuable contribution to the debate on same-sex marriages. But because the expectations of newsgroup postings are much less formal and rigorous than those of academic essays, Internet researchers need to alter the manner in which they integrate materials like this into their work. Instead of asserting that this post is a source that provides definitive evidence or extended historical analysis, a researcher would need to use Steve's message (and probably several of the other posts in the thread) as a way to gauge the different perspectives on the issue. Instead of focusing exclusively on elements such as evidence and source material, researchers might examine purpose, assumptions, and contributions to a larger conversation as a way to understand the value of such Internet sources.

For Class Discussion

"It's popular, pervasive and surprisingly perverse, according to the first survey of online erotica. And there's no easy way to stamp it out." So began the cover story of *Time* magazine's July 3, 1995, edition. For most readers, *Time* was raising a serious red flag about the state of the Internet. For Internet-savvy readers, however, the article raised another kind of red flag.

The *Time* article relied on a study done by Marty Rimm, an undergraduate researcher at Carnegie Mellon University. Unfortunately, the study was severely flawed, and the editors at *Time* were more interested in sensationalizing the information than verifying it. Here's an excerpt from the article: "There's an awful lot of porn online. In an 18-month study, the team surveyed 917,410 sexually explicit pictures, descriptions, short stories and film clips. On those Usenet newsgroups where digitized images are stored, 83.5 percent of the pictures were pornographic."

It turns out that most of these files were found on adult bulletin board systems (BBSs), not on newsgroups. Because these BBSs are devoted to pornography, finding erotic pictures on them is like finding alcohol in a liquor store or gambling in a casino. Usenet newsgroups are different than adult BBSs, but *Time* did little to clarify this distinction and gave the impression that a large part of newsgroup activity was devoted to pornography.

In the week before the article was published, several concerns about the piece's content were raised to the magazine's editors.

However, *Time* had agreed to a contract of secrecy with Rimm. No one was allowed to see or independently review the article before *Time* published its "exclusive first look" at on-line pornography. The concerns about the accuracy of the article were ignored.

Eventually, Phillip Elmer-Dewitt, the *Time* writer in charge of the story, recognized that he had "screwed up." The pressure to produce an exclusive story and the need to meet a printing deadline contributed to the publication of a major report that was full of misinformation. In the final analysis of the controversy, the on-line world pursued the truth behind the study while *Time* seemed bent on ignoring it.

Hold a discussion about the *Time* article either with your classmates or on the Net. Consider the following prompts:

- List several criteria that you could use to determine whether a source is credible.
- Are some forms of media more credible than others? How would you rate the credibility of television, radio, newspapers, and e-mail?
- Which would you say has more authority: *Time, People, National Geographic,* or *Scientific American?* Why?
- List several of the constraints that print publishers face and discuss how they affect credibility.
- List several of the factors that influence Internet publication and discuss how they affect on-line credibility.

Sources

Phillip Elmer-Dewitt. "On a Screen Near You: Cyberporn." *Time.* 3 July 1995.

<**http://pathfinder.com/@@NlI0SAUAcedaLHyW/time/magazine/domestic/1995/950703/950703.cover.html**> (15 January 1997).

The CyberWire Dispatch. 7 July 1995.

<**http://cyberwerks.com:70/Oh/cyberwire/cwd/cwd.95.07.04.html**> (15 January 1997).

BEYOND BOOKS: RESEARCHING ON-LINE

PART 2

CHAPTER 6

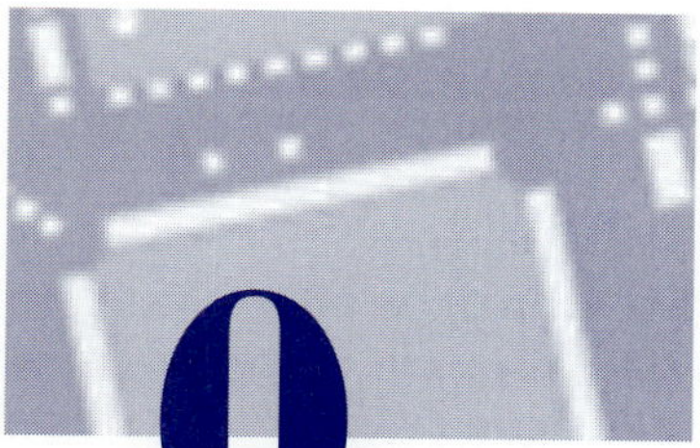

ON-LINE RESEARCH AND THE WRITING PROCESS

The Value of Research

When many students hear the words "research paper," they imagine countless hours spent digging through stacks of library books and journals to find enough facts and quotable passages to support an argument that their teacher "wants to hear."

We'd like to suggest, however, that research, particularly on-line research, is a much more dynamic, engaging, and complicated process. Research is about more than just finding a few juicy pieces of information to help fortify a ready-made position. It's about brainstorming topics, narrowing the scope of a project, communicating with others, exploring alternative perspectives, soliciting feedback, and revising claims. Perhaps most important, it is about finding a topic that strikes your interest, then uncovering its complexities and devising creative ways to incorporate these nuances into your writing.

Throughout the next four chapters, we hope to explore ways in which research can place background materials and sources into conversation with each other, allowing you to see a range of perspectives on the issues that you're writing about. We'll also look at how the conversational resources of the Net can be used in the research process. The focus will be on tapping into the vast repositories of on-line information and adapting research skills for the Net. Our goal in **Part 2**, then, is not so much to provide specific resources for you to work with (after all, these might be obsolete by the time you read this book), but instead to offer useful tips and strategies that can help guide you through the process of on-line research. Since no two people do research in the same way and no two projects demand the same approach, we suggest methods for locating, evaluating, and managing on-line resources that should prove effective in any number of different research situations.

The rest of this chapter will expand on our understanding of the research process, discuss the unique nature of on-line resources, and examine some of the challenges that Internet researchers face. **Chapter 7** explores strategies for finding and handling the many resources that are available on the World Wide Web, focusing particularly on subject sites and keyword searches. We shift to a different forum in **Chapter 8,** examining ways that Internet researchers can utilize the conversational elements of e-mail discussion lists and newsgroups. Finally, **Chapter 9** consolidates many of the strategies suggested throughout the previous three chapters by showing a hypothetical student's research project.

Getting Your Bearings

Imagine that you have to give a lecture to your classmates. If you weren't assigned a topic, you'd probably choose one that you already know something about. Perhaps you have experience canvassing for a political campaign, doing social work, or even hunting deer. If you decide to lecture on one of these familiar activities, you will be speaking as an authority. Whether it's your candidate's stance on affirmative action, the lack of funding for social agencies, or the arguments for and against wildlife population control, you will be in a position to field tough questions about your topic because you have firsthand experience with the issues that you're discussing.

Although this prior knowledge will give your lecture a strong foundation, personal experience rarely carries a complex argument on its own. To understand and articulate the full complexity of a topic, you'll probably need to bolster your position with other kinds of evidence. Scientific studies, surveys, government statistics, and scholarly articles can provide you with specific, accurate information that will enhance your credibility and help you to deliver a more persuasive lecture.

This is why we research: so that we can speak from an informed position. The research process helps us see that our topics do not exist in a vacuum, that other people are interested in and have written about the issues that concern us. Think of these people as participants in an ongoing conversation in which information is debated and ideas are reformulated. Through research, we get a sense of what this conversation is all about. We familiarize ourselves with its key terminology and develop a clearer sense of the major voices in the debate. Perhaps most important, we find out which issues are the most contested, what arguments have already been advanced, and how the various sides have responded. When we begin to write, then, we can enter into the conversation knowing what's already been said and ready to take the discussion in a new direction.

Researching to Refine and Modify Arguments

One of the basic functions of research is to complicate our understanding of an issue. Suppose that for your class lecture, you've decided to write a speech that argues in favor of deer hunting as a way to control the populations of native species of mule deer that are threatening a local ecosystem by overgrazing large sections of land. As you begin researching the project, you anticipate that your main opposition will come from animal rights advocates who argue that killing animals for any reason is unethical. However, as you begin to piece together all of the research you've found, you come across several articles pointing out that the spread of ranch land has eliminated most of the natural mule deer habitat. To support cattle grazing, large areas of land have been fenced off, and mule deer have been forced to overgraze the few remaining acres of wilderness.

You begin to realize that the issue is more complicated than you previously thought. You still might argue that hunting is necessary to control the current deer population; however, you might now suggest that the ranching industry should also be regulated to protect the environment over the long term. You began this process by looking for resources responding to the ethical arguments of the animal rights advocates (arguments you may still need to address in your lecture), but by sifting through your research, you've developed a clearer sense of the root problems, and now your argument can better reflect the depth and complexity of the issue.

We'd like you to consider research and writing as two sides of the same coin: You increase knowledge through research, and then you refine that knowledge through writing. Don't think of writing as only the moment when you finally put pen to paper. The writing process includes brainstorming, articulating a clear focus, refining that focus, and integrating resources into your work—the same activities that drive the research process. Treat research and writing as complementary and inseparable steps along the way to developing your understanding of an issue.

The Nature of Internet Resources

If you've spent any time researching in your school library, you know how difficult it can be to find useful resources. Perhaps the one item that you need is on hold or permanently checked out. Maybe it's on reserve. Or, just as likely, the library doesn't own a copy at all. Even if you do find what you need, as you begin to compose, you may end up spraining your wrist, straining your neck, and spilling your coffee as you try to hold the book with one hand and type in quotations with the other.

Despite these difficulties, however, the library is still one of the most convenient and reliable places to find information. For contrast, consider some of the problems with research on the Net. What if you discovered a terrific resource on the Web and returned the next day to find it gone? What if all the messages in a discussion group turned without warning from urban transit to transgendered playwrights? What if your search for "phosphates and the environment" returns only Web pages selling soap?

Obviously, there are some problems with Internet information. Despite these potential pitfalls, however, the Net is still an excellent place to conduct research. Because of the way information is shared on the Internet, resources can be accessed by thousands of "borrowers" every day. Additionally, since on-line resources are digitized, you don't need to "check out" anything—you can save whatever you find and keep it as long as you like. And when it comes time to write, you can copy and paste research quotations directly into your project.

You'll also find a wide variety of source materials on the Net. Documents can range from the most carefully researched and peer-edited articles about paleontology to the most passionate and articulate arguments for fluoridated Chapstick. Although there's no way to list everything you might find, you are certain to run into text documents, articles, multimedia files, and on-line conversation.

Text Documents and Articles

Many of the resources that are available on the Internet might also be found in a library—journal articles, book reviews, and press releases, for example. But the Internet houses a greater depth and variety of these documents than most libraries do. The Internet abounds with published articles, official government reports, surveys—all kinds of documents, almost all of which can be downloaded by researchers around the world in a matter of minutes.

But don't limit your definition of Internet articles to only files that you find on the official Web sites of journals, governments, or organizations. Internet researchers can also find important information on personal Web sites, postings to newsgroups, and e-mail discussion lists. These resources offer more perspectives, more current information, and a wider variety of documents than are likely to be found in printed sources.

Multimedia at Your Fingertips

If you were researching 1950s television, twentieth-century art, or even "grunge consciousness," your project would greatly benefit from the use of multimedia files. You might find many sound and video resources at your library, but how would you take them with you to study later or "quote" them in a paper? Because computer technology brings text, sound, graphics, and video together on the computer screen, the Internet works wonders for people who are interested in multimedia and research. Like the Library of Congress archives shown in Figure 6.1, there are many multimedia storehouses on the Internet.

Rather than going to an electronic catalog, trudging over to the audio-visual library, waiting for a VCR, and then taking notes, an Internet researcher can locate, retrieve, view, and even modify multimedia infor-

■ **FIGURE 6.1** Multimedia Files Available from the Library of Congress

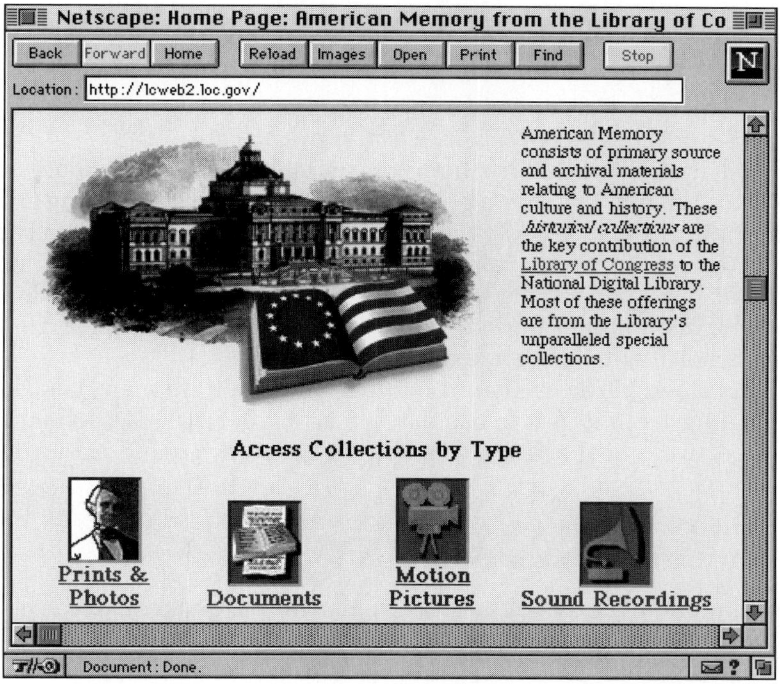

mation all from one spot, the computer terminal. Additionally, the computer lets authors weave these multimedia elements into their own compositions (a process that we discuss in **Chapter 19**).

Conversation as a Resource

One of the most striking features of the Internet is the way it opens up communication, both professional and personal. A substantial amount of the activity that takes place on-line happens in IRCs, MU*s, e-mail discussion lists, newsgroups, and Web message forums. In fact, you're likely to find more discussion on-line than on talk radio, daytime TV, CNN, and *Nightline* combined.

One exciting thing about the Internet is that these conversations themselves can become resources for writers. By tapping into existing discussions, you can get an idea about the breadth of opinions on a topic and a sense of the various controversies that circulate around an issue. Perhaps even more valuable is the fact that you can join these conversations yourself. By posting your own messages to an Internet forum, you can test your ideas, request further information, and solicit feedback about your writing. (We'll see in **Chapter 8** that there are specific strategies for successfully posting research queries.)

The Challenges of Using Internet Resources

"Great!" you're saying to yourself, "with all of this information available on-line, I'll never sweat over a research project again."

Well . . . it's true that the Internet can make researching many topics quicker and easier. And as we point out above, an ever-increasing amount of material can be accessed *only* on-line. But locating and retrieving all of this electronic information are no easy tasks. Unlike the libraries that you may be accustomed to, the Internet has no comprehensive catalog that documents its holdings and no Dewey decimal system to organize information according to subject areas.

This doesn't mean that it's impossible to find materials on the Internet—far from it. But to use the Net as an effective research tool, you should be aware of the unique challenges of accessing and retrieving on-line information.

The Shifting Status of Information

Whereas it often takes books and journals years to go through the process of publication and distribution, Internet resources can be posted with lightning speed. For instance, there are sites that update sports scores or stock prices every one or two minutes—quickly enough that you can "see" the balls and strikes at a baseball game (try looking at **http://www.fastball.com/** or **http://www.sportszone.com/**). Although this kind of minute-by-minute information probably won't be of much value for most research projects, the Internet's up-to-date coverage of many breaking news stories and issues, as at the site shown in Figure 6.2, provides the on-line researcher with more information more quickly than print media can.

The advantages of currency, however, often come at the expense of permanence and stability. Because information can be published so rapidly, the landscape of the Net is in a constant state of flux. Information that is available one day may be gone the next. Newsgroup postings, for instance, have a "shelf life" that is determined in large part by the amount of traffic on the group—when the newsgroup reaches a certain capacity, the oldest messages are replaced by new posts. Similarly, Web pages are often revised and uploaded to replace older versions. Entire sites might change locations as servers are rearranged or files are transferred from one machine to another. On top of all this, thousands of brand-new sites, users, documents, and programs join the Internet each day.

As you can imagine, all of these changes make it difficult to find, and to keep finding, on-line materials. Probably the most valuable strategy for

■ **FIGURE 6.2** On-Line News Items

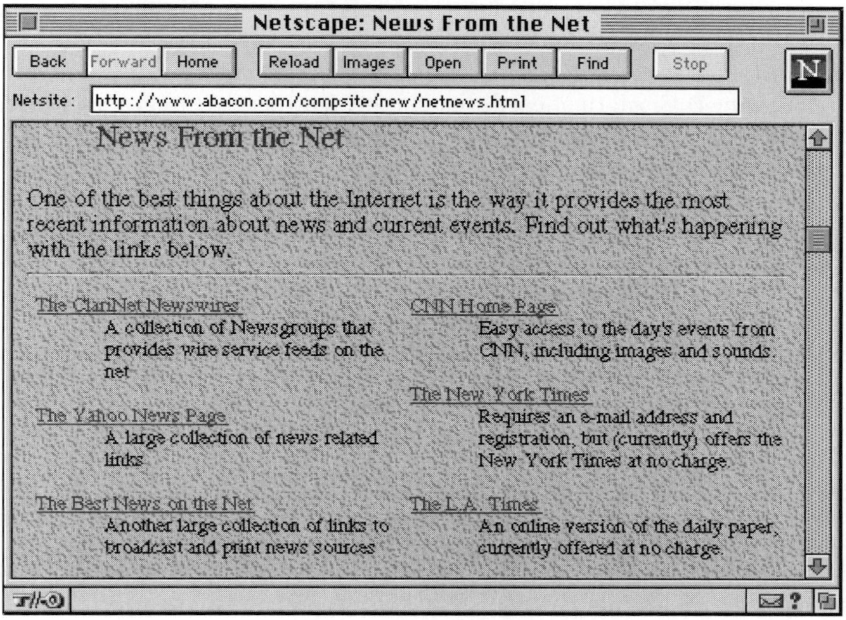

handling this lack of permanence is simply a vigilant process of charting and saving all relevant materials as you discover them (the specifics of this process are discussed further in **Chapter 7**). Remember that it is often much easier to delete unnecessary information from a disk than to relocate the material on the Net. Learn to use the Bookmark or Hotlist features that are available on many Internet software applications, or, better yet, take the time to download files (including any information needed for documentation) so that you'll be sure to have them when it comes time to write. Also, if you're working on a project for an extended length of time, be sure to check the Net regularly for new materials.

Finding a Way through the Maze

Another problem that researchers face is the difficulty of navigating through the maze of documents that make up the Net. Because these documents reside on millions of different servers around the world rather than in a centralized location, there is no comprehensive organizing principle to guide users as they try to locate on-line materials.

This problem has been compounded by the astounding growth of the World Wide Web. Since the Web allows for easy hypertextual linking, a user can jump from place to place almost without realizing it. For instance, a civil rights page set up by students at the University of Michigan could easily link to images of the 1960s Detroit riots stored on a campus server, to an African American archive in Alabama, to an article at a site in Ireland about Malcolm X's influence on Northern Ireland's civil rights movement, and to a video clip of Maya Angelou reading at President Clinton's first inauguration which is stored on a server in Washington, D.C. All of these links can be seamlessly integrated into the design of a single Web page; readers might not even know that they are experiencing a kind of collage made up of documents located all over the world.

Since most pages on the Web incorporate numerous links, it's easy to lose all sense of bearing as you research; even the most experienced Internet users can have trouble retracing their steps through a series of Web pages. You'll probably find that using Internet search engines (discussed further in **Chapter 7**) is often an easier way of locating information than just surfing from page to page. In any case, you should get into the habit of bookmarking and saving relevant information as you go.

Documentation and Intellectual Property

For any kind of research, it is essential that you give appropriate credit to your sources. Most students understand that buying a paper or using the exact words of another author constitutes plagiarism—an offense that instructors and institutions take very seriously. However, the boundaries of intellectual property extend far beyond that. You also commit plagiarism when you paraphrase someone else's ideas or use data from another source without giving the original author credit. As a rule of thumb, any information that you use in a project that is not your own and that is not generally known by the public needs to be documented.

The Internet and electronic information have introduced a whole new set of problems into what was already a pretty tricky area. Web sites, for instance, often have multiple authors collaborating to create the content and design of their pages. Let's take a hypothetical example of a *Houston Gazette* site that was designed by a fictional consulting company called WebDesigns. In this case, giving credit to the author and respecting the rights of intellectual property might be a fairly complicated task. After all, the information and data were presumably provided by the *Houston Gazette,* yet the site was "written" by WebDesigns. Who should receive the credit? What about the discussion forum in which people trade messages and debate current issues? Certainly, information from those discussions might be useful in a research project, but should you cite the authors individually or the entire *Houston Gazette* site?

Most major documentation guides, for instance, the Modern Language Association (MLA) style guide, now include citation styles for electronic resources. However, we recommend the guidelines published in "MLA-Style Guidelines for Citing Internet Sources" (reproduced in **Appendix 2** and also available on the Web at **http://www.csc.eku.edu/honors/beyond-mla/**). It is the most comprehensive and well-thought-out documentation style sheet that we have found. Another well-established Internet style sheet is written by Janice Walker from the University of South Florida available at **http://www.cas.usf.edu/english/walker/mla.html**. Numerous citation formats are rapidly being developed, though, so be sure to check with your instructor before citing your sources. At a minimum, your citations should include the author, the title, the date of your visit, and the Internet address of the materials you use.

In addition to citing your sources, you will need to decide when and to what degree it is appropriate to use the materials that you find on the Internet. For instance, "borrowing" materials from sites on the Internet is extremely easy and relatively common. Images, many of which are scanned and posted to the Net without proper copyright permissions in the first place, are often reproduced on multiple sites across the web. This practice, although very much in line with the ideals of shared information that have been central to the growth of the Internet, often conflicts with copyright law.

Furthermore, the legal criteria for reproducing copyrighted materials have not yet been adequately adapted for the Internet. Should the same standards that are used to regulate television apply to the Internet?

Should we use print standards? Are copyrighted materials that have been severely altered, edited, or sampled (perhaps mixed with other copyrighted and noncopyrighted materials) still the intellectual property of the original creator, or in their changed form do they constitute a wholly new product?

Remember that you are sailing in uncharted waters here. The future of these issues will be decided on the Net and in the courts. If you are working on a scholarly project, you may be able to rely on the "fair use" clause of the U.S. Copyright Act to excerpt certain items. The "fair use" clause is designed to allow the incorporation of small segments of copyrighted material into other projects under certain circumstances (for example, quoting a passage from a book or essay). In practical terms, this means that as long as you have a scholarly purpose and you borrow only the minimum amount that you need to support your argument or analysis, you can probably excerpt certain materials from the Internet. These laws are complicated and nuanced, though, so if you plan to work with copyrighted materials, you should familiarize yourself with the "fair use" clause and the ongoing discussions of intellectual property. (For more information about copyright and fair use, see **Appendix 3** or the *Connections* Web site.)

In the final analysis, we recommend a good faith effort to respect the principles of intellectual property. You'll need to make decisions on a case by case basis. Some sites willingly share their resources; others rigorously protect them. If you find something that you would like to use, take the time to e-mail the owner and ask permission. Often it will be granted, provided that credit is given to the original site—a small price to pay. If you don't have permission, you may be able to use the guidelines of fair use. Remember, though, that the "fair use" clause doesn't apply in every circumstance, so if you are having trouble deciding whether to use an image or other item and how to give appropriate credit, the safest bet is to ask your instructor.

FOR CLASS DISCUSSION

1. Hold a discussion either with your class or on the Net that considers the following issues:

   Intellectual property conjures up a number of different associations. When we think of property, we think of something tangible—houses, diamonds, and cars, for instance. But when we think of something intellectual, we don't necessarily think about ownership. Can someone own an idea?

It turns out that copyright law is not really geared toward ideas (say, a story about an underdog figure who makes it big); instead, it applies to the expression of those ideas (say, the movie *Rocky*). This distinction between ideas and their expression has guided the regulation of print and intellectual property for years. On the Internet, however, things are less clear. Consider a thread of discussion in a newsgroup. The person who posts a message may have written the original expression, but subsequent messages are likely to reproduce it in whole or in part. At what point do ideas become expressions or expressions turn back into ideas?

On the Web, a distinction is taking shape between content and presentation or delivery. For instance, the archives of photographs held by the Library of Congress are a reservoir of content, but a site that reproduces some of them with descriptions and explanations that add value to the original content may then own the rights to the presentation. How does the distinction between content and delivery compare to that between ideas and expression? How is the idea of ownership complicated by this shift?

2. Copyright law was instituted in response to the printing press. The ability to quickly and easily reproduce texts meant that works could be devalued as soon as they hit the street. If anyone could run off 10,000 copies of *Robinson Crusoe,* then the author and publisher stood little chance of making a living. A major function of copyright law, then, is to limit the reproduction of texts.

   But what about the medium of the World Wide Web? Since Web browsers display pages by making a temporary copy of the original document, the operating principle of the Web is based on the reproduction of texts for every browser. In many ways, this is a technological function, but it also indicates a philosophical position. After all, the Web and the Internet were created to freely share and distribute information. The recent entry of traditional publishers and corporate interests into the Web community has begun to change this sense of purpose toward a more commercial understanding of information brokerage. The Web can still be seen as the world's largest copying machine, but whether that capacity to distribute and reproduce information needs to be regulated is now the topic of much debate.

With the members of your class or on the Net, hold your own discussion about distributing information on the Web. Consider these prompts:

- What are some of the primary purposes of the Web and which do you see as the most important?
- What recommendations would you give to policy makers who are considering regulating the Web?
- What about the way files are duplicated on the Web? How does the technological makeup of the Web influence the discussion? Should it?
- How might the interests of those who would meter information in order to make a living be balanced with the interests of those who would distribute it freely?

CHAPTER 7

UNTANGLING THE INTERNET

Researching with the Web

Whether you're looking for the latest political news on Nigeria or the newest Nigerian musical group, you'll probably be able to find the information you need on the Web. That is, you'll be able to find it *if* you know where and how to look for it. Even though the Web search engines that we describe later in this chapter are powerful tools for turning up resources, getting good results requires more than just typing in "Nigeria." To be a successful on-line researcher, you will need to have strategies for using those engines, know what you are looking for, and be able to adjust your approach as you go.

Surf or Sink: Learning to Browse the World Wide Web

When most people talk about finding information on the Internet, they are generally talking about surfing the World Wide Web. There are older technologies such as Gopher and FTP that let you connect to particular

KEY TERMS

Bookmark: (1) As a verb, describes the process of marking the location of a file or site on the Internet. (2) As a noun, describes an individual address that has been saved in a browser's memory for future reference.

Boolean Operator: A connector that lets you combine terms and customize a keyword search. The principal Boolean operators are "and," "or," and "not."

Download: To transfer electronic documents from the Internet to your local machine.

Hit: An item returned from a successful keyword search.

Hotlist: Another term for a Bookmark file.

Hypertext: A composition that links pieces of information (often called "nodes") together into complex, interactive webs.

Internet Directory: An index of Internet sites cataloged by subject.

Keyword Search: An electronic search that finds occurrences of terms specified by a user.

Multimedia: (1) The combination of two or more forms of media in a project. (2) Also used to describe any file in a nontext format, such as sound, graphic, video, or animation files.

Search Engine: (1) A program that searches the Internet for occurrences of terms specified by a user. (2) Sites that provide general Internet search resources, including keyword searches and subject categories.

Targeting: Connecting directly to a particular Internet site.

URL (Uniform Resource Locator): The unique Internet address of a document on the World Wide Web.

Web Browser: Client software that allows users to navigate and interact on the World Wide Web.

World Wide Web (Often abbreviated "WWW" or "the Web"): The Internet medium that combines graphics, sound, video, and other Internet technologies such as Gopher, FTP, newsgroups, and e-mail.

sites and browse through topic-oriented directories (for more information on Gopher and FTP, see the section entitled "Internet Nuts and Bolts: Servers, Clients, and Internet Media" in **Chapter 1**). If you don't have access to the Web or if you have a particular need, Gopher and FTP can still be useful tools for locating and retrieving resources. For instance, the Veronica search engine, a keyword search designed for Gopher servers, is actually quite effective. One of the advantages of technologies like Gopher and FTP is that their information is usually organized in some kind of hierarchical structure, making it easy to locate relevant materials once you find a useful site. But this is a very rigid structure in which readers can't move easily between documents, and Gopher and FTP don't always work in conjunction with other Internet technologies.

The World Wide Web, on the other hand, is nonhierarchical; links can be made between documents anywhere on the Internet. In addition, the Web standardizes document formats, integrating Gopher and FTP along with access to newsgroups and e-mail. The Web also packages these files with a multimedia, hypertextual interface that weaves sound, video, graphics, and text together. The Web interface makes it easy to jump from page to page; a researcher might "travel" from New Orleans to New Zealand with just a click of the mouse. But with so much fluidity, how can you ever find exactly what you need?

Although surfing randomly and following every interesting link may occasionally turn up useful information, more often than not these chaotic browsing sessions lead only to frustration for a researcher who has a specific goal in mind. In addition to knowing how to click, then, serious Internet researchers need to know how to target specific sites. You do this by using the "Open Location" command in your browser and entering the Internet address, or URL, of the site you'd like to go to. Usually, the URLs of interesting Web sites are shared among Internet users by word of mouth, through e-mail, or in newsgroups. By entering the URL into a Web browser, you can move to that site immediately.

The URL (Uniform Resource Locator) tells Web browsers where to find files on the Internet. Each item on the Internet has its own URL. Examining a URL can tell you several things about the nature and location of a possible resource. It indicates whether the item came from a Web, Gopher, or FTP site. It tells you something about who is publishing the page—for example, whether it's an educational institution, a commercial site, a government agency, or a nonprofit organization. And it tells you something about the file structure of the site where the item resides.

In Figure 7.1, the URL tells us that we are looking at the Web page of a commercial soap-selling company. If the URL were gopher://gopher.eco-soap.org, we might expect to find a nonprofit organization's Gopher site.

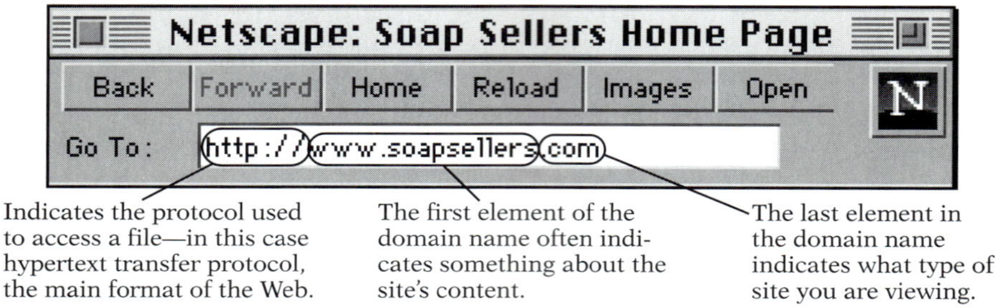

FIGURE 7.1 A Sample URL

Web Browsers

Browsers are programs that let you view documents and navigate on the World Wide Web. A number of Web browsers are available, including Lynx, Mosaic, Internet Explorer, and Netscape Navigator. Lynx is a text-only browser for users with minimal access to the Web. The majority of browsers, however, are graphical, meaning that they can integrate pictures, sounds, text, and video into their presentations. (At the time of this writing, Netscape Navigator is the browser of choice for the majority of users on the Web, so we will tend to use its terminology and conventions throughout this book. But because almost all graphical browsers share the same basic features, our discussion should apply to whatever browser you choose.)

The evolution of graphical browsers has helped to make the Internet a laboratory for exploring multimedia and hypertextual composition. Figure 7.2 not only shows the use of graphics on the Web, but also demonstrates how graphical elements can aid Web navigation. A reader can click either on the textual links or on the images themselves (for instance, clicking on the envelope and microphone icons at the bottom of the image will take a reader to the contact and discussion pages, respectively).

Browsers themselves also supply navigational aids. The "Back" command takes you back to the previous page; the "Forward" command is available only after you've gone back; and the "Home" command takes you to your browser's default opening page. Many browsers also have a "Go" or "History" command that helps you navigate by listing the pages you've visited during your browsing session.

The toolbar at the top of Figure 7.2 demonstrates several other common browser features. If the page you're on seems to be incomplete, you can use the "Reload" command to refresh the screen. The "Image" command loads any graphics on the page. When you're browsing the Web from a slow Internet connection, especially if you're using a modem at home, you might want to "turn your images off." This way, you don't have

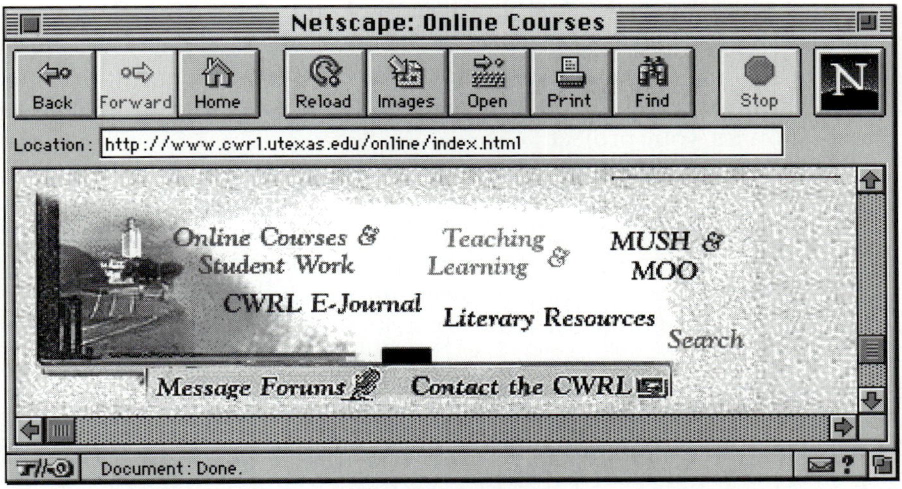

FIGURE 7.2 A Web Page with Graphics

to spend time automatically downloading large graphics files. If you decide that you want to see the images on a particular page, you can load them with the "Image" command.

The "Open Location" command lets you target the URL of a particular site. The "Find" command doesn't search the entire Internet (see the section entitled "Keyword Searches" on page 94); it locates words within the text of an open Web document. The "Stop" command (not surprisingly) stops all loading that your browser is trying to do at the moment. All of the basic functions should be available from the browser's toolbar. You'll also find additional commands listed under the browser's menus. For instance, many Web browsers have a "Mail" command that allows you to e-mail URLs or Web documents to yourself or others as you browse. Additionally, the Bookmark menu stores the addresses of Internet sites. From the menu, you can add sites to the Bookmark list or quickly jump to any of the marked locations.

Internet Directories

If you don't have a specific site in mind, a good place to begin browsing might be one of the many Internet directories that organizes information into subject categories, making it easy to quickly locate sites related to your topic. For instance, if you were writing a paper about the validity of nontraditional medical practices, you could target one of these subject directories and begin researching by looking under the broad category of

"Health." You might next look through the "Alternative Medicine" category, shown in Figure 7.3. Although the link to "Leeches" might look particularly enticing (especially if you've been to the student health center lately), the link to "Homeopathy" will probably lead to more valuable information for your project.

Usually, the process of browsing through subject directories is one of narrowing. You will probably start with the broadest category, then move through progressively smaller headings until you reach the level of specificity that is appropriate to your topic. In many ways, this progression mirrors the research process itself, in which you must continually refine your goals and narrow your focus to arrive at and fully explore a specific subject.

Some of the largest Internet directories are available at the following addresses. Check out these sites, and see the *Connections* Web site for more current information.

- Argus/University of Michigan Clearinghouse
  http://www.clearinghouse.net
- EiNet Galaxy
  http://www.einet.net

FIGURE 7.3 Subject Categories at Yahoo

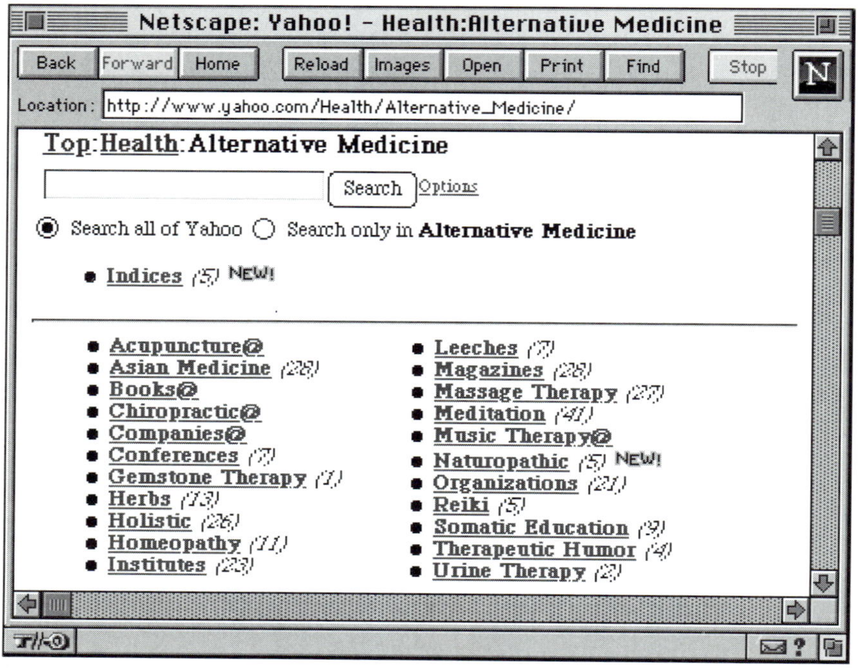

- Excite
  http://www.excite.com
- The Lycos A2Z Directory
  http://www.lycos.com
- Yahoo
  http://www.yahoo.com

There are also directories that specialize in reviewing, ranking, and giving brief descriptions of the sites they catalog. Though we suggest that you read their reviews critically (like anything else), the descriptions of the sites can give you some idea of what's available before you look through all 214 pages devoted to pigmentation in the lips of tropical fish.

- Magellan (related to Excite)
  http://www.mckinley.com
- Point (related to Lycos)
  http://point.lycos.com/categories

EXERCISE 7.1

Browsing Internet Directories

Choose one of the following topics (or come up with one on your own) and browse through the subject categories at the Lycos A2Z directory, Yahoo, and Magellan to find potential resources. Keep track of the materials you locate, and write down the path that you used to reach them (e.g., "Health," "Alternative Medicine," "Homeopathy").

(✓) Free speech on the Internet
(✓) History of jazz
(✓) Paying college athletes
(✓) Commercialism on the Web
(✓) Funding for the arts
(✓) Violence in the media
(✓) Copyright violations and intellectual property
(✓) Human rights abuses

What kinds of information did you find?

What broad categories did you move through?

Did the organization of the categories seem logical? Why or why not?

Which of the three Internet directories proved most useful? Why?

For Class Discussion

Browse through the subject categories at an Internet directory and choose an item that you would probably not find in the library. Hold a discussion with your classmates, using the following questions as prompts:

- Why wouldn't this item appear in a library?
- How would this resource be useful for a traditional paper?
- How would it be useful if you were creating a class Web project?
- How credible is the source? Why?

Keyword Searches

Most Internet researchers rely heavily on the many powerful keyword search engines of the Web. Although the term "search engine" is often used to refer to the large Internet subject sites that we mentioned above, it more specifically describes the "motor" that drives the keyword searches available at these sites. Since none of these sites is comprehensive and different engines allow different kinds of queries, we'll concentrate our discussion on helpful strategies for getting results by choosing the right search terms, trying multiple search engines, and persistently sorting through search results.

Keyword Strategies

If you've been in a library recently, you are probably already familiar with a number of keyword searches. Though each has different commands and abilities, keyword search programs all work from the same basic principle: the search engine finds all occurrences of your keyword in its database. In many ways, then, the database of words and documents is the most important part of a keyword search. For this reason, we suggest searching with the same keywords on a number of different search engines. Because almost all of these databases are huge, though, the way you compose your keyword queries will ultimately determine whether you unearth useful resources.

A few basic strategies for keyword searching will suffice in most instances. First, select your topic as narrowly as possible from the beginning. Broad keyword searches return an unmanageable number of results. Make sure, also, that you choose the most relevant keywords. If you are interested in the history of revolutions, the more specific keyword "revolution" will pull in a more manageable list of resources than the term "history."

Another keyword strategy is to come up with a list of synonyms or related people, places, and events. For instance, if you are interested in the Cuban Revolution, you might also search for "Fidel Castro," "the 26th of July movement," or even "Che Guevara." Note that the items in this list are more specific than the broad category "Cuban Revolution." As you think about related items, try to choose terms that narrow the scope of the search. Generally, a series of focused keywords often produces better results than does a single search using an umbrella term.

Also be sure to watch your spelling; even a simple typo can sabotage the most carefully thought-out keyword search. If your search term has alternative spellings, be sure to try each variant. For example, if you were interested in Cuban drama, you might try searching for "theater," "theatre," or maybe even the Spanish "teatro."

Boolean Strategies

The most valuable strategy for performing complex searches is to become familiar with Boolean operators. The term "Boolean" derives from the name of the nineteenth-century mathematician George Boole, who experimented with combinations of algebraic terms. On the Internet, Boolean (or logical keyword) searches let you combine search terms so that you can refine the way you look for information. For instance, if you were trying to find information about the history of labor unions, you could combine the search terms "history" and "labor." The search would then find documents that contain both terms.

There are three basic ways of using Boolean logic to refine searches.

Using "and" to Narrow a Search The most common strategy is to combine terms in order to limit the scope of a search. When we queried the WebCrawler search engine with the term "history," we got 58,802 hits. The term "labor" returned 7,737 items. When we combined the two terms and entered "labor and history," the search brought back only 1,882 hits. By adding a third term, "strike," we further limited our query and got just 155 hits.

Using "or" to Broaden a Search Sometimes, when working with more obscure research topics, you will need to broaden the scope of your search. By searching for multiple terms that don't appear in combination with each other, you can increase the number of results. Entering the query "picket or protest" would return hits that contained either of the two terms. On WebCrawler, "picket" returned 302 hits, "protest" brought back 2,444, and "picket or protest" returned 2,708 items.

Using "not" to Limit a Search One last approach is to exclude a search term. Usually, this is done by specifying what items *not* to look for. If your search for "labor and history and strikes" was returning reading lists from a history class that had an on-line syllabus, you could exclude them with a query such as "labor and history and strikes not syllabus." This brought down the number of hits in our search results from 155 to 96, none of which contained the word "syllabus."

These three basic strategies should get you well on your way to refining the searches that you do. Remember, however, that each search engine handles this kind of Boolean logic in different ways. Some sites will ask you to use the plus (+) or minus (–) signs to add or exclude terms, others require you to include the "and" connector, while still others let you simply combine keywords. Some search engines will also allow you to use quotation marks around a set of keywords; for example, in the search for "history of revolutions," the quotation marks tell the search engine to look only for that exact phrase. Once you understand the basic processes of limiting, broadening, or excluding items from a search, you should be able to quickly familiarize yourself with the particularities of different sites as you begin to query their search engines.

Search Engines on the Web

Although we generally try to avoid focusing on specific resources, several search engines on the Web are fairly stable and will prove particularly useful for on-line researchers. Since the possibilities for searching on the Net will surely have changed by the time you get this book, you should investigate the following sites but also get more current information at the *Connections* Web site.

- AltaVista
  http://www.altavista.digital.com
  The AltaVista engine is one of the quickest and most comprehensive on the Web. AltaVista can search not only for the titles of files, but also through the text of documents, both on the Web and on Usenet newsgroups.
- Excite
  http://www.excite.com
  Excite allows users to search both the Web and Usenet newsgroups. Additionally, the search returns offer a "more like this" feature that calculates probability ratings to help you find related pages. (Magellan's rating system is searched by Excite.)

- HotBot
  http://www.hotbot.com
  HotBot allows searches of Usenet archives and the Web. One nice feature is that HotBot can track sites which have linked to a particular URL—handy when you want to find out who has links to your site.
- Infoseek
  http://www.infoseek.com
  Infoseek offers you keyword searches, browsable subject categories, and a selection of search options that allow you to focus on the Web, Gopher, Usenet newsgroups, and e-mail addresses, to name a few.
- Lycos
  http://www.lycos.com
  Lycos is another search engine that combines keyword query capabilities with browsable subject categories. Lycos also allows you to search through selected "best of the Web" sites. (Point's rating system is searched by Lycos.)
- WebCrawler
  http://www.webcrawler.com
  WebCrawler provides subject categories for you to browse and offers a keyword search function that can scan through the entire text of documents on the Net.
- Yahoo
  http://www.yahoo.com
  In addition to providing keyword searches, Yahoo has compiled an excellent collection of subject categories. You can browse through well-organized directories such as Education, Science, or Society and Culture.

EXERCISE 7.2

Narrowing a Keyword Search

Select one of the following research topics:

(✓) Free speech on the Internet
(✓) History of jazz
(✓) Paying college athletes
(✓) Commercialism on the Web
(✓) Funding for the arts
(✓) Violence in the media
(✓) Copyright violations and intellectual property
(✓) Human rights abuses

- Go to one of the keyword search engines discussed above and search for your topic. At each stage of the process, write down the number of returns generated by the search.
- Develop a list of related terms or synonyms that will help you narrow the focus of your search. Choose several of the items from your list, and run a keyword search for each term. Write down the number of returns for these searches.
- Next refine your search using Boolean operators. At this stage, try to narrow your search so that you get a manageable set of returns.
- Finally, go to two additional search engines and repeat your refined searches.

Interpreting the Results

When you get back a list of hits from a search engine, look over the returns and try to assess the success of your query. On the simplest level, check the number of hits returned. If you end up with 8,000 possible resources for your project, you obviously should try to refine your search further. If you get just two hits from a search, be sure to check out the items—they will most likely be relevant—but also consider expanding your search to bring back more returns.

Even when you have come up with a query that brings back a manageable set of hits, you will have to put some thought into which items to ignore and which to investigate. The sample in Figure 7.4 demonstrates results from the WebCrawler search for "labor and history."

Searches often turn up numerous items, but the relevance of information can vary. You'll need to develop an eye for interpreting the results. Even the titles shown in Figure 7.4 tell us something about the resources. For instance, the first item seems to be a catalog or index of videos. The third and fourth items might lead to current information and some kind of news. The fifth hit could contain a list of scholarly publications, the eighth hit appears to be a class Web site or on-line syllabus, and the last item seems to be an on-line article.

Figure 7.5 shows how search results can be listed with descriptions and other summary information to guide Web researchers as they choose which hits to follow. Most search engines will allow you to specify the amount of textual description that is provided with each return. In this sample, the second item is of particular interest. The link is to the **H-LABOR: H-Net Labor History** discussion list. As search engines comb through Net archives, they often turn up postings to newsgroups or, in this case, information about a discussion list. If you're willing to invest some energy, you could join the list and not only find more resources, but also

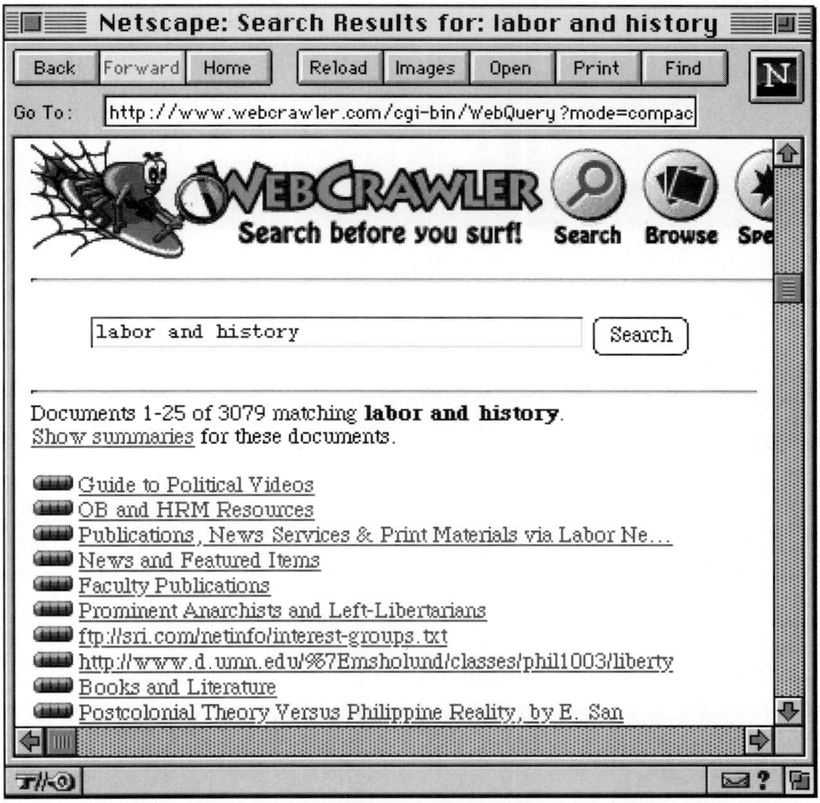

■ **FIGURE 7.4** Search Results from WebCrawler

post your own ideas in hope of gathering feedback. (For more information about researching with conversational resources, see **Chapter 8.**)

Some search engines calculate and append a probability rating to the returns (sometimes called a "score"). Even search engines that don't show a probability rating often use one to determine results. In general, items that are most likely to contain relevant information will appear first in the list of returns. These ratings, however, are often unreliable. Some ratings are calculated by the number of times a keyword appears in the document, while others seem to be determined by how fast the hamster spins the little wheel inside your computer. Don't depend on the computer's judgment to tell you which materials are the most pertinent to your work. Use your critical reading skills to evaluate each source.

Finally, be persistent. Remember that each search engine catalogs different items. If you don't have much luck with one engine, try another. Search with different keywords and combinations at each site. If one item

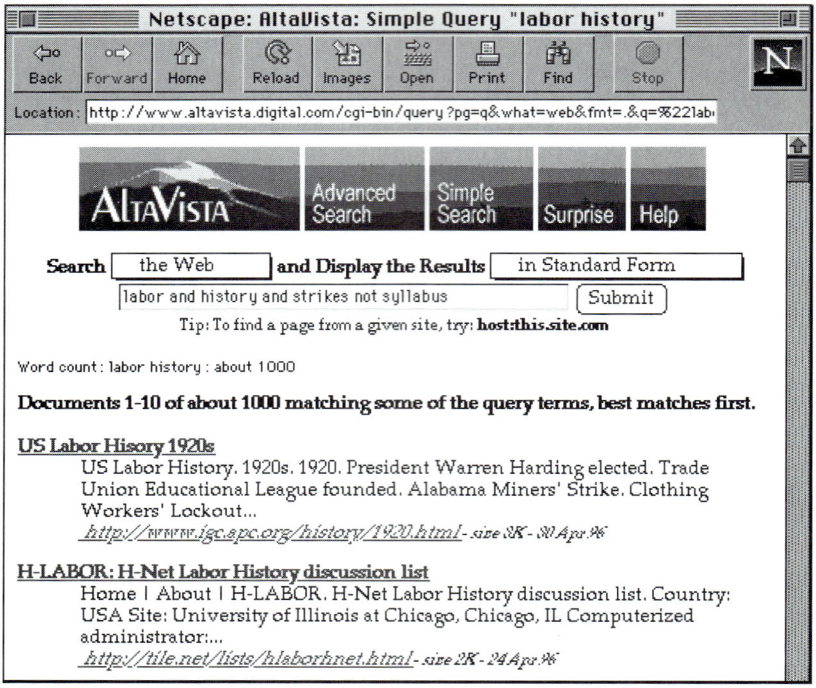

■ **FIGURE 7.5** Search Results from AltaVista

in the list of search results is a dead end, go back and try another. Browse to generate ideas and discover new search terms, then try searching again with a fresh query. If you stay flexible and keep trying, you should be able to find more than enough material for your research projects.

Keeping Track of It All

As we discussed in **Chapter 6,** the Net is always changing—new documents are constantly being added and old ones are being revised or replaced. This ebb and flow is what makes browsing the Net so interesting, but it is also the cause of some superhighway-sized headaches for Internet researchers. Using effective browsing and searching strategies can greatly improve your chances of locating information. But that's only half the battle (well, maybe two-thirds). The point of this section is to suggest several methods for keeping track of the materials that you have found. In the long run, a little effort managing and organizing your resources *while* you are collecting information will likely save you time, energy, and quite a few aspirin.

Bookmarks and Hotlists

Perhaps the simplest way to keep track of Internet resources, particularly while you are still in the process of gathering information, is to use your Web browser's Bookmark or Hotlist feature (called "favorites" in Internet Explorer). Bookmarks are like URL entries in an Internet address book. Your browser stores the URLs of useful Web pages as Bookmarks, making it easy to return to a spot without having to worry about forgetting or misspelling the address as you scribble it down. (Remember that URLs are often case sensitive, so changing even one letter from lowercase to uppercase may prompt a "File Not Found" error message from your browser.) When you find a useful site, simply add it to your list of Bookmarks so that you can return to that URL at any time.

Most browsers allow you to save Bookmark files to a diskette so that you can transport them from computer to computer. If you are working in a lab or classroom, be sure to get comfortable with keeping your Bookmarks on a diskette so you don't lose track of important information. Bookmark and Hotlist files can also be saved as HTML documents for easy incorporation into a Web site. (For more information about Web building, see **Part 4.**) Figure 7.6 shows a sample Bookmark list.

These and other Bookmark features are particularly effective for managing information gathered in the exploratory stages of your research process. As you browse the Net looking for materials or as you sift through eighty-plus hits generated from a keyword search, you probably won't have time to meticulously pore over each document. At this stage of the research process, you are generally skimming or reading quickly, looking

■ **FIGURE 7.6** Sample Bookmark File

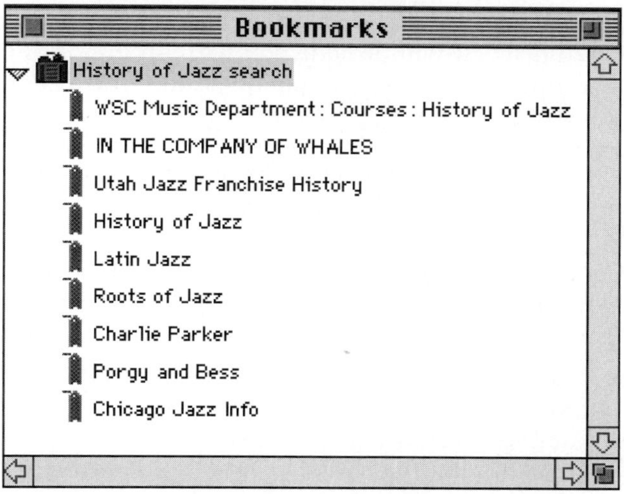

for relevant sites and weeding out any extraneous information. Bookmark the sites that seem most useful so that you can return later and examine them in more detail.

Saving Materials

Although Bookmarks are quick and convenient, they have a few obvious shortcomings when it comes to keeping track of shifting information. For example, there is very little value in having the URL of a Web page that has been moved to a different server or deleted from the Net. Similarly, because Web sites are revised so often, a Bookmark may point you to the identical location but to a page that contains very different information than the one that you initially marked.

To ensure that you will be able to relocate essential materials, we recommend saving any important information that you come across. Web browsers can now download and save almost every kind of file you will encounter on the Net—text, graphics, sound, video, software, and so on. For most files, this process is as simple as a "Save" or "Save As" command. For graphics, simply clicking on the image with your mouse may activate the "Save" command. Methods for saving images, sounds, and video will vary, however, so familiarize yourself with your particular browser's options.

Of course, you don't want to automatically save every item that you come across. You'll need to weigh the costs of storage space against the value of ensuring that you have the materials on hand. For instance, you should be careful about downloading sound or video clips, most of which are quite large, unless you are relatively certain that you will need them later. With smaller text documents, however, you might take a "better safe than sorry" approach and save more files than you will probably end up using. Although downloading any file will take up storage space on your diskette or hard drive, it will provide you with an important measure of security that you won't have if you only bookmark the location.

EXERCISE 7.3

Bookmarking and Saving Resources

Conduct a search for a topic on an Internet search engine (you can reproduce the same searches you performed in Exercises 7.1 or 7.2).

- Browse quickly through the results, bookmarking items that seem particularly relevant.
- After you've marked several sites, use the bookmark management feature of your browser to make brief annotations

of what's available at each and how the material might be useful for your topic.

- Choose at least one document that you've found and save the file to your diskette.
- Finally, export or save the entire Bookmark file to a diskette.

Citation and Documentation

Despite what you may have been told by your relentlessly cruel sixth-grade English teacher, documenting sources is not simply an exercise in discipline, designed to make sure you get all of the periods and commas in exactly the right spots. The purpose of documentation is twofold: to give credit to other authors who have provided ideas or data for your project and to help researchers who are interested in the same issues find the information that you refer to in your work.

With print media, this system is well-established and standardized, giving researchers all the information they need to find a source. Even if a library doesn't have a copy of a particular book or article, it can often use an interlibrary loan system to borrow one from another institution. Once you do find the source, the printed page helps to ensure that everyone who locates the same source will be seeing the identical information. Because books can't be updated once they have been printed, page 103 will be identical in every copy of the first edition of *Connections*.

But on the ever-shifting Net, the principles of citation have become somewhat less valuable. For instance, a researcher following a one-year-old citation to a Web site about human rights violations is likely to find a document containing substantially different information than the one that was cited a year earlier. Similarly, if a document is moved to a different server or deleted, even an accurately cited URL can become meaningless.

As you browse the Web for your research projects, collect any citation information you may need. First, it is always important to include the URL of materials you find on the Web because going back to the document's original address probably gives researchers the best possible chance of relocating the information. Along with the address, though, it is important to document the date of the visit so that researchers will be able to tell whether the page has been altered since the piece was cited (generally, Web pages have a "last modified" date to mark any recent revisions). It may also be valuable to find the e-mail address of a contact person so that if information disappears, a researcher has a way to contact the author or administrator of the page directly.

Some of these strategies are being incorporated into citation guides like the one reproduced in **Appendix 2,** but at least for now, the only way to be absolutely sure that future researchers have access to your sources is to reproduce the identical materials as part of your project. This is easier, of course, if you are writing a Web page or some other form of hypertext, but it wouldn't be too difficult, for instance, to print out several short, on-line documents and attach them to the end of your paper as a reference. Remember, however, that as with any kind of on-line borrowing, there are potential copyright issues to be considered. It never hurts to ask permission, and you should always consult with your instructor about the best way to handle the sources for your particular project.

TIPS AND TACTICS

- If you are having trouble choosing a topic, try browsing through some of the subject categories at an Internet directory.
- Successful research requires that you narrow your focus so that you won't be overwhelmed by a flood of information.
- Be persistent. Use several different search engines and Internet directories to get the fullest coverage of your topic.
- Be as precise as possible in your keyword searches so that you can turn up the best sources available. Use synonyms or related terms to further refine your search. Also try the Boolean operators "and," "or," and "not" to refine your keyword searches.
- Use your browser's Bookmark or Hotlist feature to keep track of on-line research materials. Save any files that might be important for your work, and make sure to record any citation information as you browse so that you can document your sources correctly. Things change quickly on the Net, so your research results may not be there the next time you need them.

FOR CLASS DISCUSSION

Begin by exploring the documentation issues presented at the Beyond the *MLA Handbook* site (**http://www.csc.eku.edu/honors/beyond-mla/**).

Next, as a group, try to come up with your own Internet citation style guide. Decide what information is the most important and how best to organize it into a bibliographical entry. Go through several different kinds of pages (e.g., those without an author or title) and perhaps several different types of on-line media (e.g., newsgroup postings, e-mail messages, MU* sessions) to come up with styles that accurately cite a wide range of possible Internet resources. Keep the functions of a citation guide in mind as you make your decisions. For instance, are the original date and place of publication relevant pieces of information for on-line sources? Perhaps, but you'll need to make an argument for why they should or should not be included in your style guide.

Once you decide on a set of guidelines, have someone write them up (possibly as a Web page) and then use these models as your standard documentation format for any on-line research projects. As you work with the style guide throughout the semester, think about ways to amend it so that it is an even more effective means of accurately documenting Internet resources.

When you have finished, post your thoughts to the on-line citation/documentation discussion forum at the *Connections* Web site.

CHAPTER 8

CASTING A WIDE NET

Researching with Discussion Lists and Newsgroups

E-mail discussion lists and newsgroups are electronic forums in which users exchange messages. There are literally tens of thousands of these discussion lists and newsgroups on the Net—each designed to address a specific topic ranging from the most flippant (and rather bizarre) chat on the newsgroup **alt.alien.vampires.flonk.flonk.flonk** to the most serious ethical debate on the **HPSST-L—History and Philosophy of Science and Science Teaching** e-mail list. The people who subscribe to e-mail discussion lists or who frequent newsgroups form what might be described as communities of knowledge, making these conversational forums important sources for on-line research. □

Postings as Resources

As we've said, e-mail discussion lists and newsgroups are geared toward specific topics, so if your research overlaps with one of them, you will likely find a range of useful information. Figure 8.1 provides a sense of the

KEY TERMS

E-mail (Electronic Mail): A basic form of Internet communication that allows users to send and receive messages.

E-mail Discussion List: Also known as a "list" or "Listserv." A collection of e-mail addresses managed by a program that allows users to send e-mail to a group of "subscribed" members.

Flame: A personal attack, usually sent via e-mail or on a newsgroup, that offers little or no constructive critique.

Frequently Asked Questions (FAQ): An on-line archive that collects and responds to the most commonly asked questions about a site or topic. Looking through a group's FAQ file is an easy way to get a sense of the kind of materials the group offers and discusses.

Moderated Group: A newsgroup or e-mail discussion list that uses a moderator to screen messages before they are posted.

Moderator: The individual who screens messages before they are posted to a moderated e-mail discussion list or newsgroup.

Newsfeed: An Internet posting or forum that originates from traditional news organizations such as the Associated Press or Reuters.

Newsgroup: A topic-centered forum devoted to discussion and the exchange of articles, news, and other media.

Newshost (also called a "news server"): An Internet-connected server that collects, stores, and distributes newsgroup messages.

Newsreader: Client software that allows users to read and post to newsgroups.

Post (also called a "posting"): (1) As a verb, describes the act of sending a message to a list, newsgroup, or other on-line forum. (2) As a noun, describes a message that has been sent to an on-line forum.

Query: A research question posted to the Internet.

Thread: An initial posting to an e-mail discussion list, newsgroup, or Web forum followed by a series of replies that build on each other to form a conversation.

Usenet: An extensive collection of public-access newsgroups. Most universities and colleges are connected to Usenet rather than to private or commercial bulletin boards.

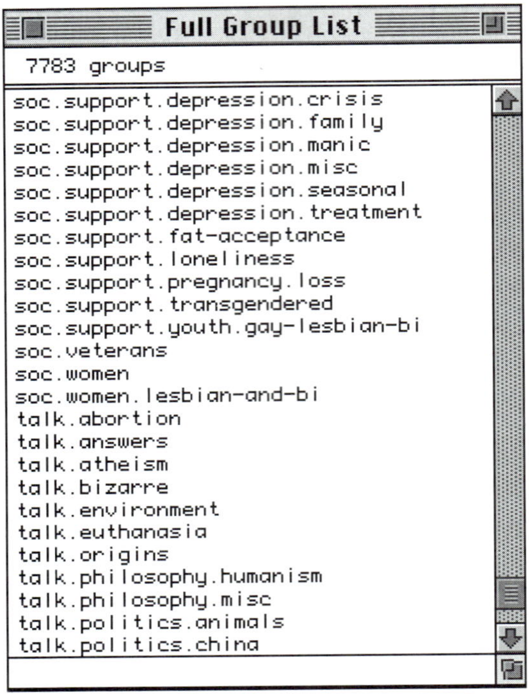

■ **FIGURE 8.1** A Sample List of Newsgroups

breadth of topics available on Usenet newsgroups. Some groups post traditional documents and articles. Others distribute multimedia. The majority of groups, however, are devoted primarily to conversation. Many of the messages that you encounter in these forums are better compared to snippets of a discussion than to articles in a magazine or journal.

Listing the Groups and Grouping the Lists

Because of the many similarities between e-mail lists and newsgroups, throughout this chapter we often talk about them as if they were interchangeable. Although there is a considerable amount of overlap between the two, there are some important distinctions to keep in mind.

First of all, there's a functional difference between e-mail lists and newsgroups. E-mail lists operate on a subscription basis; users sign on to the list much as they would subscribe to a magazine. Any message sent to the list's address is immediately distributed via e-mail to every subscriber.

If list members want to reply, they can decide whether to respond to the entire group or only to the author of a particular message. Newsgroups, on the other hand, collect messages in a central location. Rather than receiving discussion list messages via e-mail, newsgroup users log-on to a particular group, read only the messages that they are most interested in, and choose to reply either to the group or to an individual. (Note that your college or university probably subscribes to Usenet newsgroups, an extensive collection of topic-based discussion groups that is made widely available to the Internet public.)

Each forum has advantages and disadvantages. Lists, for example, offer the convenience of receiving important information every day just by checking your e-mail. However, lists may require you to invest a substantial amount of time and energy; you may have to sort through a daily flood of e-mail messages or weather long stretches when no messages are posted. You may also have to wait several days or even weeks before you receive enough messages to evaluate whether the list will be useful for your research. If you think that you have found a list that will be particularly valuable, we recommend that you subscribe to it early in the semester so that you have enough time to acquaint yourself with its dynamics.

An advantage of using newsgroups rather than e-mail lists is that previous messages are collected and stored on the newsgroup itself, making it easy for a new reader to evaluate the group without waiting for e-mail messages to accumulate. Because you can quickly get a feel for the kinds of materials that are generally posted on any given group, you can make informed decisions right away about whether a newsgroup is appropriate for your research. Additionally, you'll be able to explore several different groups, culling information from each, without having to commit to an e-mail list subscription. When you consider the tight schedules of most student projects, newsgroups generally offer an easier entry into researching with the conversational resources of the Net.

E-mail lists and newsgroups are similar, however, in that they generally encourage threads of discussion from a large group of people who are interested in a very particular subject. They are also similar in that they offer a range of resources that fall into three basic divisions.

News and Information Some e-mail lists or newsgroups distribute only news and announcements about a topic. In some cases, such as the Clarinet or "**clari**" newsgroups, these resources consist of newsfeeds from traditional news organizations such as the Associated Press and Reuters. Since many of these groups don't allow users to post replies, they are an important exception to the rule about fostering discussion. However, because they collect substantially more published articles than any single paper or news magazine, they are a remarkable resource for current information.

Scholarly Articles and Expert Discussion Some e-mail lists or newsgroups discuss topics in a serious, academic manner. Examples include the newsgroup **misc.activism.progressive** and the **H-LABOR** discussion list mentioned in **Chapter 7.** Often, these groups provide traditional resources in the form of substantial, well-researched articles and topical bibliographies. Additionally, they can offer the researcher a chance to "listen in" on conversations between experts who post informed opinions and analyses to the group.

Social Conversation The majority of e-mail lists or newsgroups focus on less serious topics and have a more social, "chat" function. While groups like **alt.culture.sardines** or **alt.penguin-fetish.recovery** will not often be of much value for researchers, this type of social group should not be totally discounted as a source of information. Even a group such as **alt.flame.newt-gingrich.dork.dork.dork** might contain a few valuable critiques of the Republican agenda, and a group such as **alt.fan.howard-stern** could be useful for a project analyzing 1990s media values.

Remember, though, that none of these categories has boundaries that are fixed in stone; in fact, the distinctions between them are often quite blurry. For example, the **IRL-News** list is devoted primarily to news and announcements about Ireland and Northern Ireland, but it regularly posts scholarly articles and interviews, and its postings often receive a fair amount of discussion. Similarly, the newsgroup **alt.fan.camille-paglia,** which carries discussions about the controversial feminist author, is something of a hybrid between the usually social "fan" groups and the more academic groups with which you would associate a figure like Paglia.

Don't just assume, however, that a "scholarly" group will be more valuable than a "social" group. Remember that full professors can as easily post a flame as recovering penguin addicts. Evaluate each post individually, judging the credibility of the author, the validity of the information, and the purpose of the message. As you evaluate the materials you find on lists and newsgroups, use these three divisions—news, scholarly discussion, and social conversation—as general guides rather than fixed categories.

Choosing a List or Group

Generally speaking, newsgroups are easier to find and use than e-mail lists. Since all of the groups are collected on a central computer at your institution (called a newshost), it is fairly simple, though often time-consuming, to look through the many thousands of groups in hopes of finding a few that will be helpful for your project. Most newsreaders (software used to access newsgroups) have a search function for locating appropriate groups, but this can be made difficult if groups use abbreviations (for example, a search for the word "environment" would not turn up the group **sci.enviro.gov**). As search functions improve, both within newsreaders and on the Web, you may have better luck uncovering relevant groups. Try a keyword search at AltaVista (using the Usenet option) or at DejaNews (**http://www.dejanews.com**) to locate groups that might be relevant to your topic. However, since each institution can subscribe to different newsgroups, searches done on the Web may turn up items that your local news server does not provide. In the end, you'll probably have to spend some time scrolling through the list of groups that are available at your school.

Finding e-mail lists is even more difficult, since there's no centralized index to browse through. However, there are several sites on the Web that have begun to catalog large numbers of lists. For instance, Tile.Net (**http://tile.net**) has a section devoted to the various e-mail discussion lists that use Listserv software (it doesn't include lists that are run using Listproc or Majordomo software). Another, more comprehensive site is shown in Figure 8.2. The LISZT Directory (**http://liszt.com**) collects information about Listserv, Listproc, and Majordomo discussion lists and

■ **FIGURE 8.2** A Catalog of Listservs at **http://liszt.com**

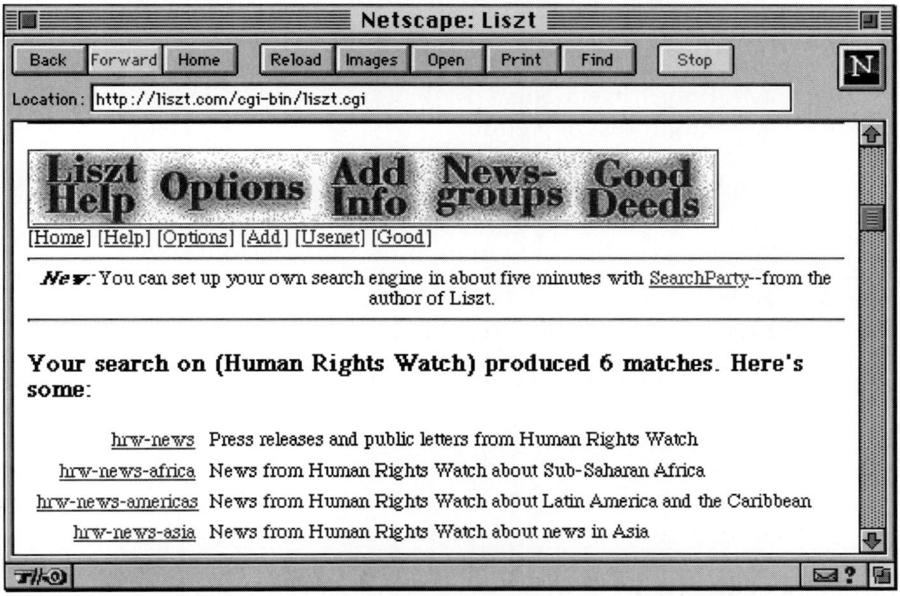

provides a brief description of each list's topic, the number of members, and information about how to subscribe. (This site, incidentally, also has a searchable list of Usenet newsgroups, making it a good place to begin looking for both lists and newsgroups.) Still, despite the thousands of lists that they catalog, these sites contain only a portion of the total number of e-mail lists that are available to Internet users.

Once you've located several promising newsgroups or lists, you'll need to decide how valuable they will be for your research. A good preliminary step is to figure out which of the three general categories seems to best describe your newsgroup or list. It will be important to determine what kinds of materials are being posted, who the intended audience of the postings seems to be, and what kind of tone is being used by the authors of the posts. (We offer more strategies for assessing the makeup of a group in **Chapter 13.**)

EXERCISE 8.1

Analyzing a Newsgroup

Working alone or in small groups, use LISZT, DejaNews, or the search functions of your newsreader to find three newsgroups that are appropriate for research in one of these subjects or another of your choice:

- (✓) Gun control
- (✓) Affirmative action
- (✓) Prayer in schools
- (✓) Rainforest depletion
- (✓) Population control
- (✓) "The MTV generation"
- (✓) World hunger
- (✓) Gender discrimination in the workplace

Remember that the strategies for Web keyword searches discussed in **Chapter 7** also apply to this kind of search.

- After you've located several groups, browse through them and categorize each group by answering the following questions:
- Is it a discussion group or does it contain mainly articles and news stories?
- What is the tone? Is it playful or serious?
- Who do you think most of the group's regular users are?
- How could you use the resources of the group in a research project?

EXERCISE 8.2

Critically Reading Newsgroup Messages

In small groups, choose one of the topics listed in Exercise 8.1 or another issue that has been in the news lately. Log onto your local news server and locate several newsgroups that might contain postings about your issue. If possible, try to find groups that would fit into each of the three broad categories so that you can get a range of news articles, scholarly debate, and social conversation. Browse through the different groups to get a feel for their materials and select three to five articles to work with. The goal here should be to select articles that offer different points of view on the issue and represent different types of messages (e.g., newsfeeds, long articles, informed discussion, activist campaigns, official statements, casual conversation).

Once you have collected this range of newsgroup postings, begin critically evaluating each message. Choose a scribe to take notes as the group discusses each of the following prompts. Once you have finished, report your findings to the full class.

- What is the purpose of each message? How does the author want the audience to react?
- Who is the intended audience of each message?
- Are there any discrepancies or contradictions between postings in terms of the information they provide? If so, what do those discrepancies tell us about each message?
- Which postings seem to have the most credibility? The least credibility? Why?
- If you were writing a paper on this topic, how might you be able to use each of the messages as a resource?

Utilizing Conversation

We all have experience using evidence from news stories or scholarly articles to support our arguments. Excerpting facts and figures, paraphrasing arguments, and quoting passages are all familiar writing skills. Integrating the conversational postings that are so readily available on e-mail lists and newsgroups into your formal writing, however, poses some additional challenges. After all, the language is often unpolished, making it difficult to quote; statements sometimes offer little supporting evidence; data may be hard to verify; and the arguments are often less coherent than those found in traditional articles and essays.

"So what's the point?" you might ask. "Why research with conversation at all?" Because lists and newsgroups offer you something beyond the static resources found in an article. Exploring these forums allows you to tap into the collective knowledge of a diverse group of people who are invested in a particular issue. You'll see the give and take that occurs when informed individuals join in conversations about complicated topics. You can get a sense of the many possible sides of any argument, and you'll also see how positions evolve as they are challenged, seconded, refuted, or modified by the other members of the group. Even a quick glance at a high-traffic newsgroup shows the number of different responses that a controversial posting may prompt. Figure 8.3, for example, shows an eleven-message "thread" of discussion building from the posting "Clinton Just Says No to Marijuana."

One helpful technique is to study the thread as a whole rather than focusing on individual messages. By considering the responses generated by each post, you will often get a sense of the many complicated arguments and nuances that surround an issue. Well-developed threads of discussion are often rich and diverse. The complex interaction in a thread can demonstrate the ways in which writers make concessions, refute arguments, and choose an appropriate voice as they debate the many facets of an issue. (See **Chapter 13** for more information about analyzing discussion threads.)

Conversational resources also highlight the ways in which you can use personal experience and anecdotes as evidence, shifting your focus

FIGURE 8.3 Several Discussion Threads on **alt.activism**

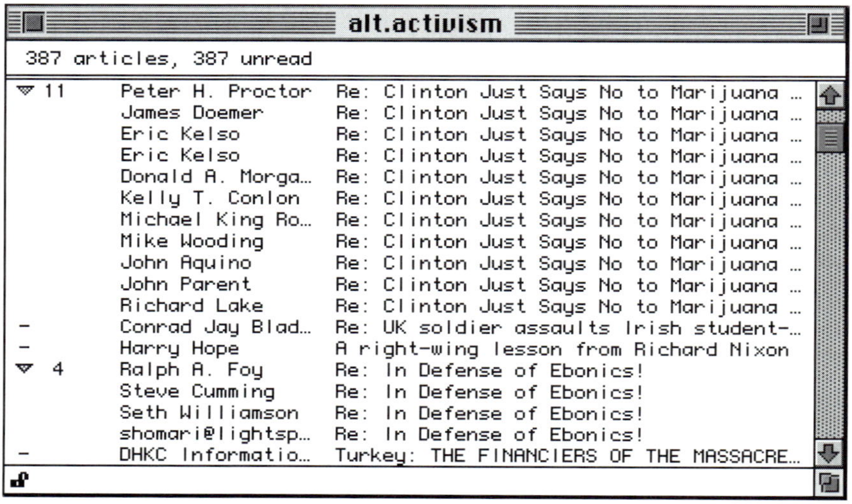

away from more "factual" statistical information or formal arguments. This type of personal experience will almost inevitably provide your writing with fresh perspectives and insights. Also, stories or anecdotes can be particularly effective as reminders that issues are more than just fuel for seminar debates. Policy decisions about capital punishment, welfare reform, or even standards for college admissions take on a new significance when we hear from people directly affected by the issues.

Conversations can be as legitimate as any other resources, but to effectively incorporate them into your writing, you will need to do some extra work. You'll have to decide whether to quote sloppy and awkward language or to rephrase a sentiment in your own words. Often, insightful posts make sense only within the context of earlier messages. You'll need to work not only with the particular argument, but also with its place in the larger thread. You might place two or more posts into conversation with one other, citing from each and then drawing comparisons and conclusions. As with any writing that incorporates research, you'll need to practice the skills of introducing, quoting, paraphrasing, and contextualizing information.

Don't forget your basic Internet research skills either. As you interact on newsgroups and discussion lists, be sure to save any messages that pertain directly to your topic. Particularly on newsgroups, since older postings are continually replaced by newer ones, you should save messages as soon as you find them. As you are saving files, be sure to get any citation information that you may need later—often the author, date, and subject of the message, as well as the list or group, are included at the top of the message. For newsgroup and discussion list citation guidelines, see **Appendix 2.**

EXERCISE 8.3

Analyzing a Thread in a Newsgroup

Choose a complicated thread in a newsgroup. Then, working alone or in small groups, follow these steps:

- Define the broad topic or issue that describes the subject of this thread.
- Begin by writing a one- or two-sentence summary of each post.
- Next, sort through your summaries and try to pick out the key arguments in the thread. Although some arguments will be repeated in more than one posting, try to chart the principal positions being outlined and the major claims being

made without reducing the thread to a simple pro and con debate.

- Finally, outline a hypothetical argument of your own that takes into account this range of positions either by conceding, refuting, or accepting the various arguments made in the thread.
- When you have finished, present your summary and the argument that you've developed to the rest of the class.

Researching through Queries and Conversations

Most writing handbooks suggest that interviews can help writers to incorporate personal insights and expert knowledge into a project. After all, you have direct access to a primary source, and you can ask that person exactly what you want to know. However, the logistics, timing, and potential awkwardness of interacting in a formal situation mean that few of us ever bother to conduct interviews as part of our research. Newsgroup and list resources, on the other hand, give us the opportunity to interact with, or "interview," numerous people simply by posting a research query.

Posting with a Purpose

Generally speaking, readers on the Net are more than willing to answer questions. To get the most worthwhile feedback, though, you will need to think carefully about the best kinds of queries to post. Although the "there is no such thing as a stupid question" rule may apply in your classroom, Internet users may not be so kind. If you waste readers' time with questions such as "Who killed JFK?" or "What's the Cuban Missile Crisis?," you can expect to be publicly flamed.

Before deciding to post a query, you should consider a few basic questions. Is this the right group? Is the content of your post relevant either to current discussion on the group or to the group's purpose? Are you likely to get useful responses from members of this group?

Also consider how receptive the group is to student queries. Some groups frown on student questions and even go so far as to ban them. If you're concerned about the decorum of a given group or list, you should check out the "Frequently Asked Questions" file (FAQ) if it's a newsgroup or the information in the introductory messages that come when you subscribe to a discussion list. The FAQ should outline the purpose of the group and offer guidelines about appropriate discussion. Also, since topics often recirculate in lists and newsgroups, you may be able to find information that already responds to your query. In general, we recommend reading FAQ as part of your familiarization with any group or list. (See **http://www.cis.ohio-state.edu/hypertext/faq/usenet/top.html** for a list of Usenet FAQs.)

Though most Usenet groups and e-mail lists are open to anyone, many academic groups are moderated. A post to a moderated group must first pass through a moderator. Since your message must be approved before it can appear on the list, there is no guarantee that group members will see it. In general, though, as long as you choose the right group and compose carefully, you can count on the good will of moderators. Whatever kind of group you are posting to, be sure that your post is interesting and relevant to the group and that it advances the existing conversation.

Writing the Post

Just as you worry about your physical appearance in certain formal situations, you should worry about the quality of writing in your posts to the Internet. Especially in a research query, your writing determines what other people "see" of you and how they are likely to respond.

Most groups will frown on a post that simply asks for information that could easily be obtained by spending a little time in the library. Before you post a message to the Net, conduct your own preliminary research. Use resources at the library, on the Web, or in previous posts so that you'll be able to compose a more informed research query. Again, at this early stage, the FAQ is a good place to start.

All queries have the potential to elicit response, so structure your post around the type of feedback you hope to receive. Are you wondering what others think about your position? Do you want to initiate dialog about an issue? Are you soliciting more information about a recent discussion topic? The answers to these questions will determine how detailed your posts are, what tone they take, how many posts you send, and even whether you reply to an existing thread or begin a new one.

Finally, be sure to follow up on any responses you receive from your research query. Remember that you're no longer working with a static resource; you'll have the opportunity to continue discussing the issues with your new correspondents. You might ask for further clarification, respectfully disagree, explain your position in more depth, or just say thanks.

Here are a few important strategies to keep in mind as you compose your query.

Ask Specific Questions Generally speaking, the more precise you make your query, the more specific the responses from your audience will be. Asking clear, detailed questions will demonstrate to your readers that you have done some prior research and that you have arrived at a focused research topic. It also limits the scope of the question so that your audience won't feel overwhelmed by the prospect of responding.

Post a Series of Questions Consider posting a series of questions so that you can tap into the range of expertise in the group. Keep your questions specific, but try asking about several closely related topics or about several angles of a single topic. By asking multiple questions, you can more precisely illustrate the scope of your project, and you will increase your chances of getting responses by providing more prompts for members to reply to.

Ask an Engaging Question One reason that student queries are frowned on in some groups is that students who are trying to gather information about a topic often ask the same broad, overly generalized questions. Since the regular members of a group are probably quite knowledgeable about its topic, they tend to be frustrated by, and therefore unlikely to participate in, discussion that is far below the level of interaction they are accustomed to. Though simple questions might seem easiest to answer, you will probably receive more useful feedback if you are able to challenge your audience.

Summarize and Synthesize One of the best ways to demonstrate that you are knowledgeable about your topic is to summarize several key arguments or positions that you have come across in your research. If you can synthesize these arguments and then position your own ideas in relation to this larger conversation, you will have gone a long way toward establishing your credibility. Contextualizing your ideas within a clear set of arguments will also help your audience to get a better understanding of which resources you have already looked through and therefore what kinds of information will be most useful to you.

Locate Intersections If possible, point out intersections between your query and any previous messages that have been posted to the group. This will show other members that you are not simply using them as a resource, but have been following the group's discussion, and that you are actively engaged in the community. Users are more likely to respond to queries that expand on existing conversations than to queries that are completely unrelated from earlier posts.

Anatomy of Two Student Posts

Here are two student research queries that were posted to newsgroups as part of a larger research project. As you read through the two messages, consider how successful each posting appears to be.

Post One

```
Hello. My name is Tim Berkman and I am interested in
Cuba (Don't ask why, I just am...sorta).  For anyone
out there, if you have any info on this wonderful
island, please, I repeat, PLEASE, send it to me as
soon as possible. Some things I am most interested
in are:

     1. any opinions or info you might have about
the United States economic blockade on Cuba

     2. info about Comecon (has to do with Russia?)
and how it pertains to Cuba.

     3. info on the conditions of Fidel Castro's
dictatorship.

If you find any extra info, I'm interested in it,
too. Thanx in advance.

                    Tim Berkman
                    tiberk@mail.utexas.edu

P.S. You can also post any info as a thread.
```

Not surprisingly, this first query received almost no useful feedback. For one thing, although Tim seems to realize that he needs to ask detailed questions, his query remains far too broad; any one of his three "specific" questions could be the subject of a separate book-length project. Note that he ends the post by asking for "any extra info," demonstrating his complete lack of focus. His posting also fails to show an in-depth understanding of the issues. He is able to ask about "Comecon," but his comment, "has to do with Russia?" shows that he is unsure about what Comecon actually is. Finally, the tone of Tim's message is damaging to his purpose. Despite the fact that he is asking the on-line community to do him a favor, he announces that he is only "sorta" interested in Cuba but almost demands that he get the information immediately—hardly an inviting request.

Post Two

> I'm doing a research paper on the current economic situation in Russia and how the U.S. is helping or hurting the current reforms.
>
> I was wondering if anyone can give me a first-person account of how the average citizen in Russia views the U.S. and how they perceive the current leadership. I know one person cannot speak for the whole country or possibly give an account of some of the things going on over there, but if you could give me your impressions or opinions, I would really appreciate it.
>
> Also, I would like to know how the people feel about Vladamir Zhironovsky and Boris Yeltsin. Here in the U.S. (Austin, Texas), we only hear and see what is available in the news media. What I would like is a more personal view and opinion and how you/they feel about the current leadership and the reforms they have implemented or proposed.
>
> I know that not everyone will be able to answer all or any of these questions, but if one answer is all you can give, that is fine.
>
> Thank You.
> Julie Coleman

This second message is a much more successful research query. Although Julie might have been able to show more of her prior research in the post, she still manages to come off sounding intelligent and interested. Her topic, the U.S. impact on economic reform in Russia, is fairly specific, and she is asking for a particular kind of response—personal opinion—that taps into the expertise of her newsgroup audience. Knowing that she will be able to find background information in the library or on the Web, Julie has written a post with the aim of soliciting responses from people who are more intimately connected with the situation and who can offer an account of their experience that will probably not be available in any other context.

TIPS AND TACTICS

- Newsgroups are generally easier to locate and use than e-mail discussion lists because they are collected on a central computer at your institution and because they store older messages.
- When you use newsgroups or discussion lists, plan on spending some time getting a feel for the dynamics of the group and the kinds of materials that are generally posted. This process takes longer with e-mail, so be sure to subscribe to any discussion lists early in the semester.
- One way of quickly assessing a newsgroup or e-mail discussion list is to place it into one of three broad categories: (1) news and information, (2) scholarly articles and expert discussion, or (3) social conversation. These headings, however, best serve as broad guidelines. Be sure to fully evaluate the character of the groups you frequent.
- When working with conversational resources, you may want to treat the thread, rather than the individual message, as the most important unit. Use the various arguments that have been posted in the discussion thread as a way of uncovering the range of perspectives that need to be considered before writing about an issue.
- When you post your own research queries to newsgroups and lists, be sure to ask specific, thoughtful questions that demonstrate some previous knowledge of your topic. Avoid queries that simply ask the on-line community to do your research for you. Before posting, consult the group's FAQ and be sure that you are familiar with the specific policies and procedures of that group.
- Know what kinds of responses you want to receive when you post a query so that you can tailor your message to fit your purpose. Remember that the more specific you can be in a query, the more likely you are to receive useful feedback.

CHAPTER 9

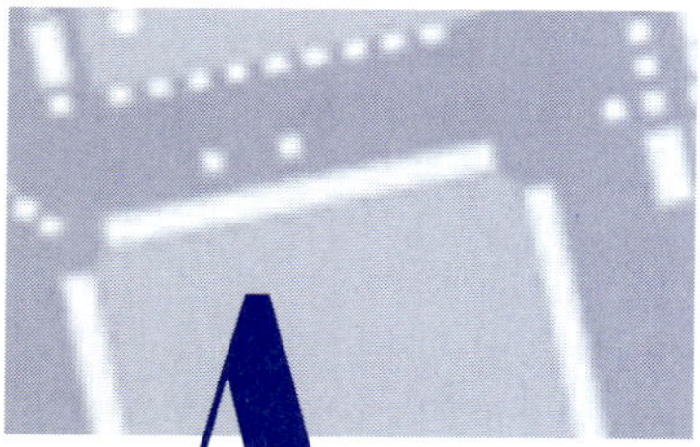

A SAMPLE RESEARCH SESSION

Instructors usually expect student research projects to have a narrow, well-defined topic. After all, a project with a limited scope is more likely to provide in-depth insight and argue with clarity. At the same time, however, instructors often give rather broad, open-ended research assignments. Although it may occasionally seem like your teachers are trying to torture you with contradictions, they probably just want you to work through the process of narrowing and focusing a topic on your own. This chapter will take you through the on-line research process of an imaginary student as she uses the various resources of the Internet to refine, clarify, and develop her own research project. Keep in mind that this example illustrates only one of many possible on-line research models. Depending on your project, you may need to vary your on-line research strategies.

Using Keyword Searches and Subject Categories

Imagine that hypothetical student—we'll call her Tara—has been given the broad assignment of researching and writing about "a topic of national importance." She initially considers some of the issues that are frequently debated in the news media—such as environmental protection, welfare reform, and crime. But these seem to be the same subjects that all of her classmates are working on, so Tara decides to look for something different.

Tara has enjoyed discussing the Civil Rights Amendment in her American history class, so she decides to research the issues of equality and discrimination. Tara starts her research by doing a keyword search for "equality" with the AltaVista Web search engine (**http://www.altavista.digital.com**). Figure 9.1 shows her results.

The returns from the search reveal a range of resources, including a project about equality and education in developing countries and information about equality on the Internet. Note, however, that the search returned about 50,000 items; this should tell Tara right away that her topic is far too broad.

Since the research process is not only about gathering materials, but also about exploring different perspectives and arguments, Tara might browse through the search results to get a feel for what's out there. When Tara looks through some of the results, she discovers that the term

■ **FIGURE 9.1** AltaVista Search Results for "equality"

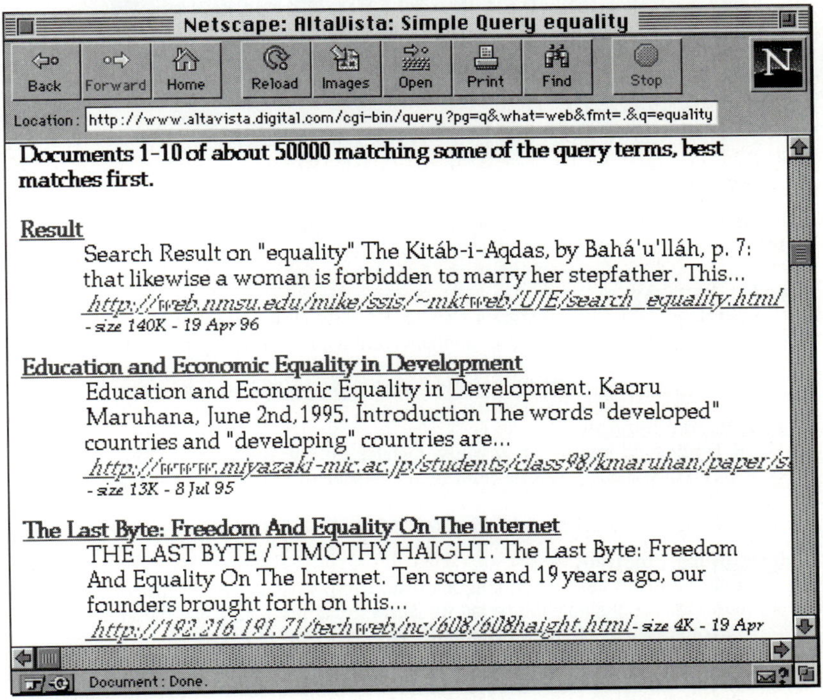

"equality" brings back items related not only to the civil rights issues she is studying, but to issues of sexual and gender equality as well. She also finds items that address equality in the workplace, at school, and on the Internet.

Let's imagine that after browsing through several items from the search returns, Tara decides to shift her focus from racial equality and the Civil Rights Amendment to issues of gender equality. She therefore refines her search query to "equality and gender."

Figure 9.2 shows that while adding the term "gender" to her query has certainly limited the search returns (the number of hits has gone from about 50,000 to about 28), the returns themselves don't seem to be closely related to each other. The first item in Figure 9.2 seems to be something about government policies, the second advertises a poster session at a

FIGURE 9.2 AltaVista Search Results for "equality+gender"

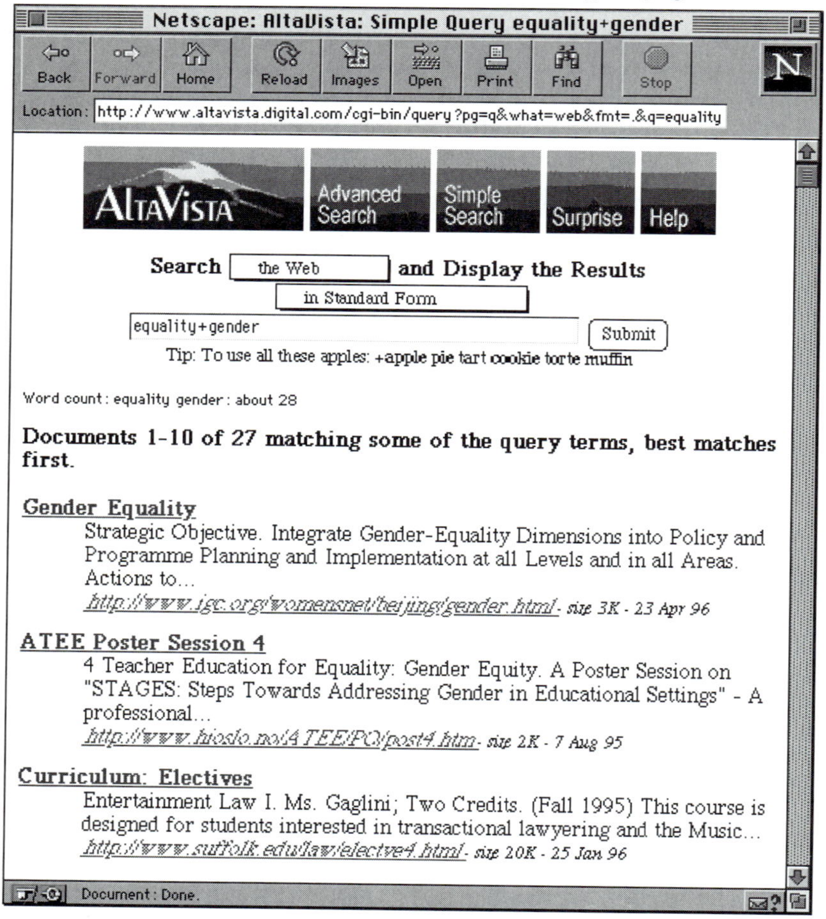

convention, and the third leads to information about a college class. Tara has narrowed the number of search returns, but she still hasn't latched on to a manageable and focused topic.

At this point, because she realizes that broad keyword searching isn't helping to narrow her topic, she decides to try another strategy: browsing through some subject categories at Internet directory sites.

Figure 9.3 shows the way that Tara is able to browse through the subject categories at the Lycos search engine (**http://www.lycos.com**). Beginning with the large list of categories, Tara goes to the "Social Issues" topic. Here she finds the category "Women's Resources." Inside that category, she comes across the item "Internet Resources for Women's Legal and Public Policy Information."

Following the link, Tara finds herself at the Internet Resources for Women's Legal and Public Policy Information homepage (**http://asa.ugl.lib.umich.edu/chdocs/womenpolicy/womenlawpolicy.html**), a Web site devoted to policy issues for women. She discovers links to other subjects, including two that particularly strike her interest: "Women and Children" and "Work Issues." Following the link to "Work Issues," she finds a number of useful articles and other links, including a Gopher site with information on the "glass ceiling," the artificial boundary that limits women's career opportunities.

■ **FIGURE 9.3** Browsing through Subject Categories at Lycos

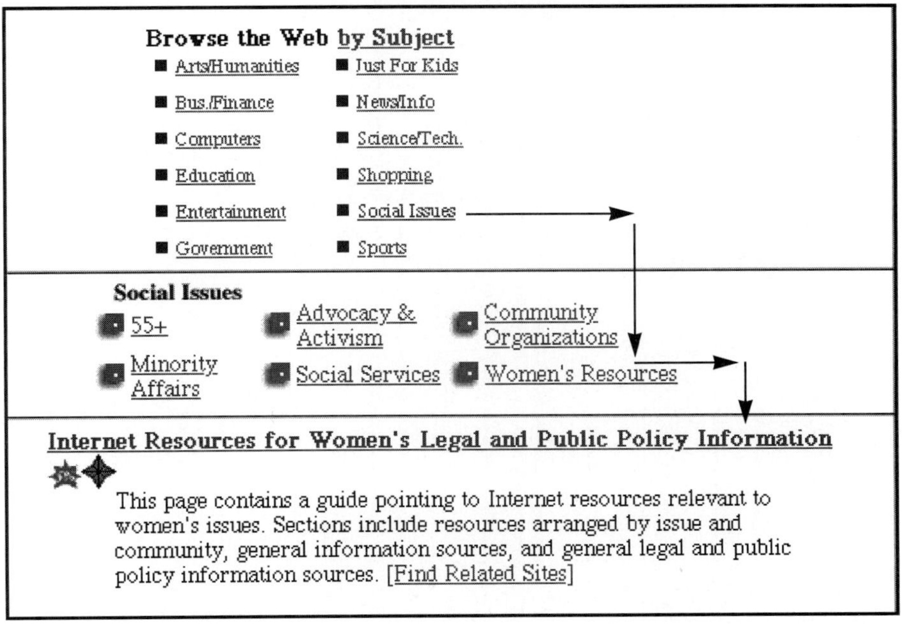

You can see that the Glass Ceiling Gopher site shown in Figure 9.4 provides a number of resources for a potential research project, including particular case information, editorials, and articles. Additionally, the site has a local search function that will help Tara browse through the files at that server.

Although she is getting closer, Tara still doesn't have an exact focus for her project. So far, the gender and workplace information seems to concentrate on issues of equal pay and sexual harassment. She might browse further through the information on the glass ceiling, trying to frame key issues and sharpen her focus. Let's imagine, however, that Tara decides to backtrack a bit. She bookmarks the Gopher site, then returns to the other item from the Internet Resources for Women's Legal and Public Policy Information site that struck her interest: "Women and Children."

The "Women and Children" link, however, has information mostly pertaining to child abuse and the rights of children. Tara realizes that she is actually more interested in the way that raising children influences the employment opportunities that women have. She jumps back to some search engines and queries with a new focus. Unfortunately, she still runs into problems. Using the keywords "women" and "work," Tara comes up with over 1,000 search returns—too many to begin saving and documenting. Figure 9.5 shows a refined query for "women," "work," and "children." When Tara tries this refined query, however, she gets no returns.

FIGURE 9.4 The Glass Ceiling Gopher Site

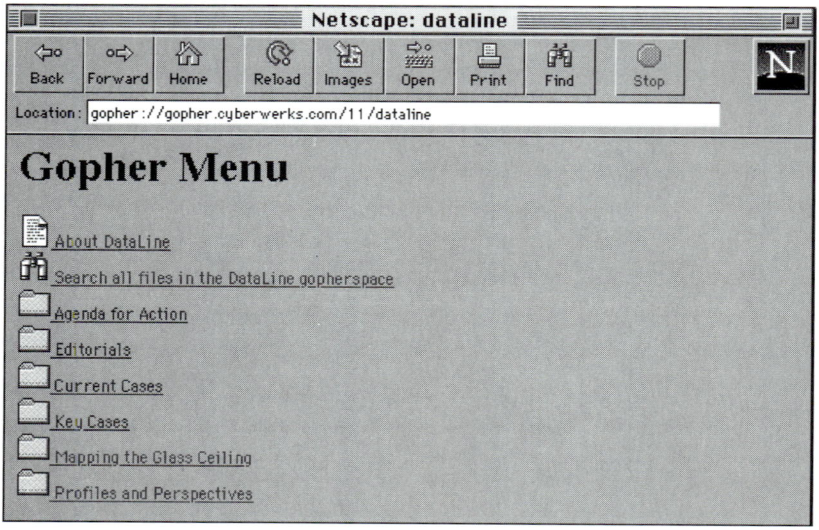

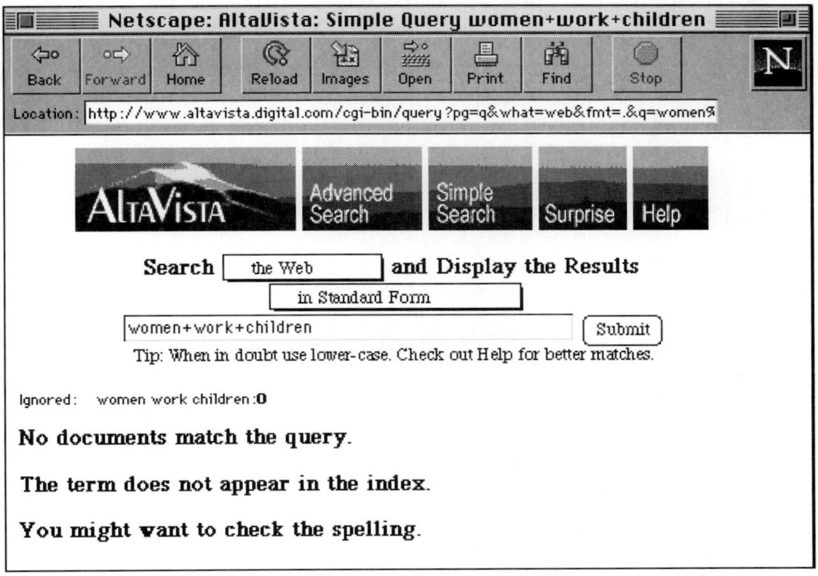

■ **FIGURE 9.5** AltaVista Search Results for "women+work+children"

Fortunately, Tara has read **Chapter 7** of *Connections* and knows that trying synonyms and other keywords as well as working with multiple search engines may be necessary. Instead of using "women" and "work," Tara tries "mothers" and "working." She tries "child care" instead of "children." She also tries the same keywords on the Lycos and Infoseek (**http://www.infoseek.com**) search engines. Tara begins to bookmark more frequently and to save a number of files to her diskette. She also opens a "notes" file, in which she pastes passages from documents and enters citation information for the items she is saving. After an hour or so of collecting information from this latest search, she has assembled the Bookmarks and files shown in Figure 9.6.

Tara has found information on the types and costs of child care and has come across an article arguing in favor of more corporate-sponsored day care centers. The article notes both a decrease in absenteeism and an increase in employee morale when companies provide on-site day care. A wide range of arguments are made in favor of on-site child care, including some based on breast feeding, divorce rates, and single motherhood. Tara decides that she has collected enough preliminary material to begin the project. In fact, she thinks that she may be closing in on a topic for her project: "Working Mothers and On-Site Day Care." At this point, she takes time to think about what she has come up with so far and begins to formalize her approach.

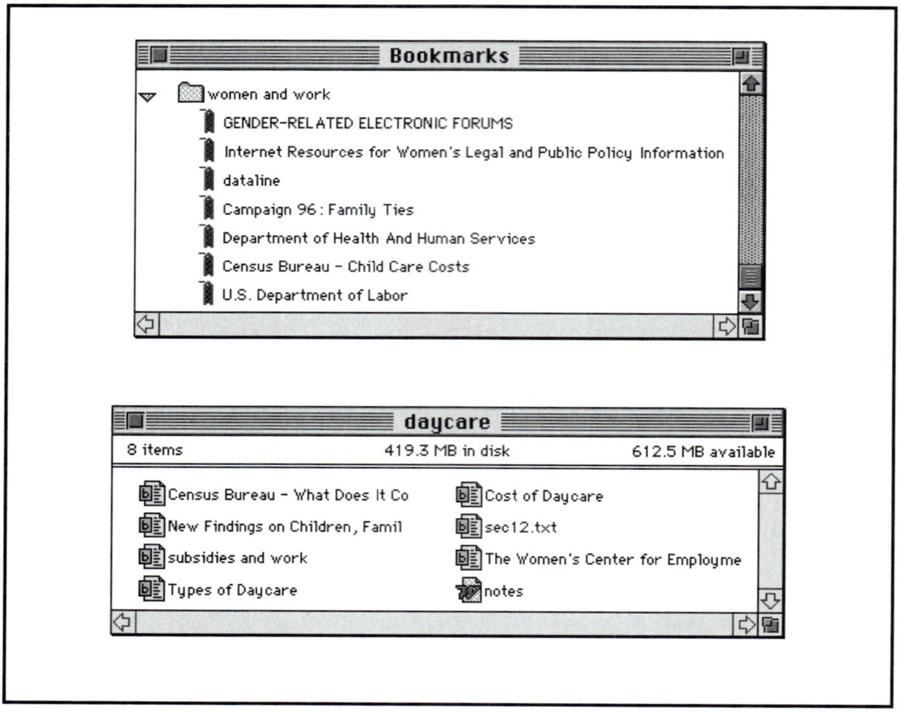

■ **FIGURE 9.6** Initial Bookmarks and Saved Files

Using Internet Conversations as a Research Tool

Writing teachers often ask students to phrase a research project in the shape of a question. Framing an issue as a research question focuses a project and guides researchers toward more relevant information. On the Internet, the power of research or focus questions is amplified; not only can these questions clarify your own thinking, they can be put to a community of interested readers. This community can respond by either providing support for your perspective, challenging you to further explain your position, or asking you to justify a particular point.

After some thought, Tara decides that she has a research question: "By not providing on-site child care for their employees, are companies discriminating against working women?"

In many ways, Tara is now in a good position to join in Internet conversations. She has done some preliminary research and narrowed her topic. She wants to see what people think of the argument that working mothers, especially single mothers, need access to on-site day care if they are going to achieve workplace equality.

To test this position, Tara sorts through the newsgroups that her school provides and comes up with a list of four: **alt.business.misc**, **alt.childcare**, **alt.support.single-parents**, and **soc.women**. Before posting, however, Tara is careful to check out the kind of activity that takes place on the different groups. She gets a feel for her audience and composes the following research query:

```
Hi everyone.  I am working on a research project
which looks at the issue of on-site daycare for
working women.  I've found some articles that show
on-site daycare benefits both parents and the
companies where they work.  Additionally, children
are more comfortable in on-site daycare situations.
What I'm trying to argue is that since these
benefits are so important, companies that don't
provide on-site daycare are discriminating against
working women. Without on-site daycare, single
mothers may not be as likely to take certain jobs
and working women will need to be absent more. It
follows that they won't be as likely to receive
important promotions, etc.

I'm hoping this group can provide some examples and
insight from personal experience. Have any of you
missed opportunities because your business didn't
provide on-site daycare?  Do any of you work where
there is on-site daycare?  Are the women there more
successful?  Thanks in advance for any help you
give.

Tara Blankenship
```

After several days, Tara receives a few interesting responses, including this one:

```
Tara.  I read your posting on soc.women and have to
respond.  I think you're correct that the benefits
of this kind of daycare reach parents, children and
corporations.  But I think there is a problem with
some of your basic logic.  When it comes to single
mothers, your point makes sense, but what about two
```

> parent families? You say that not providing on-site daycare discriminates against women. Why not against men? If the father works at a company that doesn't provide on-site care, won't he be discriminated against too? Why is it that mothers thrive more than fathers when their kids are near by? I think you'd raise a lot of red flags if you made a statement like that today.
>
> The reasons that mothers feel more compelled to sacrifice careers for the sake of family are complicated. There are any number of cultural expectations that need to be addressed, otherwise, saying that on-site daycare benefits mothers more than fathers seems to imply a biological difference between mothers and fathers that shoots down your argument. If mothers somehow need to be closer to their children, then why come to work in the first place? Stay home and watch the kids. If mothers and fathers both benefit, then providing daycare is an issue of practicality, not equality. I'm not knocking day care, just saying that it helps both mothers and fathers. Good luck with the project, Jerry Shale.

Tara was hoping for confirmation about her topic but instead receives an opposing point of view. Initially, she is taken aback. What she thought was becoming a clear focus has been muddied by Jerry's posting. What about cultural expectations for mothers? Working fathers? Biology?

When we really start to probe an issue extensively, it's easy to be overwhelmed by the amount of information and the different avenues of complexity that seem to demand exploration. Don't panic. We often make the mistake of thinking that a research project can capture every nuance of an issue or that we must somehow arrive at *the* definitive statement about a topic. Remember that some academics spend entire careers exploring topics such as "biology and cultural expectations." They see their work as a kind of evolving conversation. Rather than trying to have the final word or encapsulate every aspect of their field, they write to articulate points of dispute and to explain their own positions and claims in the context of other scholarship.

Tara realizes that rather than finding closure for her own position, she should think a while about the issues raised in Jerry's post. She sees that the benefits of on-site day care are an important part of her project.

If she wants to address child care and workplace inequality, however, she will also need to talk a bit about cultural expectations for women. Tara thinks for a while, then composes a new research question: "How do cultural expectations about child rearing affect working mothers?"

Once again, Tara takes her refined focus through the search process. Querying Lycos, WebCrawler (**http://www.webcrawler.com**), and AltaVista with combinations of terms such as "biology," "parenthood," "stereotype," "culture," "child care," and "child rearing," Tara tracks down resources that might address some of Jerry's points. She finds an article chronicling a sociological debate about genetics and motherhood and learns that this is a hotly contested topic. She comes across newsgroup archives containing still more discussion about the issue. She even finds a Web site analyzing the movie *Parenthood* in terms of gender stereotypes.

After processing some of these results, Tara realizes that Jerry's points can actually be used to support her position. She doesn't have to settle the debate about the mother's biological role in parenting. She can point out how this debate complicates her project and use it to show that cultural stereotypes do affect our understanding of motherhood. She can then argue that these stereotypes make it all the more important to create policies stressing on-site day care.

In fact, before beginning to draft her project, she bangs out a response to Jerry:

```
Jerry.  Thanks for the insightful comments about
on-site daycare.  The points you raise make sense.
I'm still not sure how the issue can be just one of
practicality, though.  You say that cultural
expectations are more important in determining
equality at the workplace. But aren't these
expectations exactly the reason why we need to
provide more opportunities for on-site daycare.

I don't think we need to argue about a biological
reason that mothers should be near their children.
That debate will probably go on for a long time. The
point is that there are stereotypical expectations
for mothers. There are expectations for fathers,
too, but the expectations for motherhood and child
rearing--whether biological or cultural are too
strong to be ignored.  If mothers are bound by a
sense that they should be the ones watching the
kids, our choices are to try to change these
expectations or to help mothers do so.  Tara.
```

We can see that by responding to Jerry, Tara is still refining the focus of her project. And although she hasn't formally begun composing her paper, by crafting her reply, she is already thinking, arguing, and writing about her topic. In fact, we would argue that this message and her earlier conversations represent components of the drafting process. Perhaps Jerry will reply with new concerns or more advice. As she moves along in the writing process, Tara can continue this conversation, bouncing new ideas off of Jerry (ouch) and others in the group, all the while collecting more resources for her project.

Saving and Documenting

Throughout this research process, Tara has been bookmarking sites and saving files that may be useful. Figure 9.7 shows how her Bookmark collection has grown, and Figure 9.8 shows the files that Tara has saved so far.

Although not every one of these resources will make it into her final project, she has saved more than she'll need because most of these items are text files that won't require much storage space. Sorting through them

■ **FIGURE 9.7** Sample Bookmark Files

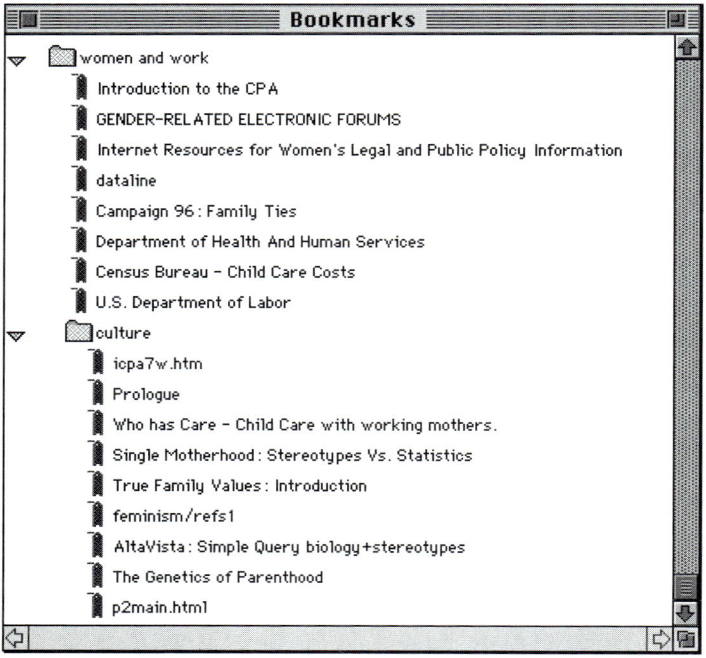

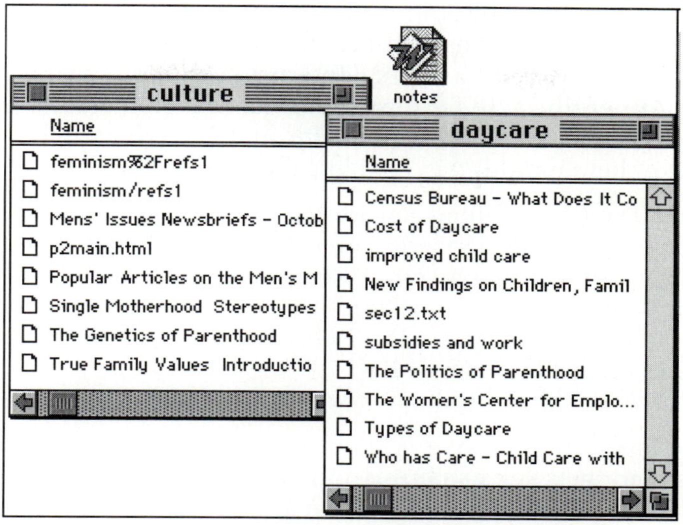

■ **FIGURE 9.8** The Resources Tara Has Collected

shouldn't be too difficult. Remember that as she has collected these resources, Tara has been writing summaries, pasting excerpts, and collecting citation information in her "notes" file. Figure 9.9 shows a section of Tara's notes.

■ **FIGURE 9.9** A Section from Tara's Notes

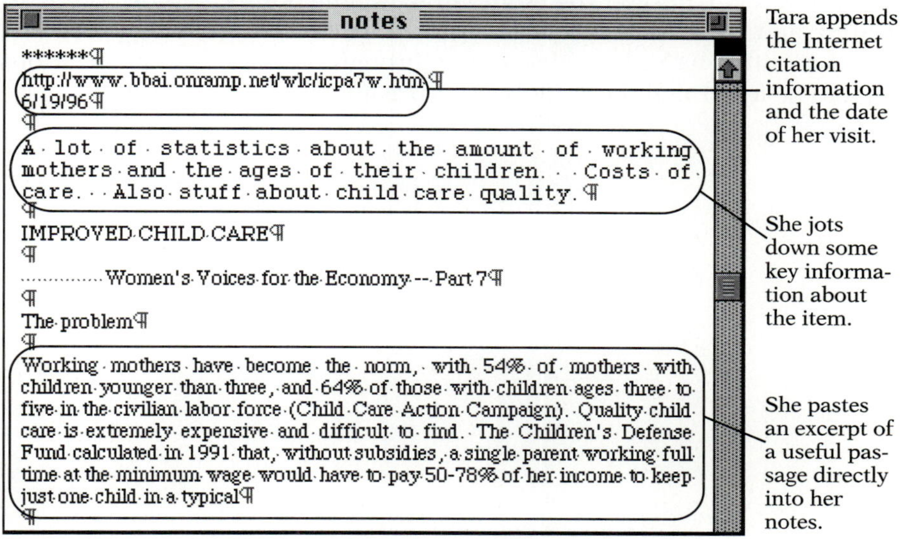

When she is finished, Tara will need to cite her sources in an appropriate format. We'll assume that her instructor has asked her to use the "MLA-Style Guidelines for Citing Internet Sources" style sheet reproduced in **Appendix 2.** If Tara uses information from Jerry's newsgroup post, from the Glass Ceiling Gopher site, and from the article "Improved Child Care," her citations will look like this:

DataLine. "The Glass Ceiling Newsletter."
gopher://gopher.cyberwerks.com/11/dataline (June 18, 1996).
Shale, Jerry. <shale@quarry.com> "Re. On-Site Daycare."
<soc.women> (June 16, 1996).
Women's Connection Online. "IMPROVED CHILD CARE ... Women's Voices for the Economy—Part 7."
<http://www.bbai.onramp.net/wlc/icpa7w.htm> (June 19, 1996).

Since the newsgroup posting is short and will likely be gone in a couple of weeks, Tara gets Jerry's permission via e-mail and attaches a printed copy of his message to the back of her paper for her instructor to refer to.

As you can see, Tara has gone through an involved process. In the course of her research, she has not only found and tracked information, but also refined and developed her topic. Remember, however, that the process of continually exploring and narrowing your topic takes time. Getting input from a newsgroup or discussion list, in particular, means posting well before you begin to draft your paper or project. Caffeine helps, but this kind of research is generally not something you do the night before a major assignment is due.

We hope you'll enjoy the hunt and that the materials you uncover along the way will keep you going. Researching on-line can be both frustrating and rewarding. But if you remain persistent and follow some of the tactics that we've been discussing throughout **Part 2,** the frustrations should be fewer and the resources surprising and useful.

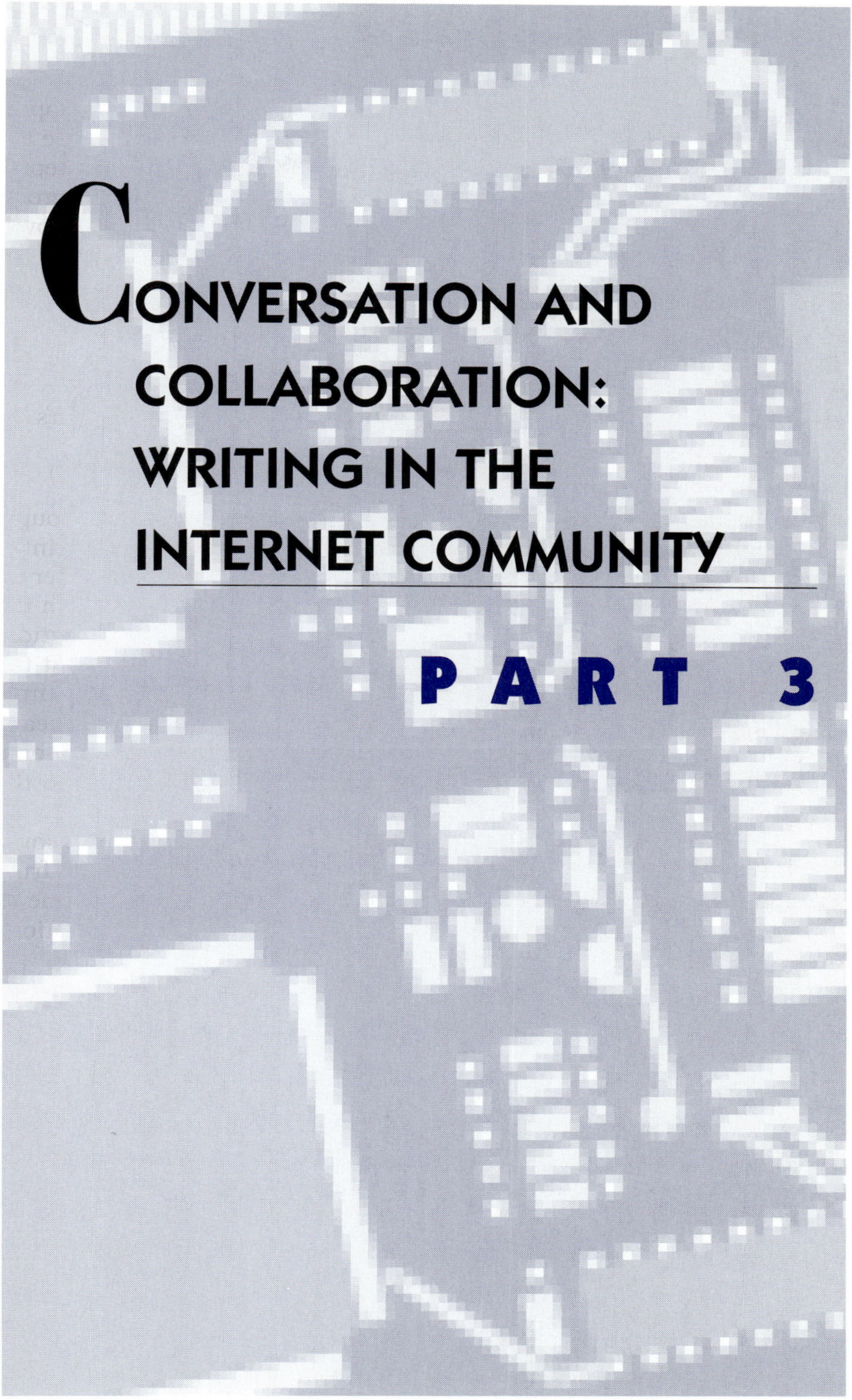

CONVERSATION AND COLLABORATION: WRITING IN THE INTERNET COMMUNITY

PART 3

CHAPTER 10

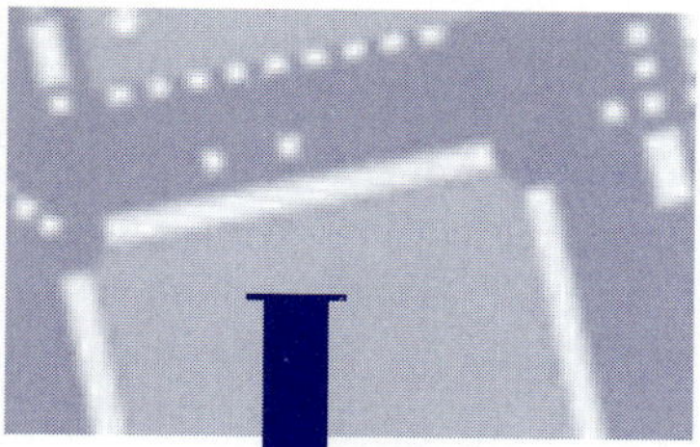

JOINING THE INTERNET COMMUNITY

The Communal Construction of Knowledge

Throughout the first half of this book, we've seen how communities construct understanding through complicated processes of thinking, writing, and conversing about concepts and issues. In **Part 2,** we focused on how research can place sources into conversation, revealing the various conflicts and debates that circulate around an issue. In this part of the book, we talk in more detail about how to use the interactive aspects of the Internet to actively participate in those debates.

We believe that our understandings are often achieved through a process of communication and based on mutual agreements. Imagine, for instance, that you are studying the wetlands ecosystem of western Florida. To learn about the habitat, you could observe the area for several days, collecting data on the variety and frequency of plant and wildlife species, the effects of tidal movement, and any evidence of pollution or other human impact on the environment. Although you would learn a tremendous amount from these observations, your understanding would still be limited by the time you were able to spend, the specific area you studied, your methods of observation, and a host of other factors. However, if you took a trip to the library when you got back (hopefully after a quick shower), you could supplement your information with the experience and observations of others. You might find studies on the evolution of the wetlands during the past fifty years, research examining the microscopic organisms sustaining the ecosystem, information about similar habitats in other areas, and environmental impact reports outlining the potential dangers of offshore oil drilling in the Gulf of Mexico.

By tapping into the collective expertise of others, you would gather much more information than you could ever collect on your own. As we discuss in **Part 2,** exploring the collective knowledge that has been developed about a topic lets you better determine your own position in relation to the various voices in a "research conversation." Further, if you were supplementing your research by taking a wetlands ecology course and you presented your observations in class, you would have the opportunity to continue this research conversation in a more interactive format. With your classmates and instructor, you could exchange ideas, share useful resources, test your positions against those of others, and critically analyze materials as a group.

By going to the library or conversing with your classmates, you can augment your own observations by engaging in a process of collaborative learning. In reality, almost all knowledge and learning rely on some form of collaboration. Even if you had been gathering data alone in the swamp, you would depend on various forms of collective knowledge. For instance, before you began your study, you would have learned about methods of scientific observation and analysis. To properly document your findings, you would have consulted detailed maps and field guides for the region. All of these lessons and materials have a collaborative component. Even the ability to record your observations depends on a shared understanding of written language. To know that the small furry animal you saw during your stay was a woodchuck, and to know that the substance he was chucking was wood, you would have to be a member of a particular language community (in this case, speakers of English who can identify certain plants and animals).

What we are trying to show with this example is that knowledge is inherently collaborative—that most of what we do and think is influenced by other people. The image of an isolated academic cloistered away in an ivory tower (or, for that matter, a swamp) is to our minds a counterproductive model of learning. By embracing the idea that knowledge is obtained through collaboration and exchange, you can become more active in the many communal conversations and debates in which understanding is created and developed.

Working within Knowledge Communities

In our hypothetical example, the budding scientist is able to share observations because she or he is a member of at least three knowledge communities: speakers of English, scientists, and students in the wetlands ecology course. Each of these communities has its own conventions and expectations. Successful writers learn to work within the requirements of different knowledge communities. As an illustration, consider the ways that a scholarly community at your college or university might differ from a group of students. Scholars might argue about whether there is a "purely linguistic basis of Eurocentric consciousness," but this debate would probably hold little meaning for most students. In fact, many academics might have trouble understanding it. For one thing, the discussion would rely on terminology and a theoretical background that are peculiar to a certain group of scholars. The debate would be taking place within a specialized community that is heavily invested in issues of linguistics and philosophy. To become a member of this community, you would need to have a set of prerequisites such as vocabulary, interest, and shared experience.

Fortunately, not all scholarly communities are as narrowly defined as the one above. As a student, it's your job to understand and acquire the prerequisites for joining a number of academic communities. Your success in college writing depends in part on how well you can master some of the basic conventions of the university community. This doesn't necessarily mean using five-syllable words or speaking with a perfect Oxford accent; but it probably does mean writing complete sentences, documenting sources, providing support for your arguments, and considering the range of complexities that are inherent in any given topic. Additionally, as you move into more specialized areas of concentration, you'll need to learn the expectations for discourse in those disciplines. In engineering, you may need to know ways of presenting statistical data. In education, you might need to learn methodologies for assessing student development. In sociology, you might need to know how to present demographic information. Whatever field you are studying, understanding its particular conventions is a necessary first step toward success.

The Benefits of Collaboration

But communities don't exist only on large institutional levels. Often, the most productive forms of collaboration take place in smaller groups. When working with others toward a common objective, we reap the benefits of constructing communal understandings. We learn to stand up for our positions, listen closely to opposing points of view, and work toward compromise. An effective group can handle very strong conflicting opinions by taking the best of each perspective and finding some sort of middle ground or by finding ways of framing the debate which are broad enough to encompass multiple perspectives. Members, then, have to be willing to modify or let go of some of their ideas to serve the best interests of the group. Through the process of exchange and negotiation, group members gain a better understanding of an issue and of the larger goals of the project.

Working in groups is also a particularly effective way of improving your writing skills. Learning to write with other authors often enhances your ability to appeal to a wider audience and gives you the benefits of careful peer review. An effective collaborative working arrangement will ensure that what you say is accurate and important for at least the people in the group, but likely for a larger audience as well. You'll learn your strengths and weaknesses as a writer, and you'll learn to revise your work in light of the group's influence.

You'll also need to constructively critique the work of your collaborators. Keep the project's goals in mind as you review your peers' materials so that you can focus on particular problems and offer specific suggestions for improvement. The roles of reviewer and author often shift back and forth in collaborative groups. As you consider the work of others, you may suggest alternative approaches or raise your own concerns about the overall project. Collaborators should be careful listeners but also actively articulate their own perspectives, with the aim of creating a free exchange of ideas that benefits the project as a whole.

Collaboration on the Internet

Collaboration and conversation are mainstays of Internet activity. We often hear people call the Internet a network of networks, but we also like to think of it as a community of communities. Along with connections between machines, the Net facilitates contacts between people. This kind of communal interaction can be seen in the various topic-centered discussion forums that are so prevalent on the Internet. For instance, there are (at last count) over 20,000 Usenet newsgroups, each devoted to a specific topic or issue. Each of these groups can be seen as a community that shares and debates its interests, ideas, expectations, and conventions. As you explore the range of media and forums that make up the Internet, you'll find that there are an enormous number of communities and collaborative activities, each of which will offer you different benefits as a writer.

For instance, the conversations that you'll find in real-time collaborative environments like MU*s and IRCs provide forums for brainstorming and exploratory writing because they bring a number of divergent perspectives to bear on any given issue. You will also find a high level of participation in these forums, since many people feel comfortable conversing in real-time electronic environments. Additionally, most of these forums allow writers to adopt on-line personas. This will give you a testing ground for presenting yourself as a speaker—a chance to experiment with style and tone so that you can influence the way an audience perceives your writing. (**Chapter 11** discusses the specifics of real-time conversation in MU*s and IRCs.)

The Net is particularly valuable for coordinating activities with your classmates and instructor. By using e-mail, newsgroups, and Web forums, you'll be able to easily contact your instructor and classmates at any time. You can also coordinate your group projects more successfully. Rather than scheduling a time when every member of the group can meet, you can use electronic communication to trade materials, plan strategies, and review each other's work. Additionally, you can use e-mail, newsgroups, and the Web to hold conversations, perhaps elaborating on discussions that were cut short by the end of class. These forums provide you with written records of your interactions, meaning that you can easily refer back to earlier points, and giving your work a kind of permanence and status not normally associated with class discussion. (See **Chapter 12** for more information about how these technologies can facilitate class interaction.)

E-mail and newsgroups also provide opportunities for interaction with a much broader audience. Engaging in dialog with the members of an Internet community will expose your ideas to a healthy process of review and revision. In addition, you can clarify your thinking about an issue by considering the multiplicity of perspectives represented by the diverse membership of the group, and you'll have to refine your analytical skills by reading messages critically. (For useful strategies about engaging with Internet communities, see **Chapter 13.**)

Chapter 14 looks at the Web as an inherently collaborative medium. On a technological level, the Web incorporates many different Internet media into a unified system of information transfer and dissemination. Because the technology of the Web allows users to easily "borrow" graphics, text, and even scripts and HTML coding, it adds a collaborative element to traditional concepts of authorship and ownership. The hypertextual capabilities of the Web allow authors to make connections between their texts and the wealth of on-line resources, bringing to life a "research conversation" and incorporating it into their presentations.

We believe the collaboration that you do on-line will make you a better communicator. It will teach you to work effectively as a member of a group, compel you to produce compositions that are informed by diverse perspectives, and enable you to compose messages and projects that clearly position themselves within ongoing conversations.

CHAPTER 11

MORE THAN JUST SLINGING MUD

Real-Time Conversation and Interaction in MU*s and IRCs

Scrivner's:

Candle-lit and smelling of wet ink and fresh paper the scrivner's shoppe is quite spartan in appearance. Behind a main counter a few desks are set, one of which is occupied by the proprietor who is meticulously penning a fine script. A display case houses some of the finer documents that have been produced while others lie drying on a large table. You should probably consult with someone more knowledgeable about this..

[Commands: Talk to Shaugnessy]

[Exits: Out to O'Connell Street SouthEnd]

talk

Shaugnessy stands up from his work and approaches you. "Interested in me work, are ye? Well, as a hobby I analyze handwriting. It is amazing what a little cursive can say about a person."

This description is taken from DragonMud, a text-based virtual environment designed at the University of California at San Diego in which users wander the streets of eighteenth-century England and Ireland. We don't have scrivener's offices around today—places where scribes meticulously hand-copy important manuscripts. But if we consider the time and effort that would have gone into copying lengthy documents by hand rather than using methods like the printing press, the photocopier, or the Internet, we can begin to understand just how much of an impact technology has on writing.

The image of a scribe producing manuscripts raises a number of issues about writing and publication that a class visiting DragonMud might discuss. For instance, how would your process of composition be different if you knew that you would have to rewrite every page by hand after each minor revision? How would you evaluate a text differently if you knew that one copy of an important document, say your employment contract, was significantly different from another copy? How would you know which words were actually chosen by the author and which may have been composed or inadvertently miscopied by the scribe? On another level, what kinds of things might this scrivener be able to express through his or her handwriting? Could those same things be conveyed through the use of typesettings or computer fonts? As a culture that has shifted almost all of its written work to computerized printing or digital display, what might we have lost by moving away from handwriting?

What better place to have this discussion than inside the scrivener's office itself? Students can learn from their surroundings, take cues from the objects that they see, and visit an environment that they would never otherwise be able to experience. Additionally, both MU*s and IRCs allow users to participate in real-time chat sessions. These synchronous exchanges can increase participation in discussions and help you interact with your audience, explore topics, and experiment with the way you present yourself as a speaker. □

KEY TERMS

Character: The persona that a user creates when logging onto a MU*. MU* users can set a description for their character to better illustrate the person they hope to adopt.

Emote: To perform an action as part of a real-time conversation on a MU*. Emoting appends the action that you wish to perform to your character name so that a third-person narrative results. For instance, "The Prof rubs her chin and wonders what to cover today in class." In IRCs, emotes are known as "actions."

Internet Relay Chat (IRC): A section of the Internet that allows users to join a chat channel and have real-time conversations.

MU*: A text-based virtual environment on the Internet. MU* is our umbrella term for the many spaces on Internet servers where users log in, explore the virtual environment, and interact with others. These spaces take their names from different versions of multiple-user software and include MUDs, MUSHs, MUCKs, and MOOs.

Nickname: The persona that a user chooses when logging onto an IRC channel.

Real-Time: Interactions that take place without any significant lapse of time between them (also known as synchronous interaction). Most of the real-time conversations on the Internet take place on IRC channels and in MU*s.

What Are MU*s and IRCs?

Before we get too far ahead of ourselves, we should briefly describe what MU*s and IRCs actually are. MU* is our acronym for the variety of text-based virtual environments found on the Internet, including MUDs, MOOs, MUSHs, and MUCKs. These environments were originally developed as a way to make role-playing games like Dungeons and Dragons more interactive. Gamers created communal spaces called Multiple User Dungeons (MUDs), which allow users from all over the world to log in and participate in collaborative role playing. Over the last several years, a number of these "virtual environments" have been developed for more social and scholarly purposes. At the same time, the meanings of the acronym have shifted somewhat. Today, MUD can stand for Multiple User Dungeons, Domains, Dimensions, or Dialogs. The basic purpose of these environments, however, has remained the same: to provide a space for multiple participants to meet and interact.

Almost all MU*s are composed as a series of programmed text descriptions. When you enter a room like the scrivener's office in DragonMud, for instance, you see a description of the space, the objects, and any people currently in the room. On a MU*, you can move through the virtual architecture, interact with the program through a set of commands, perform actions (called "emotes"), and converse with other users.

IRC channels, or "chat lines," are also electronic spaces where users log on and interact with other people. They are similar to MU*s in that IRC participants can also emote and carry on real-time electronic discussions. The fundamental difference is that the interaction does not take place in any specific textual environment. Instead, IRCs are more like CB radio channels where users carry on conversations. We've included IRCs in this chapter because much of what we will say about real-time discussion applies equally well to IRC chat lines and MU*s. However, because the spatial environment and programming of MU*s add a level of complexity that isn't found in IRCs, most of our attention will be focused on MU* environments.

Note also that the Web now provides access to a variety of real-time forums, so much of what we talk about is applicable to chat that you might do using your Web browser. In fact, it's likely that the popularity of Web chat will increase in the near future.

A Selection of MU*s

- Diversity University MOO: erau.db.erau.edu 8888
- Daedalus MOO: logos.daedalus.com 7777
- Virtual On-Line University: coyote.csusm.edu 8888
- DragonMud: dragonmud.infonex.net 4201
- CollegeTown MOO: next.cs.bvc.edu 7777
- BayMOO: baymoo.sfsu.edu 8888
- Cheshire MOOn: cheshire.cwrl.utexas.edu 7777

Connecting, Speaking, Emoting, and Navigating

Connecting to MU*s and IRCs

To connect to a MU*, you'll need to know its Internet address (such as **cheshire.cwrl.utexas.edu**) and a port number (often 7777 or 8888). You can connect either with Telnet or by using a local client program such as MUDDweller or Tinkeriview for Mac or WinMUD for Windows. We recommend working with local client software because it will make interaction, navigation, and saving transcripts easier. (For more information on clients, see the section entitled "Internet Nuts and Bolts: Servers, Clients, and Internet Media" in **Chapter 1** or the *Connections* Web site.)

Once you've entered the address and connected to the MU*, you will be prompted for a username and a password. The opening screen of most MU*s will provide specific instructions for logging on. On your first visit, you may want to log on as a "guest" so that you can quickly look around without creating a new character. If you are going to be a regular participant, though, you'll want to create a character that you can use on return visits.

To log onto an IRC channel, you'll go through a similar process. You will need to know the address of an IRC server (such as **piglet.cc.utexas.edu**) and its port number (usually 6667). Again, you can connect by using either Telnet or local client software such as Ircle for Mac or MIRC for Windows. You will be prompted to type in a nickname as you log onto the server. Once you are there, you can join a channel by typing the command

```
/join #channelname
```

If the channel that you type in does not already exist, the IRC server will automatically create a new channel by that name. If you'd like to see what channels are already open, type the command

```
/list
```

Be aware, however, that this will generally produce a huge list of channels, so be prepared to wait while the list is generated. To access on-line help about listing channels, type

```
/help/lists
```

This will provide information about modifying the "list" command so that you can bring back a manageable number of IRC channels.

Speaking and Emoting on MU*s and IRCs

Conversation on a MU* is actually a combination of speaking and emoting. To speak on a MU*, simply type in the "say" command, a single quotation mark (") followed by your message. For example, if a character named "The Prof" typed in the command

```
"Has everyone seen the assignment?
```

all the other people in the same room would see

```
The Prof says, "Has everyone seen the assignment?"
```

The "say" command simply attributes a statement to a character and sends the message to each person in the room. The conversation therefore appears as a series of messages on the computer screen. You can speak privately to a single character in a MU* with the "whisper" command, or you can "page" a character in another part of a MU*.

The "emote" command, a colon (:), is similar to the "say" command. It attributes actions to you by simply placing the name of your character before the message that you type. If a character named Jimmy typed in the command

```
:wonders if we need to cite sources in the
assignment.
```

everyone else in the room would read

```
Jimmy wonders if we need to cite sources in the
assignment.
```

It might seem a little strange at first to always talk about yourself in the third person, but you will quickly learn how to express complex actions and emotions. You can also speak with the "emote" command. For example, if Jimmy were to type in

```
:scratches his head and asks, "What documentation
style should we use?"
```

everyone else in the room would see

```
Jimmy scratches his head and asks, "What
documentation style should we use?"
```

Versions of the "say" and "emote" commands are available on IRCs as well. Since the primary function of IRCs is to facilitate discussion, however, you can forgo the quotation mark ("). Simply type in the message that you wish to send to the other users on the channel and hit "enter." To perform an action such as scratching your head, type

```
/me scratches his head and ponders the postmodern
condition.
```

The (/me) command will append the action that you enter to your character's name. Everyone else on the channel will see

```
Jimmy scratches his head and ponders the postmodern
condition.
```

Quick IRC Commands

- /join *#channel*
  Joins a user to the specified *channel;* if the channel does not exist, it will be created as a new channel.
- /list
  Lists all currently available channels. Be aware that this may produce a huge list of groups. To manage this list, type "/help/list" once you are on-line.
- /me *action*
  Makes a character "emote" whatever is typed in as the *action.*
- /msg *username message*
  Sends a private *message* to *username.*
- /nick *newnickname*
  Changes your nickname to *newnickname.*
- /who *channel*
  Shows who is on a given *channel.*
- /whois *nickname*
  Shows the identity of another user.

Navigating in MU*s

Since IRCs don't have any geographical space to move around in, navigation applies only to MU* environments. Remember that everything you "see" in a MU* is provided to you in the form of prewritten messages or descriptions. If you type the command

```
look
```

you will be shown a description of the setting and its contents, including a depiction of your surroundings, any characters who are present, and any obvious exits or special objects that the creator of the room has provided. For example,

```
You see a long dark hallway with doors to the left
and the right, labeled 'Grammar' and 'Punctuation'
respectively.
```

Often you can look in more detail at the objects in the room to get a better description. For instance, you might be able to type "look Punctuation" to get a description of the door.

Navigating in specific directions is simple; just type "n" for north, "s" for south, and so on. Similarly, to move through obvious exits, type the name of the exit—"Grammar" or "Punctuation," for example. Builders can also make "secret passages," lock rooms, or even make objects that teleport users to other sections of the MU* (for instance, picking up an urn might transport a user into a section of the MU* that depicts ancient Greece).

MOO Commands

- :*action*
  Makes a character "emote" whatever *action* is typed in after the colon.
- look
  Provides a description of the current room and its contents.
- look *x*
  Provides a description of the object *x*.
- "*message*
  Allows a user to "say" whatever *message* is typed after the quotation mark.
- page *character message*
  Sends a *message* to another *character* on the MU* regardless of where he or she is located.
- read *x*
  Is used to "read" an object **X** such as a newspaper or a sign.
- whisper "*message*" to *character*
  Sends a private *message* to the specified *character*.
- @desc me as *x*
  Provides the description *x* of yourself for the other users who "look" at you.

- @gender *genderchoice*
  Gives your character the specified *genderchoice,* usually male, female, or neuter.
- @help or help
  Gives more detailed information about MU* commands.

These commands should work with a variety of MU*s, but we've aimed them specifically at MOO environments because those seem to be the most popular formats for academic activities. Still, not all commands will work exactly the same on all MU*s, so try to get an experienced user to guide you and be sure to consult any resources your instructor has provided as well as the on-line help. (See **Appendix 4** for more MU* commands.)

The Benefits and Challenges of Real-Time Conversation

Getting the Most out of Your Real-Time

In a traditional classroom discussion, you usually have to wait your turn and share the floor with all of your classmates. This can mean that it's hard to get a word in, let alone explain a complicated point. One way to avoid this problem would be to have a class discussion in which all students could talk as much and as long as they wanted. In a traditional classroom, however, this degree of volume and chaos would probably overwhelm most students and prompt instructors to look more closely at that early retirement package.

But in MU*s and IRCs, everybody "talks" at once, and participants can choose to closely follow only the threads of discussion that they are most interested in. Additionally, messages have a certain anonymity because they look identical and lack essential features of face-to-face conversation such as tone of voice, volume, or charisma. It's harder for a few outgoing students to monopolize the conversation, so students who are normally shy will feel more comfortable adding their thoughts to the ongoing dialog. Having all of your classmates involved in a discussion means that there are more ideas to draw on. Perhaps more importantly, these real-time discussions can help you and your classmates move beyond arguments that simply shift between two poles of a conversation to a debate that uncovers the many facets of an issue.

Another advantage of IRCs and MU*s is the distinct possibility that participants from outside the class will join the conversations. Communicating with someone from outside your class, and perhaps outside of the narrow confines of the academic world, will provide even more perspectives on a topic. To accommodate the perspectives of the other users in MU*s and IRCs, you will need to think about the makeup of your audience and about how best to present yourself as a speaker. If the guest is a visiting professor, you will most likely write differently than if the guest is a student from another class. These forums make useful spaces for thinking about your audience because participants can and will respond to what you say. A statement that overlooks a key point or assumption and a character who is not well presented will likely be snubbed. Think about how your readers will react to your persona and your messages as you compose.

The last advantage of having class discussions in a real-time environment is that the whole experience can be an exercise in writing and critical reading. Everything that comes across the screen in these sessions is text written with a purpose. You can think about some of our larger rhetorical rubrics—purpose, speaker, message, audience, context, and genre—as you compose in real-time. Think, for example, about how your nickname or character affects the audience's perception of you as a speaker. How do larger social contexts influence the ways you interact in real-time? The messages that you present in these conversations will be a hybrid of informal discussion and more traditional writing, but keeping an eye toward the way that rhetorical strategies influence their composition will enhance your overall development as a writer.

Real-Time, Real Challenges

The increase in participation that accompanies real-time conversation also carries with it certain liabilities, most notably problems with the pace and depth of conversations. Because everybody can talk at once, real-time discussion may move too quickly for participants to keep up. Especially when a large group is interested in the topic, electronic discussion can sometimes be frustrating because the flow of the conversation can easily leave some of the participants behind.

The easiest way to solve this dilemma is to keep a transcript of the session. In a full class discussion, your instructor will probably already be logging a transcript for later reference. If not, or if this is a smaller group meeting, check to see whether the software you use to access IRCs and MU*s has a feature that will let you keep a log of the session. By keeping a transcript, you can return to the discussion for later analysis, revisiting ideas, solidifying a topic that was bounced around in a brainstorming session, or even quoting from the exchange.

Another way to help manage the flow of information in a real-time discussion is to focus on the messages and threads of the conversation that interest you the most. If you participate in one or two threads, you can concentrate on understanding the depth of a particular issue and writing more incisive messages yourself. Your instructor may also want to split the class into smaller groups so that discussion will have a slower, more manageable pace.

A second problem is the temptation to just bounce around from point to point, making quick, superficial comments that lack meaningful insight. Again, to counter this tendency, concentrate on a limited number of threads and try to compose longer, more thoughtful messages. Another strategy is to let the medium's tendencies work to your advantage. Instead of trying to finalize your thesis in a real-time class discussion, use the wealth of voices and perspectives to generate ideas. You'll be tapping into the strength of the medium by drawing on the benefits of increased participation.

Though it is possible to turn the sometimes superficial nature of real-time to your advantage, conversations can occasionally devolve beyond the level of superficiality and become irresponsible, even offensive. Sometimes in real-time exchanges, people send messages that actually shut down conversation. Just because you are not literally "getting in someone's face" doesn't mean that you can't do the electronic equivalent in your writing. To avoid these unproductive confrontations, or at least to keep healthy conflict from escalating to the level of a flame war, remember that your words carry weight and meaning and that they will often reach a wide audience when you send them out electronically.

Electronic conversations are curious in that messages seem strangely disembodied from their speakers. Without being able to attach a face to a statement, we often get the feeling that the words we see have been produced anonymously or created by the computer rather than by a particular person. We've seen how this can help to increase participation in a discussion; however, it also raises some important concerns about responsibility and accountability. Although it might seem that an electronic, real-time discussion has fewer constraints than face-to-face interaction, in reality, these on-line conversations have a kind of permanence that spoken discussions lack. Because it's easy to produce and archive transcripts, the messages that you send can be carefully reexamined at any time in the future, and your conversation itself becomes a text that others may read and study. Perhaps even more than in face-to-face conversations, then, you should be careful about the things you say and the way you say them.

The Effects of Interaction and Character on Writing and Discussion

An audience will often assume differing attitudes toward a message depending on their perceptions of the speaker's motivations and character. In many ways, IRCs and MU*s are a natural environment for experimenting with different writing personas. Your first opportunity begins when you log on.

Nicknames and Characters

When you join an IRC channel, you will need to choose a nickname. As you choose, consider how the audience might react to the name. If you choose a persona that projects a serious attitude, for instance, "Lord Byron," you will influence the audience differently than if you log on as "Kramer." This doesn't mean that you have to select a stuffy name. Simply be aware that your nickname will have an impact on the way that others perceive you. Make your choice in light of your purpose and audience.

MU*s provide you with more options for constructing an on-line persona because you can set a description for your character. When other MU* users "look" at your character, they will judge you in part by the description you have composed. For instance, if you log onto a MU* but don't bother setting a description, the other users will probably assume that you are a "newbie" (a term for an Internet greenhorn). In some situations, this will not be a problem; in others, it will be important to establish a description so that you can fully enter the community of the MU*.

In most MU*s, creating your description is accomplished with a command such as

```
@describe me as "A dog-faced man with glasses and a
goatee".
```

The "@describe" indicates that you are setting the description of something; "me" indicates that you are describing yourself; the information that follows, "A dog-faced man with glasses and a goatee," indicates the description you are creating. When you are finished, you can use the "look me" command to check your description. If you wish to reset your description, the easiest way is to simply repeat the process and enter a new description.

In addition to the logistics of setting your description, you'll want to think about how your actions and attitudes in the MU* further affect the way others view your character. If you come off as pompous and overbearing, your audience is likely to challenge your assertions simply on the basis of your character. If you depict yourself as overly comical, others are likely to discount what you say without fully thinking through your ideas.

EXERCISE 11.1

Describing a MU* Character

The goal of this exercise is to come up with an effective description of your MU* character. As you move through the exercise, think about the ways that your persona as a speaker influences how your messages are perceived. Perform this exercise before beginning major MU* activities so that you will be ready to set your description when you log on for the first time.

Working on your own, come up with several character names that you might use on a MU*. Consider the ways in which a name can influence your persona. For instance, if you call yourself "the brain" because you want to appear as a thoughtful person, will the idea of intelligence be overshadowed by the sense of overstuffed ego that the name carries with it?

Next, come up with descriptions for two names you have selected. First think about the persona you want to project. Then use specific details in your description to convey the appropriate character traits. For instance, if you wanted to project an image of being concerned with intellectual matters, you might "be carrying a laptop and wearing a T-shirt that says 'Eschew Obfuscation.' "

Think about the creative writer's credo: "Show, don't tell!" If you tell the audience that you are "somewhat of a rebel and ready to challenge conservative assumptions," the description will fall flat. If you show them the same idea with concrete detail, it will be stronger: "She is sporting a pierced lip and a tattoo that says 'Question Authority.' "

Take some time to flesh out the description for each character. Keep in mind the general persona that you want to present, then modify this by adding some additional personality traits. You can add a sense of mildness or assertiveness to the description. You can give some physical impressions. You might want to add some personal insights by describing something that shows your own interests. The goal will be to turn the persona into a short composition that you can use to set your character description when you join the MU*.

Actions and Emotes

One additional way in which you can affect a discussion in an IRC or MU* is by taking part in some "physical interactions." For instance, in a MU* discussion about gun control, a character might want to convey the idea that he is worried about his safety because of the spread of handguns.

Instead of just saying this, he might "put on a bullet-proof vest before grabbing his sunglasses and lacing up his walking shoes." Actions and emotes like this enhance the experience of IRC or MU* discussion. Although you can add some energy to these freewheeling discussions by "taking a match to the flag" or "tearing up a copy of the Constitution," performing with emotes or actions isn't exactly suited to developing carefully constructed arguments or convincing your audience that you have covered every angle of a topic.

EXERCISE 11.2

Role Playing

This exercise uses role-playing scenarios to help sharpen your understanding of how the construction of yourself as a speaker influences the perception of your messages and how different situations demand different approaches.

Working with your instructor and your classmates, begin by considering the following scenarios:

1. You are holding a pretrial hearing to determine whether or not a local artist should be indicted for violating community standards of decency. The artist has constructed a statue called "Justice in Chains," which characteristically depicts a figure of Justice wearing a blindfold and holding a scale. However, in this sculpture, she is also naked and wrapped in chains. Behind her, three male figures dressed in business suits are holding the chains. At the debate are members of the city council who will be trying to define the community's standards of decency, lawyers for the state who are trying to send the artist to trial, members of the defense who are trying to prevent the trial, and protesters outside the courtroom.

2. You are at a congressional hearing to determine whether or not broadcast television should be regulated. At issue is a bill that would rate the content of TV shows according to the amount of sex and violence that they contain. Shows that are deemed unsuitable by the board would be required to air after prime time. The committee is holding an open debate before voting on the bill. At the debate are members of the broadcast industry (who oppose the bill), members of the American Civil Liberties Union (who also oppose the bill), members of the Alliance for Families (who are advocating for the bill), and the congressional committee.

Now select a MU* environment in which you can act out these scenarios (your instructor will probably guide you). Assign different roles for yourselves and spend some time thinking about the different investments and motivations that your character is likely to have in the scenario. Log onto the MU* and create your character. Set a description for your character using the "@describe me as" command. Keeping your role in mind, act out one of the scenarios.

Collaborative Structures in MU*s

We've been talking about the ways in which IRC and MU* discussions take on a sense of realism and lead to effective brainstorming and exploration. In MU*s, there is an additional element that contributes to your interactions. Most MU*s contain a number of complex environments that have been constructed by other users. (In **Chapter 16,** we'll talk about some of the design considerations for building MU* spaces.)

In a MU* environment, you are likely to interact with several different kinds of structures. At the largest level, there is the MU* itself. Since most MU*s have a theme, this overriding motif will determine what types of interaction are possible. For instance, when you log onto DragonMud, you will find yourself in eighteenth-century London. This environment will not be especially useful if your class is discussing gun control. However, if you are talking about the history of urban industrialization, the setting may be appropriate. Your instructor will likely determine which tasks you should pursue in which environments, but keep the setting in mind as you work so that you get the most out of what you are doing.

At another level, there are the spaces within the MU*. For example, Diversity University MOO is modeled after a traditional college campus. When you log on, you'll find classrooms, lecture halls, and meeting spaces. These individual rooms are part of the larger MU* structure but can be built by small groups of users or even individuals. This means that as you navigate on a MU*, you will often be moving through a series of different spaces, many of which are designed collaboratively by groups of users.

Within each room or space, individual users can build any number of objects. For instance, in a classroom, a teacher may have constructed a blackboard that displays the daily assignments. A student may have built a tape recorder that keeps track of every person who comes into the space or a trick nickel that squirts dye in the face of anyone who tries to pick it up.

The collaborative nature of MU* spaces makes critical reading of the environment an important skill. Look carefully at all of the descriptions in the environment and think about how the details of these elements add to your experience. Think about the overall motif of the MU* and the descriptions of its rooms and objects. Use the various components within the MU* as a way to gauge authors' purposes. Try also to determine the intended audience for the MU*. For instance, Diversity University MOO is geared toward scholarly interaction. DragonMud provides a place to explore an historical setting. Other MU*s are designed for gaming and socializing. By considering the overall purpose of the spaces you are visiting, you can better understand how the environment influences your interactions and writing.

TIPS AND TACTICS

- Real-time conversations can be fast-paced and cover a wide range of topics. To counter these tendencies, be sure to get a transcript of the sessions and to focus on threads that interest you rather than trying to keep up with the entire discussion.
- Since real-time interactions sometimes lack the social constraints of face-to-face conversations, be sure to write responsibly and avoid participating in unproductive flame wars.
- Use MU* and IRC interactions to refine your understanding of the relationship between audience and speaker. Think of these spaces as laboratories for experimenting with personas and rhetorical situations.
- Spend time getting comfortable with the commands of IRCs and MU*s. Initially, working in these environments can seem awkward, but once this sense has been alleviated, the interactions that you have will be more productive.
- Since MU* spaces are constructed entirely of textual descriptions, be sure to read carefully as you work in these environments.

CHAPTER 12

WIRING THE CLASSROOM

Local Collaboration with E-Mail, Newsgroups, or Web Forums

One of the most practical benefits of taking a course that uses the Internet is that e-mail, newsgroups, and Web forums all provide class members with quick, effective ways to communicate with each other. Whether it's an instructor sending out announcements about coursework, a student asking for help on an assignment, a group of students collaborating on an oral presentation, or an ongoing discussion about an important course theme, electronic technology can make all of these exchanges a great deal easier and more productive. □

Working with E-Mail

Class Lists

Many instructors set up e-mail discussion lists that are specifically designed to keep the members of a class informed and in contact with each other. When a member of the class sends mail to the list, every other

KEY TERMS

Attachments: Files that are encoded and then sent with an e-mail message. The encoded document is "attached" rather than incorporated into the body of the message. The files are then decoded by the recipient's mail-reading client.

E-mail Discussion List: Also known as a "list" or "Listserv." A collection of e-mail addresses managed by a program that allows users to send e-mail to a group of subscribed members.

Newsgroup: A topic-centered forum devoted to discussion and the exchange of articles, news, and other media.

Nickname: A file created with a mail reader that contains one or more e-mail addresses. A message sent to a nickname will be forwarded to every address listed in the file.

Web Forums: Asynchronous message boards on the Web that function like newsgroups. Readers can post and respond to messages, and the conversations are instantly incorporated into the site.

member receives that message. Your instructor might use the list to update class assignments or send out important reminders. Similarly, individual students might use the list to forward any relevant e-mail to the rest of the class or to ask a question about a project or deadline. By allowing you to stay in constant contact with a large group of people, lists make classes run more smoothly. (We should note that nickname files can be used in place of class lists. See the section entitled "Nicknames" on page 161 for more information.)

Joining a List When you join almost any list, there are two e-mail addresses you'll need to know: the address of the mail server and the address of the specific list you want to subscribe to. To subscribe or unsubscribe, you send commands directly to the mail server's address.

Figure 12.1 shows a subscription message to a list named "comp-101" which is run by Majordomo software. (Other forms of discussion list software include Listproc and Listserv, just to name a few.) In this case, the student sent the subscribe command to "majordomo@lists.katmandu.edu", which is the mail server's address. The procedures for subscribing or unsubscribing to different discussion lists vary, so check with your instructor about how to join your class list.

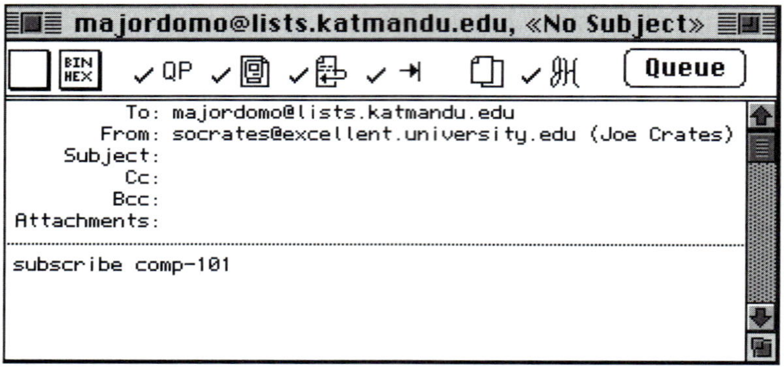

■ **FIGURE 12.1** A Subscription Message to a Majordomo List

Sending a Message to the List Once you are subscribed, to send a message to all the members of the class, you address it to the list name rather than the list server address.

Figure 12.2 shows how a message addressed to the class list can be used to easily get in touch with all of your classmates. Be sure that your message is appropriate for your audience, however. For example, if you are trying to contact your peer reviewer to set up a meeting, the rest of the class may well get annoyed if you send the message to the full list, rather than e-mailing your reviewer personally. It's also a good idea to double-check the recipient's address when sending e-mail messages. If you thought you were moaning to a classmate about the length of your recent paper assignment, you'd really start to sweat when you realized that you had accidentally sent the complaint to the full class list.

■ **FIGURE 12.2** A Message to a Discussion List

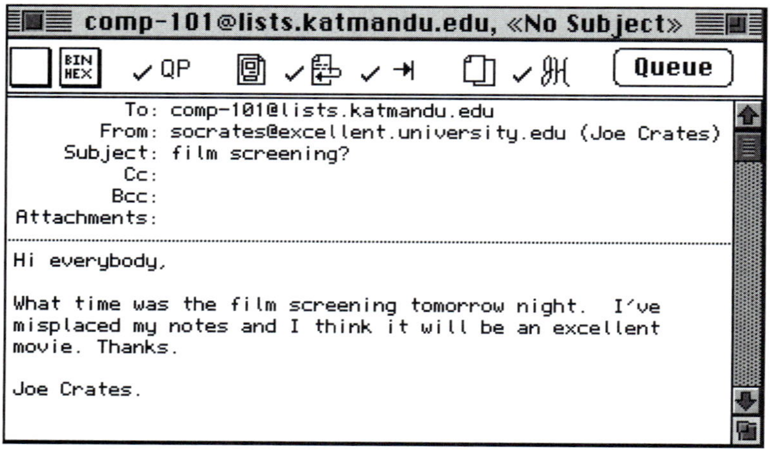

Nicknames

Most mail readers allow users to create nicknames for one or more e-mail addresses. When you send a message to the nickname, it will be forwarded to all of the addresses listed in the nickname file. Nicknames, then, can be used in much the same way as class lists. For instance, if your class doesn't have access to list software, you might set up a nickname called "comp-101" that contains the e-mail addresses of each class member. That way, by sending a message to the nickname "comp-101," you could reach the entire class without having to type in each address separately. Although class lists are generally easier for managing the addresses of larger groups, nicknames are useful for keeping track of your smaller group projects and for frequently used, or hard-to-remember e-mail addresses.

Attachments

Another feature of many mail readers is the ability to send and receive attachments. Attachments are files that are encoded and then sent with an e-mail message. The encoded document is "attached" rather than incorporated into the body of the message. The files are then decoded by the recipient's mail-reading client. Attachments allow you to send any type of file by e-mail. For instance, if you are swapping papers with a peer review partner, you can attach your draft as a Microsoft Word or WordPerfect document. Similarly, if you are working on a collaborative Web project, you might attach graphic files to a message sent to another group member.

Be aware, however, that for attachments to function properly, the person receiving the file must have a compatible program to open the attached file. In other words, if you're going to send a WordPerfect document, make sure that the recipient has WordPerfect software so that she or he can open the file. For word-processed files, you may need to save your paper in a generic format such as RTF (Rich Text Format) to ensure compatibility. Check with your instructor or decide with your collaborators which programs and file formats will be the standards for attached files. Remember also that the recipient will have to download these files, possibly with a slow modem, so think twice before attaching large files and make sure that that the recipient expects and wants the documents.

Clients

Many of the activities that we've been discussing, such as making nicknames and sending attachments, are actually features of mail readers rather than of e-mail itself. You'll probably have access to e-mail clients that run on your institution's mainframe computer (for example, Pine or Elm), but as with most Internet activities, local mail clients such as Eudora Lite (available as freeware) provide you with more options and present a more intuitive interface. (For more information about clients, see the section entitled "Internet Nuts and Bolts: Servers, Clients, and Internet Media" in **Chapter 1** or the *Connections* Web site.)

Working with Newsgroups

Like e-mail, newsgroups can be put to use on a local level. Depending on the facilities at your institution, your instructor may be able to set up a newsgroup for your class. These newsgroups are generally used more for full group discussion than for announcements and day-to-day operations.

Posting and Replying to a Message

Posting a new message to the class newsgroup is fairly straightforward. First, make sure your newsreader is configured with your name and e-mail address so that other users will be able to contact you. Next, log onto the group with your newsreader and select the command for posting a message. Compose your message, then send it on its way. Your message will be posted immediately, but you may need to reopen the group to see it. Of course, the processes will vary depending on your newsreader, so familiarize yourself with the software at your institution.

To reply to a newsgroup posting, you will need to open the message that you want to respond to. Since newsgroups are generally designed to facilitate group discussion, a default reply will probably be sent to the full group, and your message will show up as part of a discussion thread. On most newsreaders, however, you also have the option of replying privately to the author of a message, in which case your reply will be sent to the individual via e-mail.

When you reply to newsgroup postings, the newsreader will generally bring up a field that includes the message to which you are responding set off with angle brackets (>) at the front of every line. You probably won't always want to leave the full text of the previous message within your response, especially if that message is lengthy. Because users try to respond to specific points within previous messages, newsgroup replies are often composed of a series of quotes and commentary:

```
>It seems to me that the curators of the Enola Gay
>exhibit at the Smithsonian were more interested in
```

```
>revising history than celebrating the anniversary
>of the bombing

You may be right, but what's so wrong with this.
History has conveniently ignored the suffering of
the innocent people in Hiroshima and Nagasaki for
years, so correcting this seems like a worthwhile
project

>Dropping the bomb helped end the war and saved
>countless numbers of American soldiers.  We had to
>prove that we had the power in order to convince
>Japan to surrender.

Well, I agree with you that dropping the bomb may
have helped end the war, but this still doesn't mean
that the bomb had to be dropped on inhabited cities
with significant civilian populations.
```

When you "nest" your responses under a previous message, other users will understand exactly which points you are referring to and be better able to follow the conversation, even if they haven't read the previous post.

Practice some of the skills we discuss in **Part 1** as you reply to newsgroup messages. Summarize previous postings or useful information to contextualize your message for the rest of the group. Highlight major points of agreement or disagreement among the various discussion participants. Include passages that are relevant to your own message or that are necessary to fully understand the thread of discussion. In general, try to move the conversation forward by articulating your stance clearly and positioning it in relation to the other voices.

Subscribing to a Set of Groups

One handy feature of most newsreaders is the ability to limit the number of groups you have to see each time you log onto your news server. Most clients will allow you to open a window where you can store only the groups that you use most frequently.

We recommend that you set up a small subscription list like the one shown in Figure 12.3 that contains your class newsgroup and any other groups that you are likely to use frequently. It will speed up your loading time and generally make Usenet newsgroups more manageable.

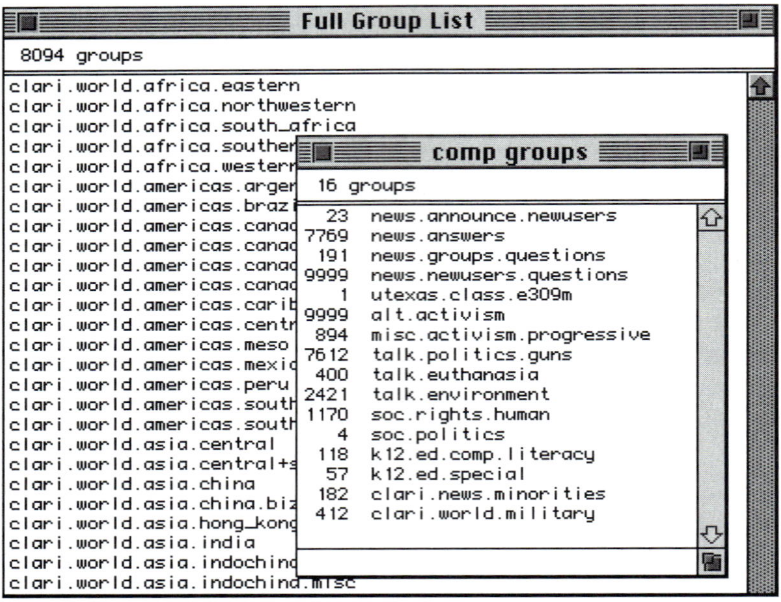

■ **FIGURE 12.3** A Selection of Subscribed Newsgroups

Working with Web Forums

As more and more courses develop class Web sites, Web forums have become increasingly important to class activities. These discussion forums look and act much like newsgroups; users can post and reply to messages from within their class site, and discussions are collected in threads (see Figure 12.4). If your class uses Web forums, you can often gather conversational resources from the messages of your classmates and use the site as an archive for course materials.

Remember, though, that a Web forum will probably be more public than a class newsgroup. Since sites are regularly hit by search engines, and since most forums allow open participation, you are likely to interact with a wider audience when you participate in discussions on the Web.

You should also know that HTML commands will work within most Web forums. This means that when you compose a message, you will be able to use certain formatting tags (such as bold, italics, or lists), include graphics, and create links. This can expand the way that discussions are held, making the class conversation more hypertextual than one carried out over e-mail or on Usenet newsgroups. (See **Chapter 17** for information about composing with HTML.)

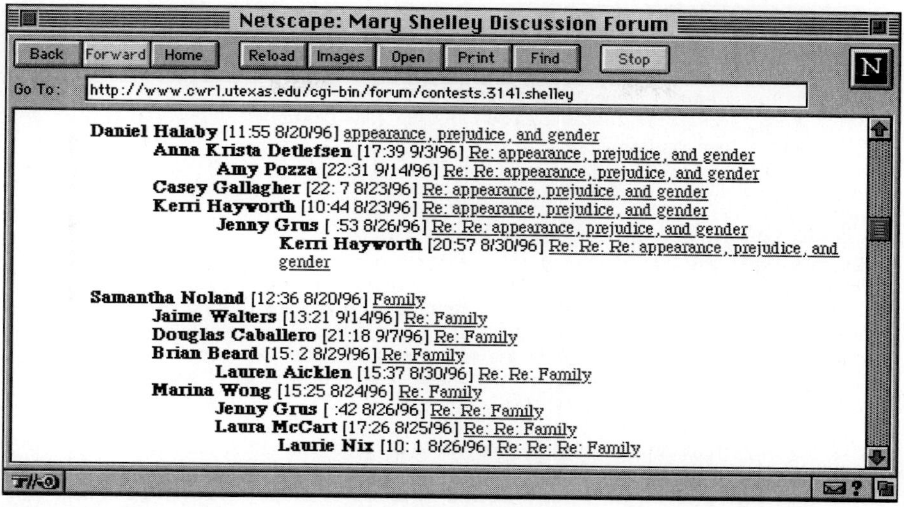

■ **FIGURE 12.4** A Web Message Forum

Reviewing the Work of Your Peers

Electronic Logistics

Internet technology can also help you collaborate with your classmates by facilitating peer critiques. Whether you're using a newsgroup, a Web forum, or e-mail, you can easily trade papers electronically without setting up a time and place to meet. You can also send copies of your peer critiques to the instructor or to other classmates. As you perform electronic peer reviews, keep some things about the medium in mind. Whereas on paper you can quickly circle a missed apostrophe or comma, it is difficult to focus on sentence-level problems on the screen. One tactic is to insert comments within the text of the piece you are reading, as shown in Figure 12.5.

Whether you use boldface, parentheses, or some other convention, weaving your comments into the text will help the author to focus on problem areas. In general, though, try to pay attention to global revisions as you respond to a paper electronically. Focus on the piece's overall organization and coherence rather than the minute details of each sentence or phrase.

Since the nature of Internet communication is especially well-suited to conversational exchange, electronic peer review offers another advantage. When a peer makes a comment about your work, you can write back

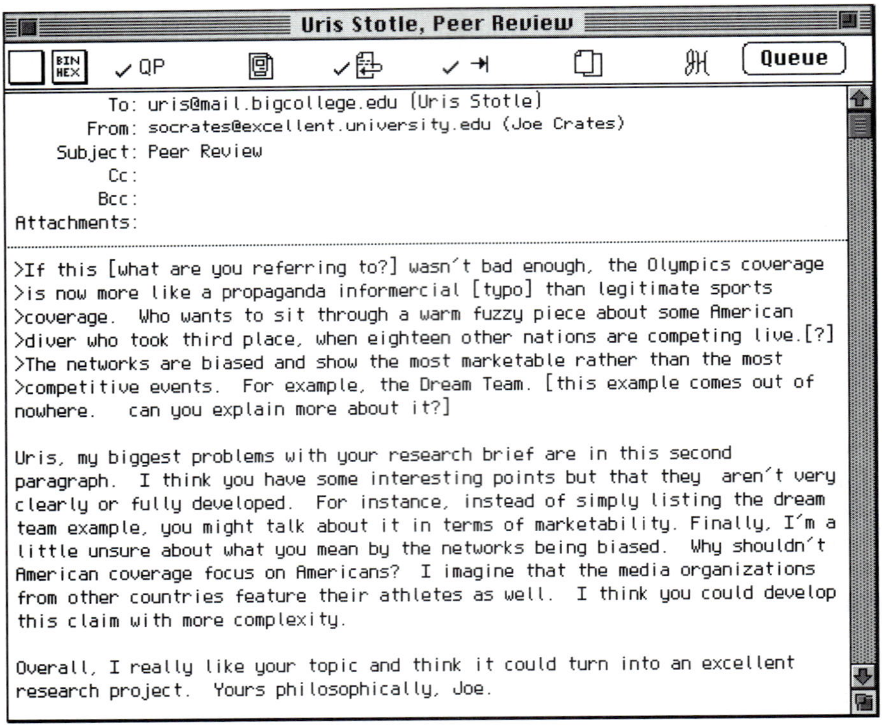
Uris Stotle, Peer Review

Queue

To: uris@mail.bigcollege.edu (Uris Stotle)
From: socrates@excellent.university.edu (Joe Crates)
Subject: Peer Review
Cc:
Bcc:
Attachments:

>If this [what are you referring to?] wasn't bad enough, the Olympics coverage
>is now more like a propaganda informercial [typo] than legitimate sports
>coverage. Who wants to sit through a warm fuzzy piece about some American
>diver who took third place, when eighteen other nations are competing live.[?]
>The networks are biased and show the most marketable rather than the most
>competitive events. For example, the Dream Team. [this example comes out of
nowhere. can you explain more about it?]

Uris, my biggest problems with your research brief are in this second paragraph. I think you have some interesting points but that they aren't very clearly or fully developed. For instance, instead of simply listing the dream team example, you might talk about it in terms of marketability. Finally, I'm a little unsure about what you mean by the networks being biased. Why shouldn't American coverage focus on Americans? I imagine that the media organizations from other countries feature their athletes as well. I think you could develop this claim with more complexity.

Overall, I really like your topic and think it could turn into an excellent research project. Yours philosophically, Joe.

■ **FIGURE 12.5** Nested Peer Review Comments

to ask for clarification, to re-explain your position, or at least to say thanks. Instead of a one-way dismantling of your work, you and your reviewer can start up a conversation about your writing that might continue for the duration of the project.

Productive Discussion and Review

Once you are comfortable with some of the logistics of electronic peer review and discussion, you should also think about some strategies for making those exchanges more productive. Remember that many people find criticism hard to take. Your goal should be to address problem areas without alienating or overwhelming your peers.

As you respond to a classmate's work, be careful to focus on the positions that are taken rather than the personalities associated with them. For instance, instead of saying that a person is naive to believe that animal testing causes only suffering, you might politely point out that experiments have potential medical benefits that might help to end other forms of suffering. If nothing else, this objection should make the author aware of the need to qualify his or her statements and perhaps prompt the author to refute this oppositional argument in a more fully articulated revision.

One helpful way of offering advice is by phrasing criticism in a conditional (if . . . , then) statement. For instance, imagine an author who has failed to provide support for most of his or her points. A reviewer could say, "You don't provide any evidence, so your argument makes no sense" or "If you provide some statistics or cite some studies to support your statements, then your argument will be stronger." The tone of the second critique is much less confrontational than that of the first because it offers suggestions for improvement.

As you review a piece, you should also consider some of the strategies of critical reading that we outline in **Chapter 5,** particularly the tactics of sympathetic and skeptical reading. Initially, try taking a sympathetic approach to a peer's paper. Rather than offering a knee-jerk reaction to the arguments you come across, take some time to hear the person out. Read first with an eye on comprehending the gist of the argument and arriving at some sense of the author's overall purpose. Once you've assessed the author's position, you can perform a more skeptical analysis, focusing on the major problems of the piece.

Similarly, avoid imposing your own agenda on the works that you review. Particularly if you disagree with the position that an author is taking, you should withhold judgment based on your assumptions about the topic and evaluate the argument in terms of its claims, reasoning, and evidence. From your opposing point of view, it will be easy to point out evidence or assumptions that the author has overlooked, but do so with the goal of strengthening the argument that the author is making rather than promoting your own ideas.

Another way to make your criticism more useful is to focus on specifics. Rather than saying, "I find the piece confusing," note the spots that gave you particular trouble. By pointing out that the transition between the first and second sections is awkward or that the third paragraph seems to contradict an earlier statement, you help the author to locate those areas that need the most attention.

Finally, as you review others' work, it is a good idea to offer alternatives whenever possible. You don't want to completely revise the work for the other person; but instead of just pointing out what is wrong, you can often point toward possible solutions. If a paper seems to lack depth, you might suggest that the author limit the scope of the project. Perhaps you could highlight one or two aspects that you found most interesting or relevant and steer the author toward these. If a piece seems incoherent, you might try to pick out the main ideas and suggest that the author revise the project in terms of these specific themes. Providing some alternatives will make your criticism less threatening and help your partner to begin thinking about revision.

Of course, these strategies are simply meant to guide you as you conduct peer reviews. Your topics and assignments will determine the way you approach the work of your peers. But if you try to focus on specifics, offer alternatives, and read with the ultimate goal of improving the author's work, then you should be able to provide worthwhile criticism.

Anatomy of a Student Peer Review

Following is a peer review of a student essay that argues for continued federal funding of paleontological research. Though this peer review represents only one of a number of options for responding to a student draft, we think it offers a reasonable critique of the argument and suggests important revisions for the paper.

> Peer Evaluation for Michael George: Funding Dinosaurs?
>
> Michael, after reading your paper it is obvious that you are for government funding for paleontology. You support your idea by saying that when this money is funded for this project it is always "well spent." You say that this project is beneficial because it provides us with a great deal of knowledge.
>
> Michael, I really like your topic and I find it very interesting. However, I can tell that this paper is something you threw together at the last minute. You provide a good example but that is only part of what you should say in your paper. You don't present or refute the opposing arguments at all. Also, when you imply that other scientific fields aren't as worthy as this one to receive money, you leave yourself open for a major beating from the opposing side. How are you able to judge which scientific field is more or less worthy of receiving the funding. You need to show how paleontology is important and more worthy of government funding.
>
> Another thing you need to work on is your reasoning for why it should receive government funding at all.

```
Simply saying that "the money invested is always
well spent" isn't enough.  Why is it "always well
spent"?

Michael, you really have a great topic, you just
need to go back and take into consideration some of
the points I've mentioned.  Once you get started
you'll have a very interesting paper.
```

Notice how the review begins by laying out the author's basic premise. While the opening avoids critique of the essay by clearly explaining the claims and support given in the paper, it also demonstrates the limitations of the argument. Since the author states only that money for paleontological research "is always well spent," the respondent has used the author's own words to point out the simplicity of this idea. She suggests that the essay lacks sufficient justification and is not specific enough about the scientific rewards of paleontological research.

Overall, the reviewer tries to maintain a sympathetic tone while offering an honest assessment of the essay's problems. She stresses that she finds the topic interesting but that the argument needs development. In particular, the reviewer points out that the author hasn't stated why paleontology is more "worthy of government funding" than other types of scientific research. By highlighting this opposing argument, she shows that the essay will be unconvincing to people who don't automatically see paleontology as a vital field of scientific inquiry.

While the global comments of this review highlight the major flaws in the essay and suggest alternatives, the reviewer might have been more specific in her critique, perhaps pointing out several arguments that would convince her of the merits of funding research in paleontology. Although it's not perfect, this review certainly provides enough thoughtful analysis to help the author revise his essay—the goal of any peer review. In fact, the aspiring paleontologist was ultimately able to support his position by more fully articulating the value of paleontological research and more persuasively justifying the need for continued government funding.

FOR CLASS DISCUSSION

Working in small groups, read the sample research brief below and perform two peer reviews. Choose a recorder to write out the reviews. Think about the suggestions for offering critique that we've been discussing, and experiment by writing one review that ignores those strategies and one that tries to implement them.

In the first review, you can be as critical and unhelpful as you wish. Find as many faults as you can in the brief, and tell the author in blunt, even unsympathetic, terms where she or he has blown it. Don't worry about hurting the author's feelings. In fact, if something seems stupid, you might want to point out just what a bonehead she or he is.

In the second review, try to present your criticisms in as helpful a manner as possible. Note the positive aspects of the brief, and phrase your criticisms with specific comments that are targeted at the brief instead of the author. Decide whether it would be more helpful to focus on global issues of organization or particular problems with the argument. Present possible alternatives and helpful suggestions for strengthening the piece.

When you have finished, compare the two critiques. List the strategies for review that you think would be the most helpful if it were your paper under the microscope. If you can think of any additional strategies, share them with your classmates.

Here is the sample research brief to be analyzed.

Research Brief on the Commercialization of the Olympics

Every four years an unprecedented event occurs. The best people in their fields come together to display their talents on a world stage. The races are fierce and the rewards are large. The competition, of course, is for the consumer dollar and the events are the 30 and 60 second ads which air during the Olympics.

If this wasn't bad enough, the Olympics coverage is now more like a propaganda infomercial than legitimate sports coverage. Who wants to sit through a warm fuzzy piece about some American diver who took third place, when eighteen other nations are competing live. The networks are biased and show the most marketable rather than the most competitive events. For example, the Dream Team.

Finally, their is the merchandising. How many logos do the athletes need to wear? Why are there so many billboards around the stadiums?

```
If the people wanted to be distracted by more
ads, they could just stay home and watch TV

I'm not trying to argue that people shouldn't
make a buck.  But when marketing begins to be
the feature presentation, we begin to wonder
just what the spirit of the games is.
```

TIPS AND TACTICS

- Using e-mail can greatly simplify your communications, but it can be frustrating when you first begin. Be sure to spend time early in the semester getting comfortable with discussion list operations, with sending and replying, and with attachments and nicknames.
- Use e-mail lists or nicknames as a way of keeping in touch with classmates and/or the instructor. Newsgroups and Web forums may be more useful for extended class discussions.
- Use electronic exchanges to practice the skills of summarizing and synthesizing information. Rather than just reproducing an earlier message, pick out and respond to the most relevant passages.
- When conducting peer reviews, focus on the piece, not the personality. Point out specific problems and try to offer alternatives and other suggestions for improvement.

CHAPTER 13

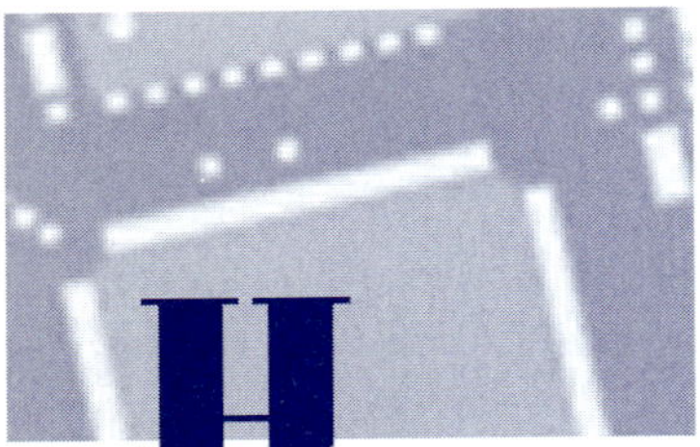

HIT 9 FOR AN OUTSIDE LINE

Dialing Long Distance with Newsgroups, E-Mail Discussion Lists, and Web Forums

One of the things that we stress throughout this book is the need to expand the number of perspectives that we consider when thinking about an issue. For this purpose, Usenet newsgroups, e-mail discussion lists, and Web forums may be the best resources on the Net. This chapter concentrates on how you can join the conversations that you find on newsgroups, lists, and Web forums as a way of honing your critical reading skills and learning to write as a member of a particular "knowledge community." □

Considering Multiple Perspectives

The Nature and Diversity of Newsgroups and Discussion Lists

The wide range of topics and the very specific nature of individual groups on Usenet mean that there are often multiple forums devoted to similar topics, allowing users to join the groups in which they feel most comfort-

KEY TERMS

Accommodation: The process of incorporating and addressing opposing points of view in your arguments.

Assumptions: The premises on which any claim is based. As the term "assumption" suggests, these premises are usually unstated.

Critical Reading: An approach to analyzing messages that looks at both their successes and their failures. Critical reading considers texts in terms of their purposes, contexts, and media and evaluates them by examining their component parts.

Flame: A personal attack, usually sent via e-mail or on a newsgroup, that offers little or no constructive critique.

Newsgroup: A topic-centered forum devoted to discussion and the exchange of articles, news, and other media.

Purpose: The motives that compel a speaker to present a message to a specific audience in a particular way. Purpose also refers to the particular goals that an author has in mind at any stage of the writing process.

Thread: An initial posting to an e-mail discussion list, newsgroup, or Web forum followed by a series of replies that build on each other to form a conversation.

Usenet: An extensive collection of public-access newsgroups. Most universities and colleges are connected to Usenet rather than to private or commercial bulletin boards.

able. For instance, postings to **rec.pets.cats** may look at the lighter side of pet ownership, while messages sent to **talk.politics.animals** may be more serious. Note, however, that there will probably be a high degree of overlap between the two groups. People on **rec.pets.cats** are likely to be personally invested in debates about animal testing and users on **talk.politics.animals** may sometimes get the urge to discuss stupid cat tricks.

Although it's harder to quickly get a sense of the range of topics covered by e-mail discussion lists, the chances are that if you have an interest in an issue or field, there is an e-mail list that addresses it. For instance, performing a keyword search for the topic "Indonesia" at the **LISZT** directory (**http://liszt.com**) of e-mail discussion groups produced information about thirty-two different e-mail lists, including lists geared toward Indonesian issues and human rights activism in Indonesia. Like newsgroups, discussion lists are composed of individuals who are committed to the topic of the group. In fact, since lists require that users subscribe to them and since participants must actively sort through the conversations that take place by reading daily e-mail, discussion lists often require a higher degree of investment on the part of members than newsgroups do.

Throughout this chapter, we treat newsgroups, e-mail discussion lists, and Web forums somewhat interchangeably. Because each of these media can be used to facilitate similar types of collaboration, the principles that we discuss apply to all three. However, since Usenet often illustrates collaborative concepts more clearly and may require less effort for you to explore, we generally draw our examples from newsgroups.

Threads and Positions

Newsgroups can help you to see the way that positions are modified as they move through a process of dialog. When a message is challenged, seconded, or refuted by a responding message, threads of discussion develop. For instance, Figure 13.1 shows a thread about racism in Joseph Conrad's novel *Heart of Darkness,* which developed on a class Web forum.

■ **FIGURE 13.1** A Discussion Thread on a Web Forum

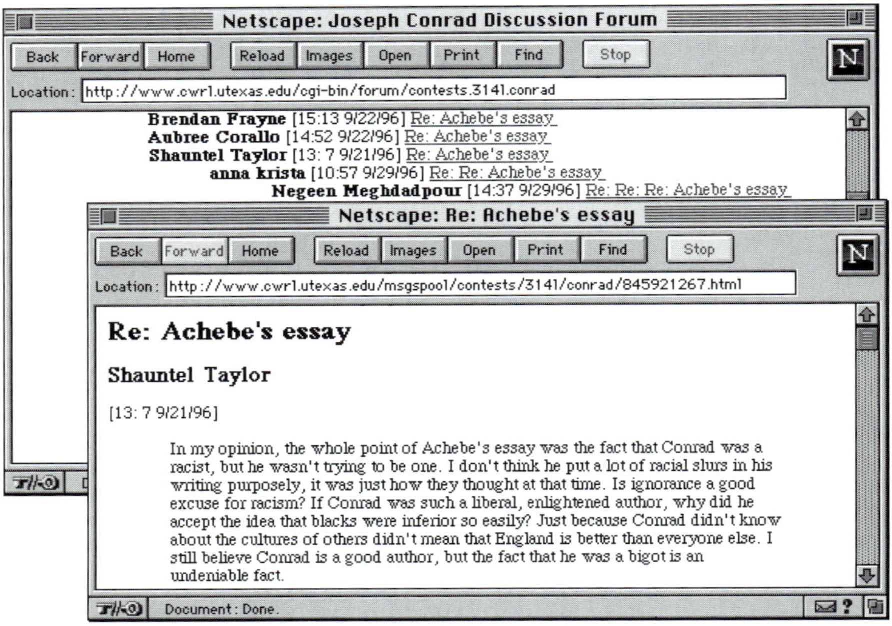

Focusing on a well-known critique of Conrad's novel by the Nigerian writer Chinua Achebe, the message by Shauntel Taylor sparked a debate that took the conversation in several new directions.

As we can see from Figure 13.1, Taylor poses some interesting questions about Conrad's intentions. She asks, "Is ignorance a good excuse for racism?" Her question is taken up in the following post by Anna Krista:

> I agree--ignorance is not a good excuse for racism. However, I tend to feel that Achebe, by focusing on this aspect of the novel, may have missed out on what was really being said/ pointed out by Conrad. I think that Conrad was trying to legitimately make some observations about the human spirit and tendencies...and I can't help but feel that Achebe tried to turn it into a "black/white" issue, when it really wasn't (in my opinion). I'm not saying that Achebe's observations weren't legitimate...I just feel that he was, himself, being a bit "racist", when he seemingly closed his eyes to Conrad's ideas (the main ones), just because there may have been contemporary controversial undertones. And the fact that he dismissed Conrad's novel, using that reasoning, really bothers me. It makes me see him as more close-minded than Conrad.

Krista accepts Taylor's suggestion that ignorance is not an excuse for racism, but she objects to Achebe's insistence on race as a central issue in the novel. She even goes so far as to turn Achebe's critique on itself, calling him "close-minded" and "racist."

After Negeen Meghdadpour seconds Krista's argument, writing, "I feel that Achebe was being a bit racist himself by finding all of the underlying reasons to call Conrad a racist," Elana Horowitz chimes in with a defense of Achebe's article. She writes:

> I really enjoyed Achebe's essay thoroughly. It gave me an entirely different perspective on the book. I do not think that Conrad was a racist,per say. However I do think that his way of unimportantly viewing minorities (like many of his contemporaries) constitutes racism. I wholeheartedly agree with Achebe's theory that Heart of Darkness merely uses Africa (inclusive of Africans) as a backdrop for the real point at issue - the degredation of the human

> mind. This plotline could have taken place anywhere - and with anything(The Irish Potatoe Famine could have even been a backdrop). To prove this point further, the movie _Apocalypse Now_ uses the same central idea, but in a different country and with a diffrerent "minority" or "other"--the Vietnamese. I do not think Conrad's intention was to spur such a huge discussion on racism, but on human morality itself. However, he does not succeed in doing so because the whole plotline of the deterioration of Kurtz's sanity and morality is underplayed by the "racist" undertones. Maybe this novel really WAS once a good look into the human mind, but I do not agree with critics who herald it as "one of the best short stories ever written in the English language."

Here, Horowitz picks up on Krista's suggestion that "Conrad was trying to legitimately make some observations about the human spirit and tendencies." Horowitz agrees that Conrad intended *Heart of Darkness* to be a psychological exploration of "human morality" but counters Krista's claim by arguing that the novel's racism undercuts the value of those psychological observations.

When you post your own messages to newsgroups, discussion lists, or Web forums, be prepared for this kind of give and take to develop. If someone raises a legitimate objection to your points, you should probably try to accommodate that perspective in any further posts. If someone is confused about what you mean, you can elaborate on your idea or try to be more specific about the way you present your information. Sometimes conversations will become heated, but in general, the process of clarification resulting from these dialogs will only make your writing stronger.

Critical Reading and Conversation

Our society places a high value on written documents. Written contracts, policies, procedures, and documentation all receive a kind of legitimacy that verbal agreements lack in our culture. Although the notion of trusting all printed texts is absurd, people still tend to grant written materials, especially those that are published, a measure of respect simply by virtue of their status as printed texts.

However, the authority of written texts becomes even more problematic on the Net. Although newsgroups and lists are forums for conversation, every exchange is a written text. Since electronic forums make it clear that we can no longer grant credibility to messages simply because they are printed (an idea that we should be critical of anyway), we need to find other methods of assessing reliability.

One strategy is to evaluate a message in terms of the group's ongoing dialog about particular issues. If a message is one of many postings in a thread, be sure to read the other posts to develop a more complete sense of the different perspectives being put forward. You can then evaluate any particular message by placing it in the context of the other posts. Never ignore a response that raises an important objection. Evaluate whether it undermines the fundamental principles of the original message or offers only a surface critique that can be easily refuted.

If a message stands alone in a group—that is, if a thread of conversation does not develop from it—you might ask yourself why. How likely is it that this one posting has been able to produce the final word about its topic? If there are no responses, is it because this is an issue that most group members are not interested in? Don't discount a lone post, but since it won't have been refined through the process of dialog, question it with added care.

If a post that you think has merit is being challenged by the other members of the group, consider the investments that the various participants may have in the matter. This will mean taking the time to critically examine the grounds on which the message is being critiqued. You might go back and look through previous controversies to get a sense of whether the regular group members have developed a rapport that goes beyond any particular issue or topic. Since some members seem to automatically disagree with each other regardless of the topic, what at first seems like a violent objection may need to be analyzed in the context of the specific conversational community.

If the larger conversation about an issue seems to be taking a turn that you find questionable, think again about the various speakers who are driving the thread. What affiliations or motivations might they have? Also consider the larger purposes of the group. Groups tend to develop collective personalities; for instance, some groups may be more conservative or more liberal than others. You'll want to familiarize yourself with the general character of the group before you evaluate a post solely on the basis of the responses that it generates.

EXERCISE 13.1

Critically Evaluating a Newsgroup

The goal of this exercise is to evaluate the tone and character of a newsgroup. In small groups, choose a fairly active newsgroup that is discussing a controversial topic. First, spend some time reading through the messages. You probably won't be able to read them all, but try to get as good a sampling as time will permit. As you analyze the group, consider the following questions. Then, focusing on these criteria and any others that you find appropriate, write a paragraph or two describing the key characteristics of the group.

- What are the issues in which the group seems most interested?
- Does the group seem to have a particular "take" on these issues? In other words, does there seem to be an overriding political philosophy?
- Does there seem to be a healthy exchange of ideas going on, or does the debate seem rather one-sided?
- What kinds of assumptions do the group members share?
- Are there any major players who seem to be regulars in the group? Do they tend to agree with each other, or do they seem to be in different camps about most issues?

Composing the Post

Posting with a Purpose

The act of conversation obviously entails more than just reading messages and evaluating groups. To reap the full benefits of these on-line communities, you'll need to add your own voice to their discussions. Before joining any kind of on-line conversation, though, consider what kind of feedback you are hoping to receive. Are you looking for particular sources of information? Are you trying out an idea? Do you want to open a debate by beginning a new discussion thread?

Your purpose will in large part dictate the kind of message you send, the manner in which you send it, and the groups or lists that you send it to. Of course, your goals may change during an extended conversation—you may start off looking for information and become embroiled in a fascinating discussion. But if you consider your purpose as you post each message, you will be better able to communicate your ideas at each stage along the way.

Soliciting Information Remember that lists and newsgroups are often composed of knowledgeable users who can refer you to important print and on-line resources or provide expertise themselves about a topic. Messages that request information or research materials, then, are quite common on many groups. Before you post such a query, however, you should try to make certain that your request is appropriate.

- Check the FAQ of the group in which you wish to post in order to verify that the list or newsgroup allows student research queries. Also make sure that your question hasn't already been answered in the FAQ.
- Try searching the archives of Usenet groups with AltaVista (**http://www.altavista.com**) or DejaNews (**http://www.dejanews.com**) to find earlier messages that may provide you with the information you are looking for.
- Post queries that can be answered only by the collective expertise of the group. Don't expect other users to do your research for you. Posting queries that could easily be answered by a trip to the library will generally produce either flames, or no results at all.

For a more comprehensive discussion of posting research queries, see **Chapter 8.**

Receiving Feedback on Your Position As you move through the composition process, you will often want feedback about some of your ideas or information. Posting messages to lists or groups can be a valuable method for testing the specifics of your argument on an interested, well-informed audience.

- As you gather your research materials, you could send out a message trying to verify an odd or anomalous piece of information that you have come across.
- Later, you might post a message advancing the basic tenets of your thesis and providing a sketchy outline of the evidence you plan to use. This way you could receive useful feedback before you begin drafting the piece.
- You might also try posting your material as you approach a final draft. You could either post the full piece or (especially if the piece is lengthy) summarize your argument to give your audience a good idea about the scope of your project. Requests for editing or proofreading comments would in most cases be inappropriate, but you could certainly ask for feedback about the quality and accuracy of your evidence, any problems with the logical structure of the argument, and/or any positions that you may have misrepresented or overlooked.

Ideally, you'll be able to use the on-line audience as a kind of sounding board to help generate new ideas and lead you toward promising resources. But don't expect the responses to always offer positive, constructive feedback. Especially on highly charged issues, you are likely to receive some rather harsh criticism. If you take these critiques for what they're worth, however, you can strengthen your arguments by incorporating opposing points of view into your project.

Selecting the Appropriate Group

One of the most important steps in the process of posting to a list or newsgroup is choosing a group that suits your needs. (See **Chapter 8** for information on how to find different types of e-mail lists and newsgroups.) When posting to a newsgroup, list, or Web forum, you probably want to target groups that have a reasonably high level of traffic and that are geared toward discussion rather than distributing news and information.

Generally speaking, there will be more than one list or group that is directly related to your topic. Since spamming (sending the same posting to multiple groups) is heavily frowned on by most Internet users, you should try to target the group or groups that are most appropriate for your purpose. Familiarize yourself with the group before you begin posting. You may find that the discussion is either too simplistic or too sophisticated for your needs.

Also, think about the group's scope. If you are just beginning to work through an issue, you may want to target groups with a broader focus. For instance, if you were writing a paper about human rights abuses, you might begin by asking for information from the broad group **soc.rights.human**. As you move further along in your writing process, you might decide to focus specifically on the human rights violations of the transnational corporation Freeport McMoRan in Indonesia. At this point, although you would still be likely to receive useful feedback from **soc.rights.human**, you might be able to find even more specific commentary about the region by sending a message to **soc.culture.indonesia**.

Anticipating and Accommodating the Opposition

Before you post, study your audience as a way of anticipating hostile or oppositional responses to your messages. For example, if you're writing to **rec.pets** about the advantages of owning a cat in an apartment, you might anticipate receiving replies from canine lovers who insist that owning a small dog is a better option. To capsize these objections before the poodle crowd has even launched them, you could accommodate their opposition in your own argument.

Since the arguments on either side of many debates are often well rehearsed (like those made by cat and dog lovers), you should be able to anticipate and declaw the major points that your opponents will raise. To those who would argue that dogs make better companions because they are more lively and affectionate, you might stress the importance of self-reliance for a pet that is cooped up inside all day. You could argue that while a cat will get just as lonely, a dog is much more likely to eat your favorite pair of shoes out of frustration and boredom.

There are times, however, when you'll need to concede certain points to the opposition in order to refute the larger argument. For instance, even cat lovers would have to concede that dogs make better protectors. But after conceding that point, the feline faction could claim that an effective watchdog would have to be a fairly large, aggressive animal and that it would be difficult to keep such a big dog in a small apartment. By conceding that dogs can be better protectors, the cat owners do two important things to bolster their argument. First, they enhance their credibility by presenting themselves as open-minded speakers. Second, the cat camp refutes the watchdog argument in a logical, rational manner, arguing persuasively that cats can be more appropriate in many circumstances.

When you're accommodating an oppositional argument, you should also focus on shared assumptions. For instance, it would be a mistake to argue that cats make better apartment pets because they hunt for themselves and therefore have a better chance of survival when left unattended for several weeks. Your audience in **rec.pets** will almost certainly assume that you're too sadistic to be giving advice about animals. For this audience, you'll want to stay focused on upholding the values of high-quality pet care. An argument that appreciates shared assumptions and successfully anticipates and accommodates opposing points of view is likely to be very convincing.

Posting with Your Audience in Mind

When you are posting to the Net, the voice that you adopt will also influence the overall success of your message. Generally speaking, your posts will generate more response if you follow a few basic guidelines:

- You can't force people to respond to your messages. When you probe the Net for feedback, you are asking other users to do you a favor; remember to be courteous and polite in your requests.
- Try to announce your purpose up front. If you are looking for a specific kind of resource, say so in your post. If you are interested in polling other group members on an issue, make it clear what kinds of responses you are hoping to gather.
- Be concise and to the point, but try to provide your audience with enough information to offer constructive feedback. This may mean going into some detail about the kinds of sources you are already familiar with, or it may mean providing a summary that outlines not only your thesis, but also some of the evidence you are planning to use.

Additionally, consider the character of your audience as you determine the tone that your message should take. For instance, if you were pursuing your research about Freeport McMoRan's mining operations in Indonesia, the group **soc.culture.indonesia** might be able to provide you with some specifics about the situation in that country that you couldn't find on the more general group, **soc.rights.human**. After reading through these groups, however, you might find that **soc.culture.indonesia** tends to be a little more politically conservative than **soc.rights.human**. As you write your posts, then, you may want to save any scathing political critique of Freeport McMoRan for the broader **soc.rights.human** and concentrate on asking questions related specifically to the region of Irian Jaya, where Freeport's mining operations are located, when you post to **soc.culture.indonesia**. This way, the audience in each group is likely to be receptive to your messages.

EXERCISE 13.2

Composing an Appropriate Post

Working in small groups or by yourself, choose a fairly active newsgroup that is discussing a controversial topic. After first evaluating the character of the group (it might be a good idea to use the same group that you evaluated in Exercise 13.1), consider what stance you would take on the controversy. Next, write a message that outlines your position. Refer to the following prompts as you compose your post:

- First, make a decision about what you want to achieve with a post to this group. What is your purpose?
- How can you tailor your message to address the most active discussion on the group?
- Judging from previous posts, are there subjects that you should avoid? Or are there ways of addressing those touchy issues without offending or angering group members?
- After considering the character of the group, what kinds of opposition might your posting meet? How might you accommodate the opposition? Are there any points you'll need to concede? How might you refute their major claims?
- How can you establish common ground between yourself and the group members? What assumptions do you share with them that would allow for productive dialog?
- What kind of tone seems most appropriate?

After answering these questions, write a draft of your post. Next describe the character of your group to the class and read your post aloud. As a full class, discuss the strengths and weaknesses of each post and determine how best to revise them. If you are interested in your topic, go ahead and revise the message, then post it. You'll be able to judge its effectiveness by the kinds of feedback you receive.

Handling Feedback

Once you've posted some messages, you'll need to think about how to handle the feedback that you will receive. Obviously there's no single "right" way to do this; quite a bit will depend on the kinds of responses you get. In most cases, however, it is considered good practice to respond to any replies that your messages generate. This may mean thanking users who gave helpful advice or critique, answering any questions that may have arisen about your post, clarifying any confusion it may have caused, or perhaps defending the validity of your position against attacks from the opposition. In these responses, try to maintain the same level of courteous, professional discourse that you used in your initial post. Fanning flames with further personal attacks will almost certainly be unproductive, whereas a measured response that uses logic and evidence to refute a position may initiate a more serious debate.

TIPS AND TACTICS

- Newsgroups and Web forums require considerably less investment than e-mail discussion lists. If you're planning to use a list, be sure to allow extra time to get comfortable with the group.
- One way to study individual messages is to examine their relationship to the larger thread of discussion. By reading messages within their context, you can get a better idea of how the audience has reacted to them.
- Evaluate messages in light of the overall personality of the group, paying close attention to the affiliations and tendencies of regular users.
- When posting, choose groups that match your purpose. Always assess the character of the group and try to appeal to the group's shared assumptions.
- Anticipate and accommodate opposition perspectives in your posts.
- Be sure to post at various stages during your writing process and respond to any feedback that you receive. Also, respect the time and conventions of the communities you are conversing with.

CHAPTER 14

STIRRING THE POT

Mixing Media on the Web

To this point, **Part 3** has explored Internet collaboration primarily in terms of the interpersonal contacts facilitated by on-line conversation and interaction. To conclude **Part 3** and begin the transition into **Part 4,** however, we'd like to examine some of the technological convergences that are taking place on the World Wide Web, a medium that can be thought of as inherently collaborative because of the ways in which it mixes media, shares information, and unifies communications technologies. □

Technological Convergences: The Process of Unifying Internet Media

Multimedia

The technological convergences that we're talking about are perhaps most visible in the preponderance of multimedia found on the Web. You'd have to do quite a bit of searching these days to find a Web page

KEY TERMS

Chat: A colloquial term that is used to describe any of the various methods for real-time conversations on the Internet.

Common Gateway Interface (CGI): Programs that allow browsers to submit information to the Web server. CGIs are actually a combination of an interface that permits the sharing of information and a script that manipulates that information. Web forums and add-link scripts are common examples of CGIs.

Hypertext: A composition that links pieces of information (often called "nodes") together into complex, interactive webs.

Link: (1) As a noun, the connection between sections, or nodes, of a hypertext. Often, links are activated by clicking on "hot text" or icons. (2) As a verb, the process of connecting pieces of information into a hypertextual form.

Multimedia: (1) The combination of two or more forms of media in a project. (2) Also used to describe any file in a nontext format, such as sound, graphic, video, or animation files.

Node: One unit of a hypertext. A node can be a document, a graphic, a sound file, or any other individual piece of information that has been linked to a hypertext.

that doesn't include at least a few multimedia elements. Graphics, backgrounds, and colors have become almost universal on the Web, and it is more and more common for Web builders to use sound clips, video clips, and special programs such as Java Applets to enhance the presentation of their pages. Because of these new opportunities, the creative possibilities of mixing media and presentation styles on the Web seem to expand every day.

Web multimedia development is due in part to increased access to multimedia design technologies such as scanners, video and sound capture stations, and high-end digital editing software. But these technologies are often too expensive for the average Web user, limiting their impact to some degree. What is actually driving the explosion of multimedia on the Web is the way authors freely share graphics, sounds, and video clips, allowing other users to integrate these files into their own compositions. Figure 14.1 shows an imagemap that incorporates image icons gathered from the Web.

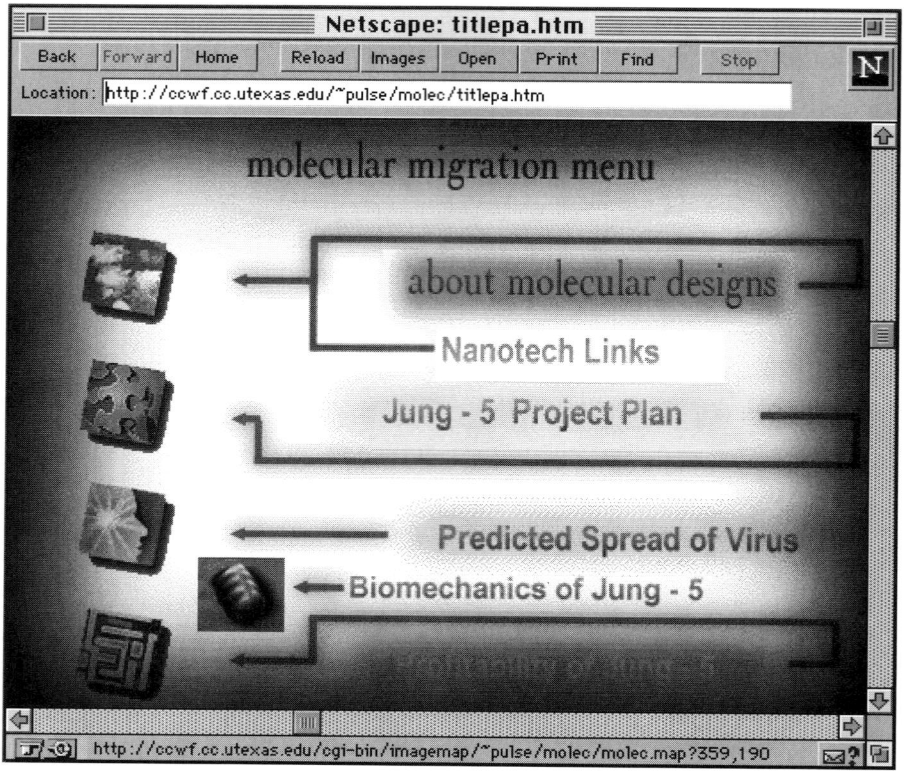

■ **FIGURE 14.1** A Student Multimedia Project

Additionally, the operating protocols of the Web itself make it simple for anyone with a graphical browser to download multimedia files to their local machines. A large percentage of these files, then, have been recycled (perhaps edited, perhaps simply reposted), meaning that the Web is not only the largest multimedia building environment in the world, but also the largest communal repository of multimedia resources. Obviously, this raises some serious questions about copyright laws and intellectual property, but because files are so easily shared, multimedia experimentation on the Web is quite often a collaborative exercise. (See **Chapter 6** and **Appendix 3** for discussions of copyright issues.)

Media Convergences

Perhaps equally remarkable is the Web's ability to subsume and unify what had once been separate Internet media. Technologies such as e-mail, newsgroups, IRCs, MU*s, Gopher, and FTP are increasingly being incorporated into the interface of Web browsers.

What this means for you is that separate mail readers, newsreaders, and FTP clients may soon be obsolete. Already Web clients provide simple interfaces for browsing FTP and Gopher sites and usable ones for managing e-mail and reading Usenet newsgroups. See, for example, the Netscape newsreading interface shown in Figure 14.2. Additionally, browsers now include chat functions that connect them to IRC lines, Web interfaces for navigating on MU*s (like the one shown in Figure 14.3), and more advanced communications technologies such as videoconferencing.

As more of these features are woven into the structure of the Web, user collaboration and interaction will become increasingly common. By expanding the number of available forums in which Net users can communicate and by allowing those forums to be connected in previously impossible ways, the Web has the potential to become the central Internet medium through which groups and individuals interact.

■ **FIGURE 14.2** Reading Newsgroups with a Web Browser

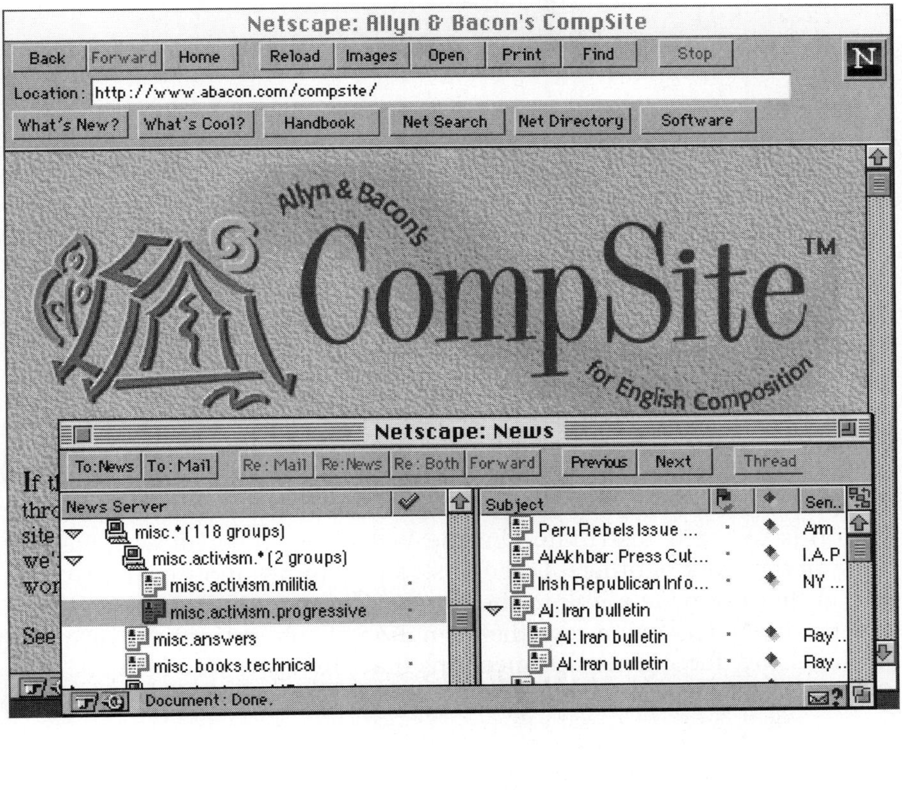

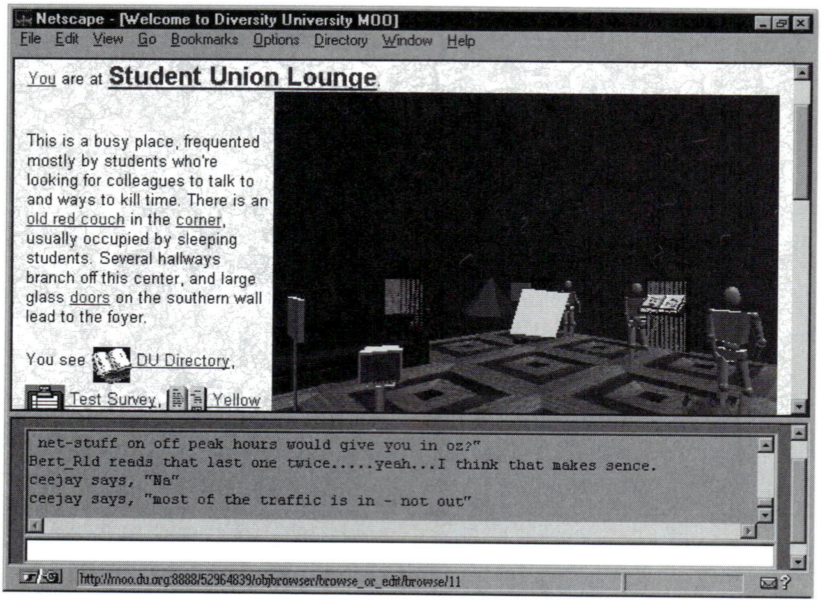

FIGURE 14.3 Navigating a MU* with a Web Browser

Hypertext as a Collaborative Medium

Hypertexts are compositions that link pieces of information together in complex interactive webs, often incorporating sound, graphics, and video. Instead of presenting information in a linear fashion, hypertexts organize materials into a series of interconnected units or nodes. Rather than beginning with the first paragraph, for instance, and proceeding through the document until the end, a reader navigates through a hypertext by selecting which nodes to follow and in what order.

Perhaps more important for our purposes, hypertext offers authors a tremendous amount of flexibility to make connections between pieces of information. For example, Web authors can provide links to any of their own documents or to other relevant sites on the Net. Because information is so easily distributed on the Web, these links allow writers to draw on the work of others. Often, instead of simply quoting and citing a text, authors provide a link to the source document in its entirety. Thus hypertextual pages encourage the formation of connections across multiple areas and documents—connections that often give web compositions a sense of collective authorship.

Figure 14.4 shows a student Web page that incorporates a number of links to outside sources. The project weaves various sources into a single hypertext, illustrating our notion that knowledge is inherently communal and collaborative. Our understandings evolve as we see the various connections, contradictions, and ambiguities that complicate a topic; Our thinking shifts and develops as we come into contact with new issues, people, books, articles, advertisements, and arguments. Hypertext, then, can be seen as a conceptual model of knowledge itself because it makes explicit some of the connections between the many pieces of information which contribute to any idea.

There is also a degree to which the writer and reader collaborate to make meaning out of the hypertext. An author must provide links in a way that gives the reader intuitive choices. Similarly, the reader's choices fundamentally influence the way that the document is perceived. Each reader may move through the nodes of a document in a different order. In a sense, readers take the choices provided by an author and create their own versions of the text. (For more information about issues related to hypertextual composition and navigation, see **Chapter 19.**)

■ **FIGURE 14.4** A Web Page Integrating Links to Outside Information

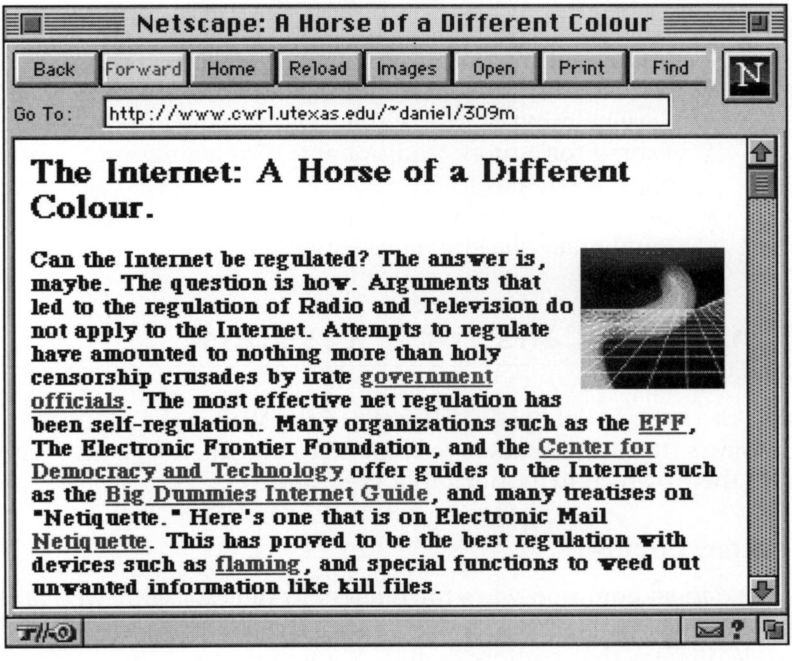

EXERCISE 14.1

Exploring Collaboration on the Web

The object of this exercise is to isolate and evaluate the collaborative elements of a Web site. In small groups or as a full class, choose a Web site to work with. If you don't have a URL in mind, we suggest looking at the Computer Writing and Research Lab's site (**http://www.cwrl.utexas.edu**).

Choose a recorder to take notes, and after spending some time browsing through the available materials, develop a list of as many collaborative elements on the site as you can find. Consider these prompts as you brainstorm about your list:

- Is the site a product of multiple authors?
- Does it link to other sites on the Web?
- Does it contain multimedia? Does it incorporate other Internet technologies such as e-mail, newsgroups, or FTP?
- Are there places where readers can contribute? If so, what kinds of contributions can they make?

After making this list, discuss the pros and cons of the site's collaborative features.

- What are the benefits of having multiple authors and including multiple documents?
- Were there times when the collaborative elements became overwhelming or distracting? Did you ever find yourself wishing for a more traditional text or a single authoritative voice? If so, why?
- Can you think of any additional collaborative features that would make the site more valuable?

Writing That Calls for a Response

Perhaps the most collaborative element of the Web is the ability to compose projects that allow readers to respond to a work, hold conversations, and add their own contributions to a Web site.

Response Forms

One of the most common ways for readers to interact with Web authors is by providing feedback about Web pages via an e-mail response form. Web style dictates that authors include their name and e-mail address on their pages so that any reader can submit comments. This function is so integral to the way that readers respond to Web compositions that many sites rely on mail forms, small programs that allow authors to prompt readers for specific types of feedback. In addition, many browsers will support a <MAILTO> command, which sends mail to Web authors. Since readers can easily contact Web authors, composition need no longer be limited to one-way delivery of information.

Common Gateways and Interactions

HTML, the scripting language that is used to create Web pages, supports a certain amount of hypertextual building (linking texts and using multimedia, for example), but it is really nothing more than a simple formatting language. Common Gateway Interfaces (CGIs) are programs run by Web servers that are written in more sophisticated computer languages (such as Perl or C++), meaning that they can handle complicated tasks. These CGIs make the Web more interactive and collaborative.

For instance, CGIs are used to create Web message forums. Similar to newsgroups, these discussion forums let readers comment publicly and exchange ideas about the content and issues at a site. When you post a message to a Web discussion forum, the CGI script processes the information and rewrites one of the pages that resides on the Web server. Thus the messages that are entered become a permanent part of the site and a record of the learning process there.

Another useful CGI script allows readers to add links to an existing Web page. By filling out a form, users submit the URL of a relevant site and perhaps a brief annotation to the CGI script, which then incorporates the link into the Web page. This provides an opportunity for the entire Web community to contribute to the construction of a site and highlights yet another way in which the Web is moving increasingly toward collaborative composition.

However, we should offer one note of caution about CGIs. Because these scripts are programmed to perform a specific task on a specific machine, they are somewhat less transferable than many other Web functions. CGIs can be shared, but to adapt them, you will need to find out how your server is set up, and you will probably need to know a little bit about programming. If you are interested in experimenting with CGIs, we recommend that you contact someone at your institution who is knowledgeable about your server and have that person walk you through the process.

Whiteboards and Chat

Even as we write this chapter, the possibilities for collaborating via the Internet are evolving. Many of these changes are being driven by Web browser developers who are creating new programs that let users talk, share written messages, work with shared programs, or compose on collaborative whiteboards. The whiteboard from Netscape's Communicator, is shown in Figure 14.5. With programs such as Communicator, users can register their name and Internet address with a central server, and other users on the Net can contact them to exchange voice messages, graphics, and other types of information, all in real time. These programs even contain answering machines, so someone can leave you a message if you're not at the computer. Microsoft's NetMeeting performs similar functions with the added benefit that multiple users can operate a single program at the same time. Users can log on and watch as you perform operations, or they can take over the controls as two or more people work collaboratively with a single application.

Collective Action

The goal of all persuasive writing is to convince an audience to think or feel a certain way. Often, though, even readers who are persuaded by effective arguments will fail to translate their feelings into action. Web compositions

■ **FIGURE 14.5** A Collaborative Whiteboard and Chat Window

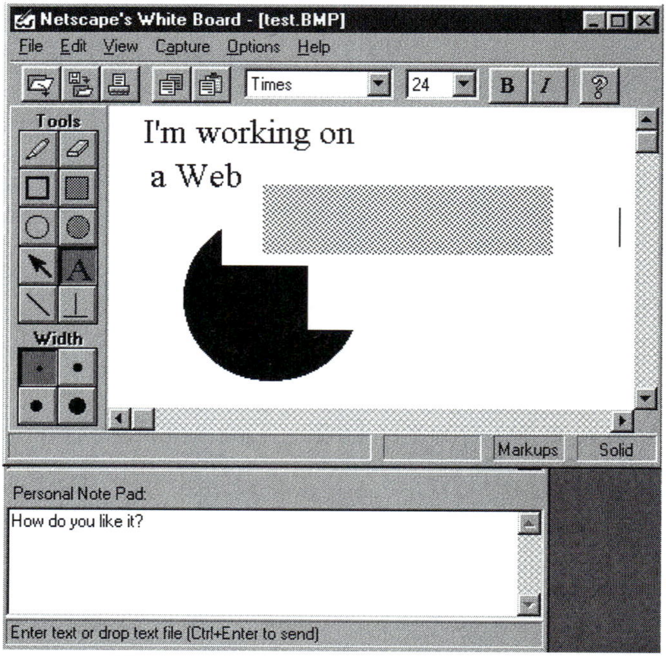

allow authors to easily include mechanisms that help readers take that next step and participate in various forms of direct action. For example, a site could provide a form to e-mail a protest letter to the board of directors of a corporation or to all the members of Congress. Similarly, users could subscribe to discussion lists or register their names with on-line databases that are designed to organize various forms of collective action.

As the sample in Figure 14.6 shows, the interactive capabilities of the Web provide you with possibilities to move readers to action. This kind of writing extends the reach of your compositions, giving you the opportunity to intervene in any number of situations by enlisting the participation of other like-minded people.

The trend is to integrate these features and programs more seamlessly into Web browsers, so real-time Web collaboration will likely become even easier in the near future. It is hard to predict exactly what these options will look like even in the short term, but we can safely say that collaboration will become more central to the ways users work with the Web.

■ **FIGURE 14.6** A Web Form for Automated E-Mailing

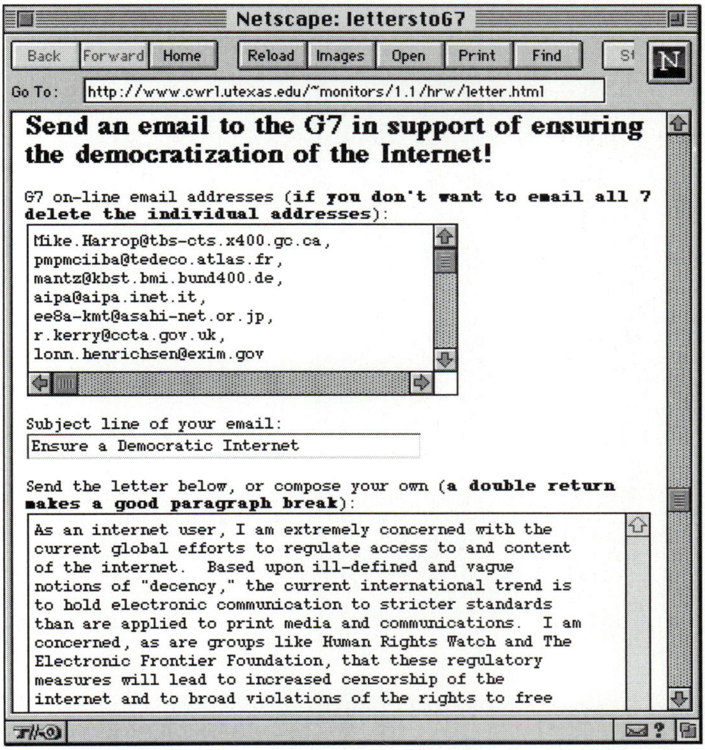

BUILDING AND DESIGN IN HYPERTEXTUAL ENVIRONMENTS

PART 4

CHAPTER 15

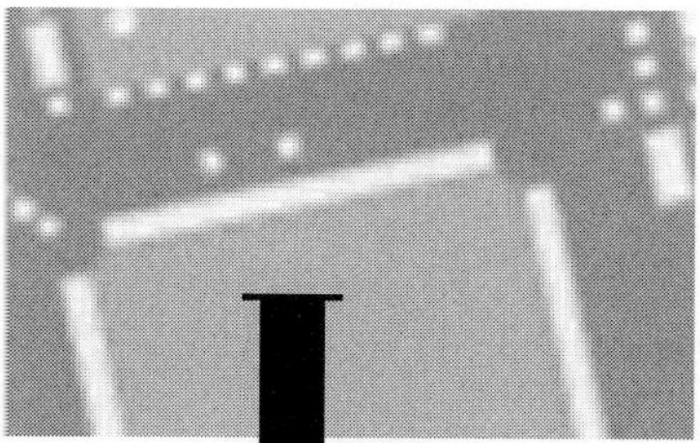

IT'S ALSO *HOW* YOU SAY IT

The Writing Process and Principles of Design

The Writing Process

As we move into **Part 4,** a section that is geared primarily toward composing larger, more fully developed projects in on-line environments, it is worth reiterating one of the core principles of this book, namely, that writing is an ongoing process through which authors, as much as anyone else, come to better understand the topics that they are working with. We realize, of course, that the need to generate a definitive product is often a practical reality. At some point, papers, articles, books—even thank-you cards—all need to be completed. And for students, this generally means that work must be turned in, evaluated, and graded. Even keeping the reality of this final product in mind, however, we feel comfortable saying that the principal value of composition comes from the process of exploring and analyzing complex issues through writing.

When we use the term "process" in this context, we are referring to the ways in which an author's level of understanding evolves as a writing project moves through a series of developmental stages. The eventual goal is to produce a rhetorically effective document, but authors frequently need to produce and revise a number of smaller documents along the way. There's no comprehensive list of stages or correct order in which these steps must be approached, but writers generally need to brainstorm ideas, narrow and focus topics, research their issues, draft compositions, solicit feedback from others, revise those compositions, polish their language and style, and edit and proofread their work.

Many of the activities that you perform on the Internet—doing keyword searches, posting research queries, conversing on a newsgroup, working on peer reviews with your classmates, or having real-time discussions—can be considered stages in the writing process if they contribute to a more fully developed project. Note that during all of these stages you'll need to practice the rhetorical principles that we outline in **Part 1:** considering your purpose, your audience, your presentation as a speaker, your medium, and the larger context in which your writing takes place.

The key to all of this is to keep an open mind and a flexible approach while you write. Don't be afraid to change course in midstream. Let yourself learn from the process of researching a topic and from the comments you receive from your reviewers. Remember that to write successfully about a difficult topic, you'll need to understand the various issues and debates that make it complex. More important, to work out a space for your voice to be heard among those of the other participants, you'll need to develop your own perspective or "take" on the topic and articulate that perspective in terms that are both meaningful and convincing to an audience.

We understand very well that this is no easy feat. It has often been said, though, that you never fully understand a subject until you've written about it. And to write, you have to wrestle both with the other voices that have weighed in on the issue and with your own decisions about how best to handle the topic. Producing a well-written document takes time and commitment. But it is only through the processes of reconceptualizing, revising, and reworking that authors can fully develop their compositions—in large part because it is those same processes that allow authors to develop a sophisticated understanding of their topics.

Design as a Process and a Product

Whether it's an architect's blueprint, an aerospace engineer's rocket, a criminal mastermind's diabolical scheme, or an author's essay, the word "design" is often used to describe the planning that goes into the development of complex projects. Design considerations can take place during every stage of a project's construction.

For instance, the criminal mastermind's initial planning or brainstorming sessions represent the beginnings of the design process in which ideas are generated and projects take shape. An architect's blueprints represent a more developed plan, somewhat akin to an outline or an early draft. In saying that the space shuttle is a "well-designed spacecraft," however, we are considering a much later stage of development—in fact, we are probably referring to the overall design of a completed project. This can mean that the craft is aesthetically pleasing, that it is durable, or more generally that its construction allows it to do the things that it was intended to do.

When we consider the importance of design principles in composition, then, we need to recognize their presence throughout the writing process, from brainstorming to drafting and, finally, to producing a finished product. In all of these stages, the process of design includes questioning, organizing, mapping, rearranging, and/or polishing to stitch the parts of a composition into a cohesive unit in which all the pieces work together to achieve the larger purposes of the project.

Note, also, that the spatial layout of a composition should have a direct correlation to its cognitive or logical organization. For instance, in print-based writing (although sometimes in hypertext composition as well), an author's ideas generally need to be presented in sequence. Before we present a solution, we have to make readers aware of the problem. If we are explaining a causal chain of events (for example, trees are cut down, which causes the soil to erode, which causes sedimentation in streams, which kills fish populations), we need to present the process step by step. If we're making a proposal, we often leave our strongest reasons for last so that they have the greatest impact. In all of these cases, the sequencing of information on the page should follow from a conceptual design of the argument's logical structure.

Design Principles in Print-Based Projects

Although the concept of compositional design is most often associated with the layouts of electronic desktop publishing or digitized multimedia projects, design principles also have a major impact on print-based writing. For instance, the academic essay is often written with the idea of closely examining complicated texts and concepts. As a genre, then, the scholarly essay is generally intended to be read in a formal and intellectually rigorous manner. Its standard design is geared toward these purposes. The fonts are generally conservative, legible, and small. The margins are relatively slim. Together, these two elements ensure that the vast majority of the page is covered with text and that a substantial amount of information will fit on every page.

Because of this density of text, readers are given cues about the nature of the argument. The first line of each paragraph will be indented to tell the audience where a new idea begins. These paragraphs, too, are usually quite dense and long (much longer, for instance, than a paragraph in a newspaper column), so an academic essay will usually require multiple pages of paper. Again, to help orient the reader, page numbers are added in a highly visible spot, as are headings that announce the beginning of different sections. These are design elements that we often take for granted, but they are important components of the academic essay. For contrast, imagine turning in a history paper about the causes of nineteenth-century Haitian slave revolts written in medieval calligraphy on a roll of paper towels. You would certainly turn a few heads, but you'd probably only distract from the seriousness and complexity of the piece.

Even within the world of academia, however, there is quite a range of design standards. Not all academic writing is completely focused on textual analysis. In engineering articles, for example, authors need to work with charts, graphs, tables, and drawings. In mathematics, it's often equations. In geography, you'll find maps. And each of these elements will introduce new problems for the project's design. Obviously, a very detailed map of a continent won't fit onto an 8.5 × 11 inch sheet of paper, meaning that authors will need to make choices about scale, placement, and which elements are most essential to the composition. Furthermore, the elements will need to work in conjunction with the text to demonstrate the concepts being discussed. In successful projects, the graphics complement or supplement the text, and the text situates and analyzes the graphics.

Design in Electronic Environments

As you begin to work with electronic compositions, it's important to have a clear sense of how the component parts of your project fit into its overall design. In general, electronic compositions tend to be more fragmented than print-based projects. Often, smaller pieces of information are connected in ways that give readers more freedom to determine how the text should be examined. Additionally, authors have to rethink the relationship between the medium they work in and the writing that they produce.

The vast majority of MU* environments, for example, are composed solely of text. Initially, you might think that these spaces would take on many of the characteristics of the text-heavy academic essays that we discussed earlier. However, MU*s and academic essays actually have very little in common. While essays present a linear progression of ideas that take the form of sequential paragraphs, MU*s usually present a multidimensional environment in which textual descriptions construct architectural or geographical spaces. Words are used to build rooms and objects—all of which continue to evolve as new users build additions onto existing structures. The spatial organization of these compositions, therefore, is far more open-ended than the linear progression found in most print-based essays.

On a superficial level, visual design features in MU*s are kept to a minimum. After all, there's not much you can do to make ASCII text look good. On a more theoretical level, however, textual descriptions in a MU* create a sense of space that allows readers to "visualize" themselves within a virtual reality. The "visual" components of the design, then, are intimately connected with the organizational structures that authors compose. As characters in a MU* move through the composition, they experience the look and feel of their surroundings, meaning that a successful design relies on carefully written prose and will coincide with the larger rhetorical purposes of the author. Each room, space, object, and character functions somewhat like a paragraph in an essay: Each introduces a new idea or concept and develops it in a way that should further the project's larger design goals.

The hypertextual compositions of the World Wide Web overlap with the conventions of an essay in different ways. On the Web the central purpose of language is not to construct architectural/geographical spaces with text (as in MU*s), so Web authors can explain, analyze, and develop ideas much as they would in a print-based essay. But because most Web pages are hypertextually linked to other pages and files, Web builders are faced with a set of organizational problems that print-based writers rarely have to grapple with.

For instance, Web authors need to think carefully about how best to split up their ideas. Along with (or instead of) the paragraph, the screen can become a major organizational unit. Additionally, the links that authors create must emphasize important information about their destinations. Like transitions between paragraphs, they should be carefully composed to maintain the document's coherence. Because most hypertexts allow readers to choose any link at any time, creating arguments that depend on a specific progression of ideas is extremely complicated. Additionally, Web authors must contend with expectations about incorporating multimedia elements into their hypertexts. As a result, they have to be conscious of the way their texts interact with sound, video, graphics, and even collaborative forums.

Web authors must also consider the aesthetics of page design. Elements like background images, colored text, and thematic icons have all become standards of Web composition. This demand for visually exciting layouts forces Web authors to consider how the look of their pages affects the rhetorical impact of their work. Again, a concern for the project's overall design becomes essential if the author is to ensure that each of the different elements has a specific purpose which works toward the larger goals of the project.

Throughout the rest of **Part 4,** we will further explore these and other on-line design issues. **Chapter 16** will go into more detail about the challenges of composing in MU* environments, paying particular attention to issues of scope, organization and descriptive language. The final four chapters are devoted to Web building, an area of on-line writing that we believe is particularly beneficial to composition students. **Chapter 17** looks at the basics of HTML scripting, demonstrating how Web pages are built. The focus of **Chapter 18** shifts to more sophisticated Web design features, concentrating on the graphical layout of a page. We continue to develop the rhetorical considerations of Web design in **Chapter 19,** in which we discuss the process of mapping arguments on the Web, working with multimedia and considering hypertextual navigation. Finally, **Chapter 20** examines some technological advances on the Web in terms of their possible impact on electronic writing.

CHAPTER 16

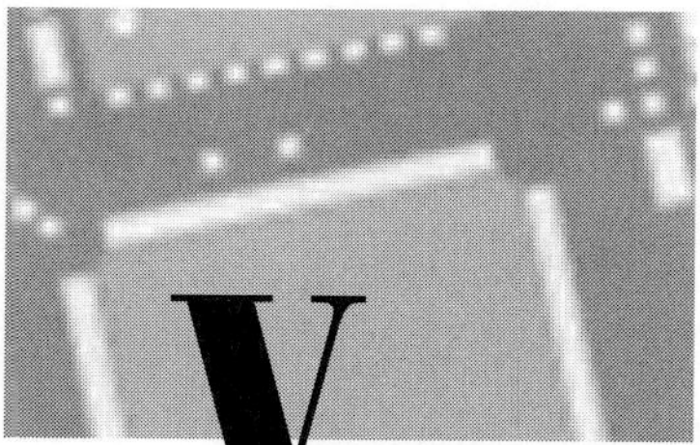

VIRTUAL ARCHITECTURE

Interior MU* Designing with a Purpose

Perhaps more than any other Internet medium that we discuss in this book, designing successful MU* projects requires that you focus carefully on your sense of purpose, the constraints and conventions of the medium, and the demands of your audience. Remember that MU*s have their roots in role-playing games, meaning that the environments were not originally meant for persuasive writing. Although more and more academic MU*s are being built, authors are still faced with the challenge of writing in an environment that was designed more for fantasy and play than for analytical composition.

Although learning MU* building commands will take a fair amount of time and energy, the process of planning your MU* projects so that their design coincides with your purpose will require the most thought and effort. Because we want to stress the conceptual organization underlying MU* projects, we are devoting this chapter to larger issues of design. MU* building requires considerably more expertise than simply interacting in virtual environments, so we're assuming that you are comfortable with navigating and conversing in MU* spaces (activities we discuss in **Chapter 11**) and that you have some time to invest in the process of construction. We provide information about MU* building commands in **Appendix 4,** but you should also check with your instructor about where to build, the level of expertise your project will require, and the availability of resources and advice from experienced users. □

KEY TERMS

Bots (short for "robot"): Programs that are designed to emulate MU* characters. By building bots, MU* authors can "people" their environments with characters who will perform programmed functions.

Channel: A "frequency" in which users on a MU* or IRC can converse with each other. Users anywhere in a MU* can create and log onto a channel where they can carry on real-time discussions without bothering other MU* users.

Framing Narrative: A story or metaphor that serves as an organizing principle for MU* designs. By constructing a framing narrative, MU* builders can provide a logical context in which to connect various rooms and objects.

Hub-and-Spoke Design: A hypertextual design that has multiple nodes (the spokes) linked from a central point (the hub). This type of organizational structure is well suited for displaying multiple perspectives or examples.

Hypertext: A composition that links pieces of information (often called "nodes") together into complex, interactive webs.

MU*: A text-based virtual environment on the Internet. MU* is our umbrella term for the many spaces on Internet servers where users log in, explore the virtual environment, and interact with others. These spaces take their names from different versions of multiple user software and include MUDs, MUSHs, MUCKs, and MOOs.

Object: An item that is placed in a MU* to flesh out the description of a room. Objects are usually just text descriptions, but they can also be programmed to perform certain tasks.

Sequential Design: A hypertextual design that limits readers' choices so that they move through an environment in a particular order. This type of organizational structure is well suited for compositions that have a clear progression of ideas.

Foundations for Construction

Organizing Your Spaces

Before you begin building, try to pinpoint what you want to accomplish with your MU* spaces. If you are trying to create a persuasive project, for instance, be aware that MU* environments don't necessarily lend themselves to the kind of linear progressions that we associate with most argumentative writing. Remember that MU* readers decide for themselves how, where, and at what speed they will move through your hypertextual environments. You'll be able to control a reader's movement to a certain degree, but you should be aware that the more navigational options you provide, the less you will be able to predict the paths that readers take.

Since MU* environments are composed of a series of interconnected rooms, you can think about your compositions as exercises in organizing pockets of information. For instance, if you were creating a MU* project to demonstrate the continued need for affirmative action policies, you might build rooms to highlight several important arenas in which minorities are underrepresented. For this type of argument, a design that relies on a hub and spokes might be the most appropriate.

In Figure 16.1, we see a design that provides a central room, with "exits" leading to other sections of the project: Higher Education, The Business World, and Government Organizations. As the project develops, each of the spokes can also become hubs. For instance, the Higher Education room might link to the Business World room or to separate spaces that talk about standardized tests, minority student enrollment, and faculty hiring practices. Keep in mind that this kind of organization places more control in the hands of readers, who will move through the rooms of the project according to their interests.

If, on the other hand, you wanted to focus on the roots of affirmative action by exploring the historical impact of discrimination and seg-

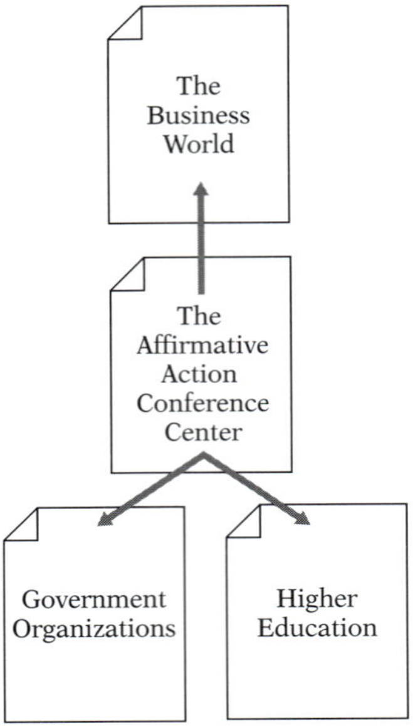

■ **FIGURE 16.1** A Hub-and-Spoke Design

regation on minority populations in the United States, you might lead readers on a kind of sequential journey from room to room.

You can see that the sequential model shown in Figure 16.2 more closely resembles the linear movement one might expect to find in a traditional paper. Here the author looks at race relations at the turn of the century, during the civil rights movement of the 1960s, and in the 1980s Reagan era, with each time period set off in its own room. Because the author has a clear sequence in mind, she or he has limited the navigational options so that readers must move through the rooms in chronological order.

For projects that chart some type of progression or development in which one space depends on information presented in the previous space(s), the sequential model may be more effective than the hub-and-spoke design. Conversely, if you are trying to demonstrate a variety of ways to look at an issue, then the hub-and-spoke model may suit your purposes better. Note, too, that these models aren't mutually exclusive. For instance, you may begin by leading your readers through a particular sequence of rooms, eventually taking them to a hub that connects to a set of adjoining rooms. The point is to design the spaces so that they best organize the information you are trying to present.

Defining Your Scope

Although some MU*s build elaborate environments—for instance, a virtual city, complete with buildings, streets, parks, and meeting spaces—it

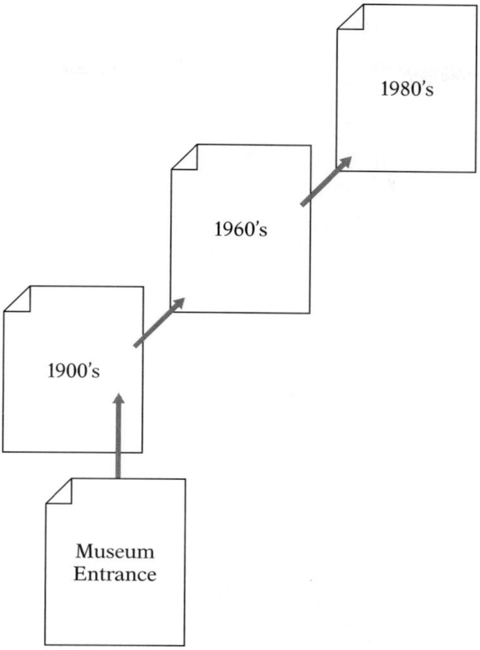

■ **FIGURE 16.2** A Sequential Design

is important to remember that (even a virtual) Rome can't be built in a day. As you consider possible structures and room designs for your MU* projects, be careful to keep their scope manageable. The old comedy acts in which characters continually shuffle in and out of a dozen doors down a long hallway may be amusing, but when navigating in MU* space, readers will quickly tire of moving through a series of hastily constructed rooms. You'll do better to scale back and concentrate on providing meaningful details and appropriate objects within the rooms that you develop.

You can also make your projects more complex by thinking of them as a kind of research project. As in other forms of research, you'll need a topic that is narrow enough to let you develop your ideas with sufficient depth. For instance, in the affirmative action rooms, you might decide to focus only on higher education, forgoing the issues related to government or the business world. You could concentrate your efforts on fleshing out your MU* spaces with relevant research. You might, for instance, provide statistics about minority enrollment and retention, historical analyses of affirmative action policies at universities, and perhaps a collection of personal narratives from students and faculty members who have been affected by affirmative action. Researching issues will allow you to describe settings and objects with an added level of specificity, making your project more believable, accurate, and appealing.

Describing Rooms and Objects

Also be sure that your room descriptions are working toward your overall purpose. For instance, in the affirmative action MU* space, you might describe a classroom with a window looking out onto Martin Luther King, Jr., Boulevard. Similarly, your description might include "an older Mexican American woman who empties the trash before class." You could contrast these two examples with a description of a white, male professor lecturing to a group of predominately white, upper-middle-class students at a prominent U.S. university, if you wanted to convey the idea that limited employment and educational opportunities are available to women and minorities.

Your larger purpose should also determine how and when you place people or objects into your rooms. For example, it might be appropriate to have Malcolm X reading a speech in your 1960s room or Ronald Reagan talking about "trickle-down" economics in your 1980s room. If you are knowledgeable about MU* design, you might also consider programming your objects to perform certain actions when a reader looks at them or picks them up. For instance, when readers in the 1960s room look at a crumpled newspaper that has been left in a corner, they might see the headline "Rosa Parks Leads Bus Protest." When the paper is picked up, it might provide them with the full text of the article. The point in each of these cases is to fill the spaces with people and objects that will demonstrate the ideas you want to convey.

Constructing Narratives

Whether you are creating open-ended spaces for readers to explore or building rooms that lead readers through a particular sequence, you will need to provide a rationale for why they are moving through the space. In the more open-ended hub-and-spoke model, consider the relationships between the different rooms and think about the transitions that readers will be making. In the sequential model, you'll need to provide a sense of logical progression as readers move from one room to the next.

Narrative Frames

Because it is so easy to create multiple rooms but relatively difficult to connect them all logically, MU* spaces often turn to "time machines" and "transporter devices" as mechanisms for moving readers from space to space. Though these devices can be useful in some instances (for example, to avoid unnecessary navigation or retracing multiple steps), we would like to encourage you to think carefully about the narrative rationale of your spaces and their overall organization and coherence.

Perhaps the best way to approach the movements between rooms is by establishing a narrative frame or an organizing metaphor to connect the various spaces. For instance, to create a logical narrative that sends readers through the affirmative action rooms of the 1900s, 1960s, and 1980s, you might design a series of museum exhibits. Readers could move from exhibit room to exhibit room, viewing the material within the context of a historical analysis. If you wanted to build a similar framing device for your discussion of minorities in higher education, the workplace, and the government, you could design each of the spaces as conference rooms at a national meeting on affirmative action or perhaps booths at a high school career fair. In either of these framing narratives, it would make sense for each the various groups to be present. And rather than beaming people from room to room, you could build a simple elevator that takes them from one floor to another. Although less flashy than a transporter, the elevator makes more sense in the context of a museum or conference hall.

MU* Space and Creative Writing

Since, in many ways, MU* readers are taken on a narrative journey, it is also helpful to think of MU* building as a form of creative writing. This doesn't necessarily mean that your creations must be fantastic mythologies peopled with gnomes and aliens. Rather, creative writing in MU* space requires that you compose descriptively and that you think about how readers will interact with your compositions. Your goal should be to create spaces where readers can picture themselves in the environment you've described.

Whatever kind of environment you are building, it will be crucial that you concentrate on the descriptive detail of the spaces and objects you build. In creative writing classes, students are constantly reminded to "show, not tell!" It's useful advice for all types of writing, but particularly for creating MU* environments, which rely so heavily on descriptive language. The more dramatically you can demonstrate your ideas and positions through concrete descriptions, the more successful your compositions will be. For instance, you might want readers entering a school board meeting to feel a high degree of tension in the room. You could provide a description such as

```
You enter the meeting room.  There is a long wooden
table in the center with eight chairs lined up on
either side and pitchers of water and glasses
arranged on top.  There is an incredible tension in
the air.
```

Although this description captures some details about the room (the pitcher and glasses, for instance), when it comes to conveying the tension, the author bluntly tells us that it is there. Providing readers with demonstrative details will create a more palpable sense of unease:

```
You enter the meeting room.  There is a long wooden
table in the center with eight chairs lined up on
either side and pitchers of water and glasses
arranged on top.  At one end, a huddled group of
people converse in whispers.  One man is thumbing
through a file folder, looking for something. In the
corner of the room two men and an older woman appear
to be arguing.  Their voices rise shrilly, and the
woman at the head of the table casts a stern glance
their way.  As you step forward, everyone in the
room suddenly becomes silent.
```

Instead of stating the obvious, let your readers decipher meaning from your descriptions and situations. Of course, there is always the danger that your language will confuse rather than clarify what you are trying to convey or that your readers will interpret your descriptions differently than you had imagined. However, if you are really trying to create a virtual reality, this is a risk you'll have to take. As long as you are aware of the potential for misinterpretation, you'll know to concentrate on choosing language that will most precisely convey your meaning.

Building for a Community

Considering Audience

One way to compose more effective MU* descriptions is to craft environments with your audience in mind. Remember that readers gather information in MU*s *only* by looking at your descriptions. This text, then, needs to both organize the space and provide the rhetorical and argumentative content. As you decide how to phrase your descriptions, balance the needs to provide structure, demonstrate ideas, and hold your readers' interest.

To test your MU* designs, have your friends or colleagues walk through the environment while it's still under construction. Doing several informal peer reviews where builders and users brainstorm about ways of improving a MU* design can be an extremely helpful process for authors who are trying to convey specific ideas in their descriptions.

Interactive and Evolving Spaces

By nature, MU* spaces are inherently collaborative—after all, the name itself is an acronym derived from the phrase "multiple user." As we discuss in **Chapter 11,** one of the primary functions of MU*s is to provide a virtual environment in which users can interact with each other. So when you're building, create spaces with an eye toward the effect that the surroundings will have on participants. Think of the environments as catalysts that might prompt readers to interact or hold discussions. By adding a level of detail to the surroundings, you'll create a relevant setting where users can draw on the environment as they interact. For instance, in a historical MU*, you might choose to focus on a printer's office in eighteenth-century England (similar to the scrivener's office shown in **Chapter 11**) rather than the whole city of London. By providing specific details about the appearance and function of various objects in the room, you could reasonably assume that the environment might prompt interesting discussions about the development of printing technology and the process of constructing and distributing books during this era.

Another way to increase the collaborative aspects of your environment is to program objects so that users can add comments or even send e-mail from within the MU*. In the eighteenth-century printing shop, then, a reader might post a comment suggesting a slightly more accurate description of the printing press you had built or remarking on the historical ramifications of a particular technological advancement that can be found on this type of press.

You can also create discussion tools that enhance opportunities for conversation. One such tool is a chat channel that allows users anywhere in the MU* to log on and interact. This could allow a class of students, for example, to explore different parts of a MU* while carrying on a dialog with each other about the strengths and weaknesses of various areas. Similarly, a group of characters in the same room could use a channel to hold a discussion without bothering other users in the room.

Depending on the type of MU* space you are building, you may also want to consider measures that would either encourage or limit construction by other users. Imagine that you were designing a virtual college campus with buildings set up to house the various academic departments. Because this is such a large project, and one that depends on an in-depth knowledge of multiple academic disciplines, you would almost certainly need help to complete the virtual campus. By designing certain template features that might be useful to other builders, you can help to facilitate collaborative work. You might be able to set up some generic classrooms, constructing features such as blackboards or overhead projectors where faculty could "plug in" data from the courses they teach. Similarly, you might set up faculty offices with built-in mail functions so that students who visited their instructor's office could send e-mail if the teacher wasn't there. With these kinds of templates in place to give builders a head start on the MU* design, it is likely that you will attract more potential collaborators.

There will also be times, however, when you want to limit the amount of construction that can be added onto a space. If your MU* is thematically based, you'll probably want to clearly announce that there are certain building codes prohibiting the construction of areas that don't fit into the setting. Obviously, it would be a little strange to find that one of the classrooms in the virtual physics building opened onto the back nine at Pebble Beach. This principle also applies when you are building in other people's MU*s. Make sure that you have permission before you begin building, and always try to keep the theme of the MU* in mind when you decide to add to preexisting MU* structures.

Anatomy of a Student MU* Project

Figure 16.3 shows a MUSH project dealing with the issue of free speech. This "free speech village" was built by a group of students as part of a collaborative writing assignment. There are a few things to note about the sample of the project reproduced here. First, the project does a good job of incorporating a narrative into the environment. By setting the project in a small village that is currently embroiled in a controversy over free speech, the students are able to craft their spaces so that they shed light on the topic.

Notice how the objects in the village square easily provide ways of addressing the issue. For instance, by including the Crowd of Protesters and the Counter-Demonstrators, the authors have a chance to articulate differing perspectives on the issue of free speech. Additionally, the objects work to further the project's narrative and provide information about the environment.

When readers look at the newspaper, it displays the headline that details an upcoming election in the village. Additionally, the headline clues readers about another object in the space: the voting booth where readers can find more information about the elections and can contribute to the site by casting their vote on the free speech controversy. Note, also, that the newspaper contains five more articles, each giving the authors another opportunity to set the scene for the project while shedding light on the issue of free speech.

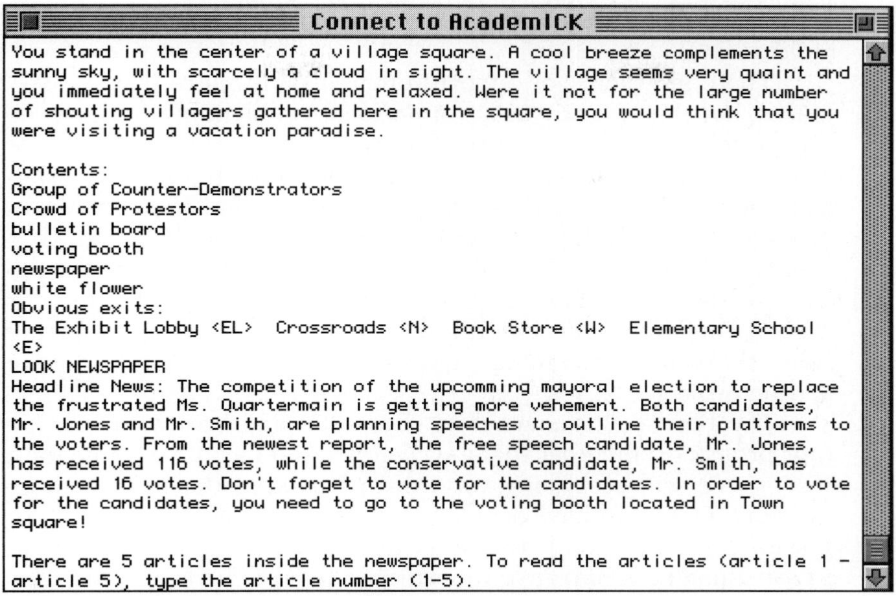

■ **FIGURE 16.3** A Student MU* Project

Of course, there are areas that might be made even stronger. Instead of mentioning that the candidates' speeches will "outline" their platforms, the authors might have filled in some details about these two important stances. They may have been able to shed additional light on the campaign by using more descriptive names than Mr. Smith and Mr. Jones. Although the authors might be more telling in their MU* descriptions, we think they do a nice job of working with a coherent purpose to provide a narrative frame for a MU* project and of using a virtual setting to explore an important issue.

EXERCISE 16.1

Constructing an Academic MU* Space

Working on your own or in a group, design an academic space in a MU* environment. You may want to make lists, take notes, or even build explanatory Web pages as part of the building process, but the assignment and the work itself will take place in a MU*. Be sure to consult your instructor about the permissions and policies for building and make sure that you have help available as you begin to build.

There are plenty of opportunities to build more playful MU* spaces, but this exercise asks you to focus on blending some of the conventions of more traditional academic writing—a sense of coherence, logical reasoning, and detailed informational prose—with the more free-flowing demands of MU* space. We don't mean that you should stifle your creative impulses and turn the MU* space into an essay. By "blend," we mean make a conscious effort to tap into the strengths of both kinds of writing as you create your spaces. Your instructor can offer more guidance, but as a starting point, think of the assignment as either a persuasive or informative writing project.

The best way to start is to choose an appropriate theme for your project. Remember that a well-conceived narrative frame for a MU* space will go a long way toward making the project more coherent. Once you have decided on a workable theme, think about possible organizational structures for the spaces that you want to create. Imagine a narrative movement through the space and consider what elements will make that movement more conducive to your own goals. Think about connections between rooms, the number of exits you want to have, and where they might lead.

You also can begin to think about any possible research that might make the project both more informative and more descriptive. After either researching for information or developing your own ideas, come up with a list of the objects that might help you to convey your thoughts. Think about possible interactions that might be programmed into each object to further the experience of readers. When readers look at objects, what details will you show them? When readers pick up objects, what will happen? How can you use the objects as opportunities for articulating your ideas?

Finally, once you have a sense of how your spaces, research, and objects might work toward the goals of the project, create your rooms and coordinate with administrators who can help you link them to the rest of the MU*. Describe your rooms using concrete details, thinking both about the narrative of your spaces and about your larger goals. As you build, be sure to set up some meeting times when your peers or instructor can review your work and talk over possible revisions. Also be sure to save your materials along the way in case you run into any unexpected technical problems.

When you have finished, take the class on a tour of the MU* and tell others on the Net who might be interested in your project.

TIPS AND TACTICS

- Before beginning to build your MU* spaces, make sure you have permission. Next, think carefully about the contexts in which you are working. What are the expectations of the MU* audience? What will your purpose be in constructing the space? What conventions exist for the medium and for the particular type of project that you want to build?
- If you are not already familiar with MU* building, be sure an experienced MU* user is available to help. You might set up a time to physically meet with someone who can get you started, or you can arrange to join someone who is logged onto the MU*.
- Carefully select a narrative frame or metaphor for your project. Think about the ways in which your particular metaphor meshes with the overall theme of the MU*. Take care to come up with a theme that provides an organizational structure that will add coherence to the spaces and objects that you build.
- Be sure that the scope of your project is manageable. Scale back when your focus seems too broad and find collaborators to help with the development of more extensive projects.
- Perform some exploratory research about your topics before deciding to build. Try to provide specific details so that your environments will have enough depth to hold a reader's interest and spark discussion.
- Practice some strategies for successful creative writing. Try to craft an environment that readers will be able to identify with. In particular, make efforts to demonstrate your points through detailed descriptions rather than overt statements (show, don't tell).
- Hold a discussion in your MU* space with peers so that they can offer criticism of the project. Also try to incorporate interactive elements into the space—for instance, a mail function that allows readers to send you comments.
- Always make backup copies of any important text you compose on the MU* to avoid losing data in the event of a crash or malfunction.

CHAPTER 17

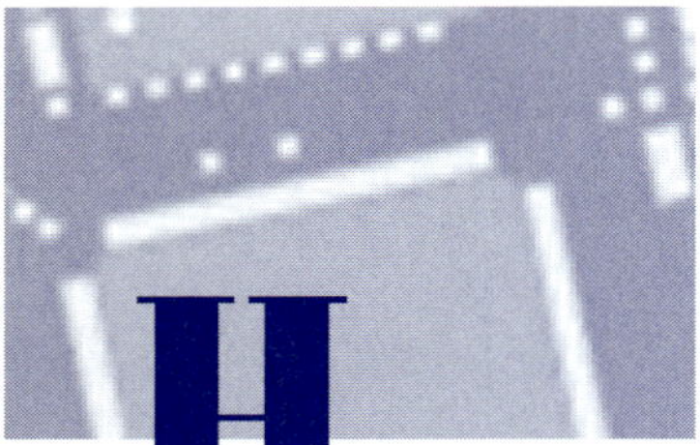

HOME (PAGE) IMPROVEMENT

The Do-It-Yourselfer's Guide to Web Building

If you've spent any time browsing the World Wide Web, you've probably come across some pretty impressive sites. As the Web has grown during the past few years, pages have become increasingly sophisticated, routinely containing elements such as graphics, tables, backgrounds, and multicolored text. Although this kind of Web design might at first seem like it would require some pretty advanced computer and graphics skills, the truth of the matter is that anyone with access to a Web server, some basic software, and a little time can put up an appealing page. □

Laying Conceptual Foundations

Understanding Hypertext Markup Language

Let's begin to think about Web composition by looking at the scripting language that is used to create Web pages. No matter how complicated or professional a page looks, it is generated using the reasonably simple scripting

KEY TERMS

Directory: An organizational structure for managing files on a disk. Some operating systems use a folder metaphor to represent a directory.

File Transfer Protocol (FTP): An Internet protocol that allows users to upload and download files.

HTML Editor: An application for composing and editing text. Though you can use any text editor to create pages for the Web, many sophisticated HTML editors that simplify Web building are available.

Hypertext: A composition that links pieces of information (often called "nodes") together into complex, interactive webs.

Hypertext Markup Language (HTML): The scripting language used to create pages for the World Wide Web. Authors insert HTML tags (commands) in a text document to change page layout, make links, and display images.

Link: (1) As a noun, the connection between sections, or nodes, of a hypertext. Often, links are activated by clicking on hot text or icons. (2) As a verb, the process of connecting pieces of information into a hypertextual form.

Source or "Document Source": The HTML file that tells a Web browser how to display a page. Most browsers allow readers to "view the source" of Web documents to see the underlying HTML tags that create the pages.

Tags: The individual HTML commands. These commands are set off in angle brackets (< >) and generally work in pairs.

URL (Uniform Resource Locator): The unique Internet address of a document on the World Wide Web.

Web Browser: Client software that allows users to navigate and interact on the World Wide Web.

Web Server: A combination of software and hardware that stores, manages, and distributes files for the World Wide Web.

of Hypertext Markup Language (HTML). HTML is a collection of commands or "tags" that, when embedded into a text file, tell a Web browser how to display what we think of as a Web page. Unlike most programming languages (which generally perform a complex series of actions), HTML is concerned primarily with formatting and page layout. For instance, a file might contain commands that tell browsers to display some of the text with a boldface font or to put a page into multiple columns. Composing Web pages, then, is a fairly straightforward process of formatting text by "marking up" a document.

Figure 17.1 shows a document that has been marked up with some basic HTML tags. The text file "basics.html" contains the HTML commands. When viewed with a Web browser, these commands display the results shown in the top window of Figure 17.1. The tags inserted in the HTML file appear in angle brackets (< >). For instance, the line "<B>Text can also be bold</B>" tells the browser to display the text between the tags in boldface type. Similarly, the text between the <I> and </I> tags will be displayed in italics.

HTML Basics: Tags, Images, and Links

As you look at the sample in Figure 17.1, note that most of the commands work in pairs—for instance, the tag <H1> appears before the phrase "A Heading Makes Text Large and Dark," after which the tag </H1> appears. This basic <TAG></TAG> pattern holds true for almost all of the HTML commands. (We'll talk about some exceptions in a minute.)

■ **FIGURE 17.1** Some Basic HTML Tags

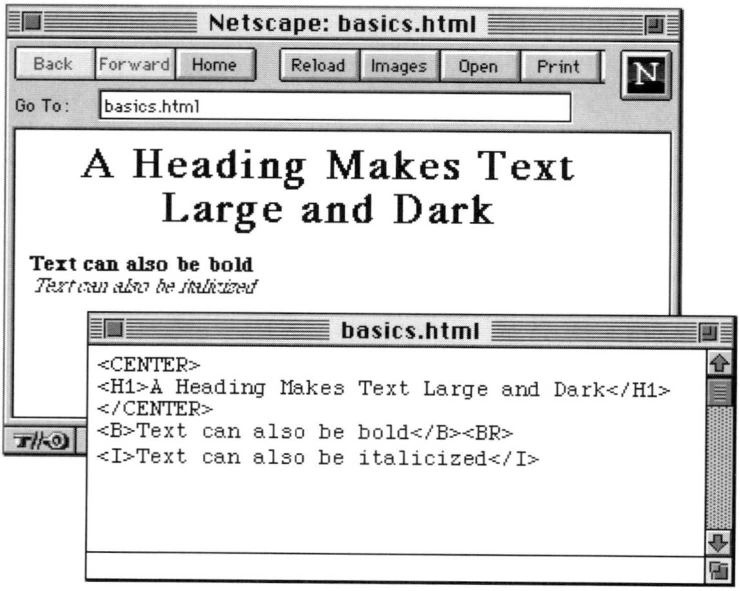

The first thing to understand about composing with HTML, then, is that most of the tags work like on and off switches. One tag initiates the command and another ends it. All the text or any other information that exists between the <TAG> and the </TAG> will be modified by the command.

Let's take a quick look at some of the other basic HTML commands that work with the <TAG></TAG> pattern.

Headings

<H1> **Size 1 Heading** </H1>

<H2> **Size 2 Heading** </H2>

<H3> **Size 3 Heading** </H3>

<H4> **Size 4 Heading** </H4>

<H5> **Size 5 Heading** </H5>

<H6> **Size 6 Heading** </H6>

Text Styles

- <B> **Boldface Text** </B>
- <I> *Italicized Text* </I>
- <U> Underlined Text </U>
- <TT> `Typewriter Text`</TT>
- <CENTER> Centered Material </CENTER>
- <STRIKE> ~~Strike Through Text~~ </STRIKE>
- ^{Superscript Text}
- _{Subscript Text}
- <BIG> Large Font </BIG>
- <SMALL> Small Font </SMALL>

HTML Exceptions

A number of other commands use the <TAG></TAG> pattern, but before we get to those, let's quickly examine the few commands that don't conform to this rule. Most single-tag commands are used for controlling the layout and appearance of the page. Let's look at another sample.

Figure 17.2 reveals the handful of commands that are exceptions to the <TAG></TAG> pattern. These single-tag commands allow you to place images, horizontal lines, hard returns, and paragraph breaks on a page. The first command, <IMG SRC="connections.jpg"> calls for an image.

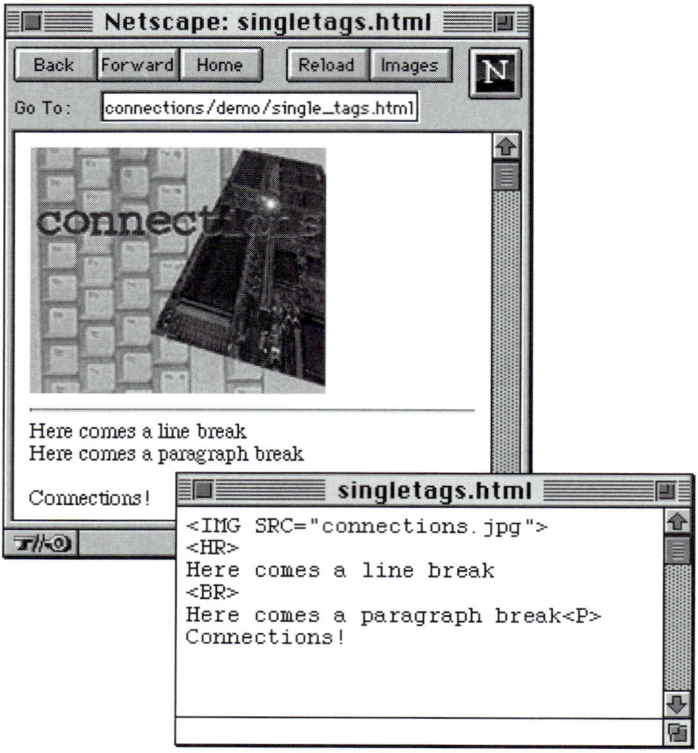

■ **FIGURE 17.2** Single-Tag HTML Commands

This displays the specified image file "connections.jpg" at the top of the page. Next, there is an <HR>, or horizontal rule, command that tells the browser to draw a line across the page. After the text "Here comes a line break," there is a <BR> command that tells the browser to place a single hard return before the next line of text. The final command in the sample, <P>, tells the browser to make a paragraph break (the spatial equivalent of two <BR> commands).

Note that browsers will display text as one continuous block unless you specify where the line breaks should occur. Generally, the paragraph break, <P>, will be sufficient, but if you need only one hard return, a single <BR> tag will force a line break. Additionally, by using multiple <BR> tags, you can create any number of line breaks, whereas using more than one <P> tag will still produce only a single paragraph break.

Images It's important to understand that images aren't physically part of the HTML page—they are separate files that are linked to the HTML document with the <IMG SRC> command. <IMG> tells the browser to place an image in the page and <SRC> tells the browser where to find the image. In our sample, "connections.jpg" is a local file, meaning that it resides in the same directory as the HTML file. You can also link to images elsewhere on the Web by specifying the full URL. For instance, you might link to the logo on the *Connections* Web site with the command

```
<IMG SRC="http://www.abacon.com/connections/
connections.jpg">
```

As long as the browser knows where to find the image file, it will be displayed on the page you are building.

Links Before we finish our overview of HTML, we should look briefly at the way that files are linked on the Web.

One of the most powerful aspects of HTML is that you can connect to any file that exists on the Web. Figure 17.3 shows a link from the *Connections* Web page to the Computer Writing and Research Labs (CWRL) at the University of Texas at Austin. Let's take a look at the HTML that constructs the link:

```
<A HREF="http://www.cwrl.utexas.edu/index.html">
The Computer Writing and Research Labs</A>
```

■ **FIGURE 17.3** An External Link

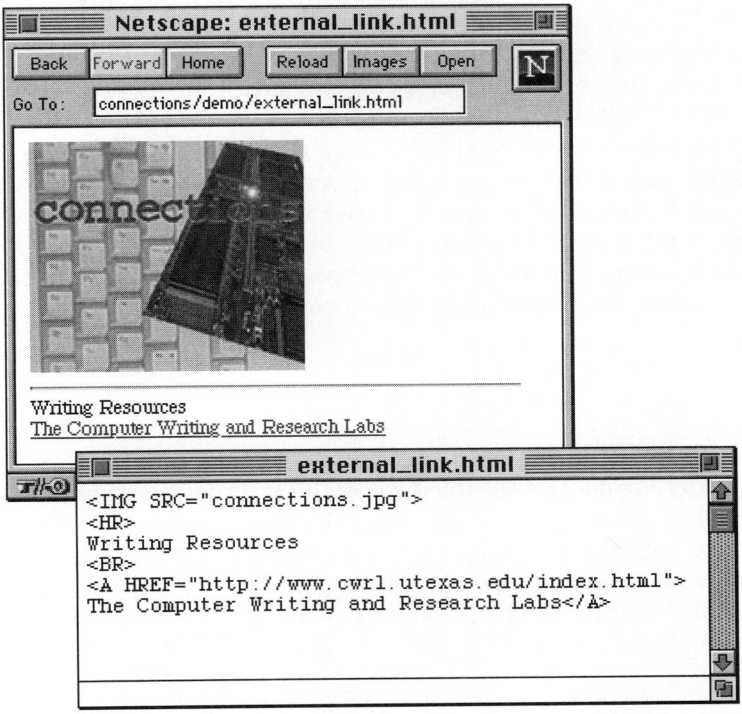

The anchor or link command follows the <TAG></TAG> pattern and, like the image command, lets us indicate which file to link to. The opening tag, <A HREF="http://www.cwrl.utexas.edu/index.html">, sets the anchor and provides the hypertext reference, or HREF, specifying the URL of the link to the CWRL home page. Next comes the text, "Computer Writing and Research Labs," followed by the </A>. The phrase between the two tags will be the "hot text" when the file is viewed by a browser. When a reader viewing the page clicks on the phrase "Computer Writing and Research Labs," the browser will load and display the CWRL home page because that is the file specified in the HREF element of the tag.

HTML Browsers and Editors

Mastering HTML commands is really not that difficult, but your understanding will come more quickly if you have a sense of the way that the Web operates. Let's begin, then, by looking at the relationship between HTML files and your Web browser. It's important to remember that you use a browser to view Web pages, but that the browser generates a Web page by interpreting information from an HTML file (a text document that has been marked up with HTML tags).

When you compose HTML files, you'll generally be working on your local machine using a text editor (for instance, a word processor) or a program designed specifically to create HTML code. As you build and revise your documents, you'll continually have to save your files on a hard drive or diskette. Though some HTML editors offer a "what you see is what you get" (WYSIWYG, pronounced "wizzywig") interface, allowing you to compose pages in an environment that resembles a Web browser, you can always check your work by opening your files with a Web browser. In any case, get comfortable with the process of editing and saving HTML files and then displaying them in the Web browser—continually shifting back and forth between editing and viewing your work.

Source Files

In addition to displaying Web pages, most browsers can also retrieve the HTML source from pages published on the Internet (usually by selecting "Source" or "Document Source" from the View menu). When you "view the source" of files that you find on the Web, you can see the HTML scripting that creates the page. This greatly increases the resources you have for learning HTML by providing a wealth of examples that you can copy or modify as you build your own pages.

HTML Editors

We recommend using an editor that will help you to compose HTML code. These editors handle HTML commands in different ways. Some operate as assistants, automating much of the tagging process but still requiring you to work with the HTML page. Other editors, often referred to as "WYSIWYG," will let you build Web pages without understanding or composing any HTML tags.

We believe, however, that it is important for you to at least understand the role of HTML and familiarize yourself with the basic commands. As a Web author, you will have more flexibility and options if you know something about HTML, and you will be better able to make use of the HTML compositions that you find on the Web. Although we believe that you should understand HTML, we also encourage you to take advantage of the automation offered by HTML editors as a way to simplify and speed up your composition process. For more information about HTML editors, see the *Connections* Web site.

So far, we've been outlining some of the basics of Web composition. We've seen that Web pages are controlled by HTML files. These files contain embedded tags that make links and control the appearance of pages. We've also seen that most HTML commands work in pairs, using the <TAG></TAG> pattern, but that a few single-tag commands are used for controlling line breaks and images. Many of these HTML tags can be supplemented with more sophisticated commands, but this overview should help you to better understand some of the basic principles of HTML. Remember that you can view the source of any Web page you come across to reveal other HTML possibilities. You can also find more comprehensive lists of HTML commands in **Appendix 5** or at the *Connections* Web site.

Getting Started with Your Own Compositions

The HTML Skeleton

Every HTML page should have a certain core set of elements that we call the HTML skeleton. Although some browsers and servers will still handle Web files if these elements are missing, we strongly recommend that you include this coding in all of your HTML documents.

The HTML skeleton shown in Figure 17.4 performs several important functions. First, the <HTML></HTML> tags at the top and bottom of the page tell the browser that it is reading an HTML document rather than some other type of file; this helps the browser to interpret and properly display all of the formatting and linking commands.

Second, the skeleton splits the HTML document into two parts: the <HEAD> and the <BODY>. The head contains information about the document that does not appear on the page itself. There can be any number of elements in the head of a document, but probably the most important is the information stored between the <TITLE></TITLE> tags—in this case, "Put Title Here." Note that when the browser displays the page, the title appears not in the text of the page itself, but in the gray title bar at the top of the screen. Always title your page with a specific description of its contents because search engines and bookmarks often rely on the title to keep track of Web documents.

The <HEAD> is also used to control more advanced operations of pages. For example, there are a number of <META> commands that pass generalized information about the page to search engines and browsers. To help search engines find your page, you can include a list of keywords with the <HEAD META KEYWORD = keyword1, keyword2, keyword3> tag. By using the <HEAD META REFRESH> command, you can also prompt a browser to load another page or reload the same page after a specified

■ **FIGURE 17.4** The HTML Skeleton

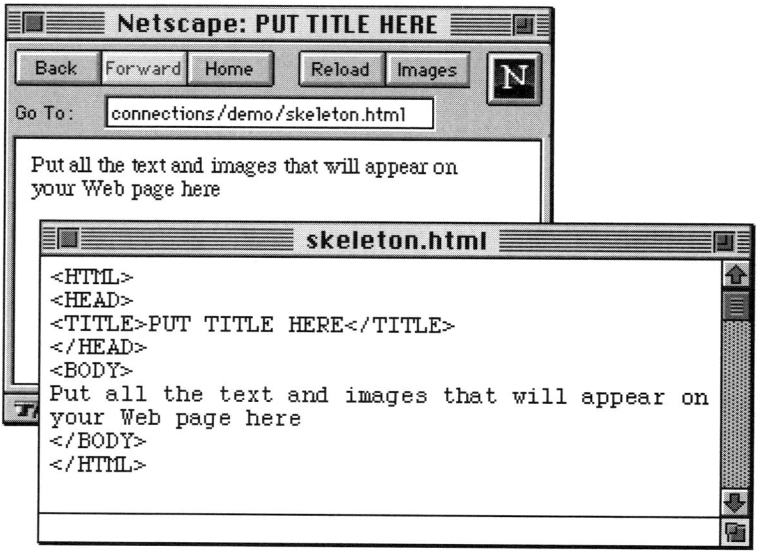

amount of time. Additionally, JavaScripts are often placed in the document <HEAD>.

The other section of an HTML document is the <BODY>. This is the portion of the HTML document containing all the information that will appear below the menu bar on a Web page. It is in the <BODY> that authors format their text, create links, and add images by using HTML commands. In this case, we've typed only "Put All the Text and Images That Will Appear On Your Web Page Here," but in general, all of your "content" will be placed between the <BODY></BODY> commands.

File Logistics

Once you understand the relationship between HTML files and browsers, you will need to learn a few strategies for naming and managing local files. Note that in this section, we are working under the assumption that most Web servers run on machines using a UNIX operating system. The recommendations that we make below are necessary in a UNIX environment but should be helpful on any Web server.

File Types and Names

As you compose, pay special attention to file naming conventions. Your instructor may have developed specific conventions for your class, but in general you should name your files and directories with lowercase characters. Since these files will eventually reside on Internet servers that are case-sensitive, saving files with lowercase letters will ensure that your pages work when they are posted to the Web. The most frequent cause of broken links and images comes from mismatches between uppercase and lowercase letters. Also be aware that the names of files created on one type of machine may be altered when transferred to another platform. (For example, file names created on DOS-based machines will switch to uppercase characters on Macintosh systems.) If you have to transfer files, double-check to make sure that all the names are still correct.

Additionally, never include spaces in your file and directory names. Both browsers and servers will have trouble interpreting file names with spaces; if you need to indicate some separation between terms in your file names, you can use the underscore symbol (_), a hyphen (-), or a dot (.), but in general you should avoid overly complex names. Also, be sure to avoid strange characters in your file names, since servers may misinterpret characters like &, /, or $ when they process your links.

Finally, you'll need to know the proper extension information to use in your file names.

File Type	Extension
HTML File	.htm/.html
Text File	.txt
GIF Image File	.gif
JPEG Image File	.jpg/.jpeg
MPEG Movie	.mpg/.mpeg
QuickTime Movie	.mov
WAV Sound File	.wav
Internet Sound File (Sun/Unix)	.au

For browsers to display files properly, the files need to have the correct extensions as part of their file names. For instance, the QuickTime movie clip "film" must be named "film.mov" for a Web browser to recognize it. The standard extensions for different file types are listed above. Note that some operating systems are limited to three character suffixes, so you may have to use the shortened version for some extensions.

One of the standards used in most Web projects is to name the opening file of any directory (the page that should be displayed first) "index.html". Browsers will automatically load an "index.html" file if no other file name is specified in the URL. The best way to avoid problems is by adhering to the conventions set forth by your instructor both in your file names and in your HTML link and image tags.

Link Strategies

The link command not only lets you incorporate the URLs of Web sites into your pages, but also allows you to make "relative" or "local" links to files on your machine. With relative links, you can simply specify the file names that you want to link to. The advantage of building local links is that you can use the folder or directory structure of a drive or diskette to help organize complex Web sites. Additionally, you can compose on your local computer and the relative links should still function when moved to a Web server. Since the links are based on the relationships between the files, if you have used the proper linking and naming conventions, you'll know that pages will work regardless of whether they're on a diskette, a hard drive, or a Web server.

The simplest model for building with relative links is to place all of your files into a single directory or folder. If all the files are in the same location, then you can construct links by simply using the file name within the HTML link tag.

Figure 17.5 shows two files that are in the same folder or directory. You can create links between these files and place images within them simply by specifying the name of the file that you want to link to. For instance, a link from the "index.html" page to the "research.html" page would look like this:

```
<A HREF="research.html">Research Information</A>.
```

The advantage of having all your files in the same directory is that it simplifies the linking process. On more extensive sites, however, a single directory can become unwieldy. If you are working on a collaborative project, for instance, you may need a directory for each member of the

■ **FIGURE 17.5** A Local Link to a File in the Same Directory

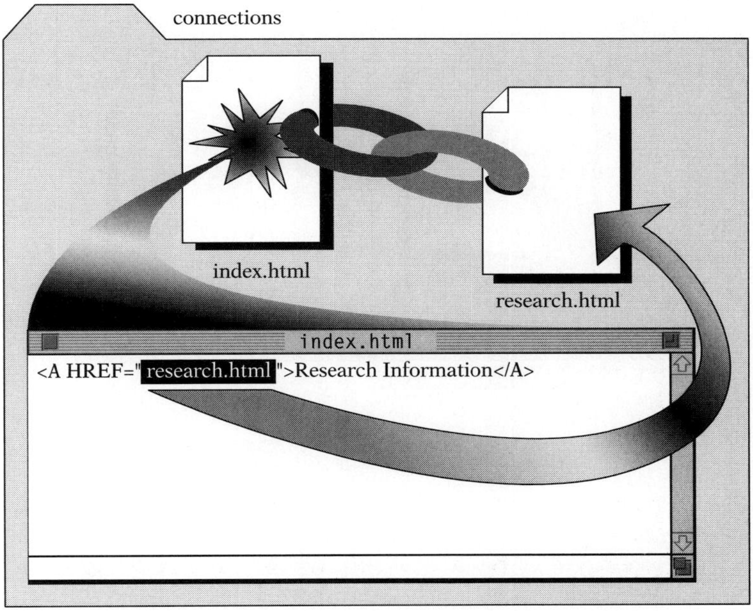

group. Even though more complex projects will have a number of directories and subdirectories, it's still advisable to connect your files with relative links.

Figure 17.6 shows a Web project that links to a file in a subdirectory. In this sample, the main page of the *Connections* site, "index.html", contains a link to a page about researching with newsgroups. In this case, however, the browser must be told to first enter the subdirectory "research" and then find the specified file "newsgroup.html" within that directory. The local link would be

```
<A HREF="research/newsgroup.html">Researching with
Newsgroups</A>
```

The command for linking to a document in a subdirectory is to specify that directory name, followed by a slash (/) and then the name of the file you want to link to.

Figure 17.7 shows the command for moving back out of a subdirectory to make a return link or a link to a file higher in the directory structure. In the sample, the link from "newsgroups.html" in the "research" directory to the contact page, "contact.html" of the "connections" direc-

■ **FIGURE 17.6** A Local Link to a File in a Subdirectory

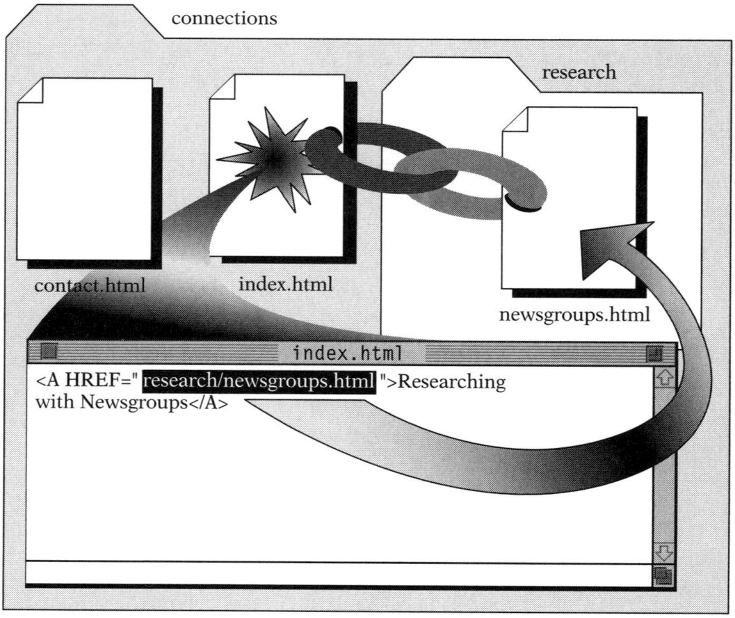

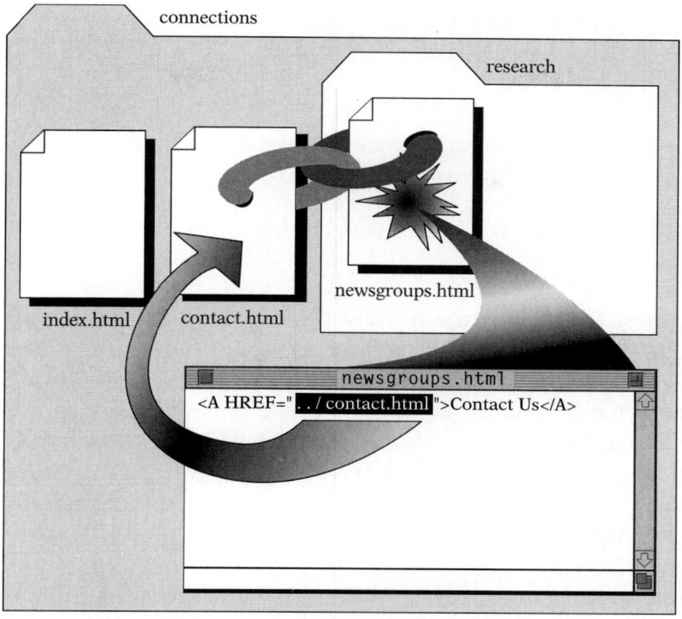

■ **FIGURE 17.7** A Local Link out of a Subdirectory

tory, is accomplished by using the ../ command. The command for linking upward in a directory structure is ../ followed by the directory or file name that you want to access. The link from the news groups page to the contact page would be

```
<A HREF="../contact.html">Contact Us</A>
```

Note that you can combine these commands any number of times if you need to make links to directories within subdirectories. For instance, from the main page, you could make a link to "research/sources/news.html". From the "news.html" page, you could back out two levels with "../../contact.html". By using the (/) command to move into directories and the (../) command to move back out, you can build projects that still utilize local links, but that also allow for more complex organizational structures.

At first, building Web sites on your own diskette or on a local drive might seem a bit tricky. You'll probably have to troubleshoot a few problems, but if you pay careful attention to the file names and your directory structures, you should be able to quickly master relative links.

Posting and Publicizing Your Work

Publication Information

To get feedback on the pages you've created, be sure to include a mail form or a <MAILTO> command:

```
<A HREF="MAILTO:bubba@whitehouse.gov">E-Mail
Bubba</A>
```

It is best to provide a contact option from all of your pages so that readers can quickly and easily offer encouragement or point out specific problems with your work. These contact forms serve several purposes. First, they act as a kind of signature for the page, demonstrating that you are taking responsibility for what you've written. Additionally, these e-mail forms add a degree of interactivity to the Web page. As you begin to receive mail from the Web, you'll be able to engage in a dialog with readers who are interested in your topic, and you can think about ways of revising your work in light of their feedback.

Along with a name and a contact form, authors usually put the date of the latest revision at the bottom of each page. This gives readers an idea of the currency of your information and helps them to determine what kinds of changes may have taken place since their last visit. Page information may also indicate whether the author is claiming copyright privileges for the content of the pages and provide information about page ownership or affiliation. Some authors will also include the URL of the page so that when readers print out a file, they will have the address handy.

Uploading and Troubleshooting

The last step in the building process is posting your files to the Web. In many cases, your instructor will be responsible for posting your files, but if you are uploading your own pages, you'll need to know something about the Web accounts at your school and File Transfer Protocol (FTP) procedures. FTP allows users to upload and download files on the Internet. Probably the best way to transfer your files is with a local FTP client such as Fetch (Mac) or CuteFTP (PC). Most of these clients have a feature that allows entire directories or folders to be uploaded at one time. If you have built projects with local links and self-contained directories, this feature will work nicely as you move files to the Web server. Of course, the procedures for uploading files will depend on the setup at your institution, so get advice from someone who is knowledgeable about your local system.

Whether you're working with a single file or an entire directory, however, you'll need to make certain that you're using the correct format when uploading files. You will want to send your HTML documents as "text" or "ASCII" and any graphics, sound, or video files as "binary" or "raw data." Make sure, too, that your client's preferences are not set to add extra suffixes such as ".txt" to the end of the file name, as this will cause problems for Web browsers when they try to read the files. Remember that you want your files on the Web server to look exactly as they do on your local machine. Once the files are up, most FTP clients have features that allow you to rename files to make minor adjustments.

Finally, use your browser to check over the files that are now on the Web server, noting any broken links or images which may not have transferred correctly. (Check with your instructor or Web server administrator to determine the URL of your site.) Often files and links that are working as you build them locally will have trouble once they reside on the server—usually, this is caused by uploading files in the wrong format or by a discrepancy between the case-sensitive file names on the server and the link information in the HTML tags. Always spend some time troubleshooting the site after it has been uploaded.

Publicizing Your Pages

If you want to attract readers to your site, you should also publicize your pages. You might contact other sites that are particularly relevant to your project—for instance, asking the administrators of the Campus Environmentalists home page to make a link to your Acid Rain project. You can also submit your site to search engines, possibly submitting to a number of engines at the same time by using sites such as Submit It (**http://www.submit-it.com/**). Remember that search engines often use the information in the <HEAD> of your document to catalog files, so be sure to include a descriptive <TITLE> and perhaps use a <META KEYWORDS= keyword1, keyword2, keyword3> tag listing additional keywords to help search engines locate your pages.

EXERCISE 17.1

Creating and Linking Pages

This assignment is designed to get you familiar with making and saving HTML files. The idea will be to build a basic Web site, linking three pages together. You can make these three pages apply to any topic; the goal here is just to get comfortable with saving, formatting, and linking HTML files. If you don't have something specific in mind, you can create an index page, a biography page, and a "cool sites" page.

- Begin by creating an "index.html" file and saving it to your diskette. This index will serve as the opening page of your site and will contain links to the other two pages. Next create and save the other two files, perhaps calling them "biography.html" and "sites.html". Once you have saved these files, set up the HTML skeleton on each page, making sure to include a short descriptive <TITLE> within the <HEAD> of the document. Also, add a heading identifying the topic of each page within the document's <BODY>.
- Next, open the "index.html" page and place some introductory information between the <BODY></BODY> tags. Don't worry about providing too much content; just try experimenting with some of the formatting tags, possibly providing headings, varying the text styles, and using horizontal rules and line breaks.
- Next, compose two short phrases that will act as hot text for the links to your other two pages. Insert the tags for creating links around the phrases. For instance, your link to the personal page might look like this:

```
<A HREF="biography.html">Find out more about
me.</A>
```

- After you have made the links to the other pages, open the index page with a browser and make sure that the links work.
- Finally, open your other two pages in your editor and add some content. At the bottom of each page, be sure to place a return link to your opening page with a command such as:

```
<A HREF="index.html">Back to the home page.</A>
```

- Once you've added your return links and additional content, check all of the pages with a browser to make sure that everything is working properly.

Although this exercise is designed primarily to get you comfortable with managing files and making links, you can continue to flesh out these pages as you learn more about HTML.

Tips and Tactics

- Composing basic HTML is a process of formatting a text document. You tell the Web browser how to display a document by putting different "on" and "off" switches around the text you want to format. Start with the skeleton, then format the body of your page. Finally, add text, images, and links to increase appeal, meaning and functionality.
- "View the source" of other pages on the Web to learn new HTML techniques.
- Use an HTML editor to automate many aspects of HTML scripting. You should also get used to the composition process of working in the editor to make changes to your document, saving the document, and then checking your work in a Web browser.
- Build files on a drive or diskette using relative or local links.
- Be sure to include a <MAILTO> command so that readers can get in touch with you, and don't forget to register your site with various Internet search engines.
- Include your name, your e-mail address, and the date of the last revision on each of your pages.
- Make sure that your file names and formats are correct and that your links and images work once your pages have been uploaded to the Web.

CHAPTER 18

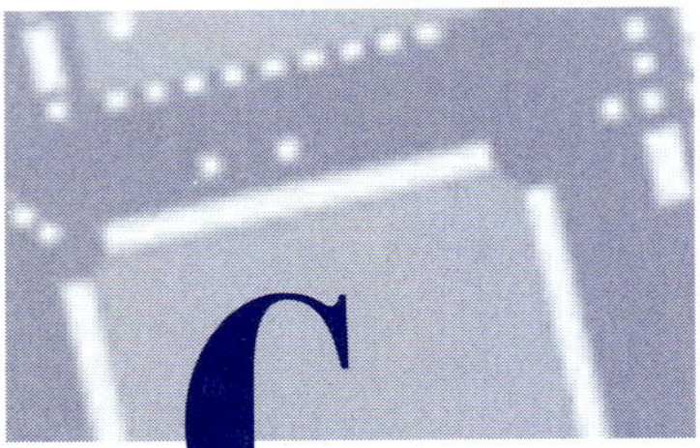

CONSIDERING PAGE LAYOUT

Once you understand the basic principles of HTML, you'll want to integrate various building elements into the design of an entire Web page. To produce Web designs that are both practical and aesthetically pleasing, you'll need to decide on the most effective ways of using space and presenting information. We'll talk in more detail about the rhetorical considerations of Web design and site organization in **Chapter 19,** but for now, let's look at some of the options for controlling page layout in HTML. □

Body Backgrounds and Font Colors

As we discussed in **Chapter 17,** most Web browsers prefer that every HTML page have a core set of elements that we call the HTML skeleton. In this chapter, we are most concerned with those elements that appear in the <BODY> section and control the look and layout of a Web page.

KEY TERMS

Background: An image or color that is tiled multiple times to form the background of a Web page.

Imagemap: An image with hot spots that activate hypertext links. Clicking on sections of the image will take readers to different Web files.

Linked Graphic: A graphic that, when clicked, activates a hypertext link to another node on the Web.

RGB (Red, Green, and Blue) Color Codes: Six-digit (hexadecimal) codes used to designate different text and background colors on the Web. RGB codes mix different proportions of the three primary colors to create the various colors of the spectrum.

Table: A Web page layout that presents information in rows and columns.

Remember, though, that all HTML files should contain this skeletal information:

```
<HTML><HEAD>

<TITLE>Put Title Here</TITLE>

</HEAD>

<BODY>

Put All the Text and Images That Will Appear On Your
Web Page Here

</BODY>

</HTML>
```

When you introduce the body of a document with the <BODY></BODY> tags, you can also specify some information about the overall appearance of the page. Most commonly, this opportunity is used to adjust background images and font colors.

The background feature allows authors to specify a color or image that will function almost like tiled wallpaper, with any text or images appearing "on top of" the background. Backgrounds can take countless forms—anything from a one-toned color to a textured pattern to psychedelic fractals to lush, red velvet. When used effectively, backgrounds can add significantly to the "feel" of the page.

The background code is included in the first <BODY> tag of the standard HTML skeleton. For instance, if we were putting up a Web page for Hot Joe's Coffee Shop, we might want to use a tiled image of a "cuppa joe" as our background. Backgrounds, like all images on the Web, must be in either GIF or JPEG format. If we had a GIF image with several cups of coffee on it, we could incorporate it as our background with the HTML scripting shown in Figure 18.1.

Although using a background image, such as the one shown in Figure 18.1, often makes a page more visually dynamic, it also poses certain challenges to authors. The most obvious of these difficulties is legibility. Although a bright, multicolored background can be a real attention grabber, it often makes it very difficult to read the text. Sometimes this problem can be eliminated by changing the text color to a contrasting shade. For instance, if you were using a black background, you would need to make the color of the text lighter and more visible. Authors can set the color of the text (<TEXT>), links (<LINK>), and links which have

■ **FIGURE 18.1** A Background Image

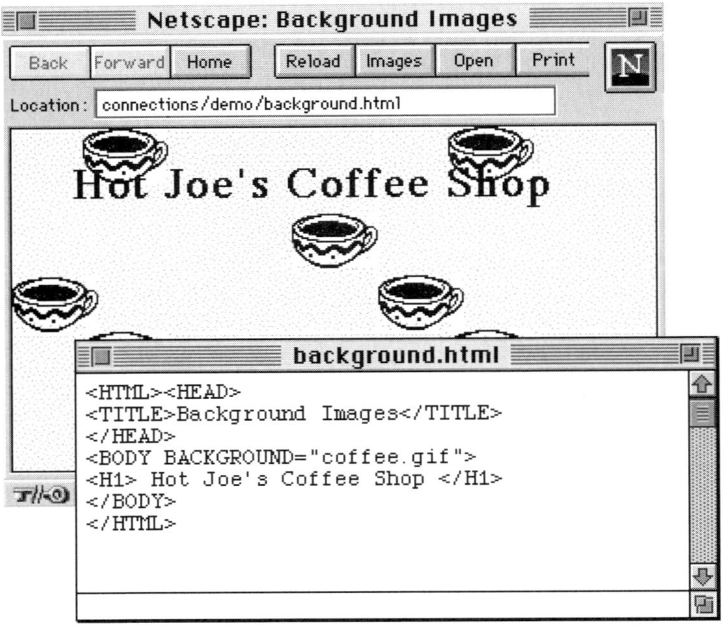

already been visited (<VLINK>) for an entire page within the initial <BODY> tag. The HTML code for putting in black text, blue links, and orange visited links on a white background is shown in Figure 18.2.

Instead of using an image file, the background in Figure 18.2 is generated by the <BGCOLOR> command, which tells the browser to set the background to a solid color—in this case, white. Notice that the text, link, and visited link colors are generated by a combination of letters and numbers. These combinations are called "RGB color codes."

These hexadecimal color codes represent a combination of red, green, and blue (the three primary colors), which blend in various proportions to create the desired shade. The first two letters or numbers represent a shade of red, the next two are green, and the final two are blue. Every color in the spectrum from black to white can be made with some combination of these three elements. As you can imagine, however, they are not very intuitive. For example, there's no way that an author who wants to use chartreuse text could figure out the appropriate code without the help of a color-picking application.

Luckily, most HTML editors now come complete with a color-generating feature. Usually, the HTML editor will display some type of color wheel that shows each color in the spectrum. Users click on the shade that they want, and the editor automatically generates the six-digit RGB color code. In case you don't have access to one of these applications, here are a few codes for some of the basic colors you might be using:

- White = "#FFFFFF"
- Blue = "#0000DD"

FIGURE 18.2 Background and Font Colors

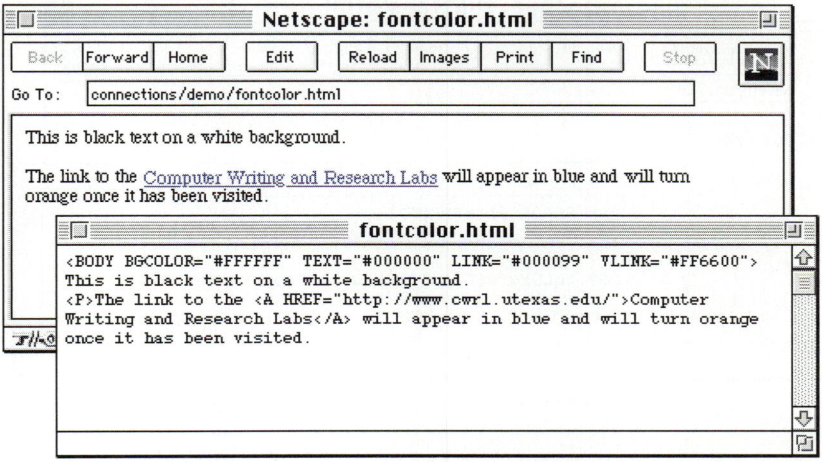

- Green = "#007700"
- Red = "#EE0000"
- Yellow = "#FFFF00"
- Brown = "#663300"
- Purple = "#990099"

By placing these color codes into the initial <BODY> tag of your document, then, you can designate the font colors for the entire Web page.

Note that different monitors process colors differently. It's extremely frustrating to see your soothing cerulean blue background turn a moldy green on your neighbor's monitor. If you use the RGB codes for the standard 216 colors that register correctly on most browsers, you should be safe. You can get more detailed information about the standard color codes at **http://www.phoenix.net/~jacobson/rgb.html** or at the *Connections* Web site.

You can also change the color of certain sections of text within the body of your document by using the <FONT COLOR></FONT> tags. For instance, Figure 18.3 shows a Web page on which one sentence appears in black and another in blue on a white background.

As you develop a color scheme for your pages, you'll need to coordinate font colors with your background images in a way that works to set an appropriate tone for your project. Some backgrounds may be too bright or "busy," making the text unreadable. Here you'll need to evaluate

■ **FIGURE 18.3** <FONT COLOR></FONT> Tags

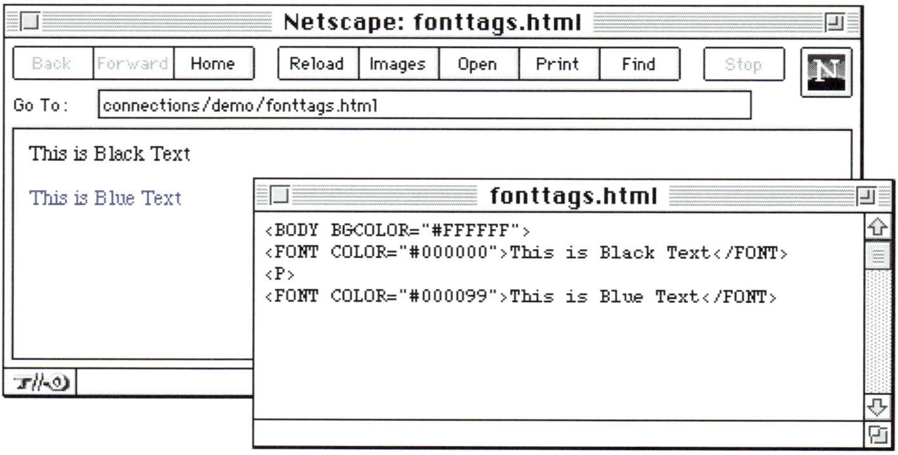

the page's purpose and decide how important legibility is. If you're building a project with a substantial amount of text, you'll probably want to use a fairly neutral background that makes it easy to read the print. In this case, you also want to avoid using excessively bright font colors that will strain the reader's eyes. If, on the other hand, you're setting up a personal page to express the elements of reckless abandon for which you've become famous, you'll have a unique opportunity to use backgrounds as a conduit through which you can express your deepest emotions and release your playful inner child. Well, at least you'll have more room to experiment.

Space on the Page

Because the Web is such a visual medium and because it allows multiple nodes of information to be collected and presented on a single page, Web users have developed different expectations for how text should be integrated into a composition. While readers of books or scholarly journals are used to finding information presented in long, continuous streams of text, Web audiences expect to find images, interesting spatial layouts, and shorter units of information that are hypertextually linked.

Rather than thinking about the paragraph or the printed page as organizational elements, it is often helpful to consider the screen as a logical unit of design. In other words, you'll want to decide how much information will fit on a single screen and how much scrolling will be distracting to a reader (this will vary depending on monitor size, but you can probably assume that most users will have at least a fourteen- or fifteen-inch monitor). The challenge is to determine how to effectively and efficiently structure the space of the Web page so that your information is presented with maximum effect.

Lists

One common method of organizing space and information on the Web is through the use of various types of lists. HTML offers several possible options for listing information.

Definition List A definition list displays items with an annotation or definition appearing on an indented line beneath each item, as shown in Figure 18.4.

Unnumbered List An unnumbered list indents and bullets each item, as shown in Figure 18.5.

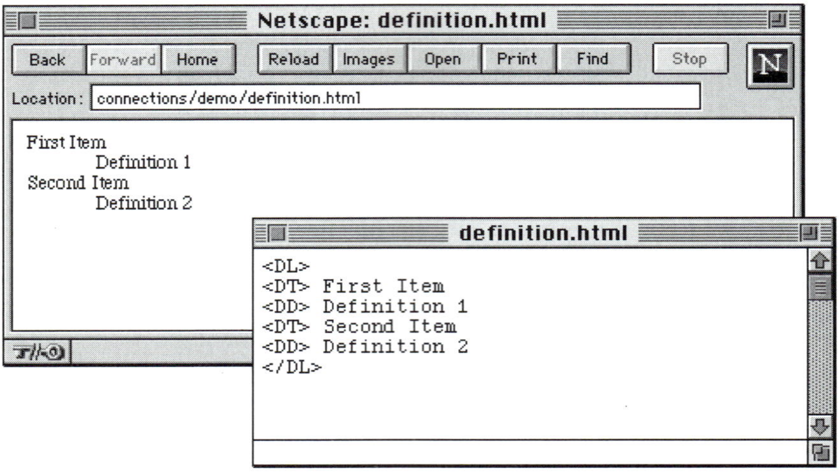

■ **FIGURE 18.4** A Definition List

Numbered List A numbered list indents and numbers each item, as shown in Figure 18.6.

Menu A menu is a list of indented items, as shown in Figure 18.7.

Note that you can use the <MENU> command multiple times to move the text toward the right-hand margin.

■ **FIGURE 18.5** An Unnumbered List

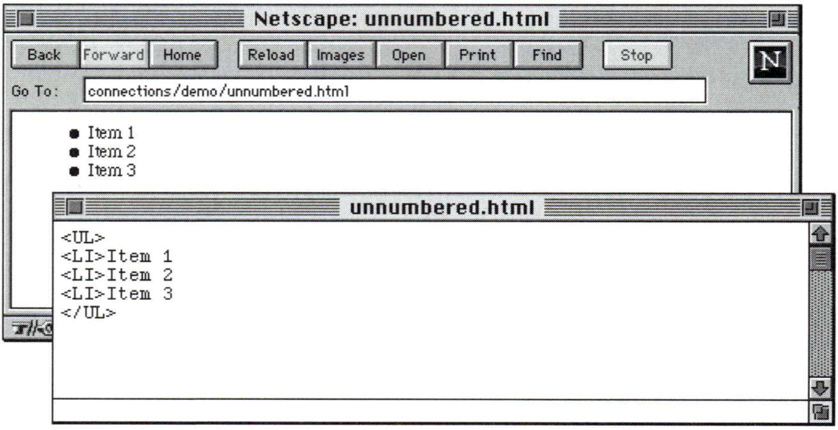

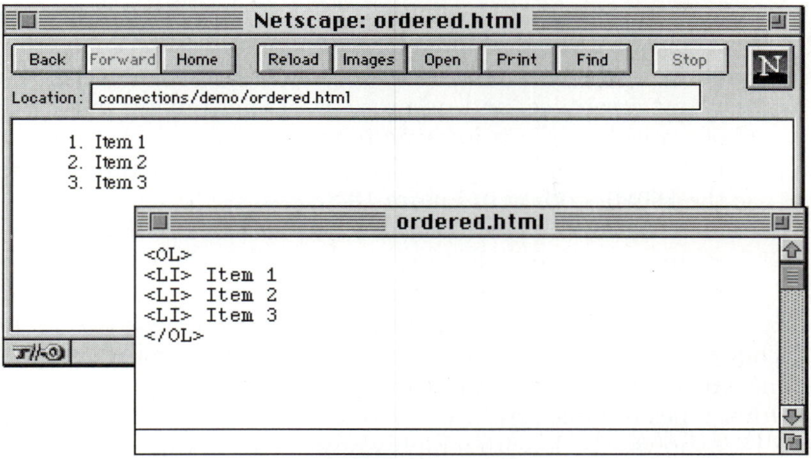

■ **FIGURE 18.6** A Numbered List

Tables

Although lists are simple and effective, they are limited in that they generally waste a certain amount of horizontal space and that they present information in a linear fashion. A more flexible method of organizing information is the table. This feature was first supported by the Netscape browser, but most other browsers now interpret tables.

■ **FIGURE 18.7** A Menu

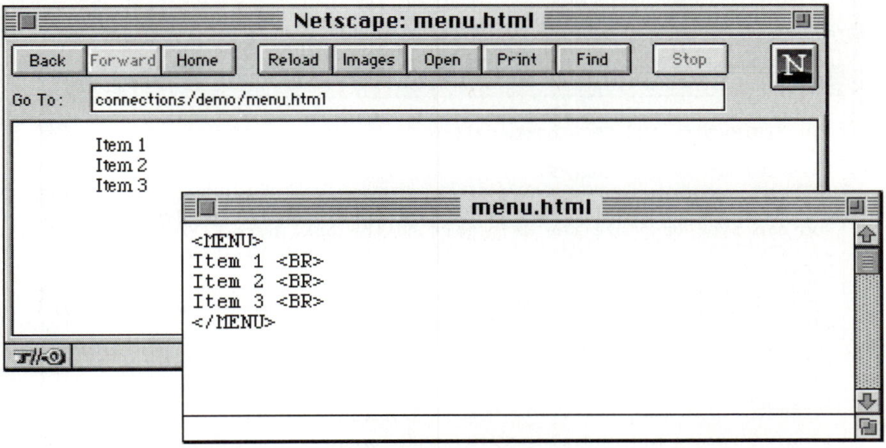

Tables allow authors to divide the screen into a series of horizontal and vertical cells (much like a spreadsheet). The individual cells can vary in size, can have different types of borders, can be visible or invisible, and can contain text, graphics, and other types of files, giving the author a great deal of control over how information is displayed on the screen. For instance, an author who wants to design a page using three columns might use the HTML coding in Figure 18.8.

In Figure 18.8, the cells are invisible, but the text and images are segmented into three columns. All three pieces of table data, <TD>, are displayed within a single table row, <TR>. The left and right columns each fill 20% of the screen, and the middle column occupies the remaining 60%. This means that regardless of browser window or monitor size, the columns will always stay in proportion.

Other types of tables show the boundaries of each cell more clearly. Figure 18.9 shows a table with a highly pronounced border.

In Figure 18.9, the "BORDER=10" command places the large shadowed border around the outside of the table. Instead of using only one

■ **FIGURE 18.8** A Three-Column Table

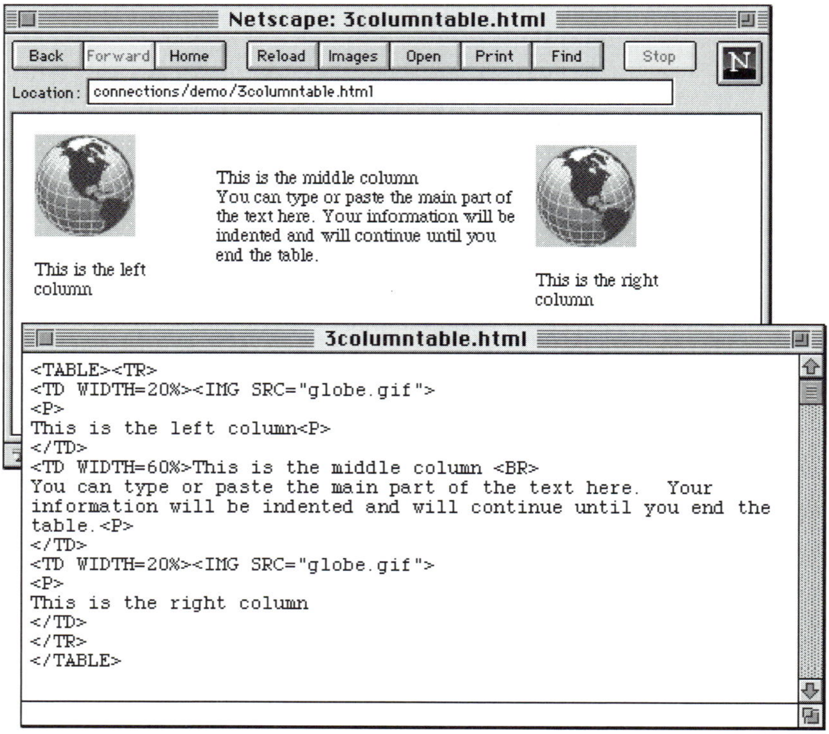

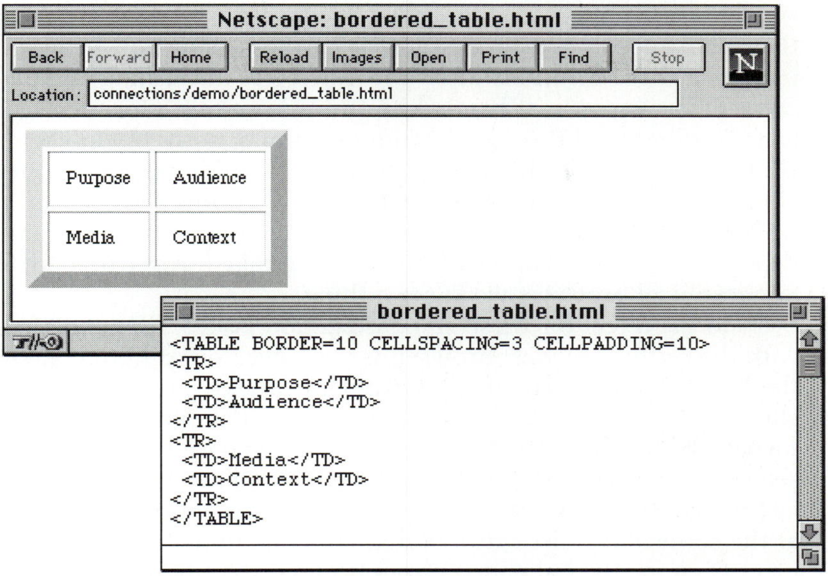

■ **FIGURE 18.9** A Bordered Table

row, this table uses two sets of <TR> commands with two cells in each row. The command <CELLSPACING> refers to the size of the line between the cells, and the command <CELLPADDING> refers to the amount of space between the text and the cell borders. By experimenting with the border, cellpadding, and cellspacing, you can develop tables which will offer you a clean, efficient way to display information on the screen.

FOR CLASS DISCUSSION

Note: This discussion requires access to different Web browsers. If your lab or classroom doesn't provide access to multiple browsers, you can download them from the Net. See the *Connections* Web site for information about current Web browsers.

Since not all browsers display text, images, and formatting in the same way, it's impossible to control every aspect of the way your pages will appear on the Web. Besides the fact that browsers interpret commands differently, variations in monitors and differences in browser window size can change the layout of a page by altering what constitutes a "screenful." Often, your efforts to make your opening graphic exactly tall enough to match perfectly with your last line of text will be thwarted when users change the size of their browser window.

There are ways to standardize the layout of your pages so that they will appear nearly identical regardless of which browser is used, but these solutions often provide fewer interesting layouts or come at the expense of bandwidth (the amount of information that can be transferred through an Internet connection). If you keep the HTML formatting so plain that all browsers will interpret the pages similarly, your site won't have much pizzazz. Conversely, if you control almost all features of the layout by making your presentation depend heavily on graphics, your site will take forever to load, and nongraphical browsers won't see a thing.

To get a feel for these standardization issues, first experiment with the settings in your browser as you check out different sites on the Web. (Your instructor may want to provide you with a list of sites.) Try browsing a few graphic-heavy sites with your images turned off. Try changing the default text size and font in your browser settings. Finally, view the site with your window sized smaller and larger than the standard setting. Next, use different browsers to look at the same sites. List features that stay functionally the same, and identify elements that change from browser to browser.

Hold a class discussion about the most important considerations for standardization. Are there times when standardization and universal access are more important than nonstandard features and vice versa? Do you prefer pages that take a more standard approach to page layout or pages that lean toward innovative design? How can you best balance standardization and innovation? As a class, come up with strategies for making your pages both interesting and accessible.

Working with Graphics

Graphics have become so universally integrated into Web building that authors are almost expected to use images in their pages. We'll discuss tactics for handling graphics files below, but for now, let's briefly review the HTML coding and then look at ways to align images on your pages.

Image Source

Remember that images aren't actually a part of the HTML file—they are separate files that are linked to the HTML file with a tag. The basic command for an image is shown in Figure 18.10.

The Web browser reads this code and displays the image "globe.gif", which in this case is a graphics file that is stored in the same directory as the HTML page.

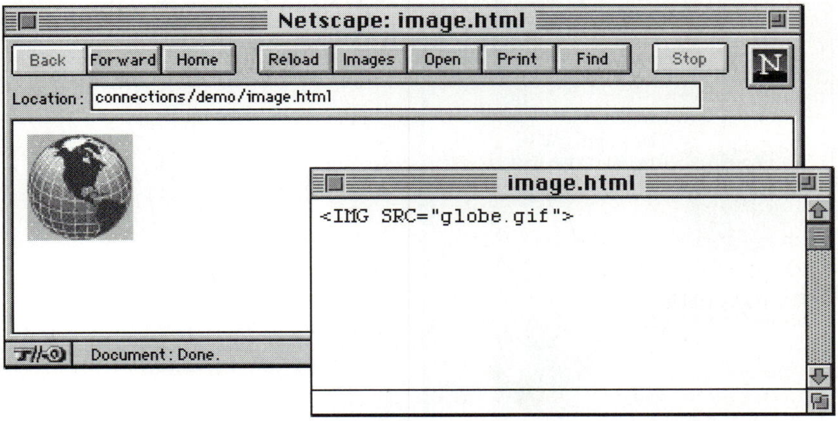

■ **FIGURE 18.10** A Basic Image

Simply placing images on the page, however, won't necessarily help you to present a complex message or argument. The key is learning how to integrate graphics with the text of your project so that each element is enhanced by the other. Again, think of the screen as the principal unit of composition, and try to make economical use of the available space by blending the text and graphics into a complementary relationship.

One way to integrate your text and images is to align the graphics in different ways. HTML gives you options for aligning graphics to the left or right of text. For instance, an author who wants to discuss two images might use the HTML code shown in Figure 18.11.

When you align an image to one side of the page, you will need to tell the browser at what point you want the text to go back to normal page alignment. This is accomplished by using either the <BR CLEAR=LEFT> or the <BR CLEAR=RIGHT> command. You can also insert space between the image and the text by using the horizontal space <HSPACE> or vertical space <VSPACE> command.

By experimenting with the various methods of alignment, you can produce the effect that you are after and find the best way of combining your text and graphics on the page.

ALT Tags

When working with graphics, don't forget that many people surf the Web with their images "turned off" to increase loading speed. Additionally, some people with limited access to the Web or with physical disabilities will be using nongraphical browsers. For these reasons, you should always

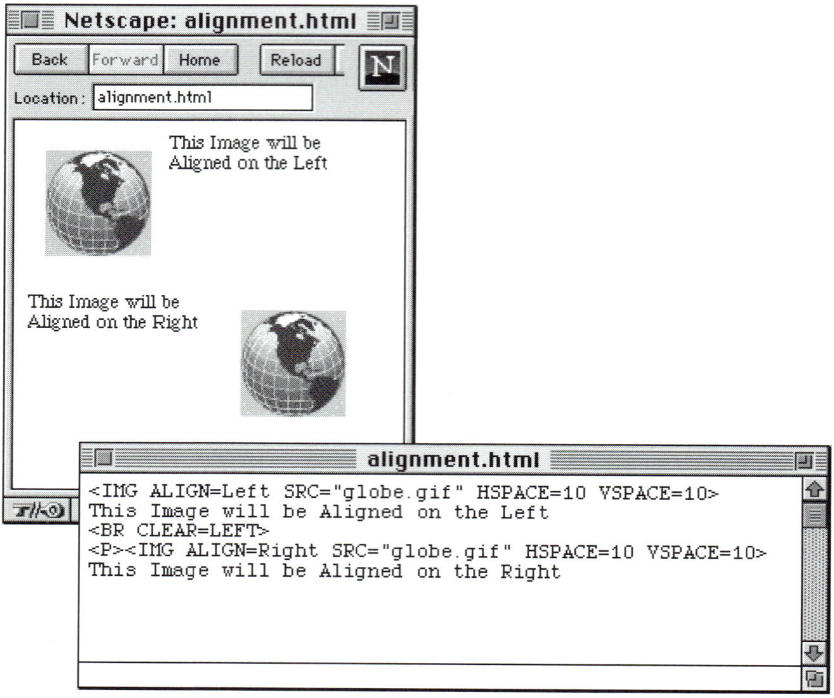

FIGURE 18.11 Image Alignment

provide an alternative description of your images. <ALT> tags appear anywhere within the image command and are commonly used both to provide a description of the image and to tell users where a linked image is pointing. Figure 18.12 displays the <ALT> description on a page being viewed with the images turned off.

By using <ALT> tags for each of your images, you will make your page more accessible to the many users who by either choice or necessity browse the Web without graphical capabilities.

Linked Graphics and Imagemaps

Another way that graphics can be integrated into the design of a Web page is by using images to create links. For instance, to take readers to the index page of the *Connections* Web site, you might link from a small image of our logo by using the following code:

```
<A HREF="http://www.abacon.com/connections/
index.html">
<IMG SRC="minilogo.gif" BORDER=0></A>
```

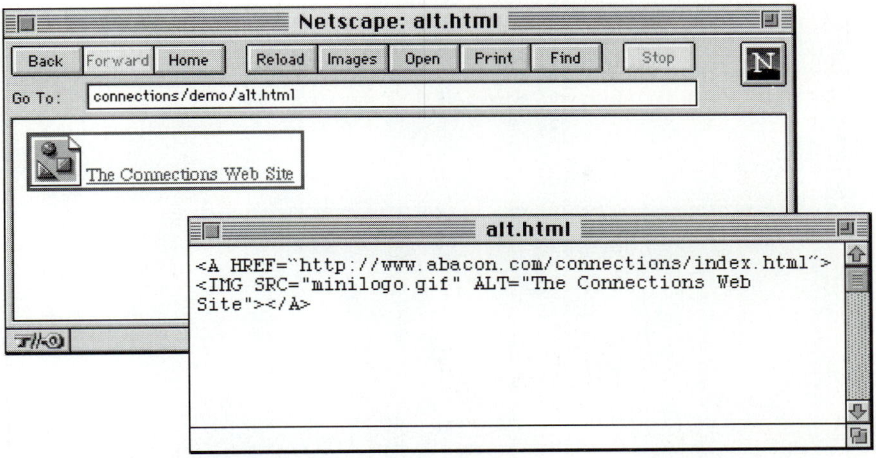

■ **FIGURE 18.12** <ALT> Tags

By default, a thin colored line will appear around the edges of the image to indicate that it's a link. We've eliminated this border by adding the command BORDER=0 to the image tag.

You can make your pages more visually appealing by using icons that act as links. Often you will see a small image of a house used to indicate "home page" or an image of an envelope to graphically illustrate "send us e-mail." More complicated concepts are obviously harder to represent, but if you are able to find images that convey the major themes of your site, you can use them as navigational aids. If you incorporate a consistent set of icons, your readers will be able to quickly locate the links to major sections of the site.

A second method of using images to facilitate navigation is to set up an imagemap. Imagemaps are single images (generally images with multiple objects in them) that are "mapped" so that a reader can go to different pages by clicking on different sections of the image. Often the opening page of a site will contain an imagemap that leads to its major nodes. For instance, the imagemap shown in Figure 18.13 was used in a composition class to provide links to student projects.

Clicking on any of the names in the image will take you to the corresponding section of the class Web site. Using imagemaps is more complicated than simply linking an image, but as you can see, it does offer some significant rewards. If you can find an image that will provide a suitable metaphor for your site and has enough elements to represent multiple nodes, you can incorporate a tremendous amount of information into a visually dramatic presentation. (For information about setting up imagemaps, see **Appendix 5.**)

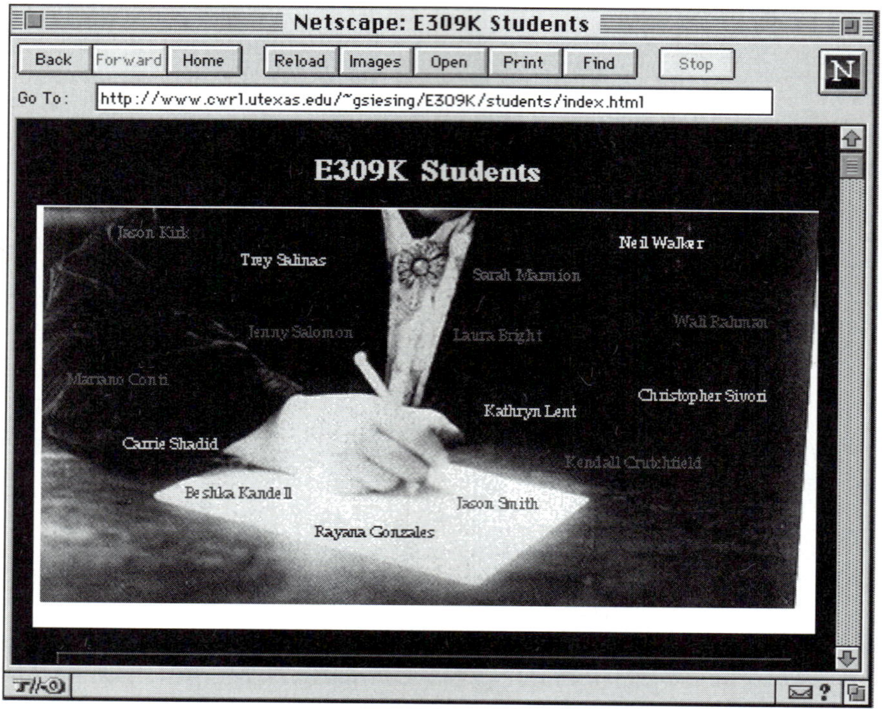

■ **FIGURE 18.13** An Imagemap from a Class Site

Tips for Working with Web Images

Once you understand how to place graphics into your HTML documents, you need to begin considering the graphics files themselves and some of the complications that will arise as you begin working with them.

Image File Size Probably the single most important concern for graphical Web composition is the size of the image file—not so much in terms of inches (we'll get to that in a moment), but in terms of bytes of stored information. The smaller the image is and the fewer images you have, the faster your page will load. Particularly for Web readers who are using modems, the amount of time it takes for pages to load is a major concern. It can be extremely frustrating to wait several minutes for a browser to download an 800 kb (kilobyte) image, only to find out that it is a flashy but nonessential part of the site. Web authors need to continually balance the desire for interesting and impressive graphics with practical concerns about the speed and efficiency of their pages.

Graphics Editors

To manipulate images, you will need a graphics editor. Several useful shareware applications for editing graphics are available on the Net, such as GraphicConverter (Mac) and LView Pro (PC). Often, colleges and universities purchase site licenses for these programs, making them available for use by students, faculty, and staff. With a simple graphics-editing program, you can crop and resize as well as change the resolution and file format of digital images. Many of these editors also allow you to create colored backgrounds and insert text into image files.

If you plan to do extensive graphics work, you may want to use a more sophisticated editor. There are several commercial applications that allow you to manipulate images by adding textures, patterns, layers, and other special effects. Unfortunately, these applications are usually expensive; check whether you have access to one at your institution. Also be prepared to invest more time in learning the operations of these more complex programs.

The idea is to think small. Ideally, you should keep most of your graphics files under 20 kb. You may need to make exceptions for an opening banner or other important images, but in general, steer away from large images unless they are essential to the page. There are a few basic strategies that can help you reduce the size of an image.

- The easiest way to reduce the number of bytes is by reducing the physical size of the image. Scaling down an image by removing an inch or two can make a significant difference in its file size.
- The Web can only display graphics at 72 dots per inch (dpi), so saving files at higher resolutions won't make the images clearer. In fact, Web browsers read all images at 72 dpi, meaning that a four-inch graphic saved at 150 dpi will turn into an eight-inch graphic on the Web.
- If you are using a transparent image or setting up an imagemap, you may need to use a GIF format. Otherwise, saving files in JPEG format will be more efficient, since they are generally smaller than GIF files. (We'll discuss file formats later in this section.)
- Use only as many colors as you need. Using 256 colors drastically reduces the size of an image that was originally created in millions of colors. Similarly, reducing an image to 64 or 32 colors will shrink its file size even further, although eventually the resolution of the image will suffer.

There are also various graphics applications that do an impressive job of compressing image files. If you are doing a significant amount of graphics work, you might want to consider investing in one of these programs so you can experiment with the resolution and size of images.

Image Scale In some ways, creating Web pages should be compared to laying out newspaper or magazine pages rather than to composing long blocks of academic text. If you think of the screen as your working space, you can better understand the need to scale down the physical size of your graphics so that no single image will overwhelm the presentation. Screen "real-estate" is a precious commodity in Web design. Placing a 6 × 6 inch graphic at the top of your page when you have only, say, a 7 × 10 inch window will leave you with almost no room to integrate the other elements of your composition.

Transparent Images You may also want to make some of your images "transparent." Transparent images allow the background of your Web page to "show through" by making one of the colors in the image "invisible." Web authors frequently use transparent images because they can be integrated more seamlessly into the page design. Because image files are saved in rectangular format, nontransparent images will be set off by this rectangular background when placed onto a Web page, resulting in an awkward appearance. There are many shareware applications that will allow you to make transparent images, such as Transparency (Mac) and GifWeb (PC). Note that transparencies require that you work with a GIF file instead of a JPEG.

Image File Formats There are two basic file formats for graphics on the Web: GIF and JPEG. Both of these formats are cross-platform, meaning that they can be read by Macintoshes, PCs, and UNIX-based computers. Since older PCs have strict naming conventions that accept only three character suffixes, files that are named .JPEG must be called .JPG on some machines.

When you're working with Web graphics, it is important to save your images as either GIF or JPEG files. As we mentioned above, JPEGs are usually smaller, so it is generally worthwhile to use this format on most of your image files. The major exception to this rule is if you want to make your image transparent, in which case you'll need to use a GIF file.

Note that, for browsers to read the image, the file extension must correspond to the format in which the file is saved. If you name a file that is saved in the GIF format "picture.jpg," the browser will be unable to properly display the image. The same, of course, goes for JPEG files that are named with the .GIF extension. Also remember that all image files must have an acceptable suffix in place. A file named "picture.gifsmall" or "jpg.pictureofme" will not be readable. The naming convention is strict in that you cannot use spaces or quotation marks in the name and you must attach the appropriate suffix.

EXERCISE 18.1

Revising the Layout of Your Personal Page

The goal of this exercise is to incorporate the aesthetic design elements discussed in this chapter into a personal home page. If you already have a home page started, you can begin refurbishing your page, using the tactics below. If not, you can get started by performing the page-building exercise at the end of **Chapter 17.**

- Begin by choosing a background for your page. If you don't already have an image or color in mind, try doing a keyword search for "background patterns" and browse through the images on the sites that you find. Once you've decided on an appropriate background, add the background to your page and adjust your font colors if necessary.
- Next experiment with various ways of presenting the information on your pages. Try using lists and tables to control the horizontal and vertical layout of the text.
- Next, try incorporating some images into your page. Experiment with the ways in which different alignments influence the layout and appearance of the text on your page. Try making images transparent. Remember to choose an appropriate scale for the images and to keep their file size to a minimum.
- If your project has more than one page, be sure to standardize the pages' appearance.

In general, try to present the information in a way that maximizes the visual appeal of the page. Remember that as you grow more comfortable with Web design, you may want to redesign your home page to present the information more clearly and attractively.

Tips and Tactics

- Use background images and font colors to enhance the look of your pages, but use them appropriately. Never sacrifice legibility to a flashy background.
- Use lists to control the vertical layout of information. Use tables to achieve even greater horizontal control of page layout. Tables make it possible to convey a great deal of information in a very small amount of screen space, but they should be small enough to work on many different sizes of monitors, and not all browsers currently support them.
- Use images to enhance your Web pages, but make sure that they are appropriate to your project. Don't use images that monopolize the screen, and don't overload the screen with too many images.
- Try using linked images or imagemaps as a way of integrating iconic representations into the design of your pages.
- Use <ALT> tags to provide alternative descriptions of your images to readers who are viewing the page with nongraphical browsers or with their images turned off.
- Be sure that your image file sizes are as small as possible to decrease the loading time of your Web pages.
- In general, use JPEG instead of GIF format and be sure that your file extensions match the image format.

CHAPTER 19

BLACK TIE REQUIRED

Web Building with Style

As we saw in the previous two chapters, building on the Web demands that authors take a new approach to the process of composition. At the same time, however, composing on the Web requires that you carefully organize and present your information, think about your audience, and consider your purpose—the same fundamental rhetorical strategies that you apply to print-based writing. □

Argument and the Web

To help you develop strategies for creating arguments on the Web, let's look at some analogies between hypertexts and more traditional print essays. For instance, most essays open with an introductory or topic paragraph. This opening usually accomplishes several things: It outlines the direction of the argument by stating the thesis; it demonstrates the importance of the project; and it works to spark the reader's interest. You can think of the opening page of a Web composition in the same terms: It situates the

KEY TERMS

Common Gateway Interface (CGI): A program that allows browsers to submit information to the Web server. CGIs are actually a combination of an interface that permits the sharing of information and a script that manipulates that information. Web forums and add-link scripts are common examples of CGIs.

Hypertext: A composition that links pieces of information (often called "nodes") together into complex, interactive webs.

Link: (1) As a noun, the connection between sections, or nodes, of a hypertext. Often links are activated by clicking on hot text or icons. (2) As a verb, the process of connecting pieces of information into a hypertextual form.

Node: One unit of a hypertext. A node can be a document, a graphic, a sound file, or any other individual piece of information that has been linked to a hypertext.

project for readers, whets their interest, and maps out the major points to be explored.

When you produce an argument in a print essay, you can usually assume that readers will encounter the information in the order in which you present it. However, hypertexts make managing the sequences in which readers move through your information more important. (See, for instance, the discussion of MU* structure in **Chapter 16.**) As an author, then, you will need to take steps to ensure that readers see the information that matters most. Figure 19.1 shows a possible structure for a Web-based argument.

You can see in Figure 19.1 that the opening page, "index.html", contains links to the subpages, "future.html" and "past.html". However, the opening page doesn't provide a link to the last subsection, "actions.html". While hypertext takes away some of an author's control by allowing readers to select which links they will follow, you can still determine which links readers have to choose from. In this case, readers must first pass through the "future" or "past" section before being able to link to the "actions" page. If it is important to your argument that readers know something about your major supporting claims before they try to understand your conclusion, then you can lead them through the claims before providing the final link.

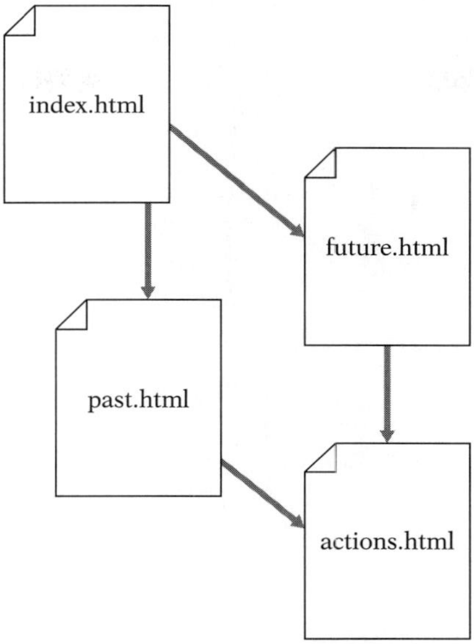

■ **FIGURE 19.1** Paths through a Web Argument

You should remember, however, that one of the strengths of hypertextual writing is that it allows readers to choose their own paths through a collection of documents. If you create a project in which the links are too prescriptive, the end result can often be a linear hypertext with a structure that resembles a print-based essay. This sort of control may be necessary on occasion—for instance, if you are composing instructions that lead readers through a step-by-step process. In general, however, Web readers expect a more fluid form of composition, one that relies on the interconnection of themes and ideas.

Figure 19.2 shows an argument that balances some of the need for sequential progression with some of the fluidity of hypertext. Although a reader must still pass through one of the two main subsections of the site ("future.html" or "past.html") to reach the "actions.html" node, there is now the possibility of more horizontal movement between the subsections. Additionally, readers can move back up through the document from the "actions" node. Although this is still a very basic model, it illustrates some of the potential for making a reader's movements through your information more fluid and hypertextual.

As you increase the number of nodes and the level of interconnectivity in a project, you may simply have to concede the fact that different readers will take different paths through the document and not all of your materials will be read. In fact, you'll need to pay specific attention to some

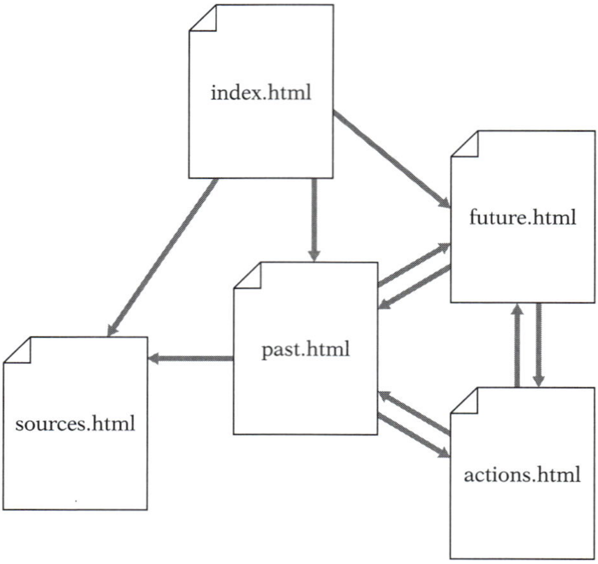

■ **FIGURE 19.2** A More Complex Argument

of the complications raised by the number of options that readers have for moving through your project. One strategy is to consider the introduction of each major subsection as a transition. Unlike the transitions between two paragraphs of an essay, however, hypertextual transitions should account for the many possible paths that readers might have taken to get to that section.

For instance, since readers of more complex hypertexts can become disoriented or miss sections, you'll probably want to provide some information about the project as a whole near the beginning of each node. In the model shown in Figure 19.2, for instance, an author composing the "actions" node might reiterate (and link back to) the major claims of the "past" and "future" pages for readers who may have missed one of the sections. By carefully composing a purpose or position statement for each major section of a hypertext, you can articulate the relevance of that section within the project as a whole and in terms of its relation to other nodes.

Challenges of Hypertext

Linearity and Complexity

Generally speaking, most Web authors try to avoid long pages of scrolling text. This is partly because long pages mean slow loading times, and partly because reading lengthy blocks of text on a computer screen can be tough on the eyes. Academic writing, on the other hand, places great value on long, uninterrupted sections of text because they allow an author to work through complicated ideas systematically. In fact, one of the reasons the Web is often criticized in academic circles is that it further emphasizes what is perceived to be a cultural trend toward the sound bite, the quick and easy encapsulation of a complex concept.

The two writing styles, however, don't need to be mutually exclusive. For one thing, as more academic writing is published on-line, the Web convention for brevity will likely be altered somewhat to account for arguments that need extended development. More important, though, length and complexity can be achieved in multiple ways. For instance, although each page of a Web site might not be particularly long, the cumulative text of sites with multiple nodes will often be quite lengthy. Additionally, complex texts can be made more accessible by carefully sectioning up the information and hypertextually linking the various pieces together. This allows an author to point readers to other parts of the project, to include relevant source materials, to suggest connections between ideas, and to develop "tangents" (perhaps relegated to a footnote or a parenthetical reference in a traditional article) in more depth without interrupting the flow of the main argument.

Problems of Navigation

As we have seen, hypertexts, particularly Web hypertexts, pose a number of navigational difficulties. When complex hypertexts are unclear about where links are leading, readers often become frustrated—unsure about which nodes they have visited and how much of the text they have explored.

It is generally a good idea to give readers clear options about how to move around in a Web site. This means providing links in visible places and carefully explaining where each link is pointing. It is especially important to tell readers when they are linking to materials on another site so that they can decide whether or not to follow the link.

One way to help readers move through your site is by providing a navigational imagemap. If you can find or create an appropriate image, these graphical maps add an air of sophistication to the site while helping readers navigate through your information.

For projects like the one in Figure 19.3 that have clearly distinguished nodes, graphical maps can be an excellent tool for navigation. Because most Web sites quickly evolve into complex structures, however, graphical maps may be hard to implement on many sites. (See **Appendix 5** for more information about how to implement imagemaps.)

If using a map seems unlikely, another option is to create a standard menu or index. One strategy for using menus is to place them at the

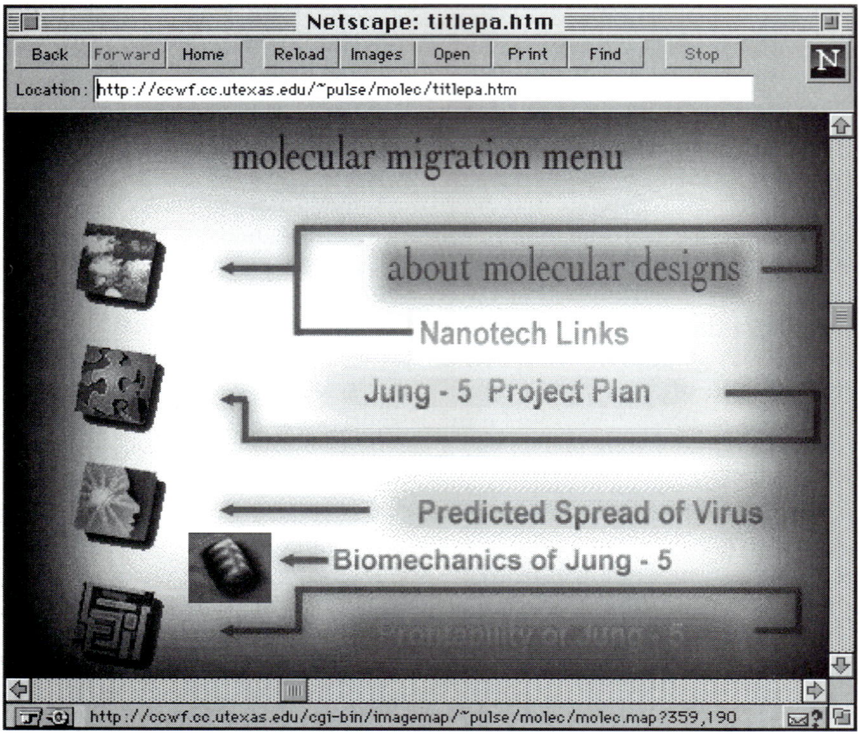

■ **FIGURE 19.3** An Imagemap in a Student Project

bottom of every page on the site. The advantage of using "footers" like this is that when readers finish scrolling through a page, they can easily choose where to move next.

Note that the footer shown in Figure 19.4 uses text to represent the various sections of a site. Although many sites link from images or icons, most of them also provide a description of the section with a word or

■ **FIGURE 19.4** A Footer

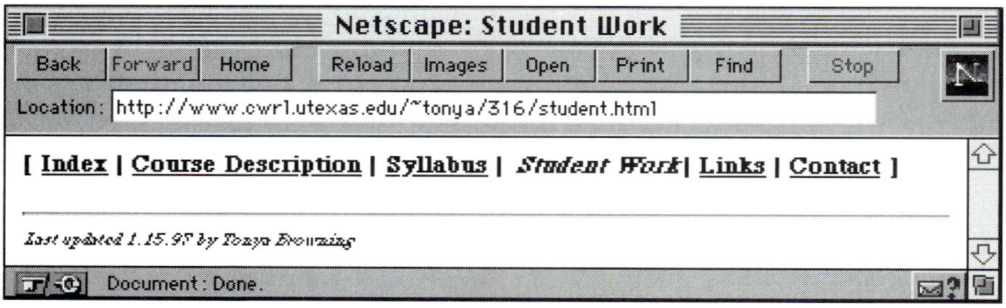

phrase. Although some icons seem to have a clear meaning (an envelope for sending e-mail, for instance), the menus that are the most successful also provide enough text to tell the reader exactly what to expect by clicking on the icon. Note, finally, that the footer in the sample has deemphasized the link for the current page. Since this footer appears on the Student Work page, that element of the footer is italicized and left unlinked to indicate the position of the reader within the site.

Another tactic is to use the table feature of most browsers to present menus that appear on the side of the page (see **Chapter 18** for more information on tables). The advantage of side menus is that readers who arrive at a page can instantly get a sense of the major elements of the site. On pages that require a fair amount of scrolling, however, menus on the side may disappear as readers move down the page.

Arranging the elements of a site in a side menu like the one shown in Figure 19.5 allows authors to include a larger number of menu options without overwhelming the layout of the page. Figure 19.5 also shows how you might complement your side menus by using a background image that sets off the menu with color.

A final way in which you can help readers navigate a site is by using frames. Frames divide the browser screen into a number of different

FIGURE 19.5 A Side Menu

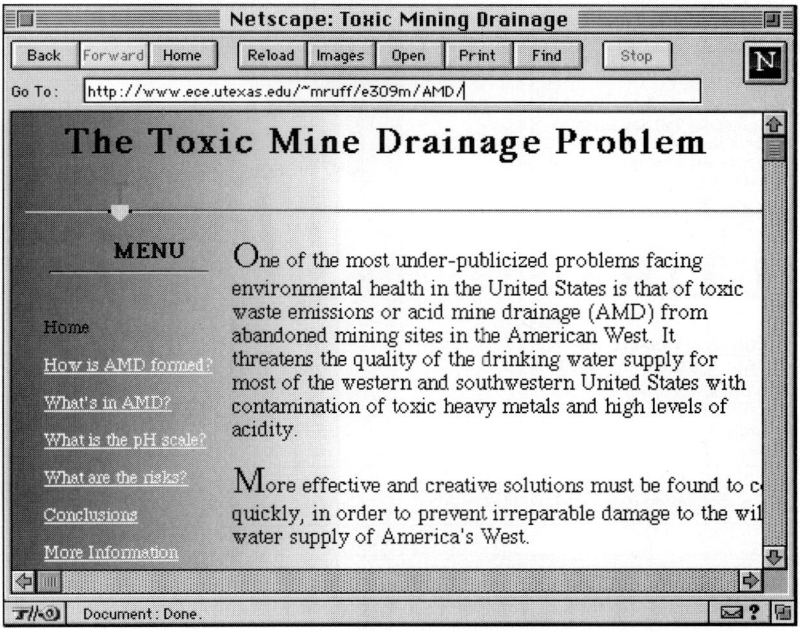

windows. For example, you can use one frame for a menu of the site and have the various pages load in a separate frame.

Figure 19.6 shows a site that uses a frame-based menu. As readers select items from the menu at the bottom, the requested pages will load in the windows above. By providing a menu in a frame, you can give your site a sense of stability because the menu frame will always remain static. Be aware, however, that not all browsers support frames and that people with smaller monitors may have trouble if your pages are divided into too many sections.

Keep your purpose and audience in mind as you decide whether or not to use frames in your designs. For example, if you are writing a page for *Wired* or some other high-tech publication, you can assume that your audience will have fairly sophisticated machinery and that they will expect a cutting-edge design. If, on the other hand, you're setting up a Web site for a local community center with the purpose of making information freely available, you might want to scale back on features such as

■ **FIGURE 19.6** A Frame-Based Menu

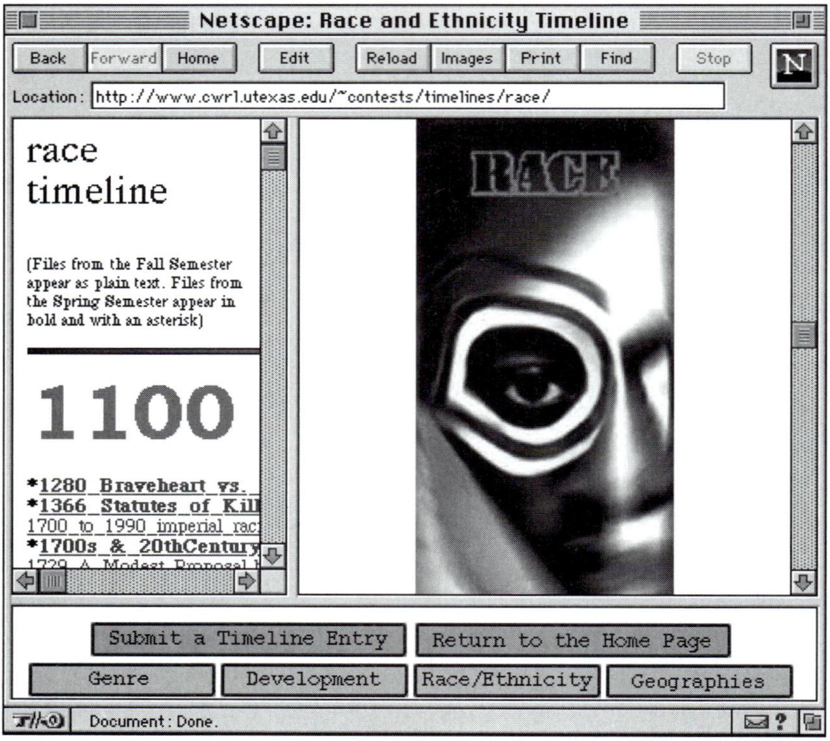

frames and concentrate on ease of use and providing the widest possible access. (For more information on using frames, see **Appendix 5.**)

Whatever type of menu you are using on your site, think carefully about organization and standardization. If, for instance, all of your menus are going to include a return link to your opening page, it makes sense to put this link at the beginning of your menu. Placing the link to the home page somewhere in the middle of a long list of elements would make it hard to find. Similarly, if the order of the menu elements shifts from page to page, readers will have more trouble intuitively using the menu and navigating the site.

Link Language and Tactics

The way that you integrate links into your Web compositions will also have an impact on a reader's ability to both navigate and absorb information. When readers don't know where links lead, they are less likely to take an educated path through your pages and more likely to get frustrated or disoriented. As a general rule, you should annotate any lists of links. By providing accurate summaries of the information that you are linking to, you can help readers to decide whether or not they should follow a given link.

A related problem can be that readers who follow links to pages elsewhere on the Web may simply never return to your site. Since you can't build "return links" on other people's pages, you always run the risk of being dumped by your reader for a more enticing site. To get around this problem, you might avoid making external links at the beginning of a page or in places where you really want your reader to digest your information. Many projects create a "related sites" page that contains links to information found elsewhere on the Web. This way, readers can fully explore the materials on your pages and then move on to other sites when they are ready.

Although the Web provides the possibility of linking to countless documents and resources, be careful to avoid overloading your pages with links to external sites. You do want to offer readers the chance of viewing the materials that you are using, but try not to place the burden of sifting through these materials on their shoulders. Use the skills of critical reading, summarizing resources, synthesizing positions, and presenting your own analysis that we outline in **Chapter 5** to work through the information about your topic and present a selection of well-annotated links to your readers.

A final point about creating successful links concerns their phrasing. Because links on the Web are highlighted, they provide authors with an opportunity to emphasize information about the materials they are linking to. For instance, a page exploring the problems of toxic mining drainage might have a link to environmental impact studies. By using a phrase such as "click here" as hot text, the author emphasizes the activity of linking rather than information about the link itself. The same project would be better served by linking from the phrase "EPA report on groundwater contamination." Articulating links with precise, descriptive phrasing will not only help your reader navigate, it will also prompt you to think about the relationship of a particular piece of information to the project as a whole.

Working with Multimedia

Gadgetry and Visual Appeal Web authors often fall into the trap of using sophisticated features simply because they want to try out the latest technology, forgetting about the larger purpose of their pages. For instance, it is common to find Web pages that are covered with high-end graphics and animated Java Applets, none of which have anything to do with the content of the page itself. These pages take a long time to load and are generally more distracting than attention grabbing.

As with all aspects of your writing, we urge you to consider the rhetorical purpose of the decisions that you make. Writing should, first and foremost, further your readers' understanding. At the same time, however, we realize that you will need to accommodate certain audience expectations if you are to create compelling Web compositions. Because the Web is a graphical as well as textual environment, the audience expects sites to have some level of visual appeal. So, while we caution against using bells and whistles for their own sake, we also recommend that you compose pages that use backgrounds, icons, and images in an appropriate way. Sometimes an icon placed before your link information does a good job of drawing attention to the major sections of your project. Similarly, a colored bar or an interesting opening image can set the mood of a page and spark a reader's interest. The trick is to balance the needs of grabbing your readers' attention with the distractions inherent in using too much gadgetry.

Multimedia Content Related to the appropriate use of visual elements is the importance of purposefully and successfully integrating multimedia content into your pages. While it's true that multimedia may enhance some compositions, there is no guarantee that using images or video and sound clips will make your writing any better. It is important to remember that, while the definition of writing is certainly expanding, there is still no substitute for well-honed verbal composition skills. Multimedia will be of most assistance to writers who also know how to present ideas and engage in discussions using traditional rhetorical strategies.

The project shown in Figure 19.7 performs an evaluation of the film *The Accused*. Since films contain both verbal and visual elements, the

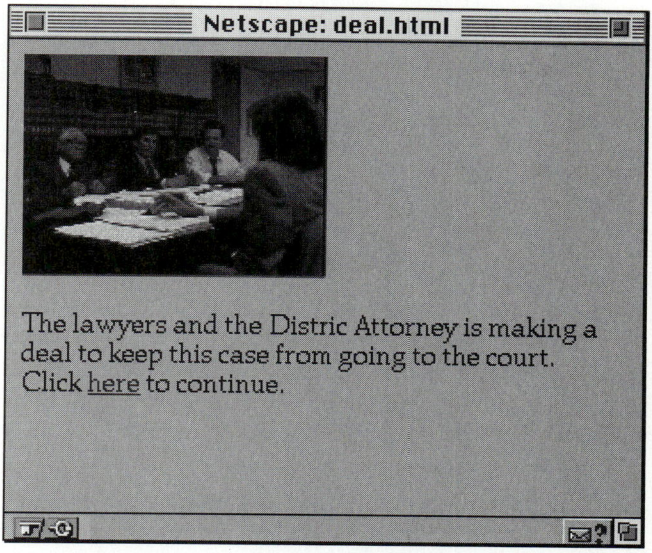

FIGURE 19.7 A Poorly Implemented Graphic

choice to include multimedia in this project seems logical. Its implementation, however, could have been much stronger. Note how the page reproduces an image from the film but does very little to evaluate that image. Just as you should never place a quotation into a traditional paper without discussing it or situating it within the larger context of your project, you should never expect a multimedia clip to make your argument for you. It is up to you to interpret that clip so that your readers know exactly how you are using it to further your analysis.

Adding multimedia elements to your presentation will likely do more damage than good unless you carefully consider the ideas you wish to convey and how the multimedia elements will contribute to your presentation. Not only does the project shown in Figure 19.7 fail to discuss the details of the image, it does not even mention the themes that are demonstrated by the scene (gender roles or the legal system, for example). Additionally, the author has overlooked both grammatical and spelling errors. Be careful not to let multimedia prevent you from clearly expressing your ideas in writing. Remember that your focus should be the development of a convincing argument. Any images that you use should complement the ideas and expressions that would otherwise be put forth in any composition.

Figure 19.8 shows a student project that does a better job of integrating a still image from a film. The project evaluates an image from the film *Blade Runner.* We can see that the student has taken some time to discuss the image. He clearly describes the subject of the image and gives some

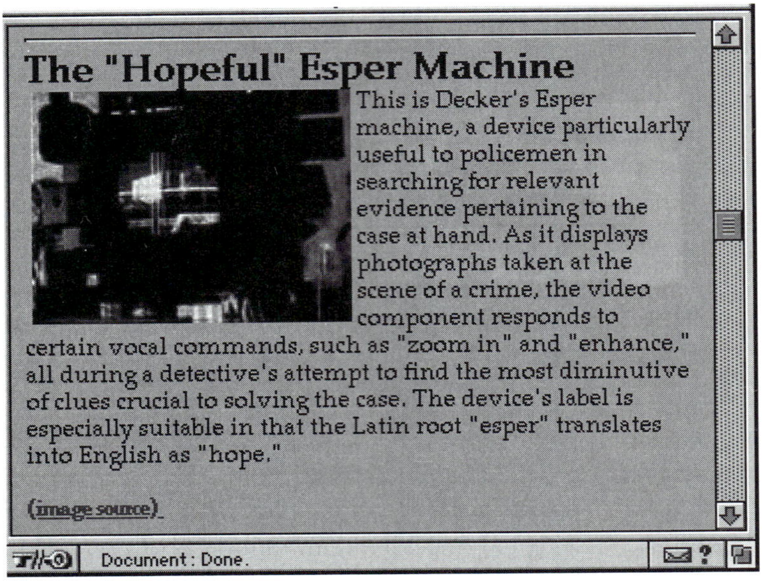

FIGURE 19.8 A More Successful Graphic

details about the machine shown in the still. Additionally, the student points out that the machine in the video still represents one of the movie's major themes: hope. He doesn't assume that all viewers will see the image the same way, but instead picks out the elements that are most important to his project and develops his analysis by using the image as an example.

Even this sample, however, has room for improvement. Although the student has discussed the details of the image and picked out a theme that it conveys, he still hasn't tied this theme to the other major ideas in his project. Instead of merely pointing out the theme of hope, the student could have shown connections with other examples of hope in the film or drawn contrasts with other themes.

Film analysis demonstrates just one possibility for incorporating multimedia into your Web compositions. Whether you are providing photographic evidence of clear-cutting operations in Oregon, a sound sample from a campaign speech, a reproduction of a famous Grecian urn, or a scanned image of a 1908 AT&T ad, remember that writing is about clarification—furthering the understanding of topics and issues for both you and your readers. Multimedia will be successful to the extent that it aids this process. Consider your purpose as you decide when and where to include images and other elements. Then consider the steps that you will need to take—explicating the images, unpacking their themes, and drawing connections with larger issues—to meet your goals.

Loading Time

One basic but extremely important Web convention is the idea that the less time it takes to load a page, the better. Although extremely long text documents can take some time to load, this issue becomes most pressing when working with graphics and higher-end multimedia elements like video or sound. You'll need to balance the desire (and, to a certain extent, the expectation) for visually dynamic Web pages with a practical concern for file size.

Video and sound files are particularly difficult to work with because of their size—generally, you'll want to give readers a choice about whether to download these clips, and you should clearly announce the size of each multimedia file that you are linking to. Remember, also, that there may be times when a sound file can be substituted for a video clip, giving readers relevant information while decreasing file size. Similarly, you might want to provide "thumbnail" versions of larger graphics that link to the full size images. This way, your pages will still load quickly, and readers can preview image files before deciding to download them. In general, avoid using large graphics unless they are essential to the project, and try not to bunch together too many images (including the background file) on a single page. It often takes as long to load ten 2 × 2 inch images as it does to load one 8 × 10 inch image. (For more information about working with graphics, see **Chapter 18.**)

Evolving Conventions

Because the World Wide Web is still a relatively new publishing medium, its style conventions are far less rigid than the longstanding rules of print-based writing. If you compare notes with a classmate, you will find that most students have been taught a very similar set of basic writing rules; we all know how and when (or at least know that there are rules for how and when) to indent a paragraph, capitalize certain letters, cite sources, even organize an argument by using an introduction, a body, and a conclusion. There are certainly variations on these rules, but most print-based writing follows a relatively fixed pattern.

Many of these conventions hold true on the Internet as well. However, as we have seen, new conventions for on-line writing are also being developed and revised to take better advantage of electronic media. Although it's easy to get caught up in the glitz and gadgetry of the Web, always remember that your priority still needs to be the content of your pages and the quality of your argument or analysis. Remember, too, that just as every essayist will have a unique style, as you become more comfortable with writing for the Web, you will have a chance to develop a voice of your own.

EXERCISE 19.1

Evaluating a Web Site

The goal of this exercise is to evaluate a Web site, looking for the concepts of rhetoric, argument, and hypertext design that we discuss above. (For some possible sites to evaluate, see the on-line exercise at the *Connections* Web site.) Working in groups or by yourself, consider the following prompts and write a short evaluation of the site.

- After finding a suitable site, first define its purpose and consider how that purpose influences the overall design. For example, is the site trying to create an argument, to provide background information, or to promote a particular product?
- How well does the site communicate its purpose? Does the design of the site help to further the purpose? What specific elements would you identify that further the goals of the site? What elements distract from the purpose?
- Does the opening page clearly communicate the contents of the site and possible options for navigation? What organizational elements and metaphors does the site use in its presentation? Are they successful? Do they contribute to the meaning as well as the organization of the site?
- How easy is it to navigate in the site? Do you get confused or disoriented? Are there clear connections between the major sections?
- Are the graphics and other multimedia elements appropriate for the site? Are they incorporated smoothly? Did the size of the files detract from the presentation because of loading time?
- If you were redesigning the site, what changes would you make? Would you add major features to the design? Would you reorganize? Would you add content? How could you enhance the appeal of the site? How would you improve the ease of navigation? What strengths of the site would you leave untouched?

Tips and Tactics

- When building Web hypertexts, consider what choices the reader will have for moving around the site. Balance the need to control a reader's progression with the convention of offering multiple choices for navigation.
- Avoid long pages of scrolling text, but be sure to develop your arguments fully. You can achieve complexity and hypertextuality by carefully constructing different nodes of your hypertext.
- Make sure your site has navigational aids, particularly when you develop multiple sections. Provide graphical maps, footers, side menus, or frame menus to help readers move through the sections of a complicated hypertext.
- Make sure you clearly annotate any lists of links, explaining what sort of information can be found by following them. Additionally, indicate which links go to other sites on the Web.
- Use precise language in your link phrasing. A link phrase should indicate what information can be found by following the link.
- Carefully consider the rhetorical significance of the multimedia elements you use. Fully explain and provide context for any elements that you put into your Web pages.
- Consider loading time when providing multimedia files or when adding graphics to your pages. Balance the value of a multimedia presentation with a concern for keeping your audience's attention while your files download.

CHAPTER 20

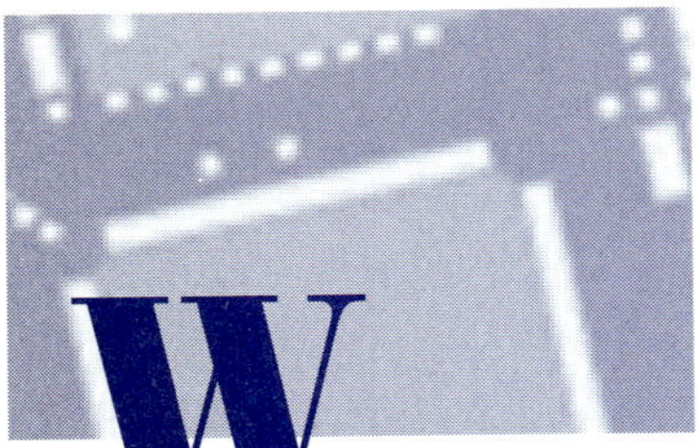

WHERE DO WE GO FROM HERE?

The Evolving Nature of Web Communication

In early 1995, before Netscape introduced the background feature into its browser, about the only way of making Web page design more visually appealing was by varying the arrangement of headings, text styles, and lists. Today, almost every Web page uses backgrounds as well as other innovative features such as tables, colored fonts, and frames. Because technologies on the Web change so rapidly, by the time you read this book, some of the technology that we discuss in this chapter will probably be as commonplace as background images are now.

While it would be presumptuous for us to predict exactly what the Web will look like even a short time down the road, we'll spend this final chapter trying to make sense of the trends that we see today with an eye toward anticipating future possibilities. The problem, of course, is that it's difficult to even locate clear trends in the fast-paced world of Web design. For example, the incorporation of features such as Java Applets and JavaScript might suggest that emphasis in Web development is shifting toward Web browsers. At the same time, however, the development of scripts that run on Web servers and the integration of database features into the operations of the Web could point to an increasing role for servers. It turns out that both browsers and servers are evolving rapidly; neither one is likely to completely outstrip the other. Because so much development is taking place in both areas, this division between browser and server technologies gives us a good way to organize our discussion about future innovations on the Web. □

KEY TERMS

Applet: An application that can be embedded in an HTML page and run from a Web browser.

Common Gateway Interface (CGI): A program that allows browsers to submit information to the Web server. CGIs are actually a combination of an interface that permits the sharing of information and a script that manipulates that information. Web forums and add-link scripts are common examples of CGIs.

Plug-in: An extension to a Web browser that allows the browser to play files created with other applications.

Script: A piece of code written in a computer programming language such as JavaScript that can be accessed from an HTML file to perform sophisticated Web operations.

Web Browser: Client software that allows users to navigate and interact on the World Wide Web.

Web Server: A combination of software and hardware that stores, manages, and distributes files for the World Wide Web.

Browser Developments

Scripting

With Netscape leading the way, the past two years have seen Web browsers become increasingly sophisticated, giving Web authors more design options than ever. Browsers can shuffle images, run programs, and manage information—tasks that until recently were handled by Web servers. One example of this increased sophistication is the implementation of scripting languages such as JavaScript. Most Web browsers can interpret these complex scripts, which can be incorporated into an HTML page. By simply placing a JavaScript inside the <SCRIPT></SCRIPT> command in your HTML file, you can manipulate information, page layout, or even other applications.

Some of the most basic JavaScripts create scrolling banners and bouncing balls. But scripts can also be programmed to perform complex operations based on interaction with the reader. For example, by incorporating the following commands into the <HEAD> of a Web page, an author would be able to use a JavaScript to open a pop-up window:

```
<SCRIPT LANGUAGE="JAVASCRIPT">
<!--
  FUNCTION WINOPEN() {
    MSG=OPEN(" ","DISPLAYWINDOW");
      }
//-->
</SCRIPT>
```

After inserting this script in the <HEAD> of the HTML file, authors can simply call for the "WINOPEN()" function in their HTML compositions to pop open a window. The HTML commands to open the window would read

```
<A HREF="JAVASCRIPT:WINOPEN()">Take Notes</A>
```

Of course, a number of additional elements would be needed to make this script fully functional.

Figure 20.1 demonstrates one possible implementation of the pop-up window: When a reader clicks on the "Take Notes" button, the JavaScript opens a new window. Though it seems simplistic on the surface—as if one window is simply placed over another—the JavaScript can be modified in any number of ways that might let readers interact with authors or contribute to a site. JavaScripts such as this have the potential to alter the experience of reading on the Web.

Be aware, however, that learning the ins and outs of a language like JavaScript requires a fair amount of investment. As even this basic pop-up window script demonstrates, the programming language is reasonably complex. But, like most things on the Web, with a little borrowing and enough experimentation, almost anyone can incorporate these more advanced functions into their pages. If you have a clear sense of the design goals for a project, technologies like JavaScript can help you achieve them. (For help with JavaScript see Netscape's JavaScript Authoring Guide at **http://home.netscape.com/eng/mozilla/Gold/handbook/javascript/.**)

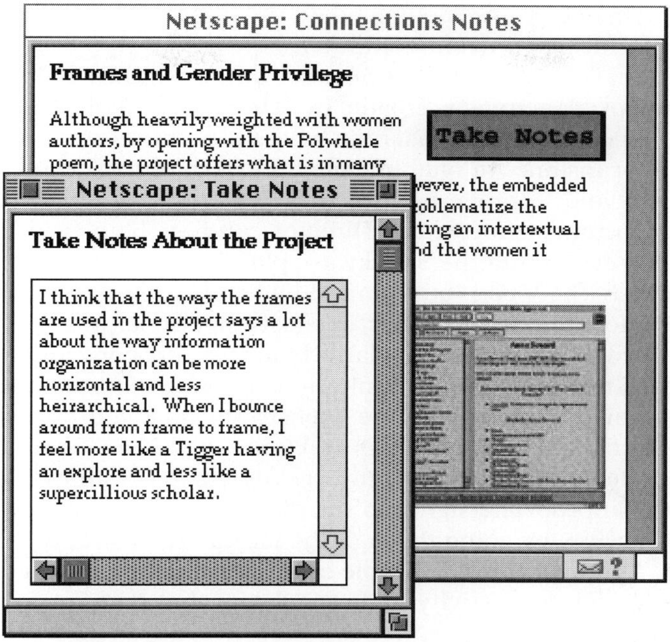

■ **FIGURE 20.1** A Pop-Up Window Created with JavaScript

Applets and Plug-ins

Another advancement supported by most browsers is the capacity to place embedded objects in Web documents. Currently, some of these objects are displayed "outside" the Web browser because they require another application to run. But the integration of embedded objects (including video streams and collaborative applications) into browser interfaces is becoming more and more seamless. One form of embedded object is the Applet. Applets are small computer programs that have been written for the Web. Users can download and run the Applet from within the interface of their browser.

The big advantage of Applets is that authors can tap into all of the flexibility and power of a complex programming language (almost all Applets are written in the Java programming language). For example, Applets might be used to show different combinations of molecules, to let readers highlight and comment on literary texts, or to let people calculate the cost of living in different cities on the basis of variables that the user selects. From a browser/server standpoint, what's nice about Applets is that they perform complex functions without having to wait for information transfers to and from a Web server. Because Applets reside on your local machine, once you've downloaded them from the Net, all your operations are performed on your computer.

Additionally, most browsers now use devices known as "plug-ins" so that they can play documents created by "traditional" applications. A plug-in is installed on your local machine where it becomes a sort of browser extension. For instance, a plug-in called Shockwave has been created for the powerful and popular multimedia authoring system Macromedia Director®. Documents created in Director can now be played by anyone who has Web access and the Shockwave plug-in.

Of course, the Web is still limited by bandwidth problems that hinder the downloading of larger files, so most early Shockwave projects and even "educational" Applets are relatively narrow in scope and appeal. As authors learn to work with the limitations in bandwidth imposed by the Internet, sophisticated projects are likely to shrink to a usable size.

The Shockwave Applet shown in Figure 20.2 is an educational tool for learning the American Sign Language Alphabet. Clicking on the letters will load the appropriate sign into the display window, allowing readers to quiz themselves by going through the interactive test that is built into the Applet. Although this is a simple example, it demonstrates the potential for increased interactivity and complexity that plug-ins and Applets bring to the Web.

Animations, 3D Graphics, and VRML

The Web is clearly evolving to support more complex graphics and animations. What is less clear is how these elements might be used in your writing projects. It's relatively easy to include an animated image or a Java Applet in your Web pages; the challenge is to incorporate those spinning balls or bouncing letters in a meaningful way. Animations that advance the goals of a project—perhaps simulations of medical procedures or instructions for performing complex tasks—will maximize the potential of these new technologies. However, the first examples of three-dimensional (3D) graphics and animations don't represent radical changes for the Web itself; Web authors are incorporating them as they would any other image.

Three-dimensional (3D) interfaces such as Quicktime VR, Hotsauce (Apple's Project X), and Virtual Reality Modeling Language (VRML) represent a more dynamic shift in Web design. Readers can navigate through these environments, looking at space "in the round," rather than the "flat" 2D presentations of most Web pages. Readers use the mouse to navigate and to activate links as they move through graphic representations of 3D environments. Especially in projects with a lot of data, these spatial representations can significantly enhance the way we present and interact with information.

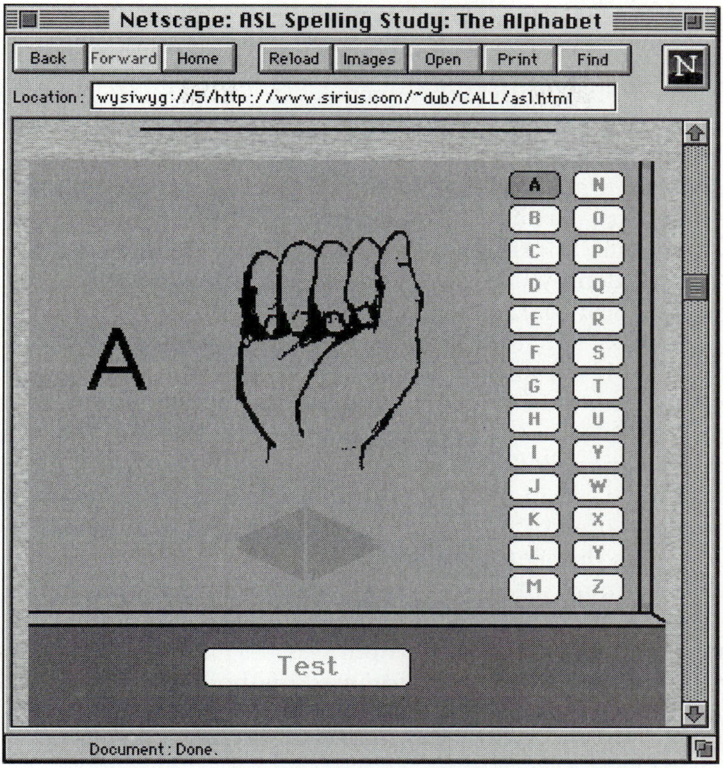

■ **FIGURE 20.2** A Shockwave Applet for Learning the American Sign Language Alphabet

Server Developments

JavaScript, Applets, and plug-ins represent the current trend to move the operations of Web interactions away from the server and toward local clients and machines. The big advantage of this movement is that large transfers of information across the Internet are kept to a minimum. The disadvantage of performing operations on local machines is that those operations lack the potential to permanently (or at least semipermanently) change the files or structure of a Web site. No matter how much information is managed and processed on the local machines of Web readers, there is little possibility that other readers will have access to it until that information is collected and organized in a central location.

CGIs and Databases

Equal in importance, then, to developments on the client side is the capacity to interface with Web servers so that information can be stored and shared through common files. To interact with servers, the Web relies on Common Gateway Interfaces (CGIs), programs that allow browsers to submit information to the Web server. CGIs are actually a combination of an interface that permits the sharing of information and a script that manipulates that information. The Web forums that we discussed in **Part 3** are created by using a CGI. Web forum users submit their comments with a form that has been integrated into a Web page. The forum CGI then processes that information and uses it to create Web pages that index and display the threads of discussion. This gives users the ability to permanently alter the content of Web sites from their browser.

Early CGIs focus predominately on guest books and discussion forums, but there are other possibilities for using these scripts. For example, CGIs can be set up to allow readers to annotate the text of a site. By using a combination of JavaScripts that control the interface of the pages and CGI scripts that submit information to the Web server, authors can make projects more interactive. Readers can highlight particular words and phrases in a project, then make comments in a pop-up window. The CGI script turns those words and phrases into hot text that links to the comments, thus providing an automated method for readers all over the world to comment on or add links to specific sections of a site. Figure 20.3 shows an example of one such site.

Many CGIs take information and create Web files, but as more and more information is exchanged via the Web, the operations taking place on servers are likely to increase in number and complexity. For instance, a number of sites use database programs to manage information. Databases allow servers to catalog large amounts of information and to quickly manipulate their holdings to suit the needs of readers. For instance, Web search engines use databases to handle complex tasks and information. The search engines collect and manage information in databases on their servers. When readers request it, the database processes the information, and the output is sent to the reader's browser.

WU*, Chat, and Collaboration

Another development is the integration of MU* space into the Web. (For more information on MU*s, see **Chapters 11** and **16.**) These features add a graphical component to the conversational and interactive elements of text-only MU* environments. Unfortunately, they generally require complex programs and powerful Web/MU* (WU*) servers. Although rudimentary in their presentations of the environment, graphical MU*s and

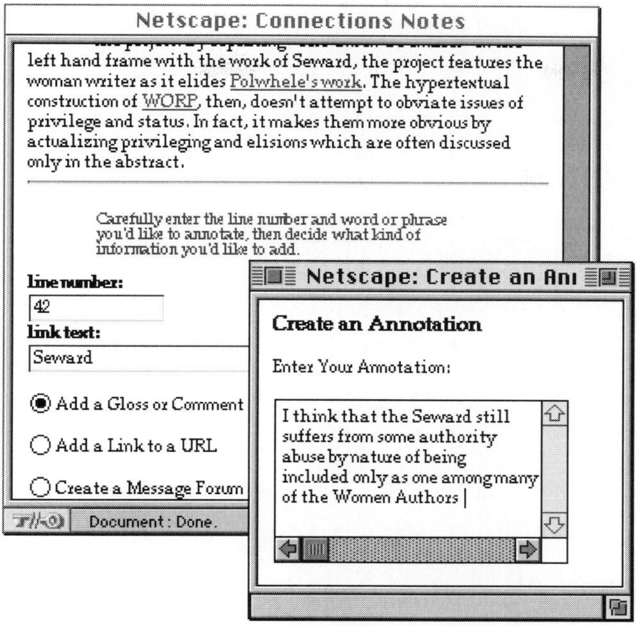

■ **FIGURE 20.3** A CGI That Allows Readers to Annotate a Site

WU*s create spaces where readers can interact with each other, follow hypertext links, and navigate through virtual environments. Once this technology becomes more widely available, Web users will be able to "WU* ~/cows/come/home".

As we close this book, we see that there is still a lot to cover. We've looked at what it means to research, collaborate, and compose on the Internet. But developments provide new possibilities for writers almost daily. We understand that it would be impossible to produce a comprehensive discussion of on-line writing—we would be aiming at a moving target. Instead, we've tried to concentrate on the skills that are required to communicate in any situation. We've talked about what it means to write as a member of a community in order to both develop our understandings and influence the people we write for.

In the end, it is not changes taking place on the Internet that are important. Although new technologies change the possibilities for composition, your ability to engage with a community will be determined not by the tools you have to work with, but by how you put these tools to work to fulfill your writing goals. In the long run, your development as a writer, rather than any on-line developments, will determine your success as a communicator.

APPENDIXES

PART 5

APPENDIX 1

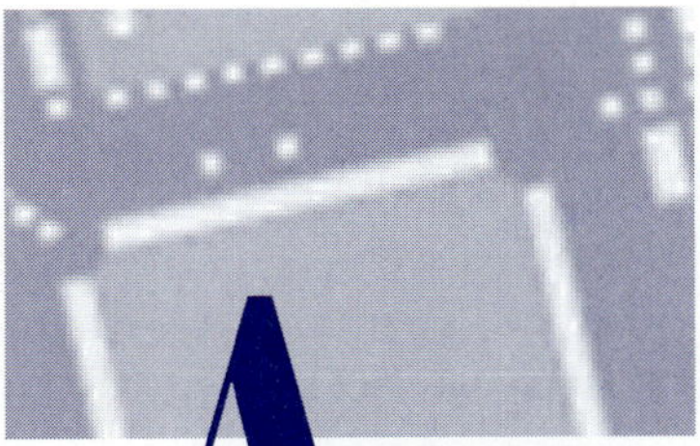

ADDITIONAL RESOURCES

We have written this book as a rhetorical guide that focuses on strategies and activities for on-line writing. However, we've provided this list so that you can quickly locate some of the most useful Internet resources. Note that for convenience and currency, this list is also available at the *Connections* Web site. □

Web Directories and Search Engines

- AltaVista (**http://www.altavista.com/**)
  In addition to providing one of the most comprehensive databases on the Net, AltaVista allows you to search archives of Usenet newsgroup postings.
- Excite (**http://www.excite.com**)
  As well as providing subject categories, this site offers a keyword search that covers both the Web and Usenet and that allows for extremely flexible queries.

- Infoseek (**http://www.infoseek.com/**)
  In addition to nicely developed subject categories, their keyword search covers the Web, Usenet, and e-mail addresses.
- Lycos (**http://www.lycos.com**)
  Lycos provides researchers with well-developed subject categories and keyword searches.
- One Search InFind (**http://m5.inference.com/ifind/**)
  This site allows simultaneous searches of WebCrawler, Yahoo, Lycos, AltaVista, InfoSeek, and Excite and removes redundancies.
- WebCrawler (**http://webcrawler.com/**)
  This site has a search feature that looks through the full text of documents on the Web.
- Yahoo (**http://search.yahoo.com/**)
  Yahoo provides a well-developed catalog of Web resources with an excellent collection of subject categories.

Links to Writing Resources

- CompSite (**http://www.abacon.com/compsite/**)
  Allyn and Bacon's on-line resource site for composition provides information about writing and researching on the Internet.
- The Computer Writing and Research Labs (**http://www.cwrl.utexas.edu**)
  The CWRL has an excellent collection of student Internet projects.
- The DeVry Online Writing Support Center (**http://www.devry-phx.edu/lrnresrc/dowsc/**)
  This is a nicely organized site offering extensive information about Internet writing.
- The Elements of Style (**http://www.cc.columbia.edu/acis/bartleby/strunk/**)
  The original version of the well-known style guide offers advice on both rules and stylistic elements of composition.
- OnLine Resources for Writers (**http://webster.commnet.edu/writing/writing.htm**)
  This site provides a list of recommended sites by the English Faculty of Capital Community-Technical College in Hartford.
- The On-line Writing Lab at Purdue (**http://owl.english.purdue.edu/**)
  This site offers an excellent collection of writing-related handouts and information.

- Paradigm On-line Writing Assistant
  (**http://www.idbsu.edu/english/cguilfor/paradigm/**)
  This is a nicely done on-line handbook and guide to many kinds of writing tasks.
- Research-It (**http://www.iTools.com/research-it/research-it.html**)
  At this site, you will find a collection of dictionaries, references, and other useful information.
- The University of Victoria Writer's Guide
  (**http://webserver.maclab.comp.uvic.ca/writersguide/starthere.html**)
  This site provides a well-developed collection of information about both the mechanical and organizational elements of writing.

Links for E-Mail Information

- The Liszt Directory of E-Mail Discussion Groups
  (**http://www.liszt.com/**)
  This site includes an extensive collection of searchable information about e-mail discussion lists.
- The Tile.Net Listserv Directory (**http://tile.net/lists/**)
  This is another searchable collection of discussion list information, but limited to lists using "Listserv" software.

Links for MU*s

- Diversity University's Cybercomp Page
  (**http://www.du.org/cybercomp.html**)
  This site has lots of information about interacting and writing in MU*s.
- LambdaMoo Programmer's Manual
  (**ftp://parcftp.xerox.com/pub/MOO/html/ProgrammersManual_toc.html**)
  This site has a fairly extensive catalog of MOO building commands and instructions.
- MOO/MU* Document Library (**http://lucien.berkeley.edu/moo.html**)
  This site has manuals, tutorials, FAQs, as well as MU* research papers.
- Yahoo's List of MUDs, MUSHs, and MOOs
  (**http://www.yahoo.com/Recreation/Games/Internet_Games/MUDs__MUSHes__MOOs__etc_/**)
  This is Yahoo's collection of links to MU* environments.

Links for Newsgroups

- DejaNews (**http://www.dejanews.com**)
  This searchable archive of Usenet newsgroup postings is a great place to go for technical questions or to find appropriate groups for research topics.
- The Indiana University's Usenet Newsgroups Resources Page (**http://sckb.ucssc.indiana.edu/kb/data/aebt.html**)
  This site provides an extensive collection of information about newsgroups, newsreaders, and netiquette.
- **news.announce.newusers**
  news.answers
  news.groups.questions
  news.newusers.questions
  These newsgroups provide Usenet newsgroup FAQs for new users.
- The Tile.Net Newsgroup Page (**http://tile.net/news/**)
  This is a well-presented searchable directory of Usenet groups.
- Usenet Info Center Launch Pad (**http://sunsite.unc.edu/usenet-i/home.html**)
  This site provides general information about Usenet and about tapping into newsgroups.
- USENET FAQs (**http://www.cis.ohio-state.edu/hypertext/faq/usenet/top.html**)
  This site offers a helpful collection of the FAQ files on many Usenet newsgroups.

Links for Web Authoring

- David W. Baker's WWW Authoring Information (**http://www.netspace.org/~dwb/www-authoring.html**)
  This site has a nice collection of links to other HTML resources on the Net.
- The Cern Guide for On-line Hypertext (**http://www.w3.org/pub/WWW/Provider/Style/Overview.html**)
  This site offers an easy-to-use collection of advice on a number of Web style conventions.
- Ian S. Grahm's Introduction to HTML (**http://www.utoronto.ca/webdocs/HTMLdocs/NewHTML/htmlindex.html**)
  You will find here a well-presented collection of the basic HTML commands.

- Netscape's Communicator Site
  (**http://home.netscape.com/flash2/comprod/products/communicator/**)
  This site provides links to information about layers, JavaScript, and other features supported by Netscape's more advanced browsers.
- Netscape's Frame Authoring Guide
  (**http://home.netscape.com/assist/net_sites/frames.html)**
  This site provides basic information about how to construct frame-based projects.
- Netscape's JavaScript Authoring Guide
  (**http://home.netscape.com/eng/mozilla/Gold/handbook/javascript/**)
  This is a helpful starting point for those who want to learn JavaScript.
- Netscape's Table Authoring Guide
  (**http://home.netscape.com/assist/net_sites/tables.html**)
  All the basic information about how to use tables in your pages is given here.
- Matt's CGI Archive (**http://worldwidemart.com/scripts**)
  This archive offers a collection of several useful CGI scripts.
- Sun Microsystem's Web Style Guide
  (**http://www.sun.com/styleguide/tables/Welcome.html**)
  This is a flexible and rhetorically sophisticated guide to Web style.

Links for News Sources

- The Atlantic Monthly (**http://www.theAtlantic.com/atlantic/**)
  This site includes an on-line version of the magazine devoted to politics and society.
- The Best News on the Net (**http://www.NovPapyrus.com/news/**)
  This is a good starting point for accessing print and broadcast news resources.
- The ClariNet Newswires
  (**http://gnn.yahoo.com/gnn/News/Newswires/ClariNet/**)
  At this site, you can find information from the newsgroups that provide wire service feeds.
- CNN Home Page (**http://www.cnn.com/**)
  CNN provides resources from the Cable News Network, including images and film and sound clips.

- The L.A. Times (**http://www.latimes.com/HOME/**)
  The on-line version of the *L.A. Times* is currently offered at no charge with no on-line registration.
- Mother Jones (**http://www.mojones.com/**)
  The Mother Jones site has the magazine in its on-line form and a cool URL to boot.
- The Nation (**http://www.TheNation.com/**)
  This on-line magazine also provides forums for reader contributions.
- The New York Times (**http://www.nytimes.com/**)
  The on-line version of the *New York Times* is currently offered at no charge, but you'll need an e-mail address to register for the service.
- The New Republic (**http://www.enews.com/magazines/tnr/**)
  This on-line magazine is geared toward editorials and opinions.
- Time Magazine (**http://pathfinder.com/time/**)
  In addition to the weekly magazine, this site offers daily news updates.
- USA Today (**http://www.usatoday.com/**)
  The on-line version of *USA Today* is currently offered at no charge.
- The Wall Street Journal (**http://www.wsj.com/**)
  This site provides resources from the business-oriented newspaper.
- The Yahoo News Page (**http://www.yahoo.com/News/**)
  This Yahoo site includes an extensive collection of news-related links.

Government Sites

- Government Information Sharing Project (**http://govinfo.kerr.orst.edu/**)
  This site contains census reports and other statistical information.
- The Library of Congress (**http://www.loc.gov**)
  This is an excellent collection of historical archives.
- National Archives and Records Administration (**http://www.nara.gov**)
  A public domain archive of text and multimedia documents from a wide range of historical and cultural periods of the United States.
- The Thomas Legislative Information Site (**http://thomas.loc.gov**)
  Presented by the U.S. Congress, this site offers a number of documents as well as legislative information.
- U.S. Government Printing Office (**http://www.access.gpo.gov/su_docs/**)
  This site provides a collection of all kinds of government documents and files.

- The White House (**http://www.whitehouse.gov**)
  You can think of this as 1600 Pennsylvania Avenue on the Web.

Links for the Humanities

- EFF: The Electronic Frontier Foundation (**http://www.eff.org**)
  This site is devoted to promoting freedom on the Internet.
- The English Server at Carnegie Mellon (**http://english-www.hss.cmu.edu/**)
  This site has a very large collection of literary resources and offers a search feature.
- Literary Resources on the Net (**http://www.english.upenn.edu/~jlynch/Lit/**)
  At this site, you will find a nice collection of resources and tools for literary study.
- Project Gutenberg (**http://www.promo.net/pg/**)
  This organization is putting the text of numerous books and articles on-line.
- Project Muse On-line Journals (**http://muse.jhu.edu/index.html**)
  This is a journal collection from Johns Hopkins University with sample on-line articles for nonsubscribers and full journal issues for subscribers.
- The Victorian Web (**http://www.stg.brown.edu/projects/hypertext/landow/victorian/victov.html**)
  Originally created with the Intermedia hypertext software at Brown University, this site features a large collection of student-created information.
- Voice of the Shuttle (**http://humanitas.ucsb.edu/shuttle/english.html**)
  This site offers an extensive collection of humanities-related resources.

APPENDIX 2

MLA-STYLE GUIDELINES FOR CITING INTERNET SOURCES

by Andrew Harnack
and Eugene Kleppinger

The following MLA-style models for documenting Internet sources are taken from Chapter 5 of *Online! A Reference Guide to Using Internet Sources* by Andrew Harnack and Eugene Kleppinger. Published by St. Martin's Press in January 1997, *Online!* also contains chapters describing APA-, Chicago-, and CBE-style documentation of electronic sources. In addition, the guide provides advice on how to connect to Internet sources (WWW, e-mail, HyperNews, Listservs, newgroups, synchronous communications, Telnet, FTP, and Gopher), recommendations for choosing and evaluating Internet sites, principles for using images and graphics in essays and research papers, and help for students who wish to publish texts on the Internet. The guide includes a glossary of Internet terms and an appendix listing important discipline-specific Web sites.

For a discussion of the principles governing the following stylistic guidelines, see Harnack and Kleppinger, "Beyond the *MLA Handbook:* Documenting Electronic Sources on the Internet," *Kairos: A Journal for*

Teaching Writing in Webbed Environments 1.2 (1996). <**http://english.ttu.edu/kairos/1.2/inbox/mla.html**>.

For more information about *Online!*, see <**http://www.smpcollege.com/-online-4styles~help/**>. Requests for examination copies of *Online! A Reference Guide to Using the Internet* may be sent by e-mail to <**facultyservices@sasmp.com**>, by fax to 212-686-9492, by calling 1-800-446-8923, or by contacting a St. Martin's Press sales representative. *Online!*'s ISBN is 0-312-15023-7. □

1 World Wide Web site

To document a file available for viewing and downloading via the World Wide Web, provide the following information:

- author's name (if known)
- title of document, in quotation marks
- title of complete work (if applicable), in italics or underlined
- date of publication or last revision (if known)
- URL, in angle brackets
- date of access, in parentheses

> **Harris, Jonathan G. "The Return of the Witch Hunts." *Witchhunt Information Page*. <http://liquid2-sun.mit.edu/fells.short.html> (28 May 1996).**
>
> **Shade, Leslie R. "Gender Issues in Computer Networking." 1993. <http://www.mit.edu:8001/people/sorokin/women/lrs.html> (28 May 1996).**

2 E-mail message

To document an e-mail message, provide the following information:

- author's name (if known)
- author's e-mail address, in angle brackets
- subject line from posting, in quotation marks
- date of publication
- type of communication (personal e-mail, distribution list, office communication)
- date of access, in parentheses

Franke, Norman. <franke1@llnl.gov> "SoundApp 2.0.2." 29 Apr. 1996. Personal e mail. (3 May 1996).

Robinette, Danny. <robinetted@ccmail.gate.eku.edu> "Epiphany Project." 30 Apr. 1996. Office communication. (29 May 1996).

3 HyperNews posting

To document a HyperNews posting, provide the following information:

- author's name
- author's e-mail address, in angle brackets
- subject line or title of posting, in quotation marks
- date of publication
- type of message (if appropriate)
- URL, in angle brackets
- date of access, in parentheses

LaLiberte, Daniel. <liberte@ncsa.uiuc.edu> "HyperNews Instructions." 23 May 1996. <http://union.ncsa.uiuc.edu /HyperNews/get/hypernews/instructions.html> (24 May 1996).

Saffran, Art. <saffran@wisbar.org> "It's Not That Hard." 5 Jan. 1996. Reply to "HyperNews Instructions" by Daniel LaLiberte. <http://union.ncsa.uiuc.edu/HyperNews/get/hypernews /instructions/90/1/1.html> (24 May 1996).

4 Listserv message

To document a Listserv message, provide the following information:

- author's name (if known)
- author's e-mail address, in angle brackets
- subject line from posting, in quotation marks
- date of publication
- address of Listserv, in angle brackets
- date of access, in parentheses

Parente, Victor. <vrparent@mailbox.syr.edu> "On Expectations of Class Participation." 27 May 1996. <philosed@sued.syr.edu>(29 May 1996).

To document a file that can be retrieved from a list's server or Web address, provide the following information after the publication date:

- address of Listserv, in angle brackets
- address or URL for list's archive, preceded by *via* and enclosed in angle brackets
- date of access, in parentheses

Carbone, Nick. <nickc@english.umass.edu> "NN960126: Followup to Don's comments about citing URLs." 26 Jan. 1996. <acw-l@unicorn.acs.ttu.edu> via <http://www.ttu.edu/lists/acw-l> (17 Feb. 1996).

5 Newsgroup message

To document information posted in a newsgroup discussion, provide the following information:

- author's name (if known)
- author's e-mail address, in angle brackets
- subject line from posting, in quotation marks
- date of publication
- name of newsgroup, in angle brackets
- date of access, in parentheses

Slade, Robert. <res@maths.bath.ac.uk> "UNIX Made Easy." 26 Mar. 1996. <alt.books.reviews> (31 Mar. 1996).

If you cannot determine the author's name, then use the author's e-mail address, enclosed in angle brackets, as the main entry. When you alphabetize such sources in your Works Cited, treat the first letter of the e-mail address as though it were capitalized.

<lrm583@aol.com> "Thinking of Adoption." 26 May 1996. <alt.adoption> (29 May 1996).

6 Synchronous communication

To document a synchronous communication, such as those posted in MOOs, MUDs, and IRCs, provide the following information:

- name of speaker(s) (if known), or name of site
- title of the event, if appropriate, in quotation marks
- date of event

- type of communication (group discussion, personal interview), if not indicated elsewhere in entry
- address, using a URL (in angle brackets) or command-line directions
- date of access, in parentheses

LambdaMOO. "Seminar Discussion on Netiquette." 28 May 1996. <telnet://lambda.parc.xerox.edu:8888> (28 May 1996).

Harnack, Andrew. Group discussion. 4 Apr. 1996. telnet moo.du.org/port=8888 (5 Apr. 1996).

7 Telnet site

To document a Telnet site or a file available via Telnet, provide the following information:

- author's name (if known)
- title of document (if known), in quotation marks
- the title of the full work (if applicable), in italics or underlined
- date of publication (if available), followed by a period
- word *telnet*
- complete Telnet address, with no closing punctuation
- directions for accessing document
- date of access, in parentheses

Aquatic Conservation Network. "About the Aquatic Conservation Network." ***National Capital Freenet.*** **telnet freenet.carleton.ca login as guest, go acn, press 1 (28 May 1996).**

California Department of Pesticide Regulation. "Pest Management Information." ***CSU Fresno ATI-NET.*** **telnet caticsuf.csufresno.edu login as super, press a, press k (28 May 1996).**

8 FTP site

To document a file available for downloading via file transfer protocol, provide the following information:

- author's name (if known)
- full title of document, in quotation marks
- date of publication (if known)
- the abbreviation *ftp*
- address of the FTP site, with no closing punctuation

- full path to follow to find document, with no closing punctuation
- date of access, in parentheses

Altar, Ted W. "Vitamin B12 and Vegans." 14 Jan. 1993. ftp wiretap.spies.com Library/Article/Food/b12.txt (28 May 1996).

You can use a URL (enclosed in angle brackets) instead of the command, address, and path elements.

Matloff, Norm. "Immigration Forum." <ftp://heather.cs.ucdavis.edu/pub/Immigration/Index.html> (28 May 1996).

9 *Gopher site*

To document information obtained by using the Gopher search protocol, provide the following information:

- author's name (if known)
- title of document, in quotation marks
- date of publication (if known)
- any print publication information, italicized or underlined where appropriate
- URL, in angle brackets
- date of access, in parentheses

Smith, Charles A. "National Extension Model of Critical Parenting Practices." 1994. <gopher://tinman.mes.umn.edu:4242/11/Other /Other/NEM_Parent> (28 May 1996).

To document the location of information with a Gopher command path format, give the following information instead of the URL:

- word *gopher*
- site name
- path followed to access document, with slashes to indicate menu selections

"Commons Sense: A Viewer's Guide to the British House of Commons." gopher c-span.org Transcripts and Publications/C-SPAN Publications/Commons Sense (29 May 1996).

10 Linkage data

To document a specific file and give linkage data showing its hypertext context, provide the following information:

- author's name (if known)
- title of document, in quotation marks
- abbreviation *Lkd.* ("linked from")
- title of the document to which file is linked, in italics or underlined
- additional linkage details (if applicable) preceded by *at*
- date of publication (if known)
- URL for source document, in angle brackets
- date of access, in parentheses

> Hoemann, George H. "Electronic Style—Elements of Citation." Lkd. *Electronic Style Page,* at "Continue" and "Citation Elements." 3 Nov. 1995. http://funnelweb.utcc.utk.edu /~hoemann/style.html> (29 May 1996).

> Miller, Allison. "Allison Miller's Home Page." Lkd. *EKU Honors Program Home Page,* at "Personal Pages." <http://www.csc.eku.edu/honors> (2 Apr. 1996).

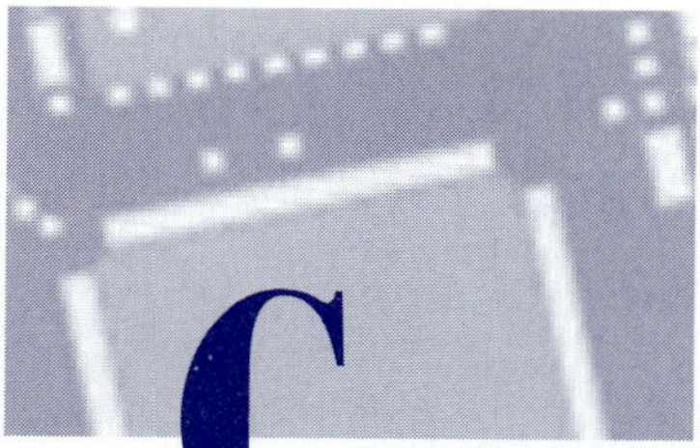

COPYRIGHT AND FAIR USE

Questions about Internet Copyright

Our emphasis on graphic-intensive Web projects might make you think that all of the images you come across while browsing the Net are available for your use. Most images, however, are protected by copyright. This means that the image of your favorite cartoon character that you got from the Warner Brothers site or that cool graphic of the computer you just downloaded from your favorite Web magazine are actually reproduced illegally on your home page.

So how do you know when it's OK to reproduce graphics, especially if you didn't see any copyright symbols or announcements on the sites and you've seen other pages that reproduce images from TV shows and movies? Why can't you just take those images?

Unless otherwise noted, you can assume that both the images and texts that you find while surfing on the Internet are protected by copyright. In general, authors, artists, and publishers do not need to indicate that they are claiming copyright privileges in order to retain reproduction rights to their work. It is your responsibility to know the copyright status of anything you wish to reproduce. Even if someone else posted the image at another site, by reproducing that copyrighted image, you are breaking copyright law. Remember that print documents are also protected by copyright, so it's also illegal to reproduce them by scanning or typing them in.

"So," you say, "what's the point? Why did you guys spend all that time telling us to include appropriate graphics when there's nothing we can use without breaking the law?"

Well, it's not quite that bleak. There are many images that are not affected by copyright restrictions.

Your Own Images

You can use a graphics program to create your own images, and there's nothing to stop you from scanning in your own texts and pictures for use on your site. If you're a budding artist, you can also scan in your artwork or create it in an illustration program and post it to the Web. You might even be able to use your graphics editor to combine, change, and manipulate a few existing copyrighted graphics into something new. Except when a previous publisher has retained copyright, you hold the rights for all of your own documents and can reproduce them at will.

Documents in the Public Domain

Images and texts that are more than seventy-five years old are considered to be "in the public domain" and can be reproduced by anyone. Government documents and images from institutions such as the Library of Congress are considered to belong to the public. In addition, many other documents have been given up for public use by their creators. (The students in our classes from whom we've taken examples in this book, for example, had to agree that their work was in the public domain.) In general, the many Web sites that are devoted to icons, backgrounds, and textures have images that are designed specifically for anyone to take and use. However, some of these sites require that you acknowledge the source of the image or provide a link to the image site (or both) on your Web page.

Permissions

Just as some sites have granted permission for all of their material to be used on the Internet, others may grant permission to writers who want to reproduce specific documents. (We had to get permission from the author to reproduce the "Ban Boxing" article in **Chapter 5,** for example.) If you find an image or article that you want to reproduce in a project and that seems to be copyrighted, you can write to the site where it is reproduced and ask for permission to use the piece. Though there is no guarantee that they will grant you permission, and it may take a while, there is still a good chance that the owners will let you use the document in a student project. This is particularly true of sites that are created and maintained by individuals and small companies. Usually, these people are more than happy to give students limited permissions.

Fair Use

If you're analyzing a document, let's say a movie still or a film clip, as part of a class project, you could justifiably include that document in your project because of the "fair use" clause of the U.S. Copyright Act. This clause puts limits on the exclusive rights of copyright holders, giving limited reproduction rights for purposes of education, scholarship, and news reporting, in particular when those uses are not-for-profit and do not substantially detract from the value of the work. The "fair use" clause of the U.S. Copyright Act reads as follows:

> 107. Limitations on exclusive rights: fair use
>
> Notwithstanding the provisions of sections 106 and 106A [17 USCS 106, 106A] the fair use of a copyrighted work, including such use by reproduction in copies or phonorecords or by any other means specified by that section, for purposes such as criticism, comment, news reporting, teaching (including multiple copies for classroom use), scholarship, or research, is not an infringement of copyright. In determining whether the use made of a work in any particular case is a fair use the factors to be considered shall include—
>
> (1) the purpose and character of the use, including whether such use is of a commercial nature or is for nonprofit educational purposes;
>
> (2) the nature of the copyrighted work;
>
> (3) the amount and substantiality of the portion used in relation to the copyrighted work as a whole; and
>
> (4) the effect of the use upon the potential market for or value of the copyrighted work.
>
> The fact that a work is unpublished shall not itself bar a finding of fair use if such finding is made upon consideration of all the above factors.

This clause means that in the work you do for traditional class assignments (scholarship), it is fair use to reproduce a portion of a copyrighted work (this is actually why quoting someone is acceptable). This isn't much of a problem when you are writing academic essays because your work will make more sense if you integrate small sections of quoted text from outside sources into your writing, rather than disrupting the flow of your argument by inserting the entire essay. But quoting from a multimedia source obviously raises another set of issues. If an image is essential to your project and you analyze and explain its significance to your work, then the fair use clause may allow you to reproduce it. In fact, Georgia Harper of the University of Texas System Office of General Counsel argues that

> Students may download, transmit, and print out images for personal study and for use in the preparation of academic course assignments and other requirements for degrees, may publicly display images in works prepared for course assignments etc., and may keep works containing images in their portfolios (quoted in *Fair Use Of Copyrighted Materials'* January 6, 1997 <**http://www.utsystem.edu/OGC/IntellectualProperty/copypol2.htm**)>.

However, this model assumes that students are producing assignments to be turned in. It also assumes that "public display" means that people can see the copyrighted material in the student's work but may not reproduce it themselves.

Complications of the Internet

The problem with this model of multimedia copyright is that it relies on the difficulty and expense of reproducing art and other media traditionally. On the Internet, all media are digital, and on the Web, all it takes is a mouse click to copy any file. Imagine that you put a project on the World Wide Web that contained a copyrighted image, say of a popular recording artist. It's quite possible that users who couldn't care less about your academic essay might find your page and download the image, just to have a picture of their favorite musician. This is exactly the type of reproduction that copyright law is designed to protect against, even though your project closely follows the traditional guidelines for reproducing copyrighted material.

We believe that the "fair use" clause and copyright law are intended to balance the rights of artists and publishers with the need for the free exchange of ideas that is necessary in a democratic society. When materials are rhetorically significant to your project and when you're exploring an issue or argument, it's a shame to let copyright laws that are based on an outdated definition of "the classroom" stifle the development of your ideas. Unfortunately, though, the balance seems to be tilting in favor of copyright holders and corporate interests. It's likely that in the next few years, copyright laws will be enforced even more strictly on the Net, making it all the more important for you to consider carefully how you use materials in your on-line projects.

For a comprehensive list of fair use resources on the Net, articles discussing the implications of fair use and reproduction, and the latest news and guidelines on fair use, visit the Stanford University Copyright and Fair Use site (**http://fairuse.stanford.edu**).

APPENDIX 4

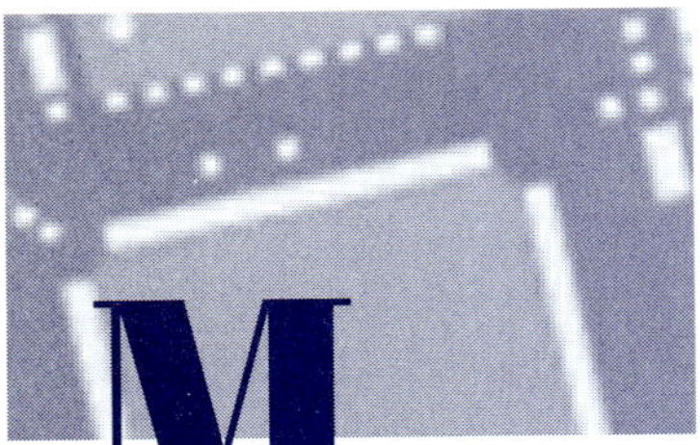

MU* COMMANDS

In this appendix, you'll find a sampling of the most commonly used MU* commands. We've chosen to publish MOO commands here because a number of academic MU*s seem to be written in this programming environment. For more details about MOO commands or commands for another programming environment (MUDs, MUCKs, MUSHs, etc.), see the on-line help files at each MU* (usually accessed by typing "help" or "@help"). Luckily, the commands for all of these environments are similar, so some of the basic commands are likely to work in almost any MU*. Also remember that there are some differences between individual MOOs, meaning that these commands may need to be modified slightly depending the MOO that you are working on.

We've split this appendix into two major sections—speaking/navigation and building—to help you distinguish between the commands you'll need for interacting on a MU* and the commands you'll need to actually construct environments in MU* space. □

Speaking and Navigating Commands

- *:action*
  Makes a character "emote" whatever *action* is typed in after the colon.
- look
  Provides a description of the current room and its contents.
- look *x*
  Provides a description of the object *x*.
- *"message*
  Allows a user to "say" whatever *message* is typed after the quotation mark.
- page *character message*
  Sends a *message* to another *character* on the MU* regardless of where she or he is located.
- read *x*
  Is used to "read" an object **x,** such as a newspapers or signs.
- whisper *"message"* to *character*
  Sends a private *message* to the specified *character.*
- @desc me as *x*
  Provides the description *x* of yourself for the other users who "look" at you.
- @drop *x*
  Allows a user to drop object *x*.
- @gender *genderchoice*
  Gives your character the specified *genderchoice,* usually male, female, or neuter.
- @help or help
  Gives more detailed information about MU* commands.
- @take *x*
  Lets you pick up the object *x*.

Building Commands

- @dig *"x"*
  Creates the new room *x*.
- @desc *x* as *"y"*
  Gives the room or object *x* the description *y*.

- @add-exit
  Creates an exit in a room.
- @add-entrance
  Creates an entrance in a room.
- @dig [direction] to "*x*"
  Gives the direction of an exit from the current room to the entrance of room *x*.
- @leave
  Defines what users will see as they go through an exit.
- @oleave
  Defines what others see when a user leaves a room.
- @arrive
  Defines what users see when they arrive in a room.
- @oarrive
  Defines what others see when a user arrives in a room.
- @lock "*x*"
  Keeps users from entering room *x* or taking object *x*.
- @nogo
  What users see if they can't move through an exit.
- @onogo
  What others see if a user can't move through an exit.
- @create [$object type] named "*x*"
  Creates the new object *x* and specifies its type (for example, $note, $letter, $thing, or $container).
- @take_succeeded
  Defines what users see when they take an object.
- @otake_succeeded
  Defines what others see when a user takes an object.
- @take_failed
  Defines what users see when they can't take an object.
- @otake_failed
  Defines what others see when a user can't take an object.
- @drop_succeeded
  Defines what users see when they drop an object.
- @odrop_succeeded
  Defines what others see when a user drops an object.
- @drop_failed
  Defines what users see when they can't drop an object.
- @odrop_failed
  Defines what others see when a user can't drop an object.

APPENDIX 5

HTML BUILDING REFERENCE

Basic Commands

The HTML Skeleton

Every HTML page should have a core set of elements that we call the HTML skeleton. Although some browsers and servers will still handle Web files if these elements are missing, we strongly recommend that you include the coding shown in Figure A5.1 in all of your HTML documents.

The <TITLE> of your page goes in the <HEAD> (remember that this is just what shows up in the title bar), and the content of your page goes in the <BODY>. You can also use a list of keywords with the <HEAD META KEYWORD=keyword1, keyword2, keyword3> tag to help Web search engines find and categorize your pages.

Headings

<H1> **Size 1 Heading** </H1>
<H2> **Size 2 Heading** </H2>

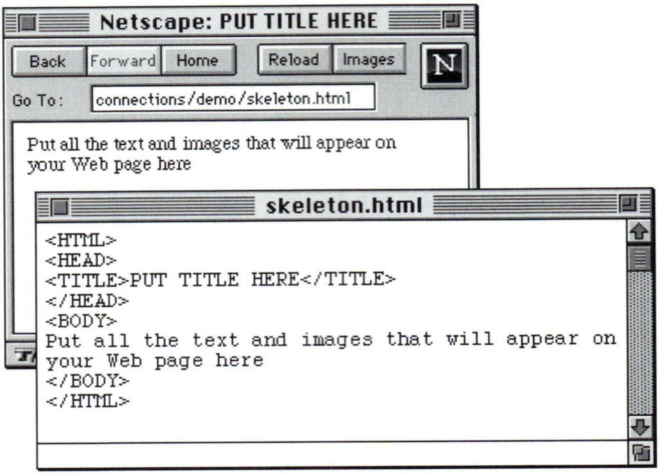

■ **FIGURE A5.1** The HTML Skeleton

<H3> **Size 3 Heading** </H3>

<H4> **Size 4 Heading** </H4>

<H5> **Size 5 Heading** </H5>

<H6> **Size 6 Heading** </H6>

Font Sizes

You can also change the relative size of the text on your pages by using the font size tag. <FONT SIZE=+1> increases the font by one. You can go up or down by 4 font sizes. You return to normal size font with the </FONT> tag. For example

```
<FONT SIZE=+4>This will be four times larger</FONT>

<FONT SIZE=-2>This will be two times smaller</FONT>
```

Text Styles

- <B> **Boldface Text** </B>
- <I> *Italicized Text* </I>
- <U> Underlined Text </U>
- <TT> `Typewriter Text` </TT>
- <CENTER> Centered Material </CENTER>
- <STRIKE> ~~Strike Through Text~~ </STRIKE>

- ^{Superscript Text}
- _{Subscript Text}
- <BIG> Large Font </BIG>
- <SMALL> Small Font </SMALL>

Single-Tag Commands

<HR> Draws a horizontal rule across the page.

 Forces a line break.
<P> Forces a paragraph break.

Lists

One common method of organizing space and information on the Web is through the use of various types of lists. HTML offers several possible options for listing information.

Definition List The definition list shown in Figure A5.2 displays items with an annotation or definition appearing on an indented line beneath each item.

Unnumbered List An unnumbered list indents and bullets each item, as shown in Figure A5.3.

Numbered List The numbered list shown in Figure A5.4 indents and numbers each item.

■ **FIGURE A5.2** A Definition List

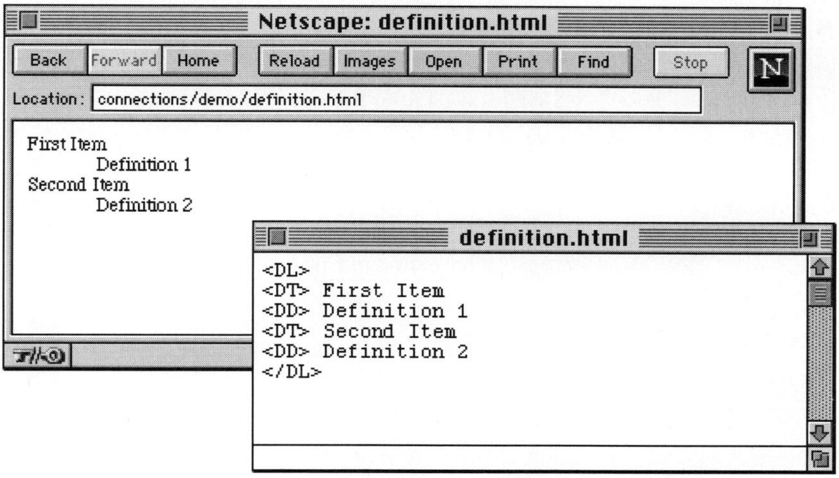

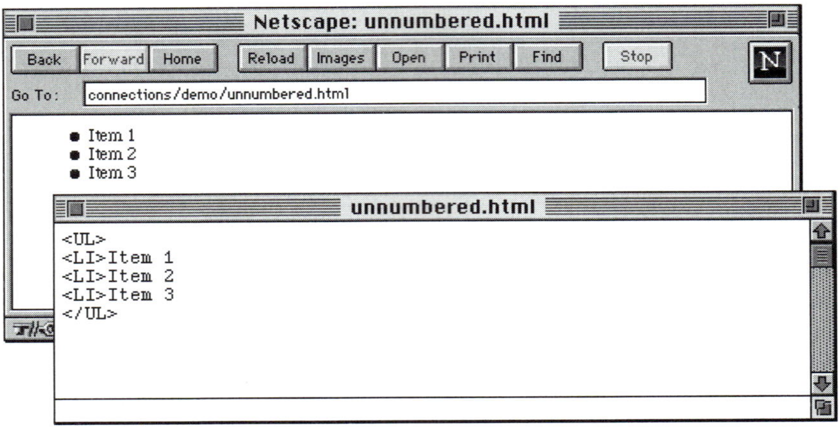

■ **FIGURE A5.3** An Unnumbered List

Menu A menu is a list of indented items, as shown in Figure A5.5. Note that you can use the <MENU> command multiple times to move the text toward the right-hand margin.

Images

It's important to understand that images aren't physically part of the HTML page; they are separate files which are linked to the HTML document with the <IMG SRC> command. Here's an example:

```
<IMG SRC="connections.jpg">
```

■ **FIGURE A5.4** A Numbered List

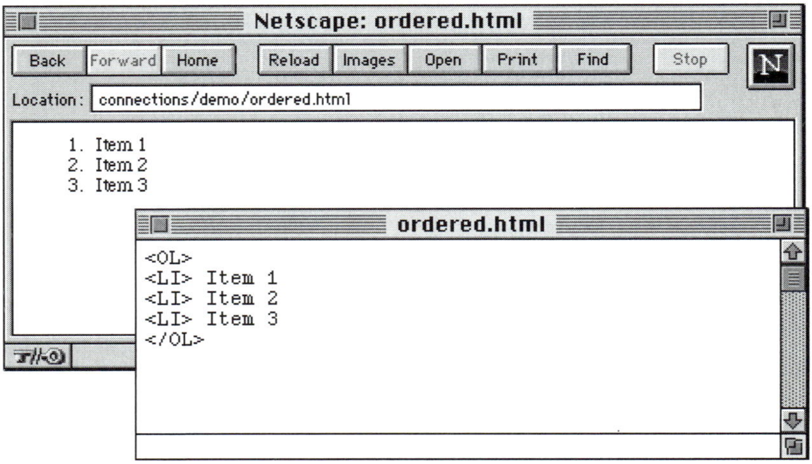

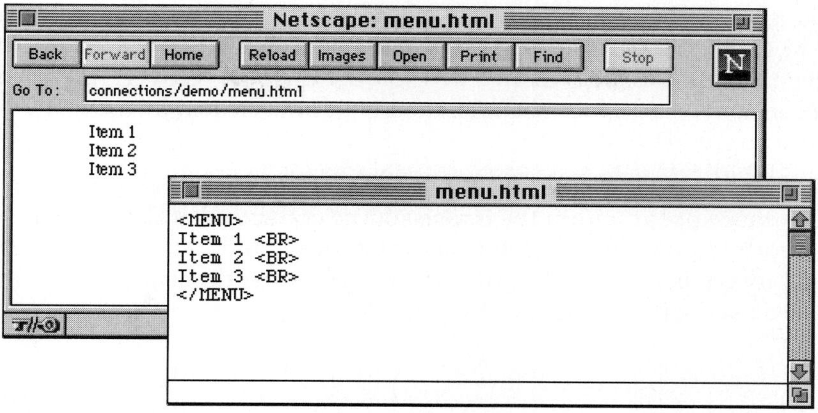

■ **FIGURE A5.5** A Menu

There are also some more advanced attributes that can be added to the image command.

Image Alignment HTML gives you options for aligning graphics to the left or right of text. For instance, Figure A5.6 shows how you can align images on the left or right of a page. When you align an image to one side

■ **FIGURE A5.6** Image Alignment

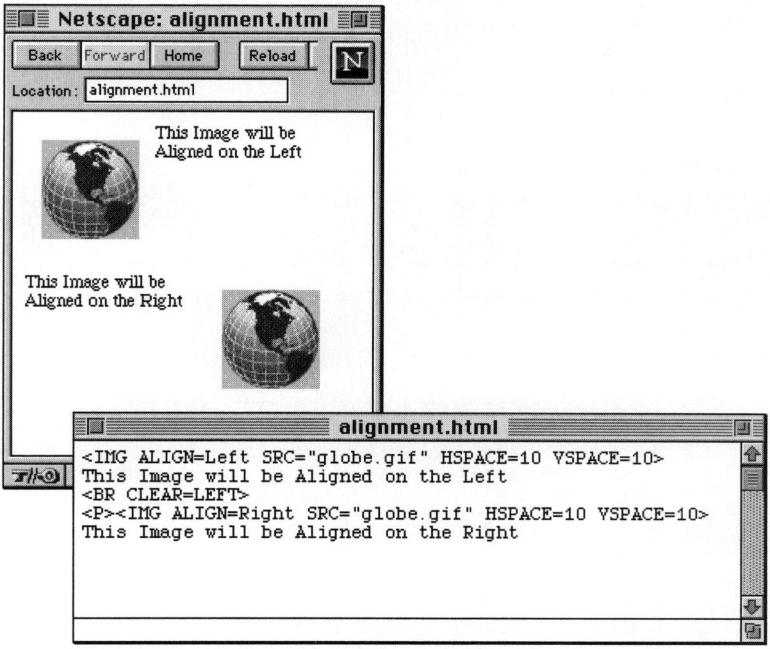

of the page, you will need to tell the browser at what point you want the text to go back to normal page alignment. This is accomplished by using either the <BR CLEAR=LEFT> or the <BR CLEAR=RIGHT> command. You can also insert space between the image and the text by using the horizontal space <HSPACE> or vertical space <VSPACE> command.

ALT Tags Always provide an alternative description of your images. <ALT> tags appear within the image source command and are commonly used both to provide a description of the image and to tell users where a linked image is pointing. Figure A5.7 displays the description on a page being viewed with the images turned off.

Links

Figure A5.8 shows a link from the *Connections* Web page to the Computer Writing and Research Labs (CWRL) at the University of Texas at Austin. Let's take a look at the HTML that constructs the link:

```
<A HREF="http://www.cwrl.utexas.edu/index.html">
Computer Writing and Research Labs</A>
```

The anchor or link command follows the <TAG></TAG> pattern and, like the image command, lets us specify which file to link to. The opening tag <A HREF="http://www.cwrl.utexas.edu/index.html"> sets the anchor and provides the URL reference for the link to the CWRL home page. Next comes the text, "Computer Writing and Research Labs," followed by the

■ **FIGURE A5.7** <ALT> Tags

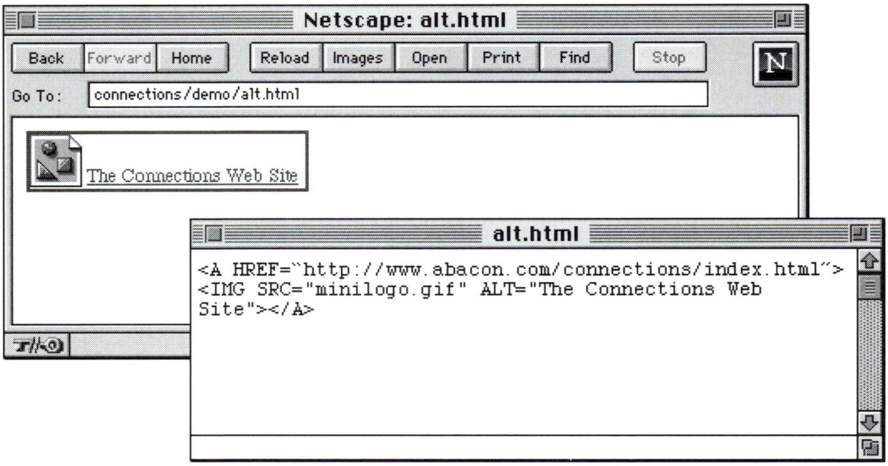

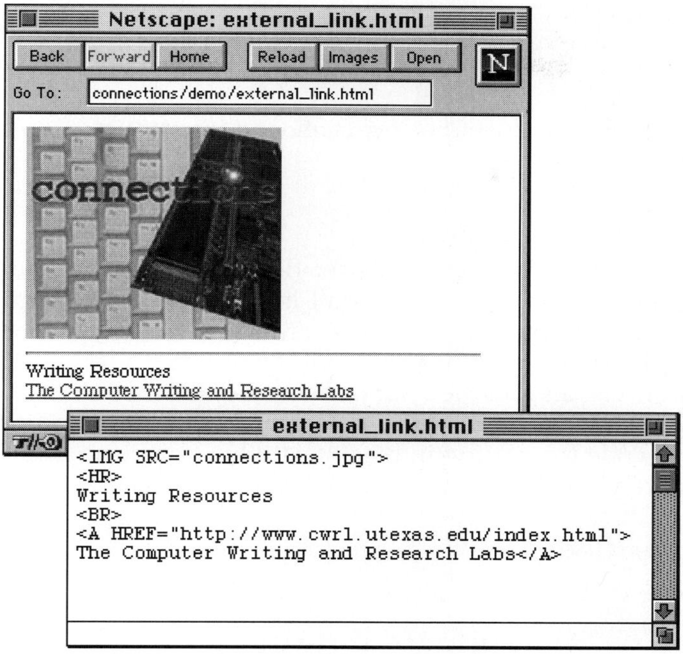

■ **FIGURE A5.8** An External Link

</A>. The phrase between the two tags will be the hot text, or linking text, when the file is viewed by a browser. In addition to HTML files, you can link to a number of different file formats that can be read by a browser.

File Types

File Type	Extension
HTML File	.htm/.html
Text File	.txt
GIF Image File	.gif
JPEG Image File	.jpg/.jpeg
MPEG Movie	.mpg/.mpeg
QuickTime Movie	.mov
WAV Sound File	.wav
Internet Sound File (Sun/Unix)	.au

MAILTO Links

To get feedback on the pages you've created, be sure to include a <MAILTO> link:

```
<A HREF="MAILTO:bubba@whitehouse.gov">E-Mail
Bubba</A>
```

Backgrounds

The background code is included in the first <BODY> tag of the standard HTML skeleton. Backgrounds, like all images on the Web, must be in either GIF or JPG format. If we had an image named "coffee.gif", we would use the HTML scripting shown in Figure A5.9.

Authors can also set the color of the text <TEXT>, links <LINK>, and visited links <VLINK> for an entire page within the initial <BODY> tag. The HTML code for putting in black text, blue links, and orange visited links on a white background would look like that shown in Figure A5.10.

RGB Color Codes

Here are the RGB codes for a few common colors.

- White = "FFFFFF"
- Blue = "0000DD"
- Green = "007700"
- Red = "EE0000"

■ **FIGURE A5.9** A Background Image

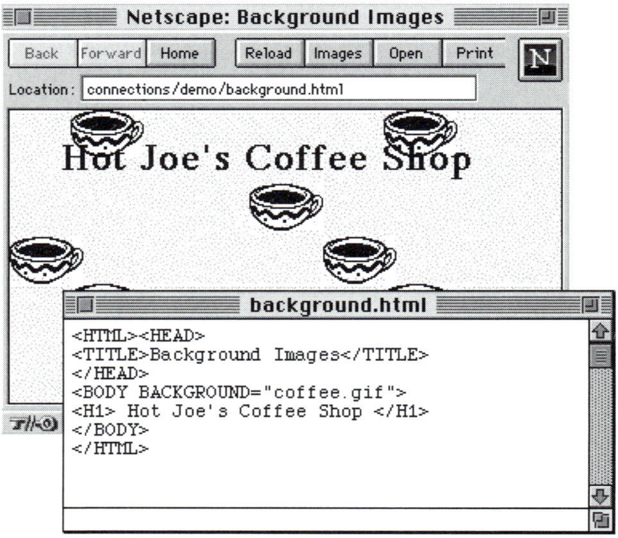

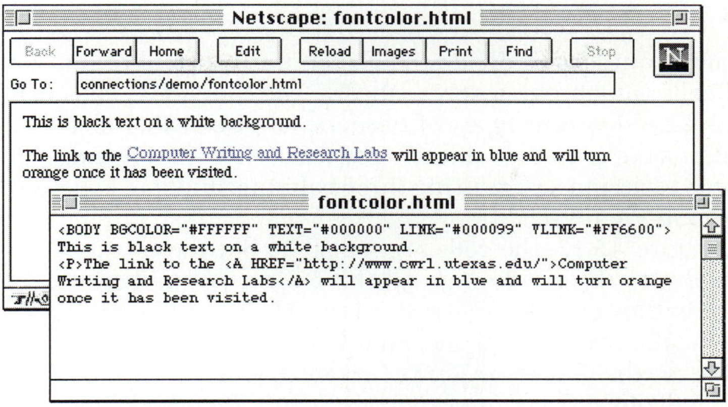

■ **FIGURE A5.10**

- Yellow = "FFFF00"
- Brown = "663300"
- Purple = "990099"

By placing these color codes into the initial <BODY> tag of your document, then, you can designate the font colors for the entire Web page.

Note that there are a number of additional colors you can use, but be aware that different monitors process colors differently. You can get more detailed information about the standard color codes at **http://www.phoenix.net/~jacobson/rgb.html** or the *Connections* Web site.

You can also change the color of certain sections of text within the body of your document by using the <FONT COLOR> </FONT> tags. For instance, Figure A5.11 shows a Web page on which one sentence appears in black and another in blue on a white background.

■ **FIGURE A5.11** <FONT COLOR></FONT> Tags

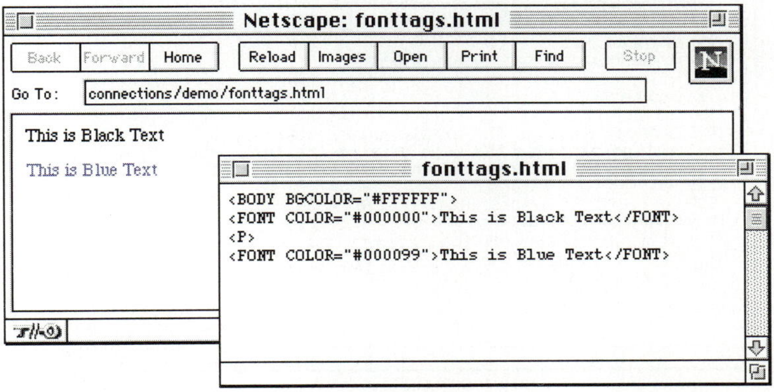

Tables

Tables allow authors to divide the screen into a series of horizontal and vertical cells (much like a spreadsheet). The individual cells can vary in size, can have different types of borders, can be visible or invisible, and can contain text, graphics, and other types of files. For instance, an author who wants to design a page using three columns might use the HTML coding shown in Figure A5.12.

In Figure A5.12, the cells are invisible, but the text and images are segmented into three columns. All three pieces of table data, <TD>, are displayed within a single table row, <TR>. The left and right columns each fill 20% of the screen, and the middle column occupies the remaining 60%. This means that regardless of browser window or monitor size, the columns will always stay in proportion with each other.

Other types of tables show the boundaries of each cell more clearly. In Figure A5.13, the "BORDER=10" command places the large shadowed border around the outside of the table. The command <CELLSPACING> refers to the size of the line between the cells, and the command <CELLPADDING> refers to the amount of space between the text and the cell borders.

■ **FIGURE A5.12** A Three-Column Table

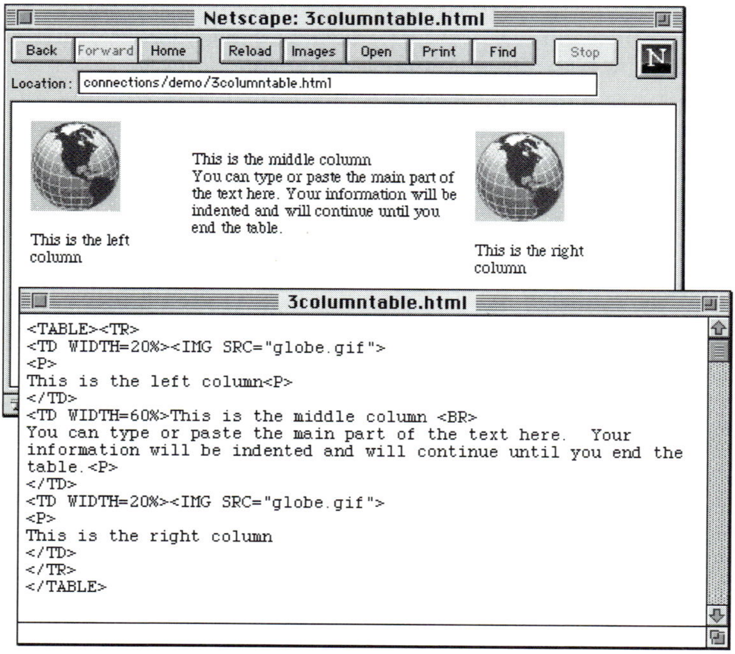

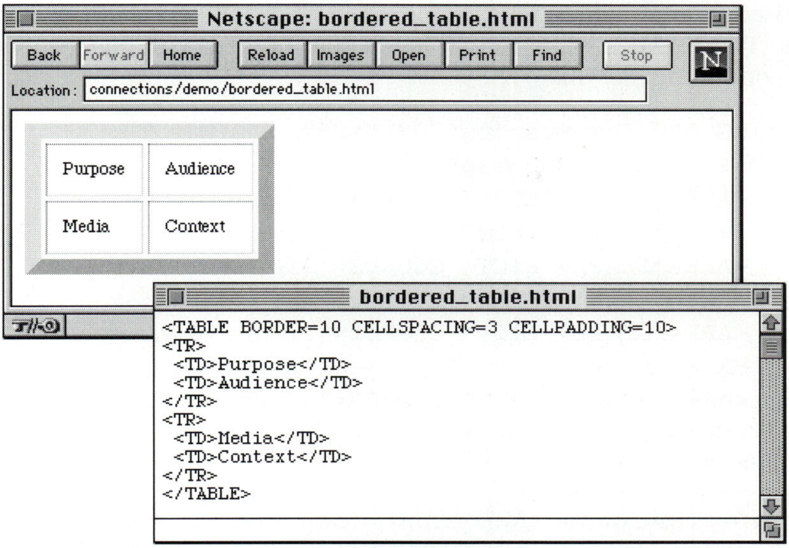

■ **FIGURE A5.13** A Bordered Table

Imagemaps, Frames, and Layers

Imagemaps

Imagemaps are single images (generally images with multiple objects in them) that are "mapped" so that a reader can go to different pages by clicking on different sections of the image. If you can find an image that will provide a suitable metaphor for your site and that has enough elements to represent multiple nodes, you can incorporate a tremendous amount of information into a visually dramatic presentation.

There are many shareware applications and WYSIWYG editors that will help you build imagemaps. Using these applications, you can set coordinates for images and specify a URL for each "hot spot." The process of creating the map will vary from application to application, but the basic HTML should be the same. The mapping application will generate a text file that includes the image coordinates and their corresponding URLs. (You can also determine the coordinates of your hot spots by using a graphics editor.) Don't be afraid if this looks like a Dow Jones stock update with numbers scrolling across the page. All you need to do is place these coordinates into your HTML document inside a <MAP></MAP> tag. You'll also need to include some additional information in the <IMG

SRC> command, which tells the browser where to find the map coordinates. The HTML coding for an imagemap named "campus.jpg" would look something like this:

```
<IMG SRC="campus.jpg" USEMAP=#campusmap>
<MAP NAME="campusmap">
  <AREA SHAPE="RECT" COORDS="15,25,40,55"
  HREF="english.html">
  <AREA SHAPE="RECT" COORDS="136,78,98,116"
  HREF="math.html">
  <AREA SHAPE="RECT" COORDS="12,52,76,24"
  HREF="physics.html">
  <AREA SHAPE="RECT" COORDS="90,85,35,11"
  HREF="socio.html">
</MAP>
```

In this case, we use <MAP NAME="campusmap"> to denote the document section where the map coordinates are stored. By including the tag "USEMAP=#campusmap" within the <IMG SRC> command, we tell the browser that the graphic file "campus.jpg" is an imagemap and that its coordinates are specified in the "campusmap" section. When a reader clicks on part of the image, the browser will know to look for the coordinates within the <MAP NAME="campusmap"></MAP> command and will load the specified page.

Frames

Like any HTML project, a frame-based design begins with an opening page. In frame structures, however, this opening page has two major components: the <FRAMESET> tag, which sets up the frame structure for the project, and the <NOFRAMES> tag, which provides an alternative for browsers that don't support frames.

Remember that not all of your audience will be able to see your frames, so you might want to provide an alternative text version for them. You'll also need to experiment a bit as you develop your frame structures. As a way of demonstrating the basics, let's look at two popular models.

A Menu in a Bottom Frame Figure A5.14 shows a structure that uses a frame at the foot of the screen to present a static menu of the site's contents. The first thing you should notice is that the <FRAMESET> command is placed after the <HEAD> of the HTML document. The <FRAMESET ROWS=90%,10%> tag determines that the structure of the page should be divided into two ROWS. This is accomplished by specify-

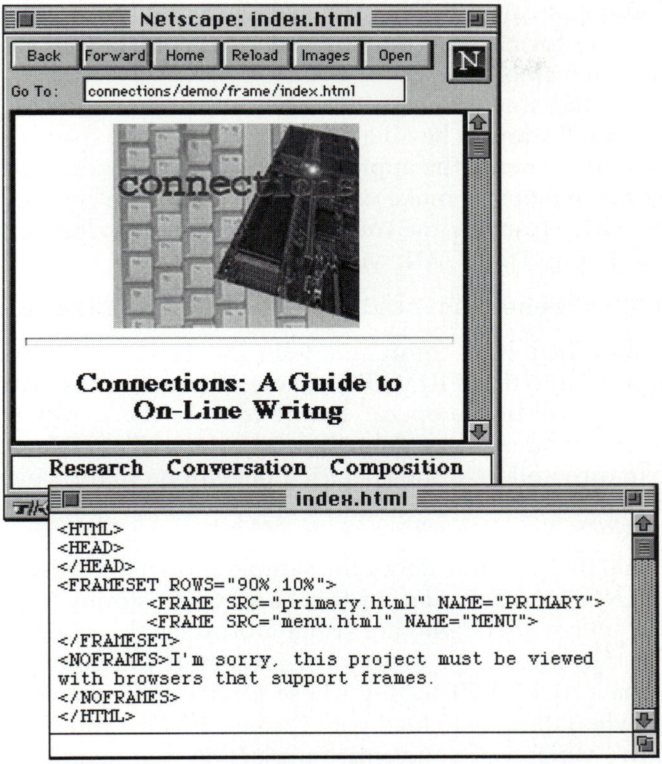

FIGURE A5.14 A Frame Menu at the Foot of a Project

ing how much space should be assigned to each of the ROWS; in this case, 90% of the browser window is given to the first frame and 10% to the second.

Next, the sample shows how the structure of the page is further controlled with the <FRAME SRC> tag. This tells the browser what information to put into each of the rows. The first tag <FRAME SRC= "primary. html" NAME=PRIMARY> specifies that the file "primary.html" should be loaded into the first frame. Like an HTML link, you can either specify a local file using relative link information or a remote file using a full URL.

The second frame in the structure is designated with the tag <FRAME SRC="menu.html" NAME=MENU>. This tag tells the browser to place the file "menu.html" in the second row of the frame structure. Note, also, that both of the frame source tags specify a name for each frame. The first frame is called "PRIMARY," and the second is called

"MENU." You can call your frames whatever you like, but you'll need to provide a name for each so that you can control the way that files are loaded into the frames.

For instance, since the second frame in the structure acts as a menu for the site, you'll want to be able to specify that when users click on one of the terms in the menu, the appropriate file will be loaded into the "PRIMARY" frame. When you make your link to "Research" in the menu, you will specify which frame name you would like the file to load into by using the "TARGET" tag. The HTML will read:

```
<A HREF="research.html" TARGET=PRIMARY>Research</A>
```

This modified link command tells the browser to load the file "research.html" into the "PRIMARY" frame. There are other TARGET tags that let you control frame operations. If you use the <TARGET= _TOP> tag in the link you are creating, the browser will break out of your frames structure and load the specified page in its main window. If you use the <TARGET=_BLANK> tag, the specified page will be loaded in a new window.

The final thing to note about the sample shown in Figure A5.14 is the use of the <NOFRAMES> tag. In this case, we've simply inserted information that tells readers who are using a browser that does not support frames why they are unable to view the project. If you don't put any message into the <NOFRAMES> tag, these readers will see nothing but a blank page when they try to load your frames. Ideally, you should provide an alternative version of your entire project so that people with limited technology will still be able to see your information. It's often easier to create a no-frames version after a site is finished; you can usually retool the frame-based pages that you've developed fairly quickly.

A Menu in a Side Frame The frame-based menu shown at the bottom of Figure A5.14 is useful because it requires very little screen space. Using such a small frame, you can create a static menu for your site without detracting from the overall layout of the pages. However, this model is somewhat limited in the number of menu options that you can provide. If your site has more than a handful of major sections, you might be better served by placing them in a side menu.

Figure A5.15 shows a project that splits the screen into two columns. This is accomplished with opening tag <FRAMESET COLS=25%,*>. Note that in addition to using the <COLS> tag to divide the page vertically, this command uses the "wildcard" or (*) symbol to designate the screen space allotted to the second frame in the structure. The initial frame will use 25% of the browser window for the first column. By using the (*) symbol, the tag tells the browser to give all the remaining space

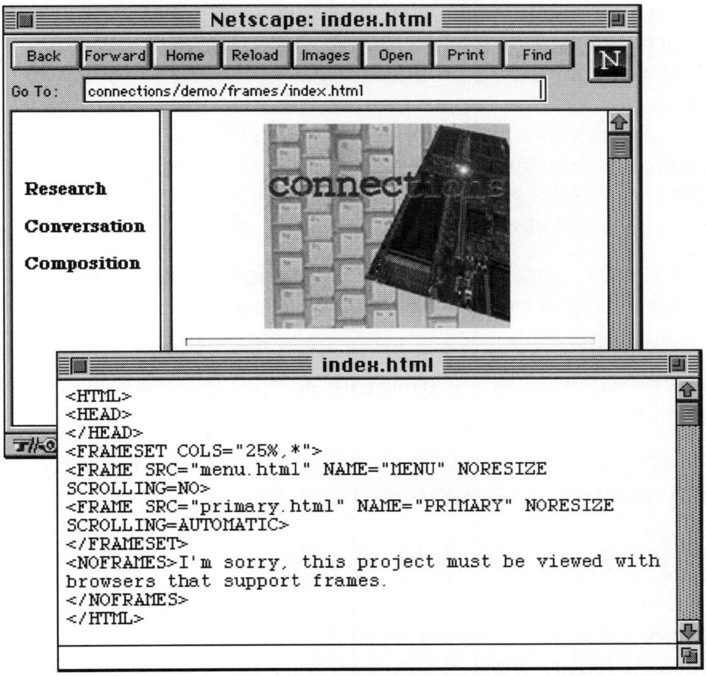

■ **FIGURE A5.15** A Frame Menu at the Side of a Project

to the second frame. Additionally, you can specify an amount of space in absolute pixels by using an integer. If you knew that your side menu requires sixty-eight pixels to display all of its images, using the tag "COLS=68,*" would make your first frame exactly sixty-eight pixels and give the rest of the space in the window to the second frame.

Figure A5.15 also shows how you can specify additional information about the frames in the <FRAME SRC> tag. The first frame in the sample is delineated with the

```
<FRAME SRC="menu.html" NAME=MENU NORESIZE
SCROLLING=NO>
```

tag. If you don't specify against it, users can resize the frames in the window of the browser. The <NORESIZE> locks the frames into place. Additionally, the default specification will give frames scroll bars if there is more information than will fit in a frame window. By adding the <SCROLLING=NO> element to the tag, you can override this option.

You can also adjust the border elements of the frame structures you create to provide more sophisticated arrangements of elements within the window of the browser. For instance, if you eliminate the border on a frame, it is possible to create a menu that blends with the rest of the pages, but doesn't disappear when users scroll down in the main frame. To eliminate the border in a frame, add the <FRAMEBORDER=0> tag to your <FRAMESET> command. In your <FRAMESET> tag, you can adjust other border elements with tags like these:

```
<FRAMESET COLS="20%,80%" BORDERCOLOR=BLACK
FRAMESPACING=30 FRAMEPADDING=20>
```

You can also adjust the spacing of the elements that will appear within an individual frame by adding attributes to the <FRAME> command with tags like these:

```
<FRAME NAME=BODY SCROLLING=NO SRC="body.html"
MARGINWIDTH=10 MARGINHEIGHT=20>
```

These added elements will specify a margin of ten pixels for the width of your frame and twenty pixels for its height.

There are many additional tags that will add quite a bit of sophistication to your frame-based projects. You should also know that you can imbed frames within frames to create any number of different arrangements. The tags and information that we've offered here, however, allow you to set up these basic structures for your own pages and get you on your way toward creating more advanced arrangements. You'll probably need to experiment with the frame structures that you develop to arrive at a final design for a presentation. Remember that you can adjust the amount of "screen real-estate" given to each frame and change the scrolling and border options for the various frames of the project. You can get more information about frames at (**http://home.netscape.com/assist/net_sites/frames.html**).

Layers

Like the frames feature supported by most HTML browsers, the layers tag is concerned with controlling the way information is presented in the window of the browser. As of this writing, Netscape versions 4.0 and greater are the only browsers which support layers. Layers allow designers to more precisely place different pieces of information within the browser window. Additionally, different layers can be treated as objects, which can be controlled by the browser using JavaScripts. So, if you wanted to have an image move from left to right across the window of a browser, you could place that image as a layer within the Web page and use JavaScript commands to control its movement.

This kind of dynamic positioning of information on the page obviously requires some sophisticated programming. Fortunately, like most things on the Web, there are a number of functions that have already been developed and that you can use as references for developing your own pages. It is not necessary to understand every aspect of a more complicated Web development language like JavaScript in order to work with layers.

As you can see from Figure A5.16, the layers tag is not overly complicated. Like other HTML commands, it works with the <TAG></TAG> pattern. In Figure A5.16 we can see that the first layer within the page is established with the <LAYER> command. A number of attributes can be added to the layer tag; for instance, here the distance from the left hand side of the browser window is specified with the <LEFT=0> attribute and the distance from the top of the window is designated by the <TOP=0> tag. In the sample shown, the first layer is associated with an HTML file with the SRC="layer1.html" tag. This allows designers to create information within the file layer1.html. In the sample shown in Figure A5.16, the </LAYER> tag closes the command for each layer. Each of the layers in

■ **FIGURE A5.16** The Netscape Layers Function

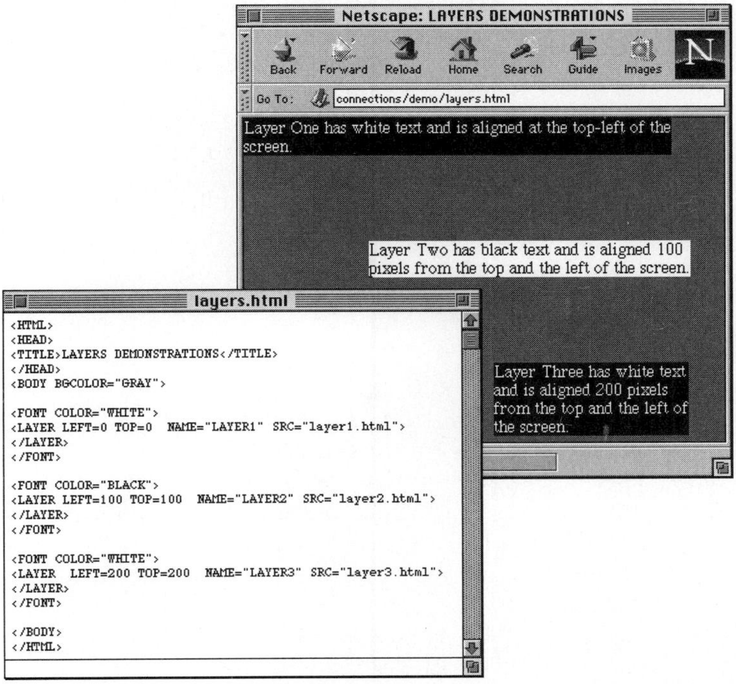

our sample is also given a name. Naming the layers allows you to control the way that the browser treats each different layer. For instance, using a JavaScript, you might tell a browser to show "Layer1" for 5 seconds and then to hide "Layer1" and show "Layer2."

In general, the process for arranging information by placing it in layers and positioning the layers relative to the top and the left of the browser window is not complicated. In order to fully understand layers and put them to use for your projects, you'll need to do some experimentation. Eventually, you'll probably also want to do some work with JavaScript so that you can take full advantage of the functionality offered by layers. Like most of the more sophisticated Web building procedures, there is a lot to learn. Fortunately, most of the information that you will need is available on-line. One of the best tutorials is Adam Rebholz's (**http://www.daily.umn.edu/~rebholz/**). You can also get more extensive information at the Netscape Communicator Site (**http://home.netscape.com/flash2/comprod/products/communicator/index.html**) and especially at the Layers and JavaScript Glossary Pages (**http://home.netscape.com/comprod/products/communicator/layers/layers_glossary.html**).

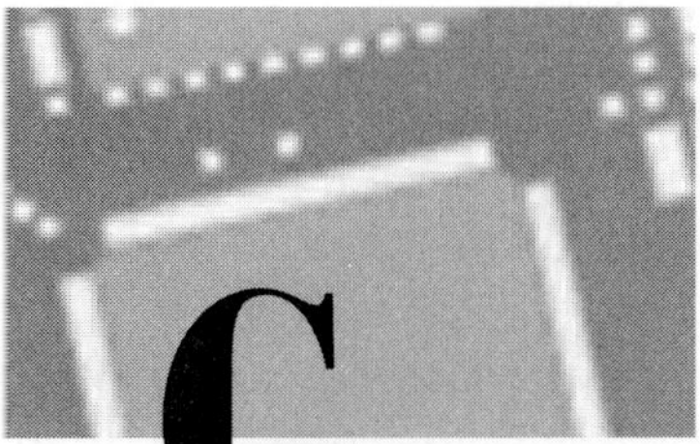

GLOSSARY

Accommodation: The process of incorporating and addressing opposing points of view in your arguments.

Applet: An application that can be embedded in an HTML page and run from a Web browser.

Arguable Position: A position that addresses a topic or issue in which some type of conflict, disagreement, or disparity exists between two or more viable positions. Those positions must share a certain amount of common ground.

Argument: A claim that is explained by logical reasoning and often supported by evidence and that is intended both to persuade an audience and to move the audience toward a clearer sense of understanding.

Assumptions: The premises on which any claim is based. As the term "assumption" suggests, these premises are usually unstated.

Asynchronous Communication: Communication that takes place over an extended period of time. For instance, newsgroup postings are asynchronous because threads develop over a period of days or even weeks.

Attachments: Files that are encoded and then sent with an e-mail message. The encoded document is "attached" rather than incorporated into the body of the message. The files are then decoded by the recipient's mail-reading client.

Audience: The recipient(s) of a message in any communication situation. The audience can range from a solitary reader of a work to an auditorium of people at a speech or a concert to thousands of readers on the World Wide Web.

Authority: The credibility and expertise with which an author speaks. Authority is influenced by an author's status, knowledge, and experience. In messages, authority is conveyed by well-wrought arguments, fair-mindedness, well-documented support, an appropriate tone, and other compositional elements.

Background: An image or color that is tiled multiple times to form the background of a Web page.

Bookmark: (1) As a verb, describes the process of marking the location of a file or site on the Internet. (2) as a noun, describes an individual address that has been saved in a browser's memory for future reference.

Boolean Operator: A connector that lets you combine terms and customize a keyword search. The principal Boolean operators are "and," "or," and "not."

Bots (short for "robot"): Programs that are designed to emulate MU* characters. By building bots, MU* authors can "people" their environments with characters who will perform programmed functions.

Byte: A unit for measuring digital information.

Channel: A "frequency" on which users on a MU* or IRC can converse with each other. Users anywhere in a MU* can create and log onto a channel where they can carry on real-time discussions without bothering other MU* users.

Character: The persona that users create when logging onto a MU*. MU* users can set a description for their character to better illustrate the person they hope to adopt.

Chat: A colloquial term used to describe any of the various methods for real-time conversations on the Internet.

Claim: A statement that stakes out a position or asserts a point.

Client: An application that contacts Internet servers and provides users with an interface to access on-line files. There are specific clients for accessing each Internet medium, such as newsreaders, mail readers, and Web browsers.

Common Gateway Interface (CGI): Programs that allow browsers to submit information to the Web server. CGIs are actually a combination of an interface that permits the sharing of information and a script that manipulates that information. Web forums and add-link scripts are common examples of CGIs.

Context: The elements surrounding and informing any act of communication. The setting, the time, related events, and any other messages about a topic all influence the way any message is constructed and interpreted.

Credibility: The amount of trust that is placed in an author's competence, motives, and fair-mindedness. Also used to refer to the reliability of resources.

Critical Reading: An approach to analyzing messages that looks at both their successes and their failures. Critical reading considers texts in terms of their purposes, contexts, and media and evaluates them by examining their component parts.

Directory: An organizational structure for managing files on a disk. Some operating systems use a folder metaphor to represent a directory.

Download: To transfer electronic documents from the Internet to your local machine.

E-mail (Electronic Mail): A basic form of Internet communication that allows users to send and receive messages.

E-mail Discussion List (Also known as a "list" or "Listserv"): A collection of e-mail addresses managed by a program that allows users to send e-mail to a group of subscribed members.

Emote: To perform an action as part of a real-time conversation on a MU*. Emoting appends the action that you wish to perform to your character name so that a third-person narrative results. For instance, "The Prof rubs her chin and wonders what to cover today in class." In IRCs, emotes are known as "actions."

Evidence: The data and materials that are used to support a claim.

Fact: Something that is verifiable within a specific group of people at a specific time.

Fair Summary: A summary that articulates the basic message of a text without critique or commentary. In general, a fair summary represents an author's argument as closely as possible.

File Transfer Protocol (FTP): An Internet protocol that allows users to upload and download files.

Flame: A personal attack, usually sent via e-mail or on a newsgroup, that offers little or no constructive critique.

Framing Narrative: A story or metaphor that serves as an organizing principle for MU* designs. By constructing a framing narrative, MU* builders can provide a logical context in which to connect various rooms and objects.

Frequently Asked Questions (FAQ): An on-line archive that collects and responds to the most commonly asked questions about a site or topic. Looking through a group's FAQ file is an easy way to get a sense of the kind of materials the group offers and discusses.

Genre: Primarily a literary term used to describe the differences between works such as plays, poems, and novels. Additionally, it can be used more specifically to distinguish subcategories such as romance or detective novels.

Hit: An item returned from a successful keyword search.

Hotlist: Another term for a Bookmark file. See also **Bookmark.**

Hot spot: The sections of an imagemap that activate hypertext links.

Hot text: Words or phrases in a hypertext that activate links. On the Web, hot text is usually underlined and set off with color. Clicking on this text takes readers to another node of the document.

Hub-and-Spoke Design: A hypertextual design that has multiple nodes (the spokes) linked from a central point (the hub). This type of organizational structure is well suited for displaying multiple perspectives or examples.

HTML Editor: An application for composing and editing text. Though you can use any text editor to create pages for the Web, many sophisticated HTML editors that simplify Web building are available.

Hypermedia: Hypertext that makes use of multimedia elements.

Hypertext: A composition that links pieces of information (often called "nodes") together into complex, interactive webs.

Hypertext Markup Language (HTML): The scripting language that is used to create pages for the World Wide Web. Authors insert HTML tags (commands) in a text document to change page layout, make links, and display images.

Imagemap: An image with hot spots that activate hypertext links. Clicking on sections of the image will take readers to different Web files.

Informative Writing: Writing that presents information without trying to persuade.

Internet Directory: An index of Internet sites cataloged by subject.

Internet Relay Chat (IRC): A section of the Internet that allows users to join a chat channel and have real-time conversations.

Keyword Search: An electronic search that finds occurrences of terms specified by a user.

Link: (1) As a noun, the connection between sections, or nodes, of a hypertext. Often, links are activated by clicking on hot text or icons. (2) As a verb, the process of connecting pieces of information into a hypertextual form.

Linked Graphic: A graphic that, when clicked, activates a hypertext link to another node on the Web.

Medium: The mode of communication for a message. The term can be used generally, for instance, to distinguish electronic communication from messages in a print medium. It can also be used specifically to distinguish subcategories of communication such as magazines and newspapers or e-mail and the World Wide Web.

Message: (1) Used to denote "what is being communicated." The message is in some ways the "content" of communication divorced from its context. (2) Also refers to the "text" that is transmitted in any act of communication.

Moderated Group: A newsgroup or e-mail discussion list that uses a moderator to screen messages before they are posted.

Moderator: The individual who screens messages before they are posted to a moderated e-mail discussion list or newsgroup.

MU*: A text-based virtual environment on the Internet. MU* is our umbrella term for the many spaces on Internet servers where users log in, explore the virtual environment, and interact with others. These spaces take their names from different versions of multiple-user software and include MUDs, MUSHs, MUCKs, and MOOs.

Multimedia: (1) The combination of two or more forms of media in a project. (2) Also used to describe any file in a nontext format, such as sound, graphic, video, or animation files.

Newbie: A colloquial expression used to describe users who are unfamiliar with the Internet and netiquette.

Newsfeed: An Internet posting or forum that originates from traditional news organizations such as the Associated Press or Reuters.

Newsgroup: A topic-centered forum devoted to discussion and the exchange of articles, news, and other media. (See also **Usenet.**)

Newshost (also called a "news server"): An Internet-connected server that collects, stores, and distributes newsgroup messages.

Newsreader: Client software that allows users to read and post to newsgroups.

Nickname: (1) The persona that a user chooses when logging onto an IRC channel. (2) A file created with a mail reader that contains one or more e-mail addresses. A message sent to a nickname will be forwarded to every address listed in the file.

Node: One unit of a hypertext. A node can be a document, a graphic, a sound file, or any other individual piece of information that has been linked to a hypertext.

Object: An item that is placed in a MU* to flesh out the description of a room. Objects are usually just text descriptions, but they can also be programmed to perform certain tasks.

Operating System (OS): The software that controls the basic operations of a computer. The OS provides an interface that allows users to operate applications and manage files. Examples include DOS, Win95, MacOS, and various versions of UNIX.

Opinion: A claim that is based on personal preference.

Persuasion: Communication that moves an audience to action or convinces audience members to think in a certain way.

Persuasive Writing: Writing that tries to move an audience to action or toward an adjustment of the audience members' beliefs.

Platform: The operating system that a computer is designed to use. For example, one program may be designed for a Macintosh platform, whereas another program would be designed for a Win95 platform.

Plug-in: An extension to a Web browser that allows the browser to play files created with other applications.

Post (also called a "posting"): (1) as a verb, describes the act of sending a message to a list, newsgroup, or other on-line forum. (2) As a noun, describes a message that has been sent to an on-line forum.

Purpose: The motives that compel a speaker to present a message to a specific audience in a particular way. Purpose also refers to the particular goals that an author has in mind at any stage of the writing process.

Query: A research question posted to the Internet.

Real-Time: Interactions that take place without any significant lapse of time between them (also known as synchronous interaction). Most of the real-time conversations on the Internet take place on IRC channels and in MU*s.

RGB (Red, Green, and Blue) Color Codes: Six-digit (hexadecimal) codes used to designate different text and background colors on the Web. RGB codes mix different proportions of the three primary colors to create the various colors of the spectrum.

Rhetoric: The study and practice of communication. Rhetoric can be used both to analyze the messages of others and to compose messages of your own.

Rhetorical Situation: The relationship between the speaker, the audience, and the message at the moment of communication. It can also refer to additional elements of communication, such as the purpose of a message and its context.

Rhetorical Triangle: The relationship among three components of any communication act: the message, the speaker, and the audience. The three are interconnected, but isolating each element for examination and evaluating their influence on each other helps us to better understand the complexities of communication.

Script: A piece of code written in a computer programming language such as JavaScript that can be accessed from an HTML file to perform sophisticated Web operations.

Search Engine: (1) A program that searches the Internet for occurrences of terms specified by a user. (2) Sites that provide general Internet search resources, including keyword searches and subject categories.

Sequential Design: A hypertextual design that limits readers' choices so that they move through an environment in a particular order. This type of organizational structure is well suited for compositions that have a clear progression of ideas.

Server: (1) Software that stores files and shares information with client programs. Together, servers and clients control the basic operations of the Internet. (2) Also refers to the machine that runs the server software.

Skeptical Reading: An approach to analyzing messages that focuses on the weaknesses of a text. A skeptical reading tries to find fault with a message in as many ways as possible.

Source or "Document Source": The HTML file that tells a Web browser how to display a page. Most browsers allow readers to "view the source" of Web documents to see the underlying HTML tags that create the pages.

Sources: The materials that authors use as they research. Academic projects generally require that authors document their sources.

Spam: To post messages (often advertisements) indiscriminately to a large number of newsgroups or e-mail discussion lists.

Speaker: The communicator in a rhetorical situation. Also refers to the ways in which an author, writer, lecturer, or any other communicator is perceived through a message. A speaker can be a single author, a spokesperson, or even an entity such as the American Medical Association.

Style: The choices of arrangement and diction that an author makes. An academic style generally uses a specialized language and constructs complicated sentences to make logically reasoned claims. An informal style, on the other hand, often uses colloquial language and less rigid conventions.

Sympathetic Reading: An approach to analyzing messages that focuses on the strengths of a text. A sympathetic reading tries to flesh out the major claims and trace the development of an argument.

Synchronous Communication: See **Real-Time.**

Table: A Web page layout that presents information in rows and columns.

Tags: The individual HTML commands. These commands are set off in angle brackets (< >) and generally work in pairs.

Targeting: Connecting directly to a particular Internet site.

Thesis: The main point that an author is trying to get across.

Thread: An initial posting to an e-mail discussion list, newsgroup, or Web forum followed by a series of replies that build on each other to form a conversation.

Tone: Similar to style, tone is the attitude conveyed in a message. Depending on the mood that the author wants to set, the tone can be frivolous, joking, serious, conciliatory, confrontational, and so on.

URL (Uniform Resource Locator): The unique Internet address of a document on the World Wide Web.

Usenet: An extensive collection of public-access newsgroups. Most universities and colleges are connected to Usenet rather than to private or commercial bulletin boards.

Web Browser: Client software that allows users to navigate and interact on the World Wide Web.

Web Forums: Asynchronous message boards on the Web that function like newsgroups. Readers can post and respond to messages, and the conversations are instantly incorporated into the site.

Web Server: A combination of software and hardware that stores, manages, and distributes files for the World Wide Web.

World Wide Web (often abbreviated "WWW" or "the Web"): The Internet medium that combines graphics, sound, video, and other Internet technologies such as Gopher, FTP, newsgroups, and e-mail.

WYSIWYG: An acronym for "What You See Is What You Get." Refers to applications that hide the complexities of document formatting. For instance, WYSIWYG HTML editors hide the tags that control Web documents, allowing users to compose without worrying about the underlying HTML commands.

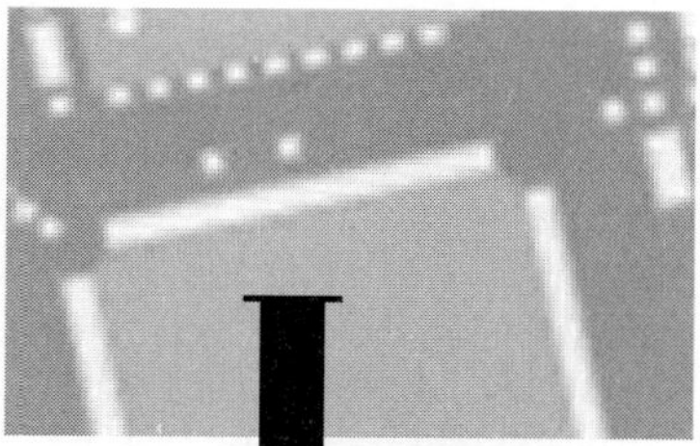

INDEX